LANDSCAPE AND POWER IN ANCIENT MESOAMERICA

LANDSCAPE AND POWER
IN ANCIENT MESOAMERICA

Rex Koontz
Kathryn Reese-Taylor
Annabeth Headrick

Routledge
Taylor & Francis Group
New York London

First published 2001 by Westview Press

Published 2018 by Routledge
605 Third Avenue, New York, NY 10017
2 Park Square, Milton Park, Abingdon, Oxon OX14 4RN

Routledge is an imprint of the Taylor & Francis Group, an informa business

Library of Congress Cataloging-in-Publication Data

Landscape and power in ancient Mesoamerica / edited by Rex Koontz,
Kathryn Reese-Taylor and Annabeth Headrick.

p. cm.

Includes bibliographical references and index.

ISBN 0-8133-3732-1 (pbk.)

1. Indian Architecture—Mexico. 2. Indians of Mexico—Religion. 3. Indians of
Mexico—Politics and government. 4. Sacred space—Mexico—History. 5. City
planning—Mexico—History. 6. Landscape assessment—Mexico—History.
7. Mexico—Antiquities. I. Koontz, Rex. II. Reese-Taylor, Kathryn.
III. Headrick, Annabeth.

F1219.3.A6 L36   2001
972'.01—dc21

00-054979

ISBN 13: 978-0-8133-3732-6 (pbk)

For Linda

CONTENTS

MAPS, TABLES, AND ILLUSTRATIONS

Maps

Tables

Illustrations

FOREWORD
Landscape and Power in Ancient Mesoamerica

DAVID FREIDEL

If states and culture ought to exist for the well-being (an esthetic condition) of their members, then society cannot preexist its arts, which determine the forms of expression by which a society is known. (George Kubler 1991:13)

Knowing Pre-Columbian societies through their arts, their architecture, and their humanmade landscapes is a goal uniting the several parts and contributions of this book into a collective effort. Some of the authors go at the task of crafting new knowledge of the pre-Columbian past with some conceptual tools that are new to me, terms such as *cultural poetics* and *aesthetic trope*. The editors go to considerable effort in the introduction to make these terms accessible, and therefore useful. Let me give just a couple of contemporary examples that make sense to me. The Vietnam War memorial in Washington, D.C., is a sacred space charged with emotional power. Its design is a culturally specific poetic layering of scales and meanings, beginning with the 58,191 individual names inscribed upon its polished black stone panels. The viewer initially moves through the monument by descending, echoing the process that each casualty of the war went through at interment. Later the viewer must ascend as she exits the monument. This fundamental movement references the basic scaffolding of narratives of death and rebirth in many cultures as well as the cultural meanings attached to actual burial rites.

Descent followed by ascent is a fundamental part of the dance of the afterlife—the poetical scaffolding on which many human belief systems are hung. In this way the monument materializes an aesthetic trope that

would resonate with most of the participants in the ceremonies of remem-
brance that occur there daily. One looks into the pure, polished black surface and sees oneself and other visitors; one observes a subdued pattern of
gray lines and columns as anonymous as the lists of the lost reported day
after day on black-and-white television newscasts during the conflict.
Then one sees the response of a visitor to the discovery of one name, the
flood of memories, of grief, that one name invokes. And then every name
stands alone and vital. This is not a memorial to the unknown or to exemplary heroes—added later in bronze—but to the very personal and singular experience of people caught up in the Vietnam War. The Wall is not an
aesthetic trope to all citizens of the United States, as the Washington Monument is, but it is just that for the generations who experienced the war
and who congregate there to perform their own private and quiet rituals
of expiation. Seeing it in the context of the other monuments in the area,
with their particular histories and memories, one has the outline of an archaeology of public U.S. life in this ceremonial center.

Acknowledging that not even all U.S. citizens can understand one of
their own contemporary national monuments, how much more difficult
it is to imagine usefully knowing the monumental art of pre-Columbian
societies as their peoples did. But there are other conceptual tools that
make this effort plausible, principal among them the prospect of continuity in meaning over time associated with images, artifacts, symbols, and
signs. For all his confidence in the centrality of art and aesthetics to the
study of ancient civilization, George Kubler generally despaired of establishing continuities of this kind from the period of the Spanish Conquest
into the deep past of Mesoamerica. However, the authors of the ensuing
chapters pose an array of arguments favoring enduring continuities, and
these arguments are the basis for opening up new fields of meaning and
function in Mesoamerican sacred spaces.

The general principle of continuity in this arena has enjoyed a strong
empirical endorsement through the decipherment of Mayan glyphic
texts of the Classic period, and several of the contributors make reference
to this material—particularly as articulated by Linda Schele. Linda
Schele was pursuing the continuities of key ideas and images in
Mesoamerica at the time of her death, and this scholarship is reflected in
her contribution to this book. Her study of Tollan, the mythical Place of
Cattail Reeds, registers a conviction, articulated many years ago by
Michael Coe among others, that historical memory in Mesoamerica transcended the rise and fall of individual civilizations and reproduced the

beliefs and icons of an enduring world vision founded more than thirty centuries ago.

Yet that common root stock, what Gordon Willey and Philip Phillips defined as an "areal co-tradition," never constrained the tangled branching of the regional cultures of Mesoamerica into a wonderful and nuanced flowering of expression. The pyramids and concourses mapping out the creation across the Teotihuacan landscape, the circle dance of great stones declaring the creation at Quiriguá, the resurrection path in Building A at El Tajín, resonate but remain distinctly localized and historically particular expressions of broadly shared and enduring tropes. The writers dealing with these subjects expertly break out the local from the Mesoamerican in ways that enrich our understanding of both.

Within the context of cosmic aesthetics as a means to legitimate power, I see two great themes in this book. First, there are explorations of the meaning of places on the landscape, both humanmade and natural, as conveyed through symbols, signs, and images—and writing in the case of the Classic Maya. Second, there are efforts to interpret places, or monuments, by means of ritual performances on or around them as these can be inferred through displayed symbolism. These two themes intertwine conceptually, and so the authors detail them to varying degrees in each chapter.

Here is an example from my own experience of how this thematic synergy can work. In late December last year, I visited the Postclassic Maya capital of Mayapan in Yucatán. Passing through the bougainvillea-laced lane to the newly cleared and consolidated buildings of the center, I faced the Temple of Kukulcan, the Feathered Serpent. By reputation, this radial pyramid is an echo of Chichén Itzá's original Castillo in north-central Yucatán. As I drew closer to the pyramid, I could see fragments of recently exposed and conserved brightly painted murals along one basal wall. An enthroned and armed god, strikingly reminiscent of one found pervasively at Chichén Itzá depicted inside an ancestor cartouche (and dubbed "Captain Sun Disk" there by Arthur Miller), was here framed by warriors lowering battle standards toward the god's celestial portal. Captain Sun Disk occurs carved on a wooden lintel in the temple on top of the Castillo at Chichén Itzá, but here at Mayapan he was prominently displayed on a version of the radial temple ethnohistorically documented as dedicated to Kukulcan. To be sure, another such scene depicted a "diving god" in the cartouche, but I saw in the seated-god mural reinforcement of the idea that Kukulcan, as the title of a legendary ruler of Chichén Itzá, might be pictured as the enthroned warrior in the ancestor cartouche.

My interest piqued, I rounded the pyramid and then regarded, up on a low corner terrace, a striding modeled stucco figure brandishing a flapstaff battle banner. Now the building came alive for me with the pageants of the month of Xul that I remembered described by Diego de Landa for the Temple of Kukulcan at Mayapan (and later at Mani):

On the evening of that day they went forth with a great procession of people, and they went very quietly to the temple of Kukulcan, which they had previously properly adorned, and having arrived there, and making their prayers, they placed the banners on top of the temple, and they all spread out their idols below in the courtyard, each for himself, on leaves of trees, which he had for this purpose, and having kindled new fire, they began to burn their incense in many places and to make offerings of food cooked without salt or pepper and of drinks made of their beans and the seeds of squashes (Tozzer 1941:158).

The battle banners of Mayapan resonated for me with those inferred for Classic El Tajín in Veracruz, as described by Kathryn Reese-Taylor and Rex Koontz in their introduction. I found my mind's eye following battle banners from Chichén Itzá to battle banners fluttering over the bundled and seated remains of revered lords in Aztec picture books like the Magliabechano (Boone 1983) to the battle banner depicted over the bundled remains of the sacrificed Maya Maize God, First Father, on a beautiful Middle Classic vase (MS 1126, Reents-Budet 1994:14–15). My mind's eye observed the banners adorning bound sacrificial victims displayed before Quetzalcoatl-Kukulcan and also decorating a tree behind the enthroned image of that god, as illustrated in the Postclassic Mexican *Codex Borgia* (plate 19). So this Mesoamerican trope blazes trails through the cultural history of the region and urges me to see in them connected understanding.

Such religious conventions and symbols served to integrate Mesoamerican states not only historically into areal co-traditions but also politically, commercially, and ritually in any given period of time. The cult of Kukulcan at Mayapan was, as seen in its successor cult at Mani, designed to solidify the elite of the Mayapan confederacy through identity with a foreign god. That same elite was committed to long-distance trade in Mexico and Central America. The trading city of Cholula in Puebla, described by Geoffrey McCafferty in this volume, housed an important cult of Quetzalcoatl, and this god's temple stood before the Templo Mayor in Tenochtitlán, the Aztec capital. How far back in time this Feathered Serpent god leitmotif can be traced is an open matter, but certainly both Mexican-style feathered serpent gods and Mexican-style battle banners are in the Maya lowlands by the fourth century AD. As it happens, the bundle burial of high lords (such as pictured on the Middle Classic vase described above) appears, albeit rarely, in the records of Kaminaljuyu, Tikal, and Waxaktun during the fifth century AD—all sites attesting significant ties to Teotihuacan.

It is difficult to find closure on such an inquiry once begun in Mesoamerican religion and ritual practice, for the connections reach out in all directions over time—the practical product of economic and social ties of importance to the local elites and their constituencies. At the same time, the sages and artisans of local traditions constantly reinvented their distinct aesthetic expressions of the myths, histories, and gods they collectively embraced as definitive of civilized life. The following articles celebrate this rich and dynamic world in ways that are both enlightening and challenging to existing precepts. The result is a hopeful and important work.

References

Boone, Elizabeth Hill.
> 1983 *The Codex Magliabechiano and the Lost Prototype of the Magliabechiano.* Berkeley: University of California Press.

Kubler, George.
> 1991 *Esthetic Recognition of Ancient Amerindian.* New Haven: Yale University Press.

Reents-Budet, Dorie.
> 1994 *Painting the Maya Universe: Royal Ceramics of the Classic Period.* Durham, N.C.: Duke University Press.

Tozzer, Alfred M.
> 1941 *Landa's* Relación *de las Cosas de Yucatan, a Translation.* Cambridge, Mass.: The Peabody Museum.

PREFACE

Recent studies of ancient landscapes have matured into well-rounded inquiries regarding humanity's engagement with the environment. Whereas many remain centered on topics such as the distribution of settlements throughout a region, the modification of the environment for agricultural purposes, and large scale water management projects, they are complemented by an array of newer studies focused on what and Wendy Ashmore and A. Bernard Knapp (1999:1) term the "socio-symbolic aspects of human environment interaction." What unites these seemingly disparate perspectives is the concept that landscapes are formed by collective human activity and, as such, are culturally constructed. This volume focuses on the culturally constructed landscapes within the civic centers of ancient Mesoamerica. Although the contributors to this volume come from varied disciplines and consider spaces created throughout the prehistory of Mesoamerican, they all share the fundamental orientation that ancient Mesoamerican landscapes were laden with meanings and that any analysis of the human relationship to the landscape must come to terms with these meanings. In particular, the studies included in this volume focus upon the specific meanings associated with the identification and expression of power embodied within landscapes. These landscapes of power are the cumulative results of encounters among individuals, the built environment (urban space, architecture, household, shrine, and so forth), and the "natural" geography.

The first two contributions form a pair of synthetic, overarching essays on landscape and power in ancient Mesoamerica. The introduction by Kathryn Reese-Taylor and Rex Koontz discusses the analytic categories used to think about landscape, space, and power. They suggest that the exploration of the more literal meanings of the environment may be balanced by the understanding of the poetics, which undergird its conception and expression. More than a site, the landscape may be considered as stage and actor in the performance, and in this way it participates in the poetics that structures the drama. This is especially true when one considers the landscape as a site for performance—such as the banner-raising ceremonies at the site of El Tajín, which Reese-Taylor and Koontz describe.

The second chapter, by Linda Schele and Julia Guernsey Kappelman, takes on the different, but no less complex, task of mapping one of the fundamental patterns of landscape organization in Mesoamerica, that of Tollan. The authors argue that the particular constellation of elements that form Tollan, the Ancient Mesoamerican paradigmatic urban plan, were used throughout ancient Mesoamerica as a "right" and powerful way of organizing urban spaces and their surrounding landscapes. Fundamental patterns, such as those embodied in the concept of Tollan, regulate mythic, architectural, iconographic, and other expressions, and in this volume are referred to as "aesthetic tropes."

In Section II, Plaza, Stelae, and Performance, the authors relate the transformation of central urban spaces and their surrounding countryside into areas of performance. In both Matthew Looper's and Kappleman's essays, the stelae format becomes the vehicle of choice for representing ritual, thus making the ritual present long after the actual performance. In this way the central space of the city (Quiriguá for Looper and Izapa for Kappelman) was turned into a permanent locus of performance, from which its meaning derived. Instead of focusing on a particular artistic medium, Heather Orr's contribution discusses the importance of the procession as defining ritual performance for Dainzú and Monte Albán, two major hilltop shrine sites in Oaxaca.

The essays in Section III, Identity and the Language of Space, treat the way space is given meanings that solidify group identities, often with the desire of promoting polity solidarity. Following on Orr's identification of procession as a chief means of inscribing meaning on the landscape, Carolyn Tate's essay shows how the importation of exotic sculptural materials at the Olmec site of La Venta was fundamental to the meaning of the sacred landscape. Tate's essay goes on to show how attitudes toward the materials themselves were part of a larger system of religious thought that bound the Olmec world together and remain central to the linguistic descendants of that crucial Formative period culture.

Annabeth Headrick's essay on the Three Temple Complex at Teotihuacan posits that this widespread architectural pattern was based on a fundamental triadic aesthetic trope found throughout Mesoamerican culture. Furthermore, Headrick shows that this pattern may be the basis for the organization of the most powerful political groups in the city. Jeffrey Stomper's essay on Copán also identifies an artifact of group identity in the Council House in the center of the site. Stomper shows how groups used the cosmological landscape of Maya myth to identify themselves and placed this identification at the heart of the Copán polity. Patricia Sarro also finds the cosmological underpinning for group identity, this time in one of the elaborately decorated multiroomed structures associated with elite groups at the site of El Tajín. Sarro proposes that the elite of Tajín reproduced their most important figure of cosmological landscape, the ballcourt, inside this building as a statement of control over the rituals associated with ballcourts and ball games. By locating these primordial spaces in the center of their restricted space, elites proclaimed not only control over but also identity with ball game ritual and its associated mythology, and thus with the Tajín polity itself.

Section IV, Paradigm and Power in Space and Narrative, concentrates on the way in which stories inscribed into the landscape were used to reify power relations. Linnea Wren, Kaylee Spencer, and Krysta Hochstetler show how serpent symbolism at the cosmopolitan site of Chichén Itzá was used to reference different areas of the Ancient Mesoamerican world, many of which were far from the Yucatán. These assertions of symbolic connection to far-away places are here seen as equivalent to the ability to trade and ally on a global level—an ability that separated the Chichén elite from others and provided an important part of their charter of legitimacy. Concomitant with this strategy was the innovative use of females as legitimating ancestors, probably in response to the need for local ties that these women gave the invading Itzá elite.

Rather than focusing on a particular group, Geoffrey McCafferty's essay on the Great Pyramid of Cholula shows how a single building's form and meaning were transformed over time to serve the needs of the various groups who based themselves at the site. McCafferty shows us the great continuities in the meaning of the building, which were based on many of the same fundamental principles of powerful space described by Schele and Kappelman. At the same time, the author is able to show how these basic patterns were modified to fit the particular political agenda of the group in power at the time. McCafferty thus offers an "archaeology of legitimacy" based on a detailed understanding of the stratigraphy and symbolism of the Tlachihualtepetl, or "man-made mountain," as the Great Pyramid was known at the time of the Spanish Conquest. The final essay, by Cynthia Kristan-Graham, investigates the spatial personality of Chichén Itzá through a detailed analysis of the relations formed by the emplacement of the glyphic record, imagery, architecture, and other forms of urban marking such as the road system. Kristan-Graham finds that the political ordering of the polity as a "multepal" or joint-ruled institution were inscribed throughout the fabric of the city.

Finally, we would like to acknowledge the assistance of many of our colleagues during the process of editing this volume. Our sincere thanks go to Laura Jankowsky and Eva de la Riva López for keeping us organized and on track with this project. Also, we would like to acknowledge the guidance and patience of our editor, Karl Yambert, during this process.

The chapters included within this volume were first presented at two separate symposia on Mesoamerican landscapes at both the American Anthropological Association and the College Art Association, and we would like to acknowledge Heather Orr for her work in co-organizing and co-chairing, along with Rex Koontz, the symposium presented at the CAA. We also would like to thank David Freidel for his unflagging support of this volume and his advice at critical junctures. Our thanks are also extended to Karl Taube, who reviewed the papers at an early stage and provided constructive comments that proved very useful in the final preparation of the volume. In addition, we are grateful for the thoughtful comments regarding the introduction to the volume provided by David Freidel, David Samuels, Denis Provencher, and Kerry Hull.

We would also like to express our thanks to our families. They have stood steadfastly by us as we worked through weekends and into the small hours of the morning. They have provided us with comfort, joy, and the occasional cup of coffee to keep us going. So to Daniela, Julian, and Lee; to Rick, Elizabeth, Schuyler, and Benjamin; and to Ross, we extend our love and appreciation.

However, in the end, we must reserve our most profound gratitude for our teacher and friend, Linda Schele. We are the results of her endeavors and her love. We hope she likes what she sees.

References

Ashmore, Wendy and A. Bernard Knapp.
  1999 "Archaeological Landscapes: Constructed, Conceptualized, Ideational."
    In *Archaeologies of Landscape: Contemporary Perspectives.* Edited by Wendy
    Ashmore and A. Bernard Knapp, pp. 1–30. Oxford: Blackwell Publishers.

The Cultural Poetics of Power and Space in Ancient Mesoamerica

KATHRYN REESE-TAYLOR
REX KOONTZ

For almost three thousand years, Mesoamerican societies have crafted spaces for ritual performance with the express purpose of forging power relations. These spaces functioned as stage sets representing paradigmatic landscapes laden with power—power that political actors would direct to a historically contingent end. Inherently present within these landscapes and the performances conducted in them are the cultural poetics of a people, embodying both the aesthetic values of a group as well as the style used to manifest these aesthetic principles.

This volume centers on examples of cultural poetics as applied to landscapes from several different societies in ancient Mesoamerica. An underlying theme that unites all of these examples is how individuals or groups fashion spaces for the purposes of accruing political power or advancing political agendas. Within this chapter we seek to define the underlying principles used by Mesoamericans to shape the landscape into effective settings for communicating power relations.

Defining Cultural Poetics

Although at times difficult to define, the cultural poetics of a people are nonetheless important to study because they can reveal aspects of culture that are not apparent at first reading. Roman Jakobson initially identified poetics as dealing with the problems of verbal structures, yet he simultaneously asserted that many poetic features, more rightly, belong to the theory of signs, or semiotics (Jakobson 1960: 350–351). With this small pronouncement, a more encompassing perspective regarding the utility of poetics for understanding signs present in all mediums arose that recontextualized the poetic, associating it with problems of semiotic structures. Thus, form and meaning were inextricably linked in Jakobson's poetics: Semiotics had embedded within it a poetics. The structuring of the communicative act, which inevitably involves a cultural poetics, could now be considered an integral part of the meaning of the communication.

Jakobson, along with his anthropologist colleague Claude Lévi-Strauss, explored the nexus of poetics and semiotics in their analysis of Charles Baudelaire's poem "Les Chats" (Jakobson and Lévi-Strauss 1962). The article divides analysis into poetic and semiotic domains (the former drawing on Jakobson's definition above, and the latter on Lévi-Straussian structuralist analysis of myth). In this short work, the authors show how particular poetical structures express particular categories of meaning in the poem (i.e., octets for animate objects, sextets for inanimate objects). All of this categorization illustrates that "each method [poetic or semiotic] may be chosen according to the circumstances, for, in the last analysis, they are substitutable one for another (Jakobson and Lévi-Strauss 1962: 5; author's translation).[1] As Robert Layton (1991:22) observed, the work of Jakobson and Lévi-Strauss was an early attempt to systematically grapple with relations of "form" and "content" (or poetics and semiotics) from a linguistic and anthropological perspective.

However, it was the work of Clifford Geertz that firmly established the use of cultural poetics as a viable approach for understanding the organization and function of culture. Geertz defines culture as a semiotic system, opening the door for the use of poetics as a means of eliciting meaning from a cultural act:

> The concept of culture, I espouse . . . is essentially a semiotic one. Believing as Max Weber, that man is an animal suspended in webs of significance he himself has spun, I take culture to be those webs, and the analysis of it to be therefore not an experimental science in search of new law, but an interpretive one in search of meaning (Geertz 1973:5).

The identification of culture by Geertz as semiotic "webs of significance" provides the means for interpreting meaning in the same manner that linguists illicit meaning from a text. Therefore, following Jakobson and Lévi-Strauss, we may view Geertz's webs of significance as both semiotically and poetically constructed. As a communicative act, the message (the literal content) must be expressed properly in order to be understood—and that proper expression is generated by a cultural poetics. Many scholars have used cultural poetics as a framework for interpreting meaning in societies based upon the premise alluded to by Geertz that cultural practices are "texted" (Volosinov 1973; Hodder 1982, 1986, 1987, 1992; Shanks and Tilley 1982, 1987; Schiefflin 1985; Bakhtin 1986; Bauman 1986; Sherzer 1987; Hanks 1989a, 1989b, 1989c; Bauman and Briggs 1990; Urban 1991)[2]. This paradigm asserts that objects are given meaning by the social interactions of individuals and may be perceived as a "text" because of their discrete form and content, which is semiotically encoded to be received by others. In this view that privileges the social construction of meaning, one may say that things embody meaning because people act as if they do. Thus a poetics must be seen as cultural: It is embedded in the agreed-upon practices of a group—practices that regulate not only what is said, but how to say it properly.

Aesthetics

Viewing culture as texted by society enables scholars to consider the cultural factors that structure the text as well as the audience reaction to those texts. Intertwined with the prosaic questions of literal content come the poetical questions of what makes a proper or powerful text. As in literary genres, two cognitive elements play important roles in the response to these questions: aesthetics and style. Aesthetic principles are often difficult to verbalize and therefore are frequently referred to by means of metaphor or trope. Meyer Schapiro has defined an aesthetic trope as ". . . a manifestation of the culture as a whole, the visible sign of its unity [that]) . . . reflects or projects the 'inner form' of collective thinking and feeling" (1953:287). Robert Plant Armstrong has revitalized the notion of the aesthetic trope by demonstrating how tropes transmute core cultural patterns through formal metaphoric properties, modalities, and media, thus providing the structuring principles for any socially effective communication (1975:45).

In a like manner, Edmund Leach has touched upon the concept of aesthetics as a structuring principle for cultural acts: "Logically, aesthetics and ethics are identical. If we are to understand the ethical rules of a society, it is the aesthetics we must study" (1977:12).[3] While using a different vocabulary, Leach is also referring to the aesthetic component of the fundamental structures of a group's self-understanding and the practices arising from that understanding.

Armstrong has also pointed out that the aesthetics and style of a group structure not only artistic endeavors, but also directly reflect group cognitive processes and shape social dynamics (1981). Aesthetic tropes encode the *metacommunicative* patterns of a people (Durkheim 1965; Lévi-Strauss 1963; Turner 1967; Keil 1979; Geertz 1980; B. Tedlock 1984, 1986, 1992; Feld 1988). People who share an aesthetic easily recognize and understand each other, and aesthetic tropes communicate to outsiders the manner in which people identify themselves and structure their daily lives.

However, following Ludwig Wittgenstein (1922), we are not only concerned with the cognitive aspects of human behavior that the study of aesthetic tropes reveals, but with the actual practices that aesthetic tropes, like ethics, direct. Wittgenstein seeks not to ascertain the supposedly true nature of what something is, but to articulate how humans conduct their practical, everyday affairs—something we usually leave unacknowledged in the background of our lives. He is concerned

> with individuals being able to 'go on' with each other (Wittgenstein 1953; nos.146–155 in Shotter 1995), with individuals being able to make 'followable', 'responsible', or 'answerable' sense to each other— simply reacting or responding in ways that makes it possible for us to continue our relationships is sufficient for him (Shotter 1995).

In this manner, aesthetics and its concomitant expression as tropes create a sense of cultural cohesiveness within a social group.

Aesthetic tropes are inherently framed in a metaphorical vocabulary that crosscuts media. Aesthetic tropes may be expressed as music, as verbal art, or as representations in two or three dimensions. The Flowering Mountain Earth, found among contemporary Maya adhering to the Costrumbrista religion, is an example of an aesthetic trope expressed as a three-dimensional representation (Reese 1996). The Flowering Mountain Earth is not merely a landscape, location, or a packet of fundamental ideas. It is a visual metaphor that embodies a concept central to the ordering of daily life by the people of Santiago Atitlan, a village located near the shores of Lake Atitlan in the highlands of Guatemala. In Atiteco myths, the Flowering Mountain Earth represents a sacred tree that stood at the center of the universe at a time before the creation of the current world. The tree became pregnant, and all the elements of the world grew from the branches. As the fruit grew larger, it became too heavy for the tree to bear and fell to the ground, scattering its seeds at its base. The sacred tree gave shelter to the young plants, but eventually the young saplings grew so abundant and large that the sacred tree was crowded out. Now, the Flowering Mountain Earth is said to exist as a stump at the center of the world and is called the Father/Mother, the beginning and ending point of all life (Carlsen and Prechtel 1991:13). The Costrumbristas believe that in this form the Flowering Mountain Earth is the ancestor of all life.

As a structuring agent, the Flowering Mountain Earth is ". . . a unifying concept, inextricably linking vegetation, the human life cycle, kinship, modes of production, religious and political hierarchy, conceptions of time, even of celestial movement" (Carlsen and Prechtel 1991:12–13). A reciprocal relationship exists between the symbolic representation of the Flowering Mountain Earth and the Costrumbristas. They believe that as long as the Flowering Mountain Earth is fed, it will continue to provide sustenance. The feeding may be literal or symbolic. Literal feeding occurs when an individual has an actual hole on his land into which offerings for the ancestors are placed. Symbolic feeding occurs during ritual performances in which dancing with sacred bundles, burning copal incense, or praying feeds the ancestral form (Carlsen and Prechtel 1991).

Likewise, it is the ritual performances of the *cofradía* that feeds and renews the community and the world. Consonant with this belief, the *cofradía* system is metaphorically expressed as vegetation in the discourse of the Costrumbristas. The trope of the Flowering Mountain Earth also encompasses temporal elements. The Flowering Mountain Earth as the stump represents death and temporally takes this form during nights and from the autumnal equinox to the spring equinox. During its death phase, the stump is called the gourd or skull. Fundamental *cofradía* rituals resurrect the Flowering Mountain Earth as the sun and help it to move across the sky. The series of deaths and births, which move the sun throughout the year, are referred to as dawnings. Individual *cofradía* are referred to as dawn houses, signifying the importance of these ritual performances. At the spring equinox, specific ceremonies are conducted to renew and rejuvenate the Earth. The world is inseminated with the gourd/skull, and during the subsequent "five delicate days,", the Earth is pregnant. If the *cofradía*s have performed the ritual and ceremonies properly throughout the year, then life again is brought forth (Carlsen and Prechtel 1991:24–25). All of the conceptual categories that structure the Costrumbrista world and their concomitant ritual obligations are encompassed within the trope of the Flowering Mountain Earth.

Fundamental to our argument is the structuring power of the aesthetic principles used to construct the trope of Flowering Mountain Earth and how those principles replicate themselves throughout Atiteco culture. Invoking the structuring power of the Flowering Mountain Earth imparts a beauty and orderliness to the communicative act. As a structuring aesthetic trope, the Flowering Mountain Earth goes beyond communally accepted literal meaning to encompass the proper, powerful grammar of any communication.

Style

Although seemingly bounded, a limitless range of variation can exist within the confines of an aesthetic trope. The variations in the material realization of the trope may be analyzed through an individual or community's style (Bourdieu 1984). Armstrong locates the nexus of stylistic variation within the actual process of creation:

> Style may . . . be seen to be a composite of media and their structures, in terms of the discipline to which those media and structures are characteristically subjected in enactment (1971:51).

Style is, in this way of thinking, the recognizable formal scaffolding on which all communicative acts are hung. In his classic definition of style in art, Meyer Schapiro observes that any particular style is ". . . a system of forms with a quality and a meaningful expression through which the personality of the artist and the broad outlook of a group are visible" (1953:287). He further defines three integral elements of style: context, form, and expression. Contextual elements consist of the spatial and temporal relationships of communicative acts. Formal elements include the properties that shape the structure of the communicative act. And finally, expressive elements are the qualities, such as color intensity, color hue, rhythm, pitch, harmony, and so forth, that participate in the meaning of any communication (Schapiro 1953).

Many scholars—such as Angel Maria Garibay (1953), Victoria Bricker (1981), Dennis Tedlock (1983, 1985), Gary Gossen (1985), Munro Edmunson (1986), and William Hanks (1989a)—have pursued the study of the style, which organizes Mesoamerican texts and oral performances. Within the formal texts of the Maya, style is critical in conveying meaning (D. Tedlock 1983). Repetitions and other stylistic features of oral narrative have implications even for those who focus on content analysis and choose to ignore style (D. Tedlock 1983:53). In tightly parallel verse, the cadence and alliteration established in one phrase must be sustained (with slight variation) in the next. At the same time, the semantic content must also be duplicated. Meaning shifts either positively or negatively using synonyms and antonyms but without disrupting completely the established meter and sound. These formal stylistics clearly organize the compositional structure and thus the content of the text.

In a similar manner, Kathryn Reese (1996) has argued that the overall design of sacred space at the Late Formative site of Cerros in northern Belize paralleled the poetic properties of formal Maya verse. She has identified structures such as episodic cycles, metaphorical stacking, formal coupletry, and triadic parallelism in the architectural program. These formal elements of style were used to convey meaning by the Late Formative architects of Cerros. Without the proper use of such formal elements, the landscape would be less intelligible to the local population, much as music composed on an octave scale is familiar or indigenous whereas music composed on a scale other than the Western octave is marked as strange or foreign. Style is not a by-product of behavior but is firmly grounded in practice and is culturally constitutive.

Therefore, the principles of an aesthetics together with its materialization through style is crucial in establishing the syntax that makes any communication intelligible with a cohesive social group. However, what is critical to understand is the interrelatedness of the two concepts. Styles are founded upon aesthetic principles, and aesthetic principles are dependent upon styles for their expression. It is the aesthetic structuring of communicative acts and their attendant social relations and the style in which these structures are expressed that cultural poetics attempts to discern.

The Structure of Power

Based upon the studies of such social scientists as Michel Foucault (1973, 1977, 1981), Clifford Geertz (1973), Pierre Bourdieu (1977, 1984), and Mikhail Bakhtin (1986), recent scholars have proposed that one of the principle structural problems posed by cultural poetics is the relationship between power and the manner in which it is represented (Dougherty and Kurke 1993). "Culture here is not cults and customs but the structures of meaning through which people give shape to their experience. Politics is not coups and constitutions but one of the principle arenas in which such structures unfold. The two being thus reframed, determining the connection between them becomes a practicable enterprise, although hardly a modest one" (Geertz 1973:312).

Geertz clearly relates politics and culture—the latter being a constitutive element of the former. Thus culture and power are not disjunctive, but instead power is expressed and manipulated through cultural categories and discourses. At this juncture one must interrogate the connection between culture and politics with a view toward constructing a field in which cultural manifestations may be read as constitutive of political power. We would argue that one of the chief loci for this expression and manipulation of power is in representation, which provides a fertile field for the exploration of the connection between culture and politics.

But how does representation constitute itself as an analytical field, and what are the elements that go into its analysis? In his study of the Paris Arcades, Walter Benjamin particularly draws upon images of power arising from dialectical structures that actualize the tensions between opposing cultural forces:

> Where thought comes to a standstill in a constellation saturated with tensions, there appears the dialectical image. It is the caesura in the movement of thought . . . it is to be sought at the point where the tension between the dialectical oppositions is the greatest (Benjamin as quoted in Buck-Morss 1989:219)

The tension of the dialectical image is an integral construct in the dynamic nature of the cultural poetic. However, in our use of the dialectical image, we expand upon Benjamin's specific definition and embrace a more encompassing exegesis.[4] We interpret the tension of the dialectic image as embodying the disjunction between that which is represented and that which represents—in other words, the signified and the signifier (Saussure 1913). The representation is intrinsically dialectic because it encodes an interior struggle between concept and conceptualization. This effort creates a rift in the image, which Kathleen Stewart has called "a space on the side of the road" (1996). This space is full of potential in that it allows for a multitude of interpretations, depending upon the audience (cf. Bakhtin 1986), for a continual reinvention of meaning consistent with a constantly changing poetics. These spaces provide for a

> . . . [R]e-entrenchment [of the image] in the particularity of local form and epistemologies, a dwelling in and on a cultural poetics contingent on a place and time . . . (Stewart 1996:6).

In this context, the disjunction between conception and representation is flooded with individual needs based upon local contingencies.

It is from the potential to direct the tension of the dialectic image towards a particular agenda that power arises. At this point, power simultaneously requires and engenders knowledge (Foucault 1973, 1977, 1981). The ability of any actor to direct the tension of an existing image or craft a powerful statement is explicitly linked to an awareness of her world.

> Perhaps we should abandon the belief that power makes mad and that, by the same token, the renunciation of power is one of the conditions of knowledge. We should admit rather that power produces knowledge . . . that power and knowledge directly imply one another; that there is no power relation without the correlative constitution of a field of knowledge, nor any knowledge that does not presuppose and constitute at the same time power relations (Foucault 1977:27).

Knowledge, for Foucault, is the control or mastery of certain cultural practices, especially those of the primary discourses regulating a culture. As we have seen, a cultural poetics is one of the fundamental constitutive elements of these discourses. Power, then, may be seen to originate in specific and localized cultural poetics that develop as a result of people and events in an exact place and time. Thus for Foucault, as for Geertz, culture is not the smokescreen behind which power and politics hide but the very embodiment of power-saturated social relations. Power rests, after Foucault, on the ability to define truth and hence knowledge, which is in the end a practice embedded at the very heart of culture. Cultural poetics, in turn, is not the epiphenomenal dressing placed on statements about incommensurable power relations to make them palatable, but may be seen instead as constitutive of those relations.

We have, we hope, established the centrality of cultural poetics in the analysis of culture and power. What remains to be done is to show how cultural poetics manifests itself in practice. To begin this task, it must first be acknowledged that the analytic category of cultural poetics is constitutive, not determinative. Whereas a work of art, political speech, or any other act of communication is structured by a cultural poetics, this structuring is done by a historical agent at a particular point in history for a particular effect. The structuring power of cultural poetics, together with the historical contingency of the politically motivated speaker, reveals the play of power in any single communicative act. Marshall Sahlins calls this meeting of structure and history "the structure of the conjuncture," in which any particular communicative event is "a relation between a happening and a structure (or structures): an encompassment of the phenomenon-in-itself as a meaningful value, from which follows its specific historical efficacy" (1985:xiv).

This approach is, perhaps, best exemplified in the work of the New Historicists who see texts as sites for the circulation of cultural energy and for the ongoing negotiation of power relations within society (Doughtery and Kurke 1993). New Historicists often detect a clash of different discourses within a single text or anecdote. Given their interest in representation, they recognize that not only can events alter the structure, but language itself and other acts of signification are also potential sites for cultural change. Thus the negotiation of power relations that the New Historicists identify in texts is a constant two-way process between text and audience, ruler and ruled, and representation and social structure (cf. Bakhtin 1986; Bourdieu 1977).[5] The cultural poetics, which structures these statements, both creates their efficacy and channels them into particular forms, which have undeniable consequences for the content itself.

The Cultural Poetics of Space

The particular form taken by a cultural poetics is dictated by the limits of the medium in which it is expressed. Space, as an expressive medium, has its own intrinsic qualities that, together with a culturally specific aesthetics and style, circumscribes its presentation within distinct societies.

Space is often charged with meaning through events. Individual actions define what the space means in relationship to society. Although the meaning inherent within any given space comes from the aesthetic values and beliefs of a people, it is the actuation of these cognitive processes that imbeds these meanings within landscapes and architecture. Therefore, all space is construed to be culturally constructed performances, both secular and sacred. Performances treat space concretely—through them space is changed, transformed, and shaped. Consequently, performance qualities are critical in constructing meaning within a spatial medium, just as they are critical in constructing meaning within a linguistic medium.

This meaning is constructed within various genres of performance by several key structuring devices. The key element is an emphasis on interaction between performer and audience during a performance event (Bakhtin 1986; Bauman 1986). Secondary structures serve to intensify this interaction and include stylistic elements of form—such as couplets, triadic clauses, metaphorical stacking, and episodic cycles—as well as stylistic elements of expression—such as vocal pitch and cadence or movement position and rhythm. All are used by the performer to engage the audience (Hymes 1975; D. Tedlock 1983, 1985; Bakhtin 1986; Bauman 1986; Hanks 1989a, 1989b, 1989c). Finally, the specific features of these elements are the result of the particular time and location in which they have been produced; the contextual environment, encompassing the general social relations; and the immediate circumstances surrounding the performance (Schapiro 1953; Volosinov 1973; Bakhtin 1986). In a similar manner, these cultural poetic features shape meaning within spaces.

Both Susan Buck-Morss (1989) and Kathleen Stewart (1996) have stressed the localization in both time and space of the cultural poetic. Extending the insight that all poetics are cultural and political in nature, these authors assert that each poetic construct reveals the social relations of a precise time and place, demanding an attention to the details of culture akin to that of "thick description" advanced by Geertz (1973:3–30). Stewart is particularly captivated by the poetic construction of landscape by the people of Appalachia, which she characterizes by the use of tropes. Her use of the concept of "chronotrope" is revealing:

> When people go out roaming the hills, whether in mind or in body
> . . . They come up against places and are stopped dead in their tracks
> by re-membered images they can't help but recall. Named places become concrete models embodying not just the literal impact of the events but the local epistemology of re-membering impacts by retracing them in graphic images that stand at once as refuse and refuge (Stewart 1996:91).

The people, then, go on to construct culturally the landscape by means of a narrative that encompasses neither an isolated account of a single event nor a chronological sequence of events. Instead, the narrative selectively recounts events and pieces of episodes that are of importance to the individual narrator in an order that is meaningful to him. This "re-membering" of the landscape constantly recontextualizes the past in the present, linking the present to the past in a nonlinear but nonetheless purposeful fashion. Thus the landscape becomes the canvas on which these people paint their conceptions of time and history.

Landscape also evokes past memories for the Australian aborigines:

> It is not simply that landscape is a sign system for mythological events, as is now understood. Rather the landscape is the referent for much of the symbolism. Too often landscape has been seen as an intervening sign system that serves the purpose of passing on the an-

cestral past. I would like to argue that landscape is integral to the
message (Morphy 1995:186).

Time was created through the transformation of ancestral beings
into place, the place being forever the mnemonic of the event.
. . . Whatever events happened at the place, whatever sequence they
occurred in, whatever intervals existed between them, all becomes
subordinate to their representation in space. Transformed into features of the landscape mythological events are represented simultaneously even if they could be said to have occurred at different
points in time (Morphy 1995:188).

Like the people of Appalachia, the Australian aborigines temporalize
space. Events are related to spatial matrices, with little attention paid to
the temporal flow. Links between the past and present are again forged by
means of narrative. Often it is the very act of recounting the past events
that creates the relationship between the past and present, as when new
people move into an area. This link is especially true of Mesoamerica,
where migration tales give meaning to multiple landscapes in order to set
up the right to inhabit a particular landscape, at the same time that these
tales create systems of political order among the inhabitants (López
Austin 1973:98). Thus groups create an identity for themselves vis-à-vis
the land and the past through narrative. They literally write themselves
into the story through the inscription of narratives onto space.

Space, then, is commonly infused with temporal signification. Furthermore, these temporal qualities are linked to the cultural construction of
history through individual and collective memories. The past is constantly being crafted by the present. Specific actions are inscribed within
landscapes, and when the acts are repeated or the locale seen again by individuals, the event from the past is recalled. Histories are created when
past events are recalled and contextualized within the present. This said,
it must be recognized that it is not a smooth, linear history that is embedded within these culturally constructed spaces. Instead, specific actions
are engraved onto specific spaces with little thought to chronological order or sequence of events. These time/space junctures are expressed
through a local aesthetic and style, rendering the composition meaningful within its social context and hence creating a powerful trope.

Space, Power, and Poetics in Practice

It is the relationship between representation—consisting of a literal message, an aesthetic, and a style—and power that is the principal focus of

the papers in this volume. Power, like aesthetics and style, can only be interpreted within a contextual environment, dependent upon the time, place, and individuals involved in the embodying communicative act (Hodder 1986, 1987, 1992). To best interpret the architectural programs of the central areas of various sites, it is critical to understand the nature of the contemporaneous public discourse, which serves as the foundation for the contextual environment.

However, in order to develop an understanding of the public discourse, Mesoamerican scholars must attend to the details of the data. "Thick descriptions" of the available cultural data are imperative to establish a meaningful context and identify the predominant public discourses (Geertz 1973). These descriptions are especially important given that incomplete data sets are inherent to working with ancient societies. To demonstrate the fruitfulness of this approach we offer below a study of the cultural poetics of the central area of El Tajín. Although it is far from our intent to provide an exhaustive reading of the ceremonial center of this site, we do wish to point out certain fundamental characteristics of central Tajín that bear directly on the theoretical issues posed earlier in the essay.

El Tajín

The site of El Tajín was a major Epiclassic urban center on the northeastern fringes of Mesoamerica. During the Epiclassic period, the entire Mesoamerican political landscape was reshaped as the Classic centers and systems fell between 700–900 AD (Jiménez Moreno 1966; Diehl and Berlo 1989). New polities in previously marginal areas, such as El Tajín in north-central Veracruz, arose to fill the power vacuum, developing hybrid, highly innovative art styles across Mesoamerica as their new urban spaces took shape. These art styles were deployed as part of a systematic program that also included performance and architecture, creating a legitimating space for the new ruling elites.

The crucible of these legitimating strategies was the ceremonial center of the city. The urban center was the principal place where Epiclassic political power was proclaimed and enacted. The messages encoded here may be viewed as fundamental political texts used to produce legitimacy in this crucial transitional period in Mesoamerican history. Even though large-scale public displays of political power had been a part of the Mesoamerican political process since Olmec times, during the Epiclassic period these displays were a strategic imperative for individuals to secure and strengthen newly formulated social roles inside of burgeoning new polities.

14

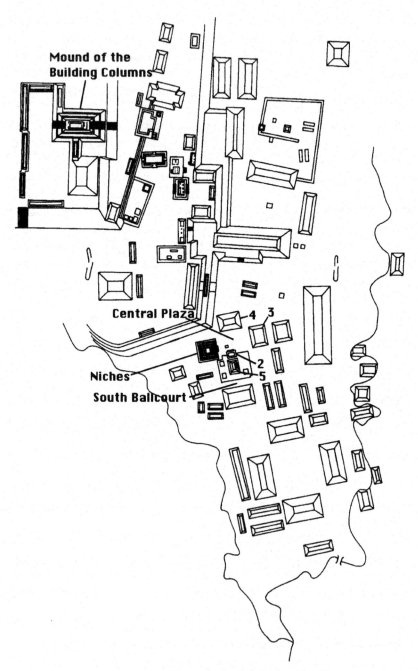

Figure 1.1   Site plan of El Tajín

The main stage set of this political theater at El Tajín is the Central Plaza (Figure 1.1). In the larger context of the site, the Central Plaza serves as the node for the groups of pyramids, plazas, and ballcourts that formed the lower ceremonial center. This public area is juxtaposed against Tajín Chico, an elevated area immediately to the north, where instead of ballcourts and pyramids, the architecture consists primarily of complex, multiroomed structures mounted on low bases (see Sarro, chapter 9 in this volume). Thus the major outdoor public spaces, such as the Central Plaza, are located in the lower area of the site, whereas the more private interior spaces, where smaller elite groups would have congregated, are situated in the upper area.[6]

The remainder of this chapter will treat the archaeological evidence for a banner-raising ritual enacted in Tajín's Central Plaza. Representations of this ritual and its archaeological residue point to two different but related audiences for the rite: one restricted and elite, the other more public and inclusive. As we will see, the elite context uses a prestige style and restricted interior space to communicate the hierarchy and legitimacy of the elite created by the rite. The more public version of the rite foregrounds instead the inclusive nature of the rite and its polity-building effects. Both of these messages draw on the fundamental legitimating power of the Snake Mountain trope, which formed the backdrop to both versions of the rite and its representations.

Snake Mountain was a central Ancient Mesoamerican aesthetic trope that regulated the shape of various mythic narratives, rituals, and ceremonial centers. Linda Schele and Julia Guernsey Kappelman analyze both the shape and the history of this trope in their contribution to this volume (see chapter 2). A central element of this trope is the sacred mountain/pyramid at the center, often viewed as a place of cosmogony, and at the base of which are raised the war banners of the polity. As we will see, the creators of the Tajín central space used this trope to frame both the elite and more popular versions of the banner-raising sequence, allowing for both hierarchy and polity building under the aegis of a proper and deeply meaningful framing space.

Dominating the Central Plaza is the most elaborately decorated monumental building at Tajín, the Pyramid of the Niches (Figure 1.2). The facade of the building consists of a variant of the talud/tablero style architecture seen throughout Mesoamerica and associated most closely with the great Classic site of Teotihuacan. Here the Teotihuacano rectangular framed tablero is replaced by a series of niches, giving the building an enhanced sculptural quality through the intense chiaroscuro effects created

Figure 1.2   Pyramid of the Niches, El Tajín

by the deep niches. This sculptural quality is amplified by the flying cornices, which surmount the niches, creating their own light/dark contrasts while serving as the base for the long, sloping talud above.

Many buildings at Tajín share this particular style of talud/tablero architecture, a fact that led George Kubler (1973) to propose that this particular architectural profile is a marker of Tajín identity. Furthermore, he posited that the Mesoamerican talud/tablero profile, regardless of variant form or attached symbolism, serves as an index of sacred architecture throughout the region. Kubler's insights fit well with what we know of Tajín's architecture: Pyramids with important religious sanctuaries are often marked with the talud/niches/flying cornice combination, and this specific architectural style seems to be restricted to the region of north-central Veracruz and the adjacent Sierra de Puebla during the Epiclassic period.[7]

Although the style is indigenous to sacred architecture at Tajín and has a regional distribution, no other building in this tradition combines the monumental size, refined finish, compositional complexity, and proportional balance of the Pyramid of the Niches. In this sense the building functions as the symbolic and aesthetic ground zero of monumental architecture at Tajín, based on the style and finish of the monument, in that, following Kubler, it communicates both "sacrality" and "Tajínness" more forcefully than any other building at the site. Viewed from the vantage point of the history of religions or semiotics, these ideas may seem basic, but they become more important when considered in the light of the political and social history of the site: Why this building, in this place, in this context?

Given its aesthetic centrality, it is not surprising to recall that the Pyramid of the Niches serves as the anchor building of the central public ritual space at the site. The main stairway ascends from the Central Plaza side of the building, marking this space as the main orientation of the building. The two buildings that flank the Pyramid of the Niches (Structures Two and Four; see Figure 1.1) each contain one sculpted relief panel that details rituals occurring in or associated with the Central Plaza. We will concentrate on one of these reliefs, the Structure Four Panel (Figure 1.3), which defines the major ritual occurring in the Central Plaza itself. Framing the composition on either side are ritual attendants who inhabit water-associated toponyms. The focal point of the composition is the central group of two facing figures with a large ceremonial object rising between them. This object rises from a turtle's carapace, through a low bench, to end capped by a roundel fringed with feathers and encircled by two serpents. I have shown elsewhere (Koontz 2001) that this central object is a war banner, similar to banners shown in ritual sequences described elsewhere at the site (Figure 1.4). Moreover, the central roundel of the Structure Four Panel is carved through the panel to create a hole in the piece, large enough for the placement of just such a banner, echoing

Figure 1.3   Structure Four Panel, El Tajín

Figure 1.4   War banner, El Tajín

the use of the panel depicted in the scene itself. Thus the Structure Four Panel not only depicts a banner-raising ceremony but is itself the base for just such a ritual.

The chief place for this banner ritual was the area fronting the adjacent Pyramid of the Niches. The archaeological remnants of this ritual are aligned along the base of the pyramid, mainly on the Central Plaza side, and consist of fifteen large cut stone blocks with holes of consistent diameter drilled into the center of the top face (Figure 1.5), comparable to the hole drilled into the central portion of the Structure Four Panel. These blocks served as the bases for the actual banner-raising ritual alluded to in the Structure Four Panel discussed above.

For Ancient Mesoamericans, war banners were highly charged objects that were seen as emblematic of the polity or political division of the group (Bricker 1981:39; Hassig 1992; Freidel et al. 1993:293–336). The political importance of the raising of these devices was fundamental, a point underscored at Tajín by their frequent representation and the importance given to other elements in the ritual, such as the banner base. Most important, the banner ritual was arranged around the central sacred mountain/pyramid of the site, the Pyramid of the Niches. A central sacred mountain with banners raised at its base echoes the shape of the fundamental Mesoamerican aesthetic trope—that of Snake Mountain—alluded to above (see Schele and Kappelman, chapter 2 in this volume). It is at the base of Snake Mountain that, according to Mexica myth and ritual, the first war was fought and won. The banners of the polity were brought together every year in celebration of that victory—a celebration

Figure 1.5   Bases of banners

that cemented the alliances of various groups to the overarching Mexica polity (León-Portilla 1987).

Yet the organization of this space and the ritual itself is not a transparent enactment of this trope. The most important depiction of the ritual, found on the Structure Four Panel, was placed at the top of Structure Four, in the now-destroyed superstructure (García Payón 1973). The audience available to see this rendering, or experience the ritual raising of that particular banner, would have been small and elite, whereas the audience available to experience the actual raising of the numerous banners at the base of the Pyramid of the Niches would have been much larger. The construction of two different audiences for such a primordial ritual raises certain questions about the political uses of the rite. How were each of these related but discrete aspects of the banner-raising ritual manipulated politically, and, perhaps more significantly, how did the deployment of the aesthetic trope denoting paradigmatic warfare help shape each of these political dramas?

The Ritual of Raising the Banners

The style used in the Structure Four Panel is typical of the fine low relief seen in important panels throughout Tajín. The use of strong double outlines in the carving, the heavy use of scroll forms, and the *horror vacui* of the composition all point to the Classic Veracruz style, defined most completely by Tatiana Proskouriakoff (1954). Far from being the originator of this style, Tajín was a late participant, applying these formal traits that had accumulated a prestige currency in both monumental and portable art for centuries before the rise of the site.[8] As noted above, the Structure Four Panel, like many low relief narrative scenes in the Classic Veracruz style at the site, was placed in a restricted, elite context, suggesting that the Classic Veracruz style itself framed specifically elite ritual contexts.[9] Thus the style itself becomes emblematic of the power and prestige of the Tajín elite.

The iconography speaks to this same interest in the elite audience. The two central participants of the Structure Four Panel (Figure 1.3) are framed by one attendant figure each—not the masses of figures who take part in the banner-raising ceremony shown at the site and in the region.[10] The two central figures are identified with insignia of the Tajín paramount ruler: The figure on the left holds the sash and sacrificial knife seen elsewhere with the ruler, whereas the figure on the right wears a cape indicative of Tajín rulership, and he holds the same type of royal cloth sash in his right hand seen with the central figure on the left. This distillation of the event into its elite core would have resonated with the small audience massed to view the single banner raised there.

The elite version of the banner rite occurred in the restrictive space at the summit of Structure Four with an elite-centered iconography expressed through the prestige Classic Veracruz style. Below, in the more popular space of the Central Plaza, the banner stones are left as undecorated, massive prismatic blocks. Instead of the focus on one banner, the Central Plaza was the place of display of the entire array of primary banners of the polity. The frame given these banners was not the elite narrative carving of the Structure Four Panel but the massive bulk of the Pyramid of the Niches, which formed the backdrop to the ceremony for the participants gathered in the Central Plaza. Instead of the focus on rulership and hierarchy, the Central Plaza proclaims the inclusion of polity groups under the aegis of the central emblem of the Tajín polity, the Pyramid of the Niches itself. The meaning and layout of this building, in turn, participated in the Mesoamerican aesthetic trope of Snake Mountain. In other words, the Central Plaza banner ritual is played out in two different spaces, for two different audiences. Above, in the sanctuary atop Structure Four, the restricted space of the highest ranking members, with its accompanying prestige style as frame and the message of legitimate hierarchy. Below, the inclusion of the major polity groups under the aegis of the personification of the sacred Tajín Snake Mountain with its inclusive, polity-building message. Both are framed by the overarching legitimacy supplied by the Snake Mountain aesthetic trope, which would have resonated with most if not all levels of society as well as outside forces active in the power structures of the polity.

This political strategy must be seen in the context of Epiclassic Mesoamerica, with its rise of new political centers, intensified elite competition, and syncretic languages of power. The Tajín strategy reveals an elite that is at once trying to proclaim their difference and legitimate their claims to hierarchical order, although the larger public proclamation omits these narratives of hierarchy and concentrates on the massing of the major groups at El Tajín. In each case, a particular variation of the fundamental aesthetic trope was foregrounded in order to convey the rightness and power of the message. In the case of the restricted elite context, the elaborate decoration in the Classic Veracruz style frames the raising of the equally elaborate single banner under the aegis of the highest ranking Tajín figures. In the case of the lower Central Plaza rite, multiple banners are framed by the emblem of the polity itself, the Pyramid of the Niches, which is an example of an even more fundamental Mesoamerican trope, that of the central sacred mountain with a banner raised at its base.[11]

It is important to note just what is at stake in the analytic strategy above, where not only are key Mesoamerican- and Tajín-specific tropes identified, but further, the context of their deployment is associated with particular social and political goals that targeted different groups. Thus the tropes, which are structuring principles of any effective communication, become political tools for a particular group's self-interested proclamations. It is here that ideals of beauty or rightness intersect with political machinations through public proclamations. This intersection is analogous to Marshall Sahlins's "structure of the conjuncture" (1985) cited above, where the conjunction of the structuring aesthetic trope and the contingent historical circumstances produce statements that proclaim both indigenous ideals of correctness and the realities of political power. Style is used to differentiate groups and reiterate group identity, as in the use of the Classic Veracruz scroll style to elaborate an elite vision of the banner-raising ceremony and in the use of the formal niche element to emphasize a ceremony uniting the entire Tajín polity. In this example, more than a simple mechanism to create polity identity, the power of this aesthetic trope was channeled to effect both social unification and the reification of hierarchy.

References

Armstrong, Robert Plant.
  1971   *The Affecting Presence: An Essay in Humanistic Anthropology.* Urbana, Ill.: University of Illinois Press.
  1975   *Wellspring: On the Myth and Source of Culture.* Berkeley: University of California Press.
  1981   *The Powers of Presence: Consciousness, Myth, and the Affecting Presence.* Philadelphia: University of Pennsylvania Press.
Bakhtin, Mikhail M.
  1986   The Problem of Speech Genres. *Speech Genres and Other Late Essays.* Translated by Vern W. McGee. Austin, Tex.: University of Texas Press.
Bauman, Richard.
  1986   *Story, Performance, and Event.* Cambridge: Cambridge University Press.
Bauman, Richard, and Charles L. Briggs.
  1990   Poetics and Performance as Critical Perspectives on Language and Social Life. *Annual Review of Anthropology* 19:59–88.
Bourdieu, Pierre.
  1977   *Outline of a Theory of Practice.* Cambridge: Cambridge University Press.
  1984   *Distinction: A Social Critique of the Judgement of Taste.* Translated by Richard Nice. Cambridge, Mass.: Harvard University Press.
Bricker, Victoria.
  1981   *The Indian Christ and the Indian King: The Historical Substrate of Maya Myth and Ritual.* Austin, Tex.: University of Texas Press.
Buck-Morss, Susan.
  1989   *The Dialectic of Seeing: Walter Benjamin and the Paris Arcades Project.* Cambridge, Mass.: MIT Press.
Carlsen, Robert S., and Martin Prechtel.
  1991   The Flowering of the Dead: An Interpretation of Highland Maya Culture. *Man* 26:23–42.
Diehl, Richard A., and Janet Catherine Berlo, editors.
  1989   *Mesoamerica After the Decline of Teotihuacan A.D. 700–900.* Washington, D.C.: Dumbarton Oaks.
Dougherty, Carol, and Leslie Kurke.
  1993   *Cultural Poetics in Archaic Greece: Cult, Performance, Politics.* Cambridge: Cambridge University Press.
Durkheim, Emile.
  1965   *The Elementary Forms of Religious Life.* New York: Free Press.
Edmunson, Munro.
  1986   *Heaven Born Merida and Its Destiny: The Book of the Chilam Balam Chumayel.* Annotated by Munro Edmunson. Austin, Tex.: University of Texas Press.
Feld, Steven.
  1988   Aesthetics as Iconicity of Style (uptown title), or (downtown title) 'Lift-Up-Over Sounding': Getting into the Kaluli Groove. *Yearbook for Traditional Music* 20:74–113.
Foucault, Michel.

1973   *The Order of Things: An Archaeology of the Human Sciences.* New York: Vintage Books.

1977   *Discipline and Punish: The Birth of the Prison.* Translated by Alan Sheridan. New York: Pantheon Books.

1981   *Power/Knowledge: Selected Interviews and Other Writings 1972–1977.* Edited by Colin Gordon. New York: Pantheon Books.

Freidel, David, Linda Schele, and Joy Parker.

1993   *Maya Cosmos: Three Thousand Years on the Shaman's Path.* New York: William Morrow.

García Payón, José.

1973. El Tablero de Montículo Cuatro. *Boletín del INAH, Series 2* 7:31–34.

Garibay K., Angel Maria.

1953   *Historia de la Literature Nahuatl.* México, D.F.: Porrua.

Geertz, Clifford.

1973   *The Interpretation of Cultures.* New York: Basic Books.

1980   *Negara: The Theatre State in Nineteenth Century Bali.* Trenton, N.J.: Princeton University Press.

Gossen, Gary.

1985   Tzotzil Literature. *Supplement to the Handbook of Middle American Indians, Volume 3.* Edited by Munro S. Edmunson. Austin, Tex.: University of Texas Press. 65–106.

Hanks, William F.

1989a   Elements of Style. *Word and Image in Maya Culture.* Edited by William F. Hanks and Don S. Rice. Salt Lake City: University of Utah Press. 92–111.

1989b   Text and Textuality. *Annual Review of Anthropology* 18:95–127.

1989c   Word and Image in a Semiotic Perspective. *Word and Image in Maya Culture.* Edited By William F. Hanks and Don S. Rice. Salt Lake City: University of Utah Press. 8–21.

Hassig, Ross.

1992   *War and Society in Ancient Mesoamerica.* Berkeley: University of California Press.

Hodder, Ian.

1986   *Reading the Past: Current Approaches to Interpretation in Archaeology.* Cambridge: Cambridge University Press.

1992   *Theory and Practice in Archaeology.* New York: Routledge Press.

Hodder, Ian, editor.

1982   *Symbolic and Structural Archaeology.* Cambridge: Cambridge University Press.

1987   *The Archaeology of Contextual Meaning.* Cambridge: Cambridge University Press.

Hymes, Dell.

1975   Folklore's Nature and the Sun's Myth. *Journal of American Folklore* 88:345–369.

Jakobson, Roman.

1960   Closing Statement: Linguistics and Poetics. *Style in Language.* Edited by T. A. Sebeok. Cambridge, Mass.: MIT Press. 350–377.

Jakobson, Roman, and Claude Lévi-Strauss.
  1962   "Les Chats" de Charles Baudelaire. *L'Homme* 2:5–21.
Jiménez Moreno, Wigberto.
  1966   Mesoamerica Before the Toltecs. *Ancient Oaxaca.* Edited by John Paddock. Palo Alto, Calif.: Stanford University Press. 1–82.
Keil, Charles.
  1979   *Tiv Song.* Chicago: University of Chicago Press.
Koontz, Rex.
  1994   *The Iconography of El Tajín, Veracruz, Mexico.* Ph.D. dissertation, University of Texas at Austin.
  2001   Epiclassic Sacred Space at El Tajín, Veracruz. *Cosmos and History: A Mesoamerican Legacy.* Edited by Andrea Stone. Tuscaloosa, Ala.: University of Alabama Press. in press. Ms. 1999.
Kubler, George.
  1973   Iconographic Aspects of Architectural Profiles at Teotihuacan and in Mesoamerica. *The Iconography of Middle American Sculpture.* New York: Metropolitan Museum of Art. 24–39.
Leach, Edmund.
  1977   *Political Systems of Highland Burma: A Study of Kachin Social Structure.* Monographs on Social Anthropology 44. London: Athlone Press.
Lévi-Strauss, Claude.
  1963   *Structural Anthropology.* Translated by Claire Jacobson and Brooke Grundfest Schoepf. New York: Basic Books.
León-Portilla, Miguel.
  1987   *Mexico-Tenochtitlán, su espacio y tiempo sagrados.* México, D.F.: Plaza y Valdes.
López Austin, Alfredo.
  1973   *Hombre-Dios: Religión y política en el mundo náhuatl.* México, D.F.: UNAM, Instituto de Investigaciones Históricas.
Matos Moctezuma, Eduardo.
  1987   Symbolism of the Templo Mayor. *The Aztec Templo Mayor.* Edited by Elizabeth Hill Boone. Washington, D.C.: Dumbarton Oaks. 185–210.
Morphy, Howard.
  1995   Landscape and Reproduction of the Ancestral Past. *The Anthropology of Landscape: Perspectives on Place & Space.* Edited by Eric Hirsch. Oxford Studies in Social and Cultural Anthropology. Oxford: Clarendon Press. 184–209.
Palacios, Enrique Juan.
  1926   *Yohualichan y el Tajín. Monumentos arqueológicos en Cuetzalan descubiertos por la Dirección de Arqueología.* México, D.F.: Secretaria de Educación Pública.
Proskouriakoff, Tatiana.
  1954   *Varieties of Classic Central Veracruz Sculpture.* Carnegie Institution of Washington, Contributions to American Anthropology and History, no. 58. Washington, D.C.: Carnegie Institute.
  1971   Classic Art of Central Veracruz. *Handbook of Middle American Indians, Volume 11.* Austin, Tex.: University of Texas Press. 558–572.

Reese, Kathryn.
1996   *Narratives of Power: Late Formative Public Architecture and Civic Center Design at Cerros, Belize.* Ph.D. dissertation, Department of Anthropology, University of Texas at Austin.
Sahlins, Marshall.
1985   *Islands of History.* Chicago: University of Chicago Press.
Sánchez Bonilla, Juan.
1993   Similitudes entre las pinturas de Las Higueras y las obras plásticas del Tajín. *Tajín.* Edited by Jürgen Brügemann, Sara Ladrón de Guevara, and Juan Sánchez Bonilla. México, D.F.: El Equilibrista. 133–159.
Saussure, Ferdinand de.
1913   *Cours de linguistique générale.* Edited by Rudolf Engler. Weisbaden: Harrassowitz.
Schapiro, Meyer.
1953   Style. *Anthropology Today.* Edited by A. L. Kroeber. Chicago: University of Chicago Press. 287–312.
Schiefflin, Edward L.
1985   Performance and the Cultural Construction of Reality. *American Ethnologist* 12(4):707–724.
Shanks, Michael, and Christopher Tilley.
1982   Ideology, Symbolic Power and Ritual Communication: A Reinterpretation of Neolithic Mortuary Practices. *Symbolic and Structural Archaeology.* Edited by Ian Hodder. Cambridge: Cambridge University Press. 129–154.
1987   *Social Theory and Archaeology.* Cambridge: Polity Press.
Sherzer, Joel.
1987   The Discourse-Centered Approach to Language and Culture. *American Anthropologist* 89:285–309.
Shotter, John.
1995   Wittegenstein's World Beyond 'The Way of Theory' Toward a 'Social Poetics.' Paper presented at the symposium, Social Construction, Culture, and the Politics of Social Identity, April 7. New York: New School of Social Research.
Stark, Barbara L.
1975   Excavaciones en los mangares del Paploapan y un estilo de volutas de Patarata. *Boletín del INAH* 14:45–50.
Stewart, Kathleen.
1996   *A Space on the Side of the Road: Cultural Poetics in the "Other" America.* Princeton: Princeton University Press.
Tedlock, Barbara.
1984   The Beautiful and the Dangerous: Zuni Ritual and Cosmology as an Aesthetic System. *Conjunctions* 6:246–265.
1986   Crossing the Sensory Domains of Native American Aesthetics. *Explorations in Ethnomusicology in Honor of David P. McAllester.* Edited by Charlotte Frisbie. Detroit Monographs in Musicology, Number 9. Detroit: Information Coordinators. 187–198.
1992   *The Beautiful and the Dangerous: Encounter with Zuni Indians.* New York: Viking Press.

Tedlock, Dennis.
    1983   *The Spoken Word and the Work of Interpretation.* Philadelphia: University
            of Pennsylvania Press.
    1985   *Popol Vuh: The Mayan Book of the Dawn of Life.* New York: Simon and
            Schuster.
Turner, Victor.
    1967   *The Forest of Symbols.* Ithaca: Cornell University Press.
Urban, Greg.
    1991   *A Discourse-Centered Approach to Culture: Native South American Myths
            and Rituals.* Austin, Tex.: University of Texas Press.
Volosinov, V. N.
    1973   *Marxism and the Philosophy of Language.* Translated by Ladislav Matejka
            and I. R. Titunik. Cambridge, Mass.: Harvard University Press.
Wittgenstein, Ludwig.
    1922   *Tractatus Logico-Philosophicus.* London: Routledge and Kegan Paul.
    1966   Article in *The New York Times.*

Notes

1. "chaque methode peut être choisie en fonction des circonstances, c'est, en
derniére analyse, parce qu'elles son substituables l'une á l'autre." The earlier
analyses of Lévi-Strauss that attempted to undo the relationship between myth
and poetics must be understood in the context of his project that shows myth out-
strips any single performance: "Its [myth's] substance does not lie in its style, its
original music, or its syntax, but in the story which it tells" (Lévi-Strauss 1963:
210). Thus myth is a sort of metalanguage or pure narrative that is not dependent
on any single performance. The latter would inevitably call into question the poetics of that performance, which the author was not willing to admit as a crucial
analytical element at the time. His work with Jakobson cited above is an express
attempt to reintegrate poetics into the structuralist analytical framework. This
would be a rather minor footnote in the history of interpretive strategies were it
not for the profound influence of structuralist modes of thought on anthropology
in general and Mesoamerican iconography and epigraphy in particular.

2. This crucial point stems from the insight that all cultural materials, and not
just textual materials, have a communicative component which is structured so
that it may be decoded by others. In this way abstract designs, common ceramics,
ritual acts, architecture, and other everyday objects and actions that may not at
first glance be seen to participate in oral or literary discourses are encoded
("texted") with meaning.

3. Leach models his relationship between aesthetics and ethics upon that proposed by Ludwig Wittgenstein (1922) in *Tractatus Logico-Philosophicus.* In this
book, Wittgenstein proposes a relationship between art and ethics which he later
summarizes in the following quote: "The work of art is the object seen *sub specie
aeternitatis;* and the good life is the world seen *sub specie aeternitatis.* This is the
connection between art and ethics." (Wittgenstein 1966).

4. Benjamin's definition of the dialectic image is founded in a late nineteenth-
century perspective that encodes all struggles as being between two opposing so-

cial forces in a very concrete external manner. We reorient the conflict, suggesting that the tension is internal, located completely within the image.

5. This struggle is external and not embodied by the image but can include the representation as an agent. The conflict fundamentally involves the question of who controls the meaning produced by any cultural act and, consequently, the power in any relationship (cf. Foucault 1981:114–115).

6. The exception to the intimate interior spaces of Tajín Chico is found in the huge enclosed court attached to the Mound of the Building Columns complex.

7. Especially important in this regard is the Sierra de Puebla site of Yohualichan (Palacios 1926).

8. For example, on the decoration of the Subterraneos at Teotihuacan and on the Pyramid of the Feathered Serpent at Xochicalco, as well as numerous portable objects from various regions of Mesoamerica which may be dated well before the rise of Tajín. See Stark (1975) and Proskouriakoff (1971:559–60) for discussions of the antiquity of this style.

9. The important exception to this observation may be the two decorated ball-courts, although these too were certainly restricted elite contexts when compared with the plaza spaces.

10. For Tajín, see the banner-raising ceremony depicted on Mound of the Building Columns Sculptures 5 and 8 (Koontz 1994). For regional depictions, see the contemporary mural program found at Las Higueras (Sánchez Bonilla 1993).

11. See Schele and Kappelman, chapter 2 in this volume, for a discussion of the time depth of the mountain/banner trope. As these authors point out, the foundational myth of the Late Postclassic Mexica, which centered around a Snake Mountain with banner (León-Portilla 1987; Matos Moctezuma 1987), has analogs that reach at least to the Late Preclassic period in the Maya area (Reese 1996). This suggests that the trope is a widespread template for creating legitimate Mesoamerican urban space.

What the Heck's Coatépec?
The Formative Roots of
an Enduring Mythology

LINDA SCHELE
JULIA GUERNSEY KAPPELMAN[1]

Myth and Context

Mesoamerican peoples throughout time viewed the shape and rhythm of the universe through the narrative of creation, played out in the movements of the sun, constellations, and planets in the sky. As a reflection back to the heavens from the Earth, they also structured the shape of their cities—and the very patterns of their civilized life—according to specific mythological narratives of primordial power. This chapter explores how one of these myths, that of Tollan, or "place of the reeds," was used to structure the aesthetics of space and form from the Formative through the Postclassic periods. Through this mythic framework, each site defined itself as a place of great civilization where the arts and good government flourished and where the right to rule and perform acts of warfare and sacrifice were divinely sanctioned.[2]

In order to understand the nature and time depth of these structuring mythologies, one must first turn to the great Aztec creation and migration stories in which these narratives are most fully elaborated. In particular, the legend of Coatépec, or "Snake Mountain," was interwoven with the myth of Tollan into the migration epic of the Aztecs. Although identified in the migration story as two stops along the journey, the locations of Tollan and Coatépec were more than just that. As Elizabeth Boone (1991) demonstrated, these locations and the movement of people through them were part of a ritual performance that not only transformed space and charged it with social and ideological significance but legitimized the rule of those who structured their sacred spaces according to its design.[3]

As with the myth of Tollan, that of Coatépec takes various forms in the Central Mexican sources, which range from pictorial codices such as the *Codex Boturini* to such chronicles as those of Sahagún, Durán, and Tezozomoc.[4] Certain consistent themes appear in each of the various versions of the Coatépec myth, however, and concern the establishment of sacred space and the divine mandate to make war and to perform sacrifice. Moreover, these themes are found throughout Mesoamerican history, suggesting that the basic structure of Snake Mountain was a central Mesoamerican aesthetic trope with enormous time depth.[5]

As illustrated in the pages of the *Codex Boturini* (Figure 2.1), the Aztecs left their island homeland of Aztlan in the year 1 Flint and canoed across the lake to Culhuacan where they erected a crude temple to their patron deity Huitzilopochtli (Boone 1991:125–127). Eight groups, each identified by a house, a seated leader, and a name sign, left together on this great migration journey. Also accompanying them were four tribal leaders, or god-bearers, one of whom carried on his back an image of Huitzilopochtli in the form of a mummy bundle and wearing a hummingbird helmet (Figure 2.2).

Figure 2.1 *Codex Boturini*, **page 1, detail. The Aztecs leave Aztlan.**
Drawing by Kappelman after *Codex Boturini* (1964)

Figure 2.2 *Codex Boturini*, **page 2, detail. God-bearer with Huitzilopochtli bundle.** Drawing by Kappelman after *Codex Boturini* (1964)

Continuing on their journey to Tenochtitlán, where they would ultimately establish their state and capital city, the Aztecs next stopped at a location named Chocayan, the "place of tears." From there they proceeded immediately to the place called Coatépec, or "Snake Mountain," that Sahagún (1950–1982, Book 3:1) tells us was very near Tollan (Figure 2.3). Page 6 of the Boturini reveals that the Aztecs spent 28 years at Coatépec (Boone 1991:Figure 8.5). Adjacent to the sign which names the year 2 Reed is the symbol for New Fire, which indicates that, in the year 2 Reed, the Aztecs celebrated the beginning of a new 52-year cycle.

The *Codex Azcatitlan* provides even more detailed information about the events that transpired at Coatépec (Figure 2.4). As it illustrates, and as we also learn from such sources as Bernardino de Sahagún (1950–1982, Book 3:1–5), Diego Durán (1967, Volume 2:218), Hernando Alvarado Tezozomoc (1975, 1980), and Juan de Torquemada (1975–1979), the Aztecs built a temple on top of Snake Mountain for their patron god Huitzilopochtli during their stay at Coatépec. In the *Codex Azcatitlan* one can see the humanmade temple built on top of the mountain that is labeled *cohuatep*, "snake mountain," and which is rendered with projecting serpent heads.

According to Tezozomoc, Huitzilopochtli then built at the base of the mountain a ballcourt, in the center of which he placed a hole called an *itzompan* or "skull place" (1980:227–229). Following Huitzilopochtli's instructions, the Aztecs dammed up the *itzompan* in order to create a "Well of Water." This Well of Water formed a lake at the base of Coatépec, making the surrounding landscape fertile and providing the Aztecs with the water necessary for the cultivation of plants and with freshwater creatures of all kinds. This description of Coatépec is echoed in the *Codex Tovar* (Figure 2.5), in which the hill is clearly labeled as Snake Mountain by the coiled serpent although water, fish, and reeds surround its base.

Figure 2.3 *Codex Boturini,*
page 5, detail. Coatépec.
Drawing by Kappelman
after *Codex Boturini* (1964)

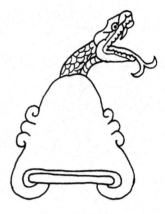

Figure 2.4 *Codex*
Azcatitlan, **page 11.**
Huitzilopochtli armed for
battle at Coatépec.
Drawing by Daniela epstein
after *Codex Azcatitlan* (1949)

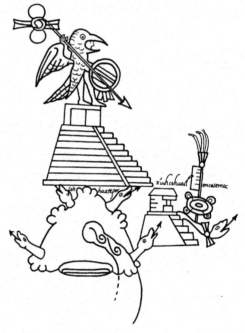

Sahagún (1950–1982, Book 3:2) recounts that a faction of the migrating Aztecs, called the *Centzon Huitznahua* or "Four Hundred Southerners," decided that they wanted to stay in this fine location, thereby ending the migration and establishing their capital at Coatépec. This greatly angered Huitzilopochtli, who came down from his mountain armed for war. The *Codex Azcatitlan* (Figure 2.4) captures this moment and simultaneously presents the narrative in two different ways. At the top of the temple on Coatépec, Huitzilopochtli is posed for battle in his war costume with

Figure 2.5   Coatépec.
Drawing by Kappelman after the *Codex Tovar*
in Matos Moctezuma (1988:Figure 17)

hummingbird helmet, lance, and shield. At the same time, one sees below the smaller temple that is labeled *xiuhcohuatl oncatemoc*, which means "there descended the xiuhcoatl, or 'fire serpent,' the weapon of Huitzilopochtli" (León-Portilla 1978:82).

Tezozomoc (1980:229) then describes in his version of the story that Huitzilopochtli surrounded the Four Hundred Southerners and their older sister, a goddess named Coyolxauhqui. Huitzilopochtli killed Coyolxauhqui in the ballcourt at midnight, destroyed the Four Hundred Southerners, and ate their hearts. Having done this, he demolished the dam in the Well of Water, causing it to dry up and forcing the Aztecs to resume their migration.

In an alternative version of the myth told by Sahagún (1950–1982, Book 3:1–5), upon arriving at Coatépec the Aztecs found Coatlicue, the mother of Huitzilopochtli, living there. One day, while Coatlicue was sweeping the temple on Coatépec, a ball of feathers floated down from the sky. Tucking it into her waistband, she conceived Huitzilopochtli. Her other children, Coyolxauhqui and the Four-Hundred Southerners, were outraged by their mother's pregnancy and decided to kill her and her child. However, warned of the children's plot, Huitzilopochtli emerged fully

**Figure 2.6   Coatlicue gives
birth to Huitzilopochtli, from
the *Florentine Codex*.**
Drawing by Kappelman after
Sahagún (1950–1982:Book 3, Figure 1)

adult from Coatlicue, armed for war with his *xiuhcoatl* and shield. An image from Sahagún (Figure 2.6) depicts the miraculous birth of Huitzilopochtli from his mother Coatlicue, or "Serpent Skirt," armed for battle with his shield, lance, and *xiuhcoatl*.

Huitzilopochtli then decapitated and mutilated his sister Coyolxauhqui at the summit of Coatépec and threw her body down the side of the mountain. He also attacked and destroyed his brothers, the Four Hundred Southerners. As in the other version of the story, the events that transpired at Coatépec ultimately forced the Aztecs to leave Snake Mountain and resume their migration. Even more importantly, the events at Coatépec engendered two primary directives: the first, a divine mandate for acts of war and sacrifice; the second, a paradigm for the construction of sacred space that included Snake Mountain, a ballcourt at its base, and a place of sacrifice. Both of these are conceptualized in the *Codex Azcatitlan* (Figure 2.4): The imagery portrays the sacred geography of Snake Mountain while also referencing the acts of paradigmatic war and sacrifice that occurred within that setting.

This paradigm for the construction of sacred space that the Coatépec myth provided was translated into the human-built landscape. For the Aztecs, this was eloquently manifested at the Templo Mayor in Tenochtitlán, their capital and the destination of their migration journey. The

Figure 2.7 The Templo Mayor from Durán's *Historia de las Indias de Nueva España.* Drawing by Kappelman after Matos Moctezuma (1988:Figure 59)

Templo Mayor was a twin temple structure whose shrines were devoted to the rain deity Tlaloc and to Huitzilopochtli (Figure 2.7). As Richard Townsend (1982) and Eduardo Matos Moctezuma (1984, 1987) discussed, the pyramid was a synthesis of "Snake Mountain" or Coatépec on the Huitzilopochtli side, and the "Mountain of Sustenance" or Tonacatepetl on the Tlaloc side. The Aztecs also referred to the Templo Mayor in its entirety as Coatépec (Broda 1987:77).

Confirming this identification of the Templo Mayor as Coatépec are the serpents that decorate the bases of the balustrades and those that undulate across the frontal platform (Matos Moctezuma 1988:Figures 44, 45, 108, 109). The Templo Mayor was, as in the image from the *Codex Azcatitlan*, the human-built version of Snake Mountain. Moreover, the construction and conceptual organization of the Templo Mayor dramatically illustrates the paradigms articulated in the Coatépec myth (León-Portilla 1978; Matos Moctezuma 1984).

At the base of the platform on Huitzilopochtli's side of the Templo Mayor, in Phase IVb that dates roughly to the 1460s, a round stone depicting Coyolxauhqui with a severed head and mutilated limbs was excavated.[6] The context and placement of this sculpture at the base of the temple stairway corresponded exactly to the Coatépec myth in which Huitzilopochtli emerged fully adult from his mother's womb, killed and sacrificed his sister, and hurled her body down the temple stairs in the first act of paradigmatic war and sacrifice. In addition, the eight standard bearers who reclined at the bottom of the stairway to Huitzilopochtli's shrine in Stage III of the Templo Mayor may have represented the Four Hundred Southerners and their mythic defeat at the base of Coatépec (Matos Moctezuma 1988:73, Plate IX). Even more likely, the standard bearers functioned as banner stones, holding the flags that were erected at the base of Coatépec during festivals celebrating the victory of Huitzilopochtli.

The Aztec seasonal festival of Panquetzalitzli re-created the myth of Coatépec and the paradigmatic acts of war and sacrifice performed by Huitzilopochtli (León-Portilla 1978:50–61; Nicholson 1985; Matos Moctezuma 1987:200, 1991:21; Koontz 1994:35–38). Both Sahagún (1950–1982, Book 2:145–148) and Durán (1967) record that during the month of Panquetzalitzli, a Huitzilopochtli impersonator descended from the Templo Mayor, carrying his *xiuhcoatl*, while prisoners were sacrificed as representatives of the Four Hundred Southerners. As part of the performance, the paradigmatic ballcourt sacrifice that Huitzilopochtli performed in the Coatépec myth was also reenacted. According to Sahagún's *Primero Memoriales*,[7] the ballcourt in which this sacrifice was performed was directly across from the Templo Mayor, analogous to its position in the Coatépec myth. In addition, as part of the Panquetzalitzli ceremony, battle banners were raised at the base of Coatépec, recalling the positioning of the standard bearers at the base of the stairs of the Templo Mayor. These banners defined the foot of Coatépec as the place of banner raising, ballcourt sacrifice, and war. Furthermore, rituals such as that of Panquetzalitzli, as Carrasco (1987) and Boone (1991) observed, transcended temporality and invoked a mythology of origins and charter. For the Aztecs, the mythological events that took place at Coatépec were not just frozen in the past but regularly reenacted in constant revalidation of the divine sanction to perform acts of war and human sacrifice. This notion is eloquently expressed, once again, in the image from the *Codex Azcatitlan* (Figure 2.4). There, the *xiuhcoatl* bears on its back the battle banner that will mark the base of Coatépec. This image perfectly summarizes the paradigmatic nature of the Coatépec myth and its translation into human landscape and ritual.

The narrative of Coatépec, as part of the origin mythology of the Aztecs, provided a conceptual model that mandated the organization of sacred space around a Snake Mountain and a ballcourt of sacrifice in which paradigmatic acts of warfare and sacrifice were performed. It also provided the supernatural validation for political and cosmological authority.[8] These themes were not limited to the Aztecs, however, but were fundamental ideals for the conceptualization of sacred space and political charter across Mesoamerica, from the Formative throughout the Postclassic periods.

The Structures of Myth

At the 1941 conference on Tollan, Jiménez Moreno (1941) argued that the original Tollan for the Aztecs—or the mythic Tollan of Quetzalcoatl—corresponded to the archaeological site of Tula, Hidalgo.[9] Since then, numerous scholars (Davies 1977; Carrasco 1982; Heyden 1983; Umberger 1987a; Florescano 1994) have demonstrated that the term "Tollan," which comes from the Aztec word *tule* meaning "reed," or "place of the reeds," was used metaphorically by the Aztecs to designate places of great governance and civilization, including their own capital of Tenochtitlán, as well as the sites of Tula, Hidalgo, and Cholula, Puebla. Likewise, the Aztecs used the term "Toltec" to refer not only to the original inhabitants of the legendary Tollan but to great artisans and artists in general.[10]

However, David Stuart (1994) recently demonstrated that the Maya also used the term "place of the reeds," which is *puh* in Mayan, to refer specifically to the site of Teotihuacan (Figure 2.8). This fact is particularly important because it demonstrates that the concept of a Tollan, or "place of the reeds," was in place long before the Aztecs entered the Valley of Mexico or encountered the site of Tula, Hidalgo. It also demonstrates that the Maya believed that certain sites, such as Teotihuacan, represented great places of learning and conceptually symbolized a "place of the

**Figure 2.8   Maya *puh* or "reed" glyphs
from (a) Tikal, Temple 1, Lintel 2; and
(b) Tikal Stela 31.**
Drawings by Kappelman after Stuart (1994:Figure 8)

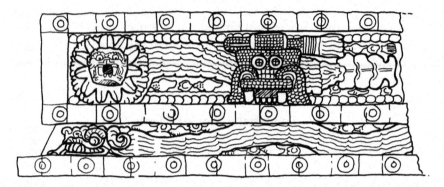

Figure 2.9   Teotihuacan, Temple of the Feathered Serpent, detail of facade.
Drawing by Kappelman after a drawing by Barbara Page in Coggins (1993:Figure 2)

reeds" where the sacred geography of Coatépec was manifested. At Teotihuacan, this concept of Coatépec was given architectural and sculptural form in the Temple of the Feathered Serpent. The facade of the structure is covered with images of a feathered serpent who bursts forth from the supernatural realm through petaled mirror portals and bears on its back a mosaic headdress, a symbol of warfare and political legitimacy at Teotihuacan (Figure 2.9) (Sugiyama 1989; Taube 1992).

Nonetheless, the concept of Tollan predates even Teotihuacan and has a time depth that stretches back into the Formative period (Schele and Mathews 1998:38). In other words, Teotihuacan was indeed a Tollan, but not the original one. The concepts of Tollan and Coatépec were in place in the Maya lowlands by at least the Late Formative period and, remarkably, were manifested in much the same manner as they would be at the Templo Mayor a millennium later. The Late Formative Maya erected Snake Mountains as part of the sacred geography of Tollan, as the place where the patron gods were born and as places of creation, foundation, and legitimatization.

For instance, the facade of Structure H-X-Sub 3 in Group H at Waxactun contains masks more than twenty-five feet tall that depict, at the bottom, a cleft mountain monster (Figure 2.10). Foliation grows out of the mountain monster's head on either side: It is an image of Sustenance Mountain, one of the great locations of creation. In the *Popol Vuh* and other Maya myths, Sustenance Mountain was the place where the gods or their assistants journeyed to retrieve maize for the first humans. Much later, the Aztecs called this same mountain Tonacatepetl, and it was rep-

Figure 2.10   Waxaktun, Structure H-X-Sub 3, detail of facade. Drawing by Schele

resented on the Tlaloc side of the Templo Mayor. At Waxaktun, Sustenance Mountain rests in water that contains sharks and represents the primordial sea, in which Sustenance Mountain floats (Freidel et al. 1993:139–140).

Above the cleft mountain is another humanmade mountain. In the mouth of this mountain is a frontal face that represents a little god with a mirror in its mouth. Nikolai Grube and Linda Schele identified this little god as the head variant for the glyph *tzuk*, which they read as "partition" (1991). This partitioning referred to the primordial acts of creation in which the divisions of the Earth, sky, sea, and, in this case, the kingdom of Waxactun itself were established (Freidel et al. 1993:140). Even more important, on either side of the mountain monster's mouth, one can see that a vision serpent penetrates it: This human-built mountain is specifically marked with a snake that identifies it as Coatépec. Thus, the two facade masks of Structure H-X-Sub 3 identify it as a Late Formative conflation of Snake Mountain and Sustenance Mountain.

The same repertoire of motifs, although inverted, also appears at Tikal on Structure 5D-33-2nd, which dates to the early sixth century (Figure 2.11) (Coe 1990:510). The bottom half of the personified mountain is bisected by a vision serpent that marks it as a representation of Snake Mountain. Kernels of maize spill forth from its cleft top, explicitly identi-

Figure 2.11   Tikal Structure 5D-33-2nd, detail of facade. Drawing by Schele

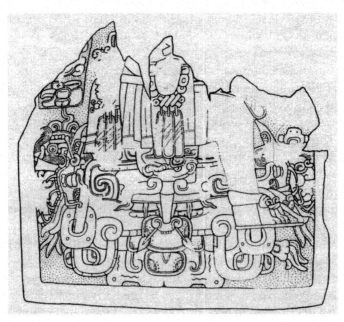

Figure 2.12   Toniná Monument 106.
Drawing by Mark Van Stone after Ian Graham

fying it as Sustenance Mountain. As at Waxaktun, the facade in its entirety is a synthesis of Snake and Sustenance Mountains. In fact, this conflation of Snake and Sustenance Mountains at both Waxaktun and Tikal anticipates the Templo Mayor at Tenochtitlán, with its twin temples of Coatépec and Tonacatepetl. Yet more important for this argument, these Late Formative and Early Classic versions from the central Peten demonstrate the time depth of this archetypal form.[11]

Monument 106 from Toniná confirms the perseverance of this symbol system into the Early Classic period (Figure 2.12). A ruler is seated in profile on a version of Snake Mountain that compares closely to that of Tikal Structure 5D-33-2nd, where serpents also penetrated the earflares in a common motif. At Toniná, it is important to emphasize that the ruler sits directly upon Snake Mountain: He is enthroned at one of the principal locations of creation, where patron gods were born and where political and cosmological authority was divinely sanctioned.

These same ideas were also expressed in the E Group at Waxaktun on the mask program of Late Formative Structure E-Sub-VII, a radial, or four-directional, pyramid (Ricketson and Ricketson 1937:Figure 33). The radial symmetry and four stairways of this structure were deliberate: "Four" in Maya is *kan*, and *kan* also means snake. Thus a radial pyramid was, literally, a *kan witz*, or "snake mountain." This Waxaktun E-Group and its symbolic design became the prototype for E-Groups across the Maya region and one of the archetypal structures for the representation of Snake Mountain (Schele and Mathews 1998:180).

The iconography of Structure E-Sub-VII reinforces these ideas. The pyramid has two levels of masks on all four sides, whereas the principal east facade has a third set of masks flanking the stairs (Ricketson and Ricketson 1937:Figure 37). The masks along the base depict snakes (Figure 2.13) and explicitly label E-Sub-VII as Snake Mountain. The middle register of masks depicts versions of Sustenance Mountain (Figure 2.14). This connection is clearly evinced on Mask 9 where maize kernels are

Figure 2.13   Waxaktun Structure E-Sub-VII, detail of snake on bottom tier of facade.
Drawing by Kappelman after Ricketson and Ricketson (1937:Figure 39)

Figure 2.14   Waxaktun Structure E-Sub-VII, detail of Sustenance Mountain masks on middle tier of facade. Drawing by Kappelman after Ricketson and Ricketson (1937:Figure 42)

contained within the forehead of the zoomorphic creature. The other masks on the middle register also reference Sustenance Mountain through various vegetal or foliage elements (Ricketson and Ricketson 1937:Figures 42–47). On the principal facade, a third register of masks depicts the Principal Bird Deity (Ricketson and Ricketson 1937:Figures 49 and 50).

When viewed as a whole, the conceptual program of Waxaktun E-Sub-VII centered around a vision of Snake Mountain rising from the swampy waters, as indicated by the snakes on the bottom registers. This imagery foreshadows much later representations of Coatépec that depict Snake Mountain with water surrounding its base (Figure 2.5) and anticipates the vivid descriptions of Hernando Alvarado Tezozomoc (1980:227–229) of the waters that then flowed from the *itzompan* in the ballcourt at the base of Coatépec.

These same paradigms for the organization of sacred space and symbolic vocabulary of monuments—well in place in the Maya region by at least the Late Formative period—also persevered into the Late Classic period at such sites as Dzibilchaltun. The House of the Seven Dolls, located in the eastern plaza of the settlement, dates to the Late Classic period, 600–750 AD (Andrews and Andrews 1980:82; Figures 83 and 89). E. W. Andrews IV and E. W. Andrews V (1980:82–127) and Clemency Coggins (1983:37–41) noted the similarities between the House of the Seven Dolls, a radial structure, and Waxaktun Structure E-Sub-VII and also commented upon the affinities between the House of the Seven Dolls and E-Groups from the central Peten.

The iconography of the entablature of the House of the Seven Dolls, as Coggins (1983:26, 36; Figures 8 and 10) pointed out, is that of the primordial sea, bound by corner masks that depict Chaks at the four corners of the world. As Linda Schele, Nikolai Grube, and Erik Boot (1998:414–415) observed, the central tower of the House of the Seven Dolls, rising as it does from this watery repertoire, represents Sustenance Mountain rising from the depths of the primordial sea. Moreover, the snakes that decorate the upper portion of the structure also mark it as Snake Mountain, once again conflated with its mythic counterpart Sustenance Mountain. The House of the Seven Dolls at Dzibilchaltun was clearly a place of creation that echoed the very sacred and old architectural forms of the Peten, where some of the most ancient examples of Sustenance Mountain and Snake Mountain were built.

The significance of this structure and its form becomes even clearer when considered in light of the Chilam Balam texts. As Schele et al. (1998:412) noted, the *Chilam Balam of Chumayel* (Roys 1933) describes an assembly of lords that was held at a site called Ichkaansiho. Ichkaansiho, or Tiho, is an ancient name for Mérida and also appears within the hieroglyphic text of Dzibilchaltun St. 19. The text names the ruler portrayed as a "chak, or corner tree . . . Holy [lord] of ???-Kan-Ti-Ho" (Schele et al. 1998:414, 429) and ends with an emblem glyph. Schele et al. (1998:414, 429) suggested that this text may give the original source for the ancient names of Ichkaansiho and Tiho for Mérida.

The *Chilam Balam of Chumayel* also relates that, at this site of Ichkaansiho, or Dzibilchaltun, the assemblage of lords established the confederacy of the Itzá. Thus the founding of the Itzá alliance was staged within the landscape of creation that depicted Sustenance and Snake Mountains rising from the primordial sea. Moreover, the E-Group arrangement and radial pyramid employed at Dzibilchaltun resonated with foundation and dynastic symbolism and legitimated the fledgling Itzá alliance by referencing the very acts of creation (Schele et al. 1998:414–415).

The design of the House of the Seven Dolls at Dzibilchaltun also anticipates the form of the Castillo at Chichén Itzá, another radial pyramid. In fact, Schele and Mathews (1998:204–205) suggested that when the Itzá first migrated to Chichén that one of their initial tasks was to create and physically document the supernatural charter for their political power. To accomplish this task, they embarked on one of the most ambitious building and sculptural programs in Mesoamerican history, which included their version of Snake Mountain that, like the one at Dzibilchaltun, echoed the same archetypal form.

Large serpent heads lie at the base of the balustrades on the northern side of the Castillo. On the evening of the vernal and autumnal equinox, the stepped terraces of this pyramid cast triangular shadows across the northeast balustrade wall, manifesting a diamond pattern that resembles the body of a giant rattlesnake (see Miller 1996:Figure 149). This construction was the Chichén version of Snake Mountain, the place of origin, foundation, and legitimization.

This same idea is expressed on an interior column in the Lower Temple of the Jaguar at Chichén (Figure 2.15). The sides of the column depict four versions of the old god Pawatun, the father of the Maize God and the grandfather of the Hero Twins, standing on a personified mountain monster with a cleft head (Schele and Mathews 1998:212). Plant stalks emerge from the mountain monster's eyes and become waterlily pads on which fish nibble and birds and turtles frolic: It is an image of the cleft Mountain of Sustenance floating in the primordial sea. Furthermore, a snake emerges from the cleft and undulates up behind the old god. The entirety represents the union of Snake Mountain and Sustenance Mountain once again, here supporting the father of the Maize God.[12]

Although the Late Formative antecedents for the conflation of Snake and Sustenance Mountains are well documented, so too are the Formative roots for the articulation of paradigmatic warfare within the sacred landscape, specifically through the raising of battle banners at the base of Coatépec. At the site of Cerros, Belize, Snake Mountain was manifested in the

Figure 2.15   Chichén Itzá, Lower Temple of the Jaguar, interior column.
Drawing by Schele

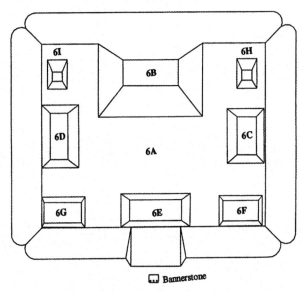

Figure 2.16   Cerros Structure 6 platform showing location of battle banner at base of stairs.
Drawing by Kathryn Reese-Taylor

form of the elaborate Structure 6 Complex (Figure 2.16) (Reese 1996; Schele and Mathews 1998:331, n.24). The architectural complex consists of eight structures, situated in the cardinal and intercardinal directions, that ring the top of a large truncated platform. Structure 6B, the largest of the group, sat at the apex of the platform (Reese 1996).

Two large stucco masks originally adorned the tiers of Structure 6B, and David Freidel (1986) argued that they were terminated at the time of the abandonment of the civic center. All that remains on the upper tier is a twisted cord motif. On the bottom tier, a snakehead is visible adjacent to the now-eroded main mask (Figure 2.17). The snake sits at the base of the mask and appears to emerge from the remnants of a mouth or chin strap (Reese 1996). The iconography of Structure 6B, in which serpents emerge from the maws of zoomorphic masks, recalls that of Waxaktun H-X-Sub 3 and also anticipates Early Classic versions of Coatépec.

Perhaps even more interesting, however, is the banner stone that was placed at the base of the truncated platform of Structure 6A (Figure 2.16) (Reese 1996). The large, rectangular banner stone sat on a low-lying stone platform and contained circular holes that appear to have been deliberately cut into the rock.[13] The presence of this banner stone at the base of

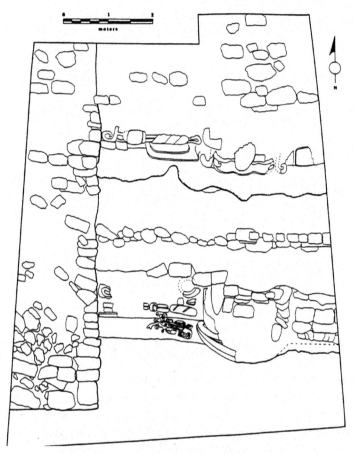

Figure 2.17   Cerros Structure 6B facade.
Drawing from Freidel (1986)

the main platform of Structure 6 explicitly associates the public space of
this complex with warfare (Reese 1996). It also archaeologically documents, during the Late Formative period, the basic organization of sacred
space in which a banner stone was placed at the base of Coatépec. Moreover, this fundamental structure for the articulation of divinely sanctioned warfare would persevere in Mesoamerica through the Postclassic
period, as manifested at the Templo Mayor and through rituals such as
that of Panquetzalitzli, in which battle banners were raised at the base of
Coatépec in recreation of the first mythic acts of warfare and sacrifice.
The entire complex of Structure 6 at Cerros, by adhering to a mythic paradigm for the organization of sacred space, successfully provided a the-

ater in which warfare and sacrifice were supernaturally ordained and sanctified.[14]

In conclusion, whereas the fundamental structuring principles of Snake and Sustenance Mountains can be traced from the Late Formative period through the Postclassic period with a consistency and duration of form that is truly remarkable, the origin of these paradigms is even more ancient. It is, in fact, founded in the physical geography of the Olmec heartland (Schele and Mathews 1998:39–40). In the Olmec region, the sudden, jutting volcanoes of the Tuxtla Mountains dramatically interrupt the swampy, lowland environment. There are no real slopes or foothills in this region, just an abrupt shift from marshy areas filled with reeds to tall volcanic peaks.

Certainly the Olmecs themselves emulated this natural environment and recreated it in the human-built landscape (Freidel et al. 1993:132; Reilly 1994). At the site of La Venta, for example, one can see the Middle Formative antecedents for the structure of the mythic landscape of Tollan. Rising out of the main plaza at La Venta is a large mound that replicates a mountain (Figure 2.18). At its base lie two long parallel mounds that Frank Reilly III (1994) identified as a ballcourt. This Middle Formative organization of sacred space, which included a pyramid mountain with a ballcourt at its base, became the model for civilized life—and for the space of Tollan and Coatépec—that would be reproduced for thousands of years across Mesoamerica.

Thus landscapes modeled upon the ideals of Snake Mountain and Sustenance Mountain can be traced back into the Formative period of Mesoamerica. Late Formative Maya were constructing their versions of Coatépec long before the Teotihuacanos built their great temples and

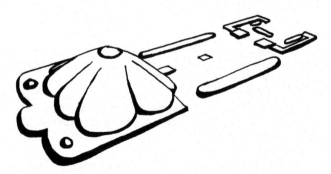

Figure 2.18   La Venta, map.
Drawing by Kappelman after Freidel et al. (1993:Figure 3:4)

pyramids. Moreover, they were modeling their versions of Coatépec after the great civilization of the Olmec and were reestablishing a landscape of creation and political legitimatization. The myths of Tollan and Coatépec provided archetypal symbolism that Mesoamerican peoples used to design and construct the sacred centers of their cities and which served to invest their buildings with a profound symmetry. Within these cosmologically charged spaces, rituals were performed, governance was ordained, and history unfolded.

References

Andrews, E. W., IV, and E. W. Andrews V.
   1980   *Excavations at Dzibilchaltun, Yucatán, Mexico.* Middle American Research Institute Publication 48. New Orleans: Tulane University.
Boone, Elizabeth.
   1991   Migration Histories as Ritual Performance. *To Change Place: Aztec Ceremonial Landscapes.* Edited by Davíd Carrasco. Boulder: University of Colorado Press. 121–151.
Broda, Johanna.
   1987   Templo Mayor as Ritual Space. *The Great Temple of Tenochtitlán: Center and Periphery in the Aztec World.* Edited by Johanna Broda, Davíd Carrasco, and Eduardo Matos Moctezuma. Berkeley: University of California Press. 61–123.
Carrasco, Davíd.
   1982   *Quetzalcoatl and the Irony of Empire: Myths and Prophecies in the Aztec Tradition.* Chicago: University of Chicago Press.
   1987   Myth, Cosmic Terror, and the Templo Mayor. *The Great Temple of Tenochtitlán: Center and Periphery in the Aztec World.* Edited by Johanna Broda, Davíd Carrasco, and Eduardo Matos Moctezuma. Berkeley: University of California Press. 124–162.
Codex Azcatitlan.
   1949   El Códice Azcatitlán. Facsimile edition with a commentary by Robert Barlow. *Journal de la Société des Américanistes* 37:101–135, Atlas.
Codex Boturini.
   1964   Códice Boturini. *Antigüedades de México, basadas en la recopilación de Lord Kingsborough, Volume 2, Part 1.* Edited by José Corona Núñez. México, D.F.: Secretaría de Hacienda y Crédito Público.
Coe, William R.
   1990   *Excavations in the Great Plaza, North Terrace and North Acropolis of Tikal, Volume 2.* Tikal Report Number 14, University Museum Monograph 61. Philadelphia: University Museum and University of Pennsylvania.
Coggins, Clemency.
   1983   *The Stucco Decoration and Architectural Assemblage of Structure 1-Sub, Dzibilchaltun, Yucatán, Mexico.* Middle American Research Institute Publication 49. New Orleans, La.: Middle American Research Institute, Tulane University.

1993 The Age of Teotihuacan and Its Mission Abroad. *Teotihuacan: Art from the City of the Gods.* Edited by Kathleen Berrin and Esther Pasztory. New York: Thames and Hudson. 140–155.

Davies, Nigel.
1977 *The Toltecs, Until the Fall of Tula.* Norman, Okla.: University of Oklahoma Press.

Durán, Diego.
1967 *Historia de las Indias de Nueva España e islas de la tierra firme.* Translated and edited by Angel María Garibay K. México, D.F.: Porrúa.

Florescano, Enrique.
1994 *Memory, Myth, and Time in Mexico: From the Aztecs to Independence.* Translated by Albert G. Bork, with the assistance of Kathryn R. Bork. Austin, Tex.: University of Texas Press.

Freidel, David A.
1986 The Monumental Architecture. *Archaeology of Cerros, Belize, Central America, Volume I: An Interim Report.* Edited by Robin Robertson and David Freidel. Dallas: Southern Methodist University Press. 1–22.

Freidel, David A., Linda Schele, and Joy Parker.
1993 *Maya Cosmos: Three Thousand Years on the Shaman's Path.* New York: William Morrow.

Gillespie, Susan D.
1989 *The Aztec Kings: The Construction of Rulership in Mexica History.* Tucson, Ariz.: University of Arizona Press.

González Torres, Yólotl.
1975 *El culto de los astros entre los mexicas.* Mexico City: Sep-Setentas.

Grube, Nikolai, and Linda Schele.
1991 Tzuk in the Classic Maya Inscriptions. *Texas Notes on Precolumbian Art, Writing and Culture* 14. Austin, Tex.: The Center for the History and Art of Ancient American Culture of the Art Department of the University of Texas.

Heyden, Doris.
1983 Reeds and Rushes: From Survival to Sovereigns. *Flora and Fauna Imagery in Precolumbian Cultures, Iconography and Function.* Edited by Jeanette F. Peterson. BAR International Series 171. Oxford: British Archaeological Reports. 93–112.

Jiménez Moreno, Wigberto.
1941 El problema de Tula. *I Mesa Redonda,* Boletín 1:2–8.

Klein, Cecelia F.
1988 Rethinking Cihuacoatl: Aztec Political Imagery of the Conquered Woman. *Smoke and Mist: Mesoamerican Studies in Memory of Thelma D. Sullivan.* Edited by J. Kathryn Josserand and Karin Dankin. BAR International Series 402. Oxford: British Archaeological Reports. 237–278.

Koontz, Rex A.
1994 *The Iconography of El Tajín, Veracruz, Mexico.* Ph.D. dissertation, University of Texas at Austin.

León-Portilla, Miguel.
1978 *Mexico-Tenochtitlán, su espacio y tiempo sagrados.* México, D.F.: Plaza y Valdes.

López Luján, Leonardo.
1993 *Las ofrendas del Templo Mayor de Tenochtitlán*. México, D.F.: Instituto Nacional de Antropología e Historia.
Matos Moctezuma, Eduardo.
1984 The Templo Mayor of Tenochtitlán: Economics and Ideology. *Ritual Human Sacrifice in Mesoamerica* Edited by Elizabeth H. Boone. Washington, D.C.: Dumbarton Oaks. 133–164.
1987 The Templo Mayor of Tenochtitlán: History and Interpretation. *The Great Temple of Tenochtitlán: Center and Periphery in the Aztec World*. Edited by Johanna Broda, Davíd Carrasco, and Eduardo Matos Moctezuma. Berkeley: University of California Press. 15–60.
1988 The Great Temple of the Aztecs: Treasures of Tenochtitlán. London: Thames and Hudson.
1991 Las seis Coyolxauhqui: Variaciones sobre un mismo tema. *Estudios de Cultura Nahuatl* 21:15–30.
Milbrath, Susan.
1980 Star Gods and Astronomy of the Aztecs. *La antropología americanista en la actualidad: Homenaje a Raphael Girard, Volume 1*. México, D.F.: Editores Mexicanos Unidos. 289–303.
1997 Decapitated Lunar Goddesses in Aztec Art, Myth, and Ritual. *Ancient Mesoamerica* 8:185–206.
Miller, Mary Ellen.
1996 *The Art of Mesoamerica, from Olmec to Aztec*. rev. edition. London: Thames and Hudson.
Nicholson, H. G.
1971 Pre-Hispanic Central Mexican Historiography. *Investigaciones contemporáneos sobre historia de México: Memorias de la tercera reunión de historiadores Mexicanos y Norteamericanos*. Austin, Tex.: University of Texas Press.
1985 The New Tenochtitlán Templo Mayor Coyolxauhqui-Chantico Monument. *Indiana* 10:77–98.
Paso y Troncoso, Francisco del.
1905- *Fray Bernardino de Sahagún: Historia de las cosas de Nueva España, Volumes 1–4*. Madrid: Hauser y Menet.
1907 *Fray Bernardino de Sahagún: Historia de las cosas de Nueva España, Volumes 5–8*. Madrid: Hauser y Menet.
Reese, Kathryn Victoria.
1996 *Narratives of Power: Late Formative Public Architecture and Civic Center Design at Cerros, Belize*. Ph.D. dissertation, University of Texas at Austin.
Reilly, Frank Kent, III.
1994 *Visions to Another World: Art, Shamanism, and Political Power in Middle Formative Mesoamerica*. Ph.D. dissertation, University of Texas at Austin.
Ricketson, Oliver G., and Edith B. Ricketson.
1937 *Uaxactun, Guatemala Group E–1926–1931*. Carnegie Institution of Washington Publication 477. Washington, D.C.: Carnegie Institution.

Roys, Ralph L.
1933   *The Chilam Balam of Chumayel.* Carnegie Institution of Washington Publication 438. Washington, D.C.: Carnegie Institution.

Sahagún, Bernardino de.
1950–   *Florentine Codex: General History of the Things of New Spain.* Translated and
1982   edited by Arthur J. O. Anderson and Charles E. Dibble. Santa Fe, N.Mex.: School of American Research and the University of Utah.

Schele, Linda, Nikolai Grube, and Erik Boot.
1998   Some Suggestions on the K'atun Prophecies in the Books of Chilam Balam in Light of Classic-Period History. *Memorias del Tercer Congreso Internacional de Mayistas.* México, D.F.: Universidad Nacional Autónoma de México.

Schele, Linda, and Peter Mathews.
1998   *The Code of Kings: The Language of Seven Sacred Maya Temples and Tombs.* New York: Scribner's.

Seler, Eduard.
1960–   *Gesammelte Abhandlungen zue Amerikanischen Sprach-und Altertumskunde.*
1961   Graz, Austria: Akademische Druk-u. Reprinted from 1902–1903 edition, Berlin.

Stuart, David.
1994   The Texts of Temple 26: The Presentation of History at a Maya Dynastic Shrine. Paper presented at the School of American Research seminar, Copan: The Rise and Fall of a Classic Maya Kingdom, October.

Sugiyama, Saburo.
1989   Iconographic Interpretation of the Temple of Quetzalcoatl at Teotihuacan. *Mexicon* 11(4):68–74.

Taube, Karl.
1992   The Temple of Quetzalcoatl and the Cult of Sacred War at Teotihuacan. *RES* 21 (Spring):53–87.

Tezozomoc, Hernando Alvarado.
1975   *Crónica Mexicana.* México, D.F.: Editorial Porrúa.
1980   *Crónica Mexicayotl.* México, D.F.: Editorial Porrúa.

Torquemada, Juan de.
1975–   Monarquía indiana. De los veinte y un libros rituals y monarquía indiana, con los
1979   guerras de los indios occidentales, de sus poblazones, descubrimiento, conquista, conversión y otras cosas maravillosas de la mesma tierra. Edited by Miguel León-Portilla. México, D.F.: Universidad Nacional Autónoma de México.

Townsend, Richard.
1982   Pyramid and Sacred Mountain. *Ethnoastronomy and Archaeoastromony in the American Tropics.* Edited by Anthony F. Aveni and Gary Urton. Annals of the New York Academy of Sciences 385. New York: New York Academy of Sciences. 37–62.

Umberger, Emily G.
   1987a Antiques, Revivals, and References to the Past in Aztec Art. *RES* 13
      (Spring):63–105.
   1987b Events Commemorated by Date Plaques at the Templo Mayor: Further
      Thoughts on the Solar Metaphor. *The Aztec Templo Mayor*. Edited by
      Elizabeth Hill Boone. Washington, D.C.: Dumbarton Oaks. 411–450.

Notes

1. This paper, written by Kappelman shortly before the death of Linda Schele
in April of 1998, is based upon a presentation given by Schele and Kappelman on
12 March 1998 at the annual Maya Meetings at The University of Texas at Austin.
Kappelman would like to thank Kathryn Reese-Taylor and Rex Koontz, who
carefully read a draft of the manuscript and inserted their editorial comments
and suggestions in an attempt to faithfully reflect as best as possible the ideas
that Schele presented in her portion of the presentation. Thanks also go to Khristaan Villela who read an early draft of the oral presentation and provided helpful
comments.

2. For various discussions of the concept of Tollan in a Mesoamerican world
view, see Carrasco (1982), Matos Moctezuma (1987), Florescano (1994), Koontz
(1994), and Schele and Mathews (1998).

3. The myth of Tollan and the myth of Coatépec are distinct episodes in the origin mythology of the Aztec people, which describes the migration of the Aztecs
into the Valley of Mexico and the founding of their capital at Tenochtitlán. Although in the narrative the events at Coatépec actually precede the founding of
Tollan by the Aztecs, in spatial and conceptual terms Coatépec is imbedded
within Tollan. In other words, the construction of a Coatépec became an essential
element in the establishment and definition of a city as a Tollan, or place of great
learning. Therefore, the specific features that defined Coatépec and the events
that transpired there had a direct bearing on the landscape of a Tollan.

4. See Boone (1991:122–123) for a more complete discussion of sources for the
migration history of the Aztecs, including pictorial codices, textual sources, and
various sixteenth-century documents.

5. See the introduction of this volume, Carrasco (1982), Florescano (1994), and
Schele and Mathews (1998).

6. See Matos Moctezuma (1988:74, Figure 14 and Plate III). This theme is
echoed in the associated offerings of the temple that feature the severed heads of
females (López Luján 1993). For a discussion of other Coyolxauhqui sculptures
found within the context of the Templo Mayor, see Milbrath (1997), who notes
that one Coyolxauhqui fragment shows Huitzilopochtli's *xiuhcoatl* penetrating
her body, per Sahagún's (1950–1982) version of the myth.

7. See Paso y Troncoso (1905–1907, Volume 6, Part 3:Plate 11) or Matos
Moctezuma (1988:Figure 20).

8. Although discussion of the Coatépec narrative has been limited to the
themes above, other approaches include the astronomical symbolism of the myth
(Seler 1960–1961, Book 3:320–329; Nicholson 1971; León-Portilla 1978; Milbrath
1980, 1997; Gillespie 1989), as well as its metaphors for ancient political conflicts

(González Torres 1975; Nicholson 1985; Umberger 1987b; Klein 1988; Matos Moctezuma 1991).

9. The main historical sources Jiménez Moreno used to build his argument include *Los Anales de Cuauhtitlan*, the *Historia Tolteca-Chichimeca*, and the writings of Sahagún, as well as other sixteenth-century Nahuatl sources. For the history of this debate, see Davies (1977) and Schele and Mathews (1998:39, 198–199).

10. See Umberger (1987a:69), who quotes Sahagún (1950–1982, Book 10:165–166): "Their name is taken from—it comes from—their manner of life, their works. The Tolteca were wise. Their works were all good, all perfect, all wonderful, all marvelous. . . ."

11. As Schele and Mathews (1998:337, n.28) noted, during this period at Tikal there was an unobstructed view of Structure 5D–33–2nd from the ballcourt in the East Plaza. This fact offers further support for the suggestion that basic structuring principles or mythic paradigms—such as a ballcourt at the base of Snake Mountain—were well in place by this early date. This same fusion of the two fundamental creation locations also appears at Copán on Rosalila, where bright yellow kernels of corn emerge from the cleft of their version of Sustenance Mountain, whereas above an enormous serpent undulates, marking the structure as Snake Mountain (Khristaan Villela, personal communication 1997).

12. Schele and Mathews (1998:217) further noted that the snakes' mouths open at the top of the column and emit tiny scenes of the Maize God's resurrection from the Cosmic Turtle. In each of the four registers at the top, a resurrected Maize God rises from the turtle shell and grasps squash vines growing from the heads of gods who are themselves emerging from the ends of the turtle carapace. As they wrote, "Farmers plant maize, squash, and bean seeds together in their *milpa*, or cornfields. The squash spreads out along the ground to preserve moisture, while the beans climb the stalk of maize. Here both maize and squash come together into the world at the moment of First Father's rebirth in the company of his parents, who stand on Snake Mountain" (Schele and Mathews 1998).

13. According to Reese (1996:53–54), the banner stone is a large, rectangular monolith with rounded corners that measures approximately 1.4 x 1.4 meters. The northeast corner of the stone is crushed and falls off the platform, and several large cracks run through the surface. This condition led Reese to conclude that the monolith was either intentionally destroyed at some time in the history of the center or suffered postdepositional weathering of a nature not noted on other stone surfaces or in other structures. Inset 40 centimeters from the west edge and 60 centimeters from the south edge of the banner stone is a circular hole that appears to have been cut. The hole is approximately 15 centimeters in diameter and between 10 and 15 centimeters deep. Twenty centimeters to the east of the hole and inset 60 centimeters from the south edge is another carved hole of the same approximate dimensions. The spacing of the two holes implies that a third hole should have been present, establishing a triadic pattern. No third hole was detected on the surface, but the area where the third hole should have been is heavily damaged.

14. Also see Reese (1996) for a discussion of the architectural organization of Complex 6, as well as complexes at Waxaktun and Tikal, in terms of the Maya creation story.

Procession Rituals and Shrine Sites: The Politics of Sacred Space In the Late Formative Valley of Oaxaca

Heather S. Orr

The study of processionals, like the study of pilgrimages, can enable penetrating insights into political, social, and cultural processes. In this chapter, I discuss the Valley of Oaxaca sites of Dainzú and Monte Albán in their capacity as hilltop shrines and sacred places that were the focus of procession ceremonies. I suggest that the power of these shrine sites was wielded as a political tool. This study is intended to contextualize the Late Formative sculptural/architectural programs at Monte Albán and Dainzú. The chapter opens with a framework for the discussion of procession rituals in the Valley of Oaxaca region. The relationship between processionals and petitions for rainfall is next considered, followed by a discussion of shrine sites, and finally an examination of sacred space and politics at Dainzú and Monte Albán.

Rituals of Procession

Several manners of organization are possible in procession rituals. Because "processions transform movement from a functional, physiological act into a cultural performance," formal organization in a procession "depicts socio-cultural themes" (Morinis 1992:15). For example, participants are frequently arranged in a way that directly replicates social hierarchies or groupings. Indeed, as A. Morinis (1992:24) has stated for pilgrimage, rituals of procession, with exceptions, are typically a conservative, stabilizing force in society that operate to reinforce the existing social order (see also Turner 1974:171, 196; Morinis and Crumrine 1991:7; Crumrine

1991; Urbano 1991). Processional ceremonies can be powerful centralizing and unifying agents that serve to strengthen inter- and intracommunity ties. First and foremost, the goal of these rituals is the unification of the human community with the sacred or supernatural. Given this goal, processions centralize and unify in essentially two ways—although these may be accomplished simultaneously: 1) disperse groups can be brought together under the umbrella of shared convictions to engage in a common spiritual experience; and/or 2) processions can reinforce community identity as something distinct from other local communities.

The first general principle of unification through procession is best observed where procession takes place in the context of pilgrimage, but it can also be seen on the local level. For example, all pueblos under the authority of the *cabecera* of Etla process with their saints to that town's church on Easter Sunday for Easter Mass; the saints are said to visit with one another on this occasion (cf. Allen 1988:190ff.).

The use of procession to demarcate formal territorial boundaries is one aspect of the second principle. Local Oaxacan authorities, together with community members, walk present-day municipality *linderos* in a formal, annual processional boundary check (Kowalewski, personal communication 1995). During Bishop Gillow's *visitas pastorales* of his diocese (1888–1890, 1892–1913), he noted that visitor hosting customs among the villagers included processions with the images of their saints along the *rayas*, or boundary lines, of their communities (Esparza 1985:40–57). Processions are characteristically initiated in the region by the celebration of Catholic ceremonials and funerary rituals. In addition, community crises will sometimes spark processions—particularly periods of drought.

Procession and Rainfall

Given the semiarid highland climate of the Valley of Oaxaca, it is not surprising that petitions for rainfall seem to be a powerful motivational force for procession rituals, both in recent and ancient history. During the spring (i.e., the beginning of the rainy season: April–May in the Valley) of 1995, I observed that sparse rainfall and poor crop growth prompted quietly held processions with images of patron saints up *mogotes* (pre-Columbian pyramidal mounds) and hills in several Valley of Oaxaca pueblos. John Monaghan (1987:426; see also 1995) documented that a shortage of rainfall can induce the Mixtec to hold processions accompanied by saints who are identified with rain (e.g., Santiago, Santa Ana, Caballeria; see also de la Fuente 1939; Ingham 1986:157ff.). Processions are particular to rituals assuring adequate rainfall in the adjunct highlands state of Guerrero (Cordry 1980:154–157; Oettinger and Parsons 1982; Esser 1988:302–305; see also Martínez 1972); these are held directly before the rainy season each year.

Stephen Kowalewski et al. (1989) observed a marked, Late Postclassic increase of hilltop ritual centers in some parts of the Valley of Oaxaca during their survey of the region. They attribute this occurrence in part to possible Monte Albán V changes of religious emphasis toward rain clouds and lightning, which are generally associated with high places (Kowalewski et al. 1989, Volume 1:340ff.; Flannery and Marcus 1983:345–347). The investigators do not indicate whether they also tested for corresponding patterns of drought, but such a relationship should be examined because the association between high places, caves in hills and mountains, and lightning (i.e., rain) is well documented for this region (e.g., de Burgoa 1934, Volume 1:359, 361, 341–342, 356; Parsons 1936:211ff., 328–330; Cruz 1946; Dahlgren de Jordan 1966:244–248; *Multiples* 1981). Kowalewski et al. noted significantly that many of these known Period V ritual centers are located on or above tributary streams whose waters depend upon rainfall. I believe that this observation can also be extended to a number of earlier hilltop shrines, especially those associated with sites reliant upon rainfall farming and rainfall-dependent water sources, such as Dainzú. Undoubtedly, ceremonial processions of some form were made to these sacred places. Archaeological evidence of ritual activity is present at the sites, such as high numbers of *sahumadores* (incense burners; see Kowalewski et al. 1989, Volume 1:342).

Considering both the unpredictability of rainfall in the Central Valleys, together with an apparent correlation between drought and ritual processions, it is intriguing that two major processionals occur here near or at the beginning of the rainy season: April 5 and May 3, Holy Friday and The Holy Cross respectively. Indeed, Elsie Clews Parsons recorded that the appearance of the New Lightning of the New Season was associated with *Semana Santa* (Holy Week, April 1–7), marking the beginning of the rains and the agricultural season: "Sometimes there is much rain in *la semana santa*" (1936:277). It is noteworthy that Holy Week is temporally related to the regional cycle of rainfall and agricultural fecundity (cf. Adams 1991:109–110). Furthermore, there are profound sacrificial and penitential undertones to the appurtenant processions and rituals of Holy Friday. In general, a relationship can be noted between rainfall/agricultural fecundity-related processionals, penitence, and sacrifice, at least in the southern highlands of Mesoamerica (cf. Barker 1957;

Turner and Turner 1978; Sallnow 1987; 1990; Allen 1988; Crumrine and Morinis 1991; see also Durán 1971).

Sacrifice can take multiple forms in processional ceremonials. For example, the processional routes up to many hilltop shrines today often involve some purposeful degree of difficulty, such as pathways that are deliberately rugged or steep. In addition, depending upon the specific ritual occasion, offerings of food or sacrifices of chickens (or, on rare occasions, turkeys) are usually made at the shrine; a mass is typically held at the site, or in town upon descent. Innumerable pre-Hispanic, colonial, and ethnographic documents attest to the use of turkeys, chickens (post-contact), or human sacrifices for petitions to rain deities in Oaxaca and throughout Mesoamerica (e.g., *Codex Vaticano Ríos*, *Codex Yanhuitlán*; de Burgoa 1934; Parsons 1936:211, 222, 324ff.; Tozzer 1941; Dahlgren de Jorden 1966:244–245, 247–248; Durán 1971; Monaghan 1987; Spero 1987; Looper 1991; Masson 1994).

The relationship between acts of penitence and rainfall might be elucidated by cases that suggest that *Rayo* (Lightning/Rain) is conceived of as a moral authority—an aspect of Mesoamerican rain deity complexes that has deep roots in antiquity (see Parsons 1936:213; Esparza 1985:52; Spero 1987; Taube 1992:17ff., 1996). For example, the town of San Marcial Osolotepec, in the Sierra Madre del Sur, is known regionally as a place in which "nadie pelia o roba, por que luego los castigen el Rayo" ("nobody fights or steals, because later Lightning punishes them"). Lightning stays in a cave above the town. The people visit this cave to "hacer sus demandas," to make petitions or to ask wishes from Lightning. Two individuals from San Marcial recounted (not without a certain amount of zeal) that in January 1995, two youths who had robbed an elderly man were struck dead in punishment by el Rayo afterwards, while their mother was preparing their *comida* (Orr field notes 1995; cf. Cruz 1946; Esparza 1985:52).

Shrine Sites

Common to all sacred places is what James Preston (1992:33ff.) has termed "spiritual magnetism," or the power of a shrine to attract devotees. Spiritual magnetism derives from human concepts and values via historical, geographic, social, and other forces that coalesce in a sacred center. Preston outlined four general variables associated with spiritual magnetism: 1) miraculous cures; 2) apparitions of supernatural beings; 3) sacred geography; and 4) difficulty of access. However, he acknowledged that other factors may also be included, such as 5) cases in which the presence of relics at shrines may enhance their spiritual magnetism; and 6) the role of national identity in forming spiritual magnetism (e.g., Urbano 1991). The latter could be extended to include community identity and cultural identity, in terms of active resistance, or cultural continuity (e.g., Konrad 1991). I additionally believe that another variable might be considered at the local community level, within circumscribed regions: the role of mythical/historical events occurring in association with certain locations. That is, as A. H. Betteridge (1992) discussed for the specialized characteristics of pilgrimage centers, each shrine develops a body of legend and lore to account for its distinctive character and capability. Preston stressed that it is uncommon for all variables to appear at any given single shrine site (1992:38).

The spiritual magnetism of a sacred place can decline or intensify over time, depending upon sociocultural factors and changes:

> Pilgrimage sites strongly associated with sacred geography may diminish in importance as civilizations decline. Many of the great places of pilgrimage of antiquity have faded away after periodic episodes of stellar florescence (Preston 1992:35).

Conversely:

> ... (the) intensity of spiritual magnetism may increase as a shrine becomes better known for miracles or when it develops a focus of intensifying cultural activity ... during certain historical periods some sacred centers become increasingly associated with supernatural efficacy (Preston 1992:37).

Preston also identified a principle that he termed "spiritual synthesis" to describe temporal and cultural continuity and syncretism in the spiritual magnetism of a shrine site. Places that undergo spiritual synthesis are transformed repeatedly under new or imposed cultural and religious circumstances, principally because they are "focal points for movements of large numbers of people toward centers of civilization" (Preston 1992:35).

These principles may be applied to ancient sacred places in the Valley of Oaxaca. For example, the Xoo Phase–Monte Albán V decline in importance of Cerro Dainzú corresponds directly with the population shift to Macuilxóchitl. Moreover, it is at this time also that a shrine complex is established upon the hill above the center of Macuilxóchitl (Dan Zun, Cerro Calvario, Hill of Reeds/Hill of Five Flowers; see Kowalewski et al. 1989). Whereas this example serves to illustrate Preston's principle of diminishing spiritual magnetism that can occur at shrines associated with sacred geography, I suggest below that Monte Albán is a striking example of a sacred place that rapidly gains preeminence through increased spiritual magnetism. In addition, this hilltop metropolis was located at a geographic and economic center of the valley, a situation that appears to have contributed greatly to its having retained a fair degree of political consequence during a relatively extensive period of time (Flannery and Marcus 1983; Byland and Pohl 1994; Joyce and Winter 1996). Indeed, Monte Albán is still considered a sacred place by some of the valley population (see, for example, Orr 1997), and the capital city of Oaxaca de Juarez itself is strategically situated near the base of the ancient sacred hills.

Pre-Hispanic Processionals, Shrine Sites, and Politics: Dainzú

In the artistic record, pre-Hispanic processional rituals typically show named individuals, in linear formations, with apparent social ranking (e.g., Urcid Serrano 1994:87–88). Processions occurred during funerary rituals (e.g., Caso 1938; Miller 1996); in relation to warfare and sacrifice (e.g., Urcid Serrano 1992:273); to mark political events (see Urcid Serrano 1994:87–88); and as part of the handball game documented at Dainzú, Monte Albán, and Cerro de la Campana (see Orr 1997). These ancient processionals were linked to larger sequences of events and should therefore be considered contextually. There is perhaps no other site in the valley system where this is better tested than at Dainzú.

Dainzú is singular for its preservation of an artistic and archaeological record that documents a ceremonial sequence involving a ritual type of ball game that had penitential and sacrificial overtones, a procession enacted as part of that ritual, and a demarcated processional route that led to a hilltop architectural grouping archaeologically identifiable as a shrine complex (Orr 1997). An analysis of patterns of distribution, the ritual sequence itself, and the ideological principles tied to the Dainzú handball game highlights the potential of this cultural complex for political maneuvering (Orr 1993, 1997).

The only surviving *in situ* pictorial documents of the handball game in the valley are found at sites that are located upon sacred hills: Dainzú, Monte Albán, and Cerro de la Campana (Orr 1997).[1] In all three cases, elite residences are situated on or near the hilltops of the centers. As A. Morinis points out:

> . . . since sacred places tend to enshrine collective ideals, shrine sites can be valuable resources in socio-political processes . . . [the] position [of the pilgrimage center] outside ordinary social boundaries lends power to [it], yet, ironically, belief in the power of the place makes it a target for social manipulations (1992:24–25; see also Crumrine and Morinis 1991:7–8; Kendall 1991; Vreeland 1991).

Most particularly, through direct control and explicit associations made by local polities between their group or cause with specific sacred places, the legitimacy of those polities is sanctioned—both to resident and non-resident populations—by a power that is seldom questioned. Empirical evidence cannot verify or disprove the power of something that is sacred; it is this very absence of material corroboration that both distinguishes the sacred from the secular and can underlie passionate convictions of its veracity (e.g., Rappaport 1971; Drennan 1976; Flannery 1976).

I have suggested that procession is recorded as one aspect of the Dainzú handball game, both iconographically and archaeologically (Orr 1997). The ritual act of procession establishes a profound social bond, separating individuals from the normal world and placing them in a different world in which the expression of religious devotion and communication with the divine are a shared, community experience. As mentioned above, social ranking and political organization can be registered or reaffirmed through the performance of formal processions. Religious processions also lend themselves well to political reconciliation, both in cases where fission has occurred within a social group or where the integrative process can assist conflict and dispute resolution between factions. This view of procession as a mechanism for social integration, achieved through religious sanctions, shares traits with David Freidel's pilgrimage-fair, in that relatively diverse groups from different levels of society may be brought together for material, as well as ideological, purposes (see Freidel 1981:378).

However, Freidel's model reaches into the broader geographic spectrum of long-distance trade affiliations. The framework I suggest is most relevant to populations located within a smaller, restricted radius. These are brought together for religious festivals specific to particular, locally acknowledged sacred places. Such festivities would be hosted by the resident community and therefore would have a direct impact upon the political (and divine) prestige of the local polity(ies). Ultimately, the roots of these ceremonies during the Formative period are probably found in the alliance-building, rank affirming feasting rituals of "big-man" early chiefdoms (cf., for example, Fox 1996).[2]

The effectiveness of processionals as tools for social reconciliation or integration is dependent upon the part they play within the larger ceremonial sequences to which they belong. This point is demonstrable, for example, with the Dainzú handball game and other ritual sequences wherein mock combats are central events alongside processions (Orr 1997). Apart from an inherently penitential character, some degree of competition typically underlies these ritual battles; opponents may originate from rival parties in a social group or from different competing communities (e.g., Cordry 1980:154–157; Allen 1988:203ff.). [3]

In pre-Hispanic Mesoamerica, the outcome of staged ritual battles was often fixed. These spectacles often seem to have served as means for public participation in the socially restricted activity of warfare, as the venue for human sacrifice, and as intimidating displays of physical power. Symbolic combat, however, also provides a controlled mechanism for the release of intergroup tensions and potential conflicts or may actually function as a substitute for true warfare (e.g., Hunt 1977:144–145; Gowans 1981:220, 223; Chagnon 1983; Kertzer 1988:125–127, 129–130). In mock combat/procession ceremonial sequences, the ritual combat is a safety valve or outlet that frames the recognition of schism, whereas the procession component, with its common goal of reaching a recognized sacred place for purposes relevant to shared religious convictions, has the effect of underscoring the essential unity of the larger group. Social integration can thus be achieved through both events, in the context of the ceremonial whole—under the auspices of hosting polities or communities.

Some researchers have proposed that the Dainzú-type of handball game was a ritual combat (Orr 1993, 1994, 1997; Taube personal communication 1994; see also Kubler 1984:161). I believe that this combat game was directly associated with warfare and human sacrifice and was conducted in connection with petitions for rainfall. I posited that a productive, specific historical ethnographic analogy may be made between Dainzú handball and the *tigre* battle enacted in certain present-day Guerrero pueblos immediately prior to the rainy season (Orr 1997). The villagers consider this event to be a sacrificial act, with the specific purpose of ensuring the coming of the rains. Strikingly, in the village of Zitlala, the combat was originally timed to correlate with the Holy Cross procession through town. Where the *tigre* battle involves members from the three competing districts of the village fighting one another as representatives of their *barrios*, the procession involves participants from the three districts joining together at the town's mountain-top shrine to share in oblations and sacrifices to the *tigre* rain deity (Cordry 1980: 154–157; Esser 1988: 302–305).

Shrine Sites and Sacred Geography: Monte Albán

Shrines are raised, steps are cut, topography is altered, and settlement patterns change, all as a result of the historical development of the pilgrimage. Here we trace the swells and recessions of flows of people, and the impacts which these tides register on sites elevated to the status of divine abodes on earth (Morinis and Crumrine 1991:9).

The concept of sacred geography as it is employed here was developed for the study of Hindu pilgrimage sites by Vidyarthi (1961, 1979; Preston 1992; see also Kashnitz-Weinberg 1944). As discussed by James Preston: "[in] those traditions where the earth is associated with powerful religious sentiments, spiritual magnetism is strongly linked to sacred geography" (1992:34). In Mesoamerican tradition, human-built sacred spaces were typically located on or near sacred geographic features, and they attempted to replicate the sacred natural environment in site-planning schemes with inherently political resonances (e.g., Benson 1981; Heyden 1981; Ashmore 1989, 1991; Schele and Freidel 1990; Bernal-García 1992; Reilly 1994; Freidel, Schele, and Parker 1993; Koontz 1994).

The foundation of Monte Albán and the rapid growth in size and population density of the hill-top site during Period I (ca. 500–200 BC) corresponds temporally with a sharp population drop at previously important valley floor sites (Winter 1974:982; Flannery and Marcus 1983; Kowalewski et al. 1989; Flannery and Marcus 1990:52–53). In particular, the major Rosario Phase (700–500 BC) Etla Valley center of San José Mogote experienced a notable decline until Monte Albán II (ca. 200 BC–200 AD; see Flannery and Marcus 1983, 1990, 1994). These phenomena have generally been explained by archaeological evidence for increased interregional and extraregional conflict, which was accompanied by a shift from valley floor to piedmont and hilltop sites (Blanton et al. 1982; Spencer 1982; Flannery and Marcus 1983; Kowalewski et al. 1989; Joyce 1991, 1994; Joyce and Winter 1996). However, these archaeological data are actually limited to a few cases of human sacrifice throughout the valley system, the demographic shift itself, the appearance of supposed defensive walls at some hilltop sites, and the iconographic evidence provided by the Danzantes carvings representing sacrificed captives (see below) at Monte Albán and San José Mogote (e.g., Joyce 1991:558–567).

Because the hill cluster of Monte Albán is strategically located at the juncture of the three main valley arms, researchers believe that the site was ideal for the control of trade and traffic and was suitable to fortification (Winter 1974; Blanton 1978; Blanton et al. 1982; Flannery and Marcus 1983, 1990; Joyce and Winter 1996). Some scholars suggest that the center was actually established as the capital of an incipient, expansive militaristic state (Marcus 1976; Spencer 1982:12–31; Flannery and Marcus 1983, 1990), whereas others argue against this position (Sanders and Nichols 1988). Richard Blanton proposed that Monte Albán was a neutral central place where representatives from various previously disparate valley polities purposefully unified to form a regional confederacy for economic and military purposes (1976, 1978:39, 1983; Blanton et al. 1982:69–71; see also Wright 1977; Willey 1979; Santley 1980; Joyce and Winter 1996). Blanton based this argument on evidence derived from an extensive surface survey, which he believed to indicate the presence of three distinct *barrios* (1976, 1978). Marilyn Masson (1994) posited that Blanton's *barrios* suggest the emergence of corporate kinship groups at the urban center.

Arthur Joyce and Marcus Winter (1994, 1996) proposed that emerging elite groups were responsible for the establishment of Monte Albán. These groups soon attracted a steadily growing population of laborers and craft specialists. They posited that the Monte Albán nobility monopolized ritual authority and manipulated religious symbolism to assert their position as mediators between the human and divine worlds. They believe that religion and warfare were part of a complex ideology that Monte Albán's elite employed to support and maintain their authority over nonelite sectors. Within this actor-based perspective, a shared world view functioned to create and assert social distinctions (Winter and Joyce 1994; Joyce and Winter 1996). In addition, Joyce and Winter are among the few writers to acknowledge the inherent sacred power of the location itself:

> The most sacred of institutions may have been the Monte Albán hilltop itself, which visually and perhaps symbolically dominated the valley . . . The Main Plaza with its impressive public buildings visible throughout much of the valley below would have been a kind of permanent, immovable source of prestige and sacred power that could not have been accessed by other elites except through cooper-

ation with Monte Albán's rulers or by conquest (1996; see also Kowalewski et al. 1989, Volume I:344).

Most writers concede that the Main Plaza at Monte Albán was a focus for regional festivals and ceremonies. However, this aspect of function tends to be underemphasized in relation to economics, redistribution of goods, and political strategy (e.g., Blanton 1978, Flannery and Marcus 1983, Winter 1984, Joyce and Winter 1996). I proposed that the area be reconsidered as first and foremost having served the requirements of a pilgrimage center (Orr 1996, 1997). The conflict-based arguments discussed above minimize the possibility that the role of the site location as a sacred place and probable pilgrimage shrine could have, in fact, been fundamental and decisive to the florescence of Monte Albán. The very traits elucidated by Blanton, Joyce, and Winter, for example, coincide with salient features of shrine centers.

The choice of location and layout of the Main Plaza center suggests that the area was probably known and visited as a sacred place well before the urbanization of Monte Albán. The enormous expenditure of labor and planning that went into the construction of this great public space (see Acosta 1965:818) was certainly motivated by needs beyond those of administrative activities or even the requirements of a principal market center (cf. Winter 1984, 1989). The design of such a space simultaneously addressed economic, marketing, and political needs. The Main Plaza space, in fact, is very suitably designed to accommodate the massive temporary influxes of people that are typical of pilgrimage and procession ceremonials (cf. Silverman 1991).[4] For example, the architecture that delimited the periphery of the Main Plaza created a bounded space, with monumental facades, high platforms, and limited access to some structures, that effectively controlled the movement of people through the area (e.g., Blanton et al. 1982). Passage around the plaza was additionally restricted by the development of the structures along the central spine, which would have eventually forced human traffic to move in a circular pattern. Certainly sheer intimidation, spectacle, and social distinction made manifest in physical space were keyed into this architectural arrangement. But all factors considered, this spatial layout conforms with the constituents of pilgrimage centers throughout Europe, Asia, and Latin America:

In traditional societies, a pilgrimage center is a bounded place apart from ordinary settlement, drawing pilgrims from great distances as

well as nearby. It must have some place of congregation, some symbols on display readily understood by the congregated pilgrims,
common activities (often conducted *en masse*) and myth which the
other elements (site, symbols, and activities) evoke; such myths are
narratives commonly known (Moore 1980:207).

That the impressive architecture, monumental sculptural displays, and
painted imagery which originally enlivened the center were concomi-
tantly employed by Monte Albán's leading lineages for self-aggrandize-
ment only highlights my points.

I do not discount conflict-related explanations for Late Formative social and demographic shifts that occurred in the Valley of Oaxaca. However, I believe that, in seeking to understand the relatively dramatic rise
to prominence that Monte Albán experienced, more attention should be
given to ideological principles that are especially particular to this region.
For example:

Both sociologically and theologically, the sacred place has a power
which secular groups seek to tap and channel for their own temporal
purposes. It is an irony of being a place apart that this otherworldli-
ness is the source of the power which ultimately leads pilgrimage
centers to become embroiled in political rivalries, in which any kind
of power is a potential resource (Morinis and Crumrine 1991:8).

Deep-level structure is made manifest in the magnification of the holy
that separates the sacred place from the mundane world. As points of
contention, powerful shrine sites can have significant effects upon population flows and changes.

I have suggested this general scenario: Around 500 BC, Monte Albán
acquired increased spiritual magnetism due to any one of Preston's variables discussed above, together with reasons of internal polemics. Enter-
prising groups would have soon converged upon the site, attracted by
the potential for economic gain and prestige through assuming control
and operation of the sacred place. Having established themselves, these
groups were *a priori* at a social, political, and economic advantage over
incoming residents; however, they had to employ several strategies to retain their advantages. Thus, in the later part of Monte Albán I, enormous
architectural and sculptural enterprises were undertaken in ostentatious
displays of accumulated wealth and the implicit authority that was sanctified by the very location the patrons pioneered (see Joyce and Winter
1996; Orr 1997).

This scenario also accounts for a soon-thriving local ceramics industry and workshops within the site center devoted to the production of exotic goods. The consumption of these products rapidly intensified (Winter and Joyce 1994; Joyce and Winter 1996). Joyce and Winter (1996) and Masson (1994) note that ceramic effigies of Cociyo, the Zapotec rain-lightning deity, appear with increasing frequency through the Late Formative and Classic periods; by Monte Albán III, these were mold-made and mass produced (see also Caso et al. 1967; Urcid Serrano 1992). This type of small-scale art form, which bears images of principal deities and supernaturals, belongs to the class of materials commissioned or purchased for personal rites and spiritual merit at pilgrimage shrines worldwide throughout history. Indeed, the pilgrimage industry typically provides a large market for artisan products and religious paraphernalia.

Sacred Space and Politics: The Danzantes of Monte Albán and Dainzú Ballplayers

The earliest known monumental art at Monte Albán is represented by the Danzantes carvings.[5] These depictions of mutilated sacrificial victims appear with the foundation of the great center, around 500 BC (Period Ia, the Danzantes Wall). Dates for carved Danzantes stones range from Monte Albán I through Period II (Scott 1978; Garcia Moll et al. 1986). Only one example of the sculptural type is found outside of Monte Albán, at the site of San José el Mogote (SJM-3, Marcus 1976, 1980; Flannery and Marcus 1983, 1990, 1994; Cahn and Winter 1993).[6] This carving attests to an understanding of Danzante iconography in other parts of the valley, along with an acknowledged connection between Monte Albán and San José Mogote.

I have suggested that the individuals represented in the Danzantes carvings were victims of mock combat rituals; these were single events in a warfare-sacrifice ritual sequence, enacted as public spectacles (Orr 1993, 1997). I believe that, like Dainzú handball, the objectives of agricultural fertility and dependable rainfall lay at the heart of these events, in the context of a divine covenant or sacrificial exchange (Orr 1994, 1996, 1997). For example, the unusual practice of genital mutilation or castration graphically represented on many Danzantes carvings both supports, and is explained by, this postulation (cf. Scott 1978, Volume I:25–26). The relationship between bleeding of the male genitals and fertility is a common theme throughout Mesoamerican art (e.g., Schele 1996).

I additionally believe that the Danzantes mock combat ritual sequence included processionals within the Monte Albán shrine center. This ritual sequence closely parallels that which I have suggested for the ballplayers carvings of Dainzú. At both centers, these carvings were exhibited in similar grand, architectural schemes that were designed like codices writ large.

Although many interpretations of the Danzantes carvings have been presented, scholars generally agree that the figures represent sacrificed individuals (discussed in Scott 1978; Garcia Moll et al. 1986; Urcid Serrano 1992). Most researchers suggest that the victims were captives of warfare (Marcus 1976, 1980; Flannery and Marcus 1983). Hieroglyphic texts identify many of the figures, supplying dates, names, and the victims' places of origin (Marcus 1980; Flannery and Marcus 1983; Urcid Serrano 1992, n.d.). These slack-faced individuals, whose contorted, naked bodies were pecked onto stone surfaces, conform entirely with pan-Mesoamerican iconographic conventions for the depiction of prisoners and sacrificial victims (Coe 1962; Marcus 1976, 1983; Scott 1978; Schele and Miller 1986; Flannery and Marcus 1990).

One researcher suggested that the Danzantes might portray lesser village men, taken in raids and skirmishes, rather than nobles from rival polities or factions (Marcus 1976). However, as mentioned, numerous Danzantes are accompanied by hieroglyphic toponyms identifying these individuals with specific locations. Furthermore, this proposal is not consistent with the careful depiction of elite adornments on most Danzantes. For example, large earspools are particularly emphasized; even though many figures have been stripped of their regalia, holes are clearly delineated on the earlobes where spools would have hung (Orr 1997). Indeed, during excavations at Monte Albán in the 1970's, Marcus Winter uncovered a pair of greenstone earspools from an Early Period II elite burial (Burial MA 77–14) that are 8 centimeters in diameter and identical to those portrayed on Danzantes figures (personal communication 1994).

Joyce Marcus interpreted the carvings as a ritual and symbolic display of potential power, intended to legitimize the as yet uninstitutionalized power of the newly founded elite who established Monte Albán (1976, 1980). Her interpretation employs a reconstruction in which all (nearly 400) known Danzantes sculptures originate from the east-facing Danzantes Building facade (Flannery and Marcus 1983:89). Marcus and others view this enormous structure, with its awesome display of slain captives, as a commemorative monument (Marcus 1976; Blanton 1978). However, most of these carvings are individualized virtual portraits of specifically identified persons—rather than symbols of potential victims. In addition, a number of Danzantes stones are carved on several sides— evidence that they were reused multiple times for different constructions (see Scott 1978; Garcia Moll et al. 1986; Urcid Serrano 1992). The figures also tend to form stylistic groupings or categories, which, according to Javier Urcid Serrano, indicate independent sculptural programs pertaining to unique structures (1992, n.d.; Orr 1993; see also Scott 1978).[7]

The Danzantes Wall is the only remaining indication of what were more than likely several such facades decorating pyramidal platforms in the Main Plaza of Monte Albán. This wall is also the earliest surviving monument from the great Mesoamerican artistic tradition of representing war captives and sacrificial victims in large sculpted or painted "galleries"—exemplified by such Classic Period Maya works as the captive sculptures in the Palace at Palenque and the murals of Bonampak (Marcus 1976, 1980; Flannery and Marcus 1983, 1990; Miller 1986; Schele and Miller 1986). The Ballplayers Wall at Dainzú also belongs to this tradition (Orr 1993). As Marcus pointed out, this type of architectural programming relies upon staged, ritual interaction by religious practitioners with the structures themselves to reveal the full significance of the imagery (Marcus 1974; Flannery and Marcus 1983:89–90, 1990; see also Scott 1978, Part 1; Schele and Freidel 1990:105ff.; Urcid Serrano 1992; Orr 1993).

The narrative aspect of these sculptural programs was brought to life, and inherent ideological precepts were elucidated and enhanced, by ritual practitioners physically ascending the immense platforms plastered with Danzantes or Ballplayers carvings and performing the ritual actions depicted on those monuments (Orr 1993, 1997; Winter and Joyce 1994; Joyce and Winter 1996). Independently, the sculptures are didactic tallies that could be understood syntactically, like the pictorial lists of conquered sites recorded in the Mixtec codices.

Marcus has argued that the iconographic themes at Monte Albán are almost exclusively militaristic, whereas those at other valley centers emphasize ritual and religion (1976, 1983:113). She proposed that styles and themes in the sculpture of the Central Valleys are unified by Period IIIA when, she suggested, the previously autonomous valley floor centers were subjugated by Monte Albán (Marcus 1976:137). Blanton referred to Marcus's conclusions to corroborate his neutral central place hypothesis for Monte Albán:

Not only were there more carved stone monuments at the new capital than at any other valley center, but they differed from those of the other centers in portraying exclusively military themes. Monuments from other centers prominently include ritual themes. This makes sense for a neutral institution, since subjects are best avoided for which there may have been no regional consensus; ritual may have been one such area (1978:39).

These arguments are problematic for several reasons. First, the writers presume a complete, *in situ* artistic record in a region where it is well established that this record is undependable (Urcid Serrano 1992, n.d.). Second, the acts of warfare and human sacrifice were clearly ritualized—as attested by the very iconography of the Danzantes. These practices were founded in deeply held religious convictions throughout Mesoamerican history and cannot, therefore, be separated as something fundamentally exclusive from other types of ritual. Third, although the scale in numbers of Danzantes carvings is not replicated elsewhere, sacrifice is depicted in the sculpture of other sites, such as San José Mogote and Dainzú. Sacrifice formed a central part of the Dainzú handball game; this ball game was also known at Monte Albán (Orr 1997). Finally, Marcus and Blanton's arguments do not place the images of sacrifice at Monte Albán within their broader ritual context. It is clear that the sequence of events encompassing the Danzantes sacrifices calls for a deeper consideration than merely acknowledging the presence of militarism.

In the previous discussion, I have suggested that, through associations between place and polity, the sacred power of Dainzú and Monte Albán as shrine sites lent itself well to political strategization. I consider the distributional link between handball iconography and hilltop shrine sites in the valley to be the key to an understanding of the handball complex. Procession and sacrifice were integral components of the Dainzú type of handball game. In addition, I have attempted to demonstrate links between the possible ideological premises of the ritual acts recorded by the Danzantes and by the Dainzú Ballplayers. I have reframed the Formative Period iconography of sacrifice and the handball game in the Valley of Oaxaca within a paradigm that does not distinguish religious concerns from political motives. In so doing, it has been necessary to readdress the role of the valley's greatest Late Formative center, Monte Albán.

The examination of sacred geography at Monte Albán made above underscores weaknesses in exclusively militaristic hypotheses for the city's rise to power and similar interpretations of the Danzantes. I presented a hypothesis that the rapid settlement and florescence of Monte Albán around 500 BC was due primarily to a sudden rise in the religious importance of this sacred hilltop shrine. As the site gained importance, the urban population expanded likewise. I do not negate the impact of warfare and internal conflict during this period, however; the two hypotheses are not necessarily mutually exclusive. Beyond basic power displays, for example, what was the underlying motivation for erecting the huge carved Danzantes and Dainzú ballplayers programs that characterize architectural sculpture at this time? Furthermore, why specifically is this type of imagery found only at sites that are demonstrably hilltop shrines? I believe that these shrine sites were dedicated to the Zapotec Cociyo, and I suggest that processions and ritual combats ending with sacrifice were held there as part of the ritual sequence of supplication to the rain deity. Political aspirations were woven into the ideological fabric of these centers, and competing or aspiring polities found ripe fodder for self-promotion and legitimization.

References

Acosta, Jorge.
    1965   Preclassic and Classic Architecture of Oaxaca. *Handbook of Middle American Indians, Volume 3.* Edited by Robert Wauchope and Gordon R. Willey. Austin, Tex.: University of Texas Press. 814–836.

Adams, W. R.
    1991   Social Structure in Pilgrimage and Prayer: Tzeltales as Lords and Servants. *Pilgrimage in Latin America.* Edited by N. R. Crumrine and A. Morinis. Contributions to the Study of Anthropology 4. Westport, Conn.: Greenwood Press. 109–122.

Allen, Catherine.
    1988   *The Hold Life Has: Coca and Cultural Identity in an Andean Community.* Washington, D.C.: Smithsonian Institution Press.

Ashmore, Wendy.
    1989   Construction and Cosmology: Politics and Ideology in Lowland Maya Settlement Patterns. *Word and Image in Maya Culture.* Edited by William F. Hanks and Don S. Rice. Salt Lake City: University of Utah Press. 272–286.
    1991   Site-Planning Principles and Concepts of Directionality Among the Ancient Maya. *Latin American Antiquity* 2(3):199–226.

Benson, Elizabeth, editor.
    1981   *The Olmec and Their Neighbors: Essays in Memory of Matthew W. Stirling.* Washington, D.C.: Dumbarton Oaks.

Betteridge, A. H.
    1992   Specialist in Miraculous Action: Some Shrines in Shiraz. *Sacred Journeys: The Anthropology of Pilgrimage.* Edited by A. Morinis. Contributions to the Study of Anthropology 7. Westport, Conn.: Greenwood Press. 189–210.

Blanton, Richard.
1978 *Monte Alban: Settlement Patterns at the Ancient Zapotec Capital.* New York: Academic Press.
Blanton, Richard, Stephen Kowalewski, Gary Feinman, and Jill Appel.
1982 *Monte Alban's Hinterland, Part I: The Prehispanic Settlement Patterns of the Central and Southern Parts of the Valley of Oaxaca, Mexico.* Memoirs of the Museum of Anthropology, University of Michigan, 15. Ann Arbor, Mich.: University of Michigan.
Burgoa, Francisco de.
1934 *Geográfica descripción.* Publicaciones del Archivo General de la Nación 25–26. México, D.F.: Talleres Gráficos de la Nación. Reprint.
Byland, Bruce, and John Pohl.
1994 *In the Realm of 8 Deer: The Archaeology of the Mixtec Codices.* Norman, Okla.: University of Oklahoma Press.
Cahn, Robert, and Marcus Winter.
1993 The San Jose Mogote Dancer. *Indiana* 13:39–64.
Caso, Alfonso.
1938 *Exploraciones en Oaxaca, quinta y sexta temporadas, 1936–37.* Instituto Panamericano de Geografía e Historia Publicación 34. México, D.F: Instituto Panamericano de Geografía e Historia.
1947 Calendario y escritura de las antiguas culturas de Monte Alban. *Obras Completas de Miguel Othon de Mendizabal, Volume 1.* México, D.F.: INAH.
Caso, Alfonso, Ignacio Bernal, and Jorge Acosta.
1967 *La ceramica de Monte Alban.* Memorias del Instituto Nacional de Antropología e Historia 13. México, D.F.: INAH.
Chagnon, Napoleon.
1983 *Yanomano: The Fierce People.* 3rd ed. New York: Holt, Rinehart, and Winston.
Coe, Michael.
1962 *Mexico.* New York: Frederick E. Praeger.
1965 The Olmec Style and Its Distribution. *Handbook of Middle American Indians Volume 3.* Austin, Tex.: University of Texas Press.739–775.
Cordry, Donald.
1980 *Mexican Masks.* Austin, Tex.: University of Texas Press.
Crumrine, N. Ross.
1991 Fiestas and Exchange Pilgrimages: The Yorem Pahko and Mayo Identity, Northwest Mexico. *Pilgrimage in Latin America.* Edited by N. R. Crumrine and A. Morinis. Contributions to the Study of Anthropology 4. Westport, Conn.: Greenwood Press. 71–90.
Crumrine, N. Ross, and Alan Morinis, editors.
1991 *Pilgrimage in Latin America.* Contributions to the Study of Anthropology 4. Westport, Conn.: Greenwood Press.
Cruz, Wilfredo.
1946 *Oaxaca Recondita: Razas, idiomas, costumbres, leyendas y tradiciones del Estado de Oaxaca, Mexico.* México, D.F.: INI.
Dahlgren de Jordan, B.
1966 *La Mixteca: Su cultura e historia prehispanicas.* México, D.F.: UNAM.

Drennan, Robert D.
1976   Religion and Social Evolution in Formative Mesoamerica. *The Early Mesoamerican Village.* Edited by K. V. Flannery. New York: Academic Press. 345–368.

Durán, Fray Diego.
1971   *Book of the Gods and Rites of the Ancient Calendar.* Translated by Fernando Horcasitas and Doris Heyden. Norman, Okla.: University of Oklahoma Press.

Esparza, Manuel.
1985   *Gillow durante el Porfiriato y la Revolution en Oaxaca, 1887–1922.* México, D.F.: SAGEO.

Esser, Janet Brody, editor.
1988   *Behind the Mask in Mexico.* Santa Fe, N.Mex.: Museum of New Mexico Press.

Flannery, Kent V., editor.
1976   *The Early Mesoamerican Village.* New York: Academic Press.

Flannery, Kent, and Joyce Marcus.
1990   Borron y cuenta nueva: Setting Oaxaca's Archaeological Record Straight. *Debating Oaxaca Archaeology.* Edited by Joyce Marcus. Anthropological Papers, Museum of Anthropology, University of Michigan. Ann Arbor, Mich.: University of Michigan. 17–69.

Flannery, Kent, and Joyce Marcus, editors.
1983   *The Cloud People: Divergent Evolution of the Zapotec and Mixtec Civilizations.* New York: Academic Press.

Fox, John Gerard.
1996   Playing with Power: Ballcourts and Political Ritual in Southern Mesoamerica. *Current Anthropology* 37(3):483–506.

Freidel, David, Linda Schele, and Joy Parker.
1993   *Maya Cosmos: 3000 Years on the Shaman's Path.* New York: William Morrow.

Fuente, Juan de la.
1942   Las ceremonias de la lluvia entre los zapotecas de hoy. *Actas, 27th International Congress of Americanists* 5:479–489.

Garcia Moll, R., D. W. Patterson Brown, and M. Winter.
1986   *Monumentos Escultoricos de Monte Alban.* Munich: Verlag C. H. Beck.

Gowans, Alan.
1981   *Learning to See: Historical Perspectives on Modern Popular/Commercial Arts.* Bowling Green, Ohio: Bowling Green University Popular Press.

Hunt, Eva.
1977   *Transformation of the Hummingbird: Cultural Roots of a Zinacatan Mythical Poem.* Ithaca: Cornell University Press.

Joyce, Arthur.
1991   *Formative Period Occupation in the Lower Rio Verde Valley, Oaxaca, Mexico: Interregional Interaction and Social Change.* Ph.D. dissertation, Department of Anthropology, Rutgers University.
1994   *Ideology, Power, and State Formation at Monte Alban.* Paper presented at the 59th Annual Meeting of the Society for American Archaeology, Anaheim, Calif.

Joyce, Arthur, and Marcus Winter.
  1996   Ideology, Power and Urban Society in Prehispanic Oaxaca. *Current Anthropology* 37(1):33–86.
Kashnitz-Weinberg, Guido Freiherr Von.
  1944   *The Mediterranean Foundations of Ancient Art.* Translated by John R. Clarke. Frankfurt Am Main: Vittorio Kostermann.
Kendall,C.
  1991   The Politics of Pilgrimage: The Black Christ of Esquipulas. *Pilgrimage in Latin America.* Edited by N. R. Crumrine and A. Morinis. Contribution to the Study of Anthropology 4. Westport, Conn.: Greenwood Press. 139–156.
Kertzer, David.
  1988   *Ritual, Politics, and Power.* New Haven: Yale University Press.
Konrad, H. W.
  1991   Pilgrimage as a Cyclical Process: The Unending Pilgrimage of the Holy Cross of the Qintana Roo Maya. *Pilgrimage in Latin America.* Edited by N. R. Crumrine and A. Morinis. Contributions to the Study of Anthropology 4. Westport, Conn.: Greenwood Press. 123–138.
Koontz, R.
  1994   *The Iconography of El Tajín, Veracruz, Mexico.* Ph.D. dissertation, University of Texas at Austin.
Kowalewski,Stephen, et al.
  1989   *Monte Alban's Hinterland, Part II: Prehispanic Settlement Patterns in Tlacolula, Etla, and Ocotlan, The Valley of Oaxaca, Mexico.* Memoirs of the Museum of Anthropology, University of Michigan, 23. Ann Arbor, Mich.: University of Michigan.
Kubler, George.
  1984   *The Art and Architecture of Ancient America: The Mexican, Maya, and Andean People.* New York: Penguin.
  1985   Pre-Columbian Pilgrimages in Mesoamerica. *Fourth Palenque Round Table.* Edited by M. C. Robertson. San Francisco: The Pre-Columbian Art Research Institute. 313–316.
Looper, Matthew.
  1991   *The Dances of the Classic Maya Deities Chak and Hun Nal Ye.* M.A. thesis, University of Texas at Austin.
Marcus, Joyce.
  1973   The Iconography of Power Among the Classic Maya. *World Archeology* 6(1):83–94.
  1976   The Iconography of Militarism at Monte Alban and Neighboring Sites in the Valley of Oaxaca. *Origins of Religious Art and Iconography in Pre-Classic Mesoamerica.* Edited by H. B. Nicholson. Los Angeles: UCLA Latin American Center. 123–139.
  1980   Zapotec Writing. *Scientific American* 242(2):50–64.
  1983   Monte Alban II in the Macuilxóchitl Area. *The Cloud People: Divergent Evolution of the Zapotec and Mixtec Civilizations.* Edited by K. V. Flannery and J. Marcus. New York: Academic Press. 113–115.

Martinez Marin, C.
  1972 Santuarios y peregrinaciones en el Mexico Prehispanico. *Religion en Mesoamerica, Volume XII: Mesa Redonda.* Edited by J. Litvak King and N. Castillo Tejero. México, D.F.: Sociedad Mexicana de Antropología. 161–178.
Masson, Marilyn.
  1994 Cocijo, Ancestors, and the Annual Cycle: Reflections of Secular and Religious Divisions of Power Among the Classic Period Zapotec. Paper presented at the 57th Annual Meeting of the Society for American Archaeology, Anaheim, California.
Masson, Marilyn, and Heather Orr.
  1998 The Writing in the Wall: Political Representation and Sacred Geography at Monte Alban in Programs of Building Dedication, Nahual Transformation, and Captive Sacrifice. *The Sowing and the Dawning: Termination Process in the Archaeological and Ethnological Record of Mesoamerica.* Edited by Shirley Boteler Mock. Albuquerque, N.Mex.: University of New Mexico Press. 165–175.
Miller, Arthur.
  1996 *The Painted Tombs of Oaxaca: Living with the Dead.* Cambridge: Cambridge University Press.
Monaghan, John.
  1987 *We Are the People Who Eat Tortillas: Household and Community in the Mixteca.* Ph.D. dissertation, University of Pennsylvania.
  1995 *The Convenants with the Earth and Rain: Exchange, Sacrifice, and Revelation in Mixtec Sociality.* Norman, Okla.: University of Oklahoma Press.
Moore, A.
  1980 Walt Disney World: Bounded Ritual Space and the Playful Pilgrimage Center. *Anthropological Quarterly*:207–218.
Morinis, A.
  1992 Persistent Peregrination: From Sun Dance to Catholic Pilgrimage Among Canadian Prairie Indians. *Sacred Journeys: The Anthropology of Pilgrimage.* Edited by A. Morinis. Contributions to the Study of Anthropology 7. Westport, Conn.: Greenwood Press. 1–18.
Morinis, A., and N. R. Crumrine.
  1981 *De las multiple formas de nuestra religion.* Oaxaca, Mexico: INI.
  1991 La Peregrinacion: The Latin American Pilgrimage. *Pilgrimage in Latin America.* Edited by N. R. Crumrine and A. Morinis. Contributions to the Study of Anthropology 4. Westport, Conn.: Greenwood Press. 1–18.
Multiples Formas.
  1981 *De las multiples formas de nuestra religion.* Oaxaca, Mexico: INI. Oettinger, M., Jr., and P. A. Parsons.
  1982 Una guia para rituales de la lluvia en Petlacala, Guerrero. *Tlalocan* 9:373–384.
Orr, Heather.
  1993 The Ballplayers of Dainzú: Evidence for Inter-site Elite Competition in the Late Formative Valley of Oaxaca. Paper presented at the 58th An-

nual Meeting of the Society for American Archaeology, St. Louis, Missouri.

1994　Stone Balls and Masked Men: Initial Observations of a Combat Ritual in Precolumbian Oaxaca. Paper presented at the 59th Annual Meeting of the Society for American Archaeology, Anaheim, California.

1996　The Long Winding Road: Rituals of Procession and Pilgrimage in the Ancient Valley of Oaxaca. Paper presented at the 61st Annual Meeting of the Society for American Archaeology, New Orleans, Louisiana.

1997　*Power Games in the Late Formative Valley of Oaxaca: The Ballplayer Carvings at Dainzú.* Ph.D. dissertation, University of Texas at Austin.

Parsons, Elsie Clews.

1936　*Mitla, Town of Souls and Other Zapoteco-Speaking Pueblos of Oaxaca, Mexico.* Chicago: University of Chicago Press.

Pozorski, T., and S. Pozorski.

1995　An I-Shaped Ball-Court Form at Pampa de las Llamas-Moxeke, Peru. *Latin American Antiquity* 6(3):274–280.

Preston, James.

1992　Spiritual Magnetism: An Organizing Principle for the Study of Pilgrimage. *Sacred Journeys: The Anthropology of Pilgrimage.* Edited by A. Morinis. Contributions to the Study of Anthropology 7. Westport, Conn.: Greenwood Press. 31–46.

Rappaport, R. A.

1971　*Ecology, Meaning, and Religion.* Richmond, Va.: North Atlantic Books.

Reilly, Kent F., III.

1994　*Visions to Another World: Art, Shamanism, and Political Power in Middle Formative Mesoamerica.* Ph.D. dissertation, University of Texas at Austin.

Sallnow, M. J.

1987　*Pilgrims of the Andes.* Washington, D.C.: Smithsonian Institute Press.

1990　*Contesting the Sacred: The Anthropology of Christian Pilgrimage.* London, Routledge.

Sanders, W. T., and D. L. Nichols.

1988　Ecological Theory and Cultural Evolution in the Valley of Oaxaca. *Current Anthropology* 29(1):33–80.

Santley, R. S.

1980　Disembedded Capitals Reconsidered. *American Antiquity* 45(1):132–145.

Schele, Linda.

1996　The Olmec Mountain and the Tree of Creation in Mesoamerican Cosmology. *Olmec World: Ritual and Rulership.* Princeton: The Art Museum, Princeton University. 105–119.

Schele Linda, and David Freidel.

1990　*A Forest of Kings: The Untold Story of the Ancient Maya.* New York: William Morrow.

Schele, Linda, and Mary Ellen Miller.

1986　*Blood of Kings: Dynasty and Ritual in Maya Art.* Fort Worth, Tex.: Kimbell Art Museum.

Scott, John.
1978   *The Danzantes of Monte Alban.* Dumbarton Oaks Studies in Pre-Columbian Art and Archaeology 19. Washington, D.C.: Dumbarton Oaks.

Silverman, H.
1991   The Ethnography and Archaeology of Two Andean Pilgrimage Centers. *Pilgrimage in Latin America.* Edited by N. R. Crumrine and A. Morinis. Contributions to the Study of Anthropology 4. Westport, Conn.: Greenwood Press. 215–228.

Spencer, C. S.
1982   *The Cuicatlan Cañada and Monte Alban.* New York: Academic Press.

Spero J.
1987   *Lightning Men and Water Serpents: A Comparison of Maya and Mixe-Zoquean Beliefs.* M.A. thesis, University of Texas at Austin.

Taube, Karl.
1992   *The Major Gods of Ancient Yucatan.* Dumbarton Oaks Studies in Pre-Columbian Art and Archaeology 32. Washington, D.C.: Dumbarton Oaks.
1996   The Rainmakers: The Olmec and Their Contribution to Mesoamerican Belief and Ritual. *The Olmec World: Ritual and Rulership.* Princeton: The Art Museum, Princeton University. 83–104.

Tozzer, Alfred.
1941   *Landa's* Relación *de las Cosas de Yucatán: A Translation.* Papers of the Peabody Museum of American Archaeology and Ethnology, Volume XVIII. Cambridge, Mass.: Harvard University. Reprinted New York: Kraus Reprint Corporation, 1966.

Turner, V.
1974   *From Liminal to Liminoid in Play, Flow, and Ritual: An Essay in Comparative Symbology.* Princeton, N.J.: Humanities Press.

Turner, V., and E. Turner.
1978   *Image and Pilgrimage in Christian Culture: Anthropological Perspectives.* New York: Columbia University Press.

Urbano, H.
1991   Mythic Andean Discourse and Pilgrimages. *Pilgrimage in Latin America.* Edited by N. R. Crumrine and A. Morinis. Contributions to the Study of Anthropology 4. Westport, Conn.: Greenwood Press.

Urcid Serrano, Javier.
1992   *Zapotec Hieroglyphic Writing.* Ph.D. dissertation, Yale University.
1994   Monte Alban y la escritura Zapoteca. *Monte Alban: Estudios Recientes.* Edited by Marcus Winter. Oaxaca, Mexico: Proyecto Especial Monte Alban. 1992–1994.
n.d.   Corpus of Zapotec Hieroglyphic Writing. Manuscript in possession of the author.

Vidyarthi, L. P.
1961   *The Sacred Complex in Hindu Gaya.* New York: Asia Books.
1979   *The Sacred Complex of Kashi.* New Delhi, India: Concept.

Vreeland, J. M., Jr.
    1991 Pilgrim's Progress: The Emergence of Secular Authority in a Traditional
        Andean Pilgrimage. *Pilgrimage in Latin America.* Edited by N. R. Crum-
        rine and A. Morinis. Contributions to the Study of Anthropology 4.
        Westport, Conn.: Greenwood Press.
Winter, Marcus.
    1974 Residential Patterns at Monte Alban, Oaxaca, Mexico. *Science*
        186:981–986
Winter, Marcus, and Arthur Joyce.
    1994 Early Political Development at Monte Alban: Evidence from Recent Ex-
        cavations. Paper presented at the 93rd Annual Meeting of the Ameri-
        can Anthropological Association, Atlanta, Georgia.

Notes

1. I consider this distribution to be significant, particularly because large-scale monuments depicting sacrificial themes in general follow the same pattern during the Formative Period—viz. the Danzantes of Monte Albán and Monument 3 of San José Mogote.

2. For example, the architectural ballcourt (i.e., a bounded space), composed of a central alley flanked by two long parallel mounds, may find its origins in Early and Middle Formative period earthen structures identified as ballcourts, which are significantly found at sites considered to be foci of emerging and paramount chiefdoms (Freidel, Schele, and Parker 1993; Reilly 1994; Blake et al. 1996; cf. also Pozorski and Pozorski 1995). However, the form and situation of these early structures can likewise be considered to conform with the functional requirements of processional ways. The architectural type is typically located at or near the site center and is closely related to ceremonial or civic/ceremonial public edifices. Reilly, for example, believes that the main South Court of Complex A at La Venta was intended both as a false, or ritual, ballcourt and as a processional way leading to the North Court (personal communication 1996; see Orr 1997). Indeed, Kubler made some notable insights along these lines:

> . . . At the ballcourt, a small-scope pilgrimage could be performed as a com-
> munal effort to insure continuity . . . the ballgame courts provided a setting
> for a ritual of action expressive of commonly held beliefs about the meaning
> of existence—but within the pleasurable frame work of play and sport at-
> tractive to large crowds . . . These games between and among neighbors
> were surely a surrogate for hostility. Like a pilgrimage, the ballgame was a
> form of associative convergence for worshipful action at a sacred place, but
> its competitive nature inevitably dominated any religious content
> (1985:315).

3. At Least six toponyms associated with carved ballplayers survive at Dainzú, indicating an identification with different locales or community sectors (Orr 1997; see also Urcid Serrano 1992).

4. Kubler observed that:

Architectural evidence. . . supports the argument that both highland and low-land sites were, in some cases, designed to receive large crowds of visitors at regular periods. The plazas and concourses of Teotihuacan, Cholula, Tikal, and Copán suggest crowds of many thousands swarming to ceremonies required by the calendar (1985: 316).

However, he goes on to support Blanton's view that Monte Albán was designed to restrict general access. Although some degree of restriction is evident, recent findings, in particular those of the Proyecto Especial Monte Albán, 1992–1994, suggest the city center had formal access-ways (e.g., Joyce and Winter 1996). Indeed, the summit may be breached from several approaches.

5. Danzantes ("dancers") is employed here as the commonly used term because early research at Monte Albán referred to the well-known Monte Albán I and II stone slabs carved with human figures considered by many researchers to represent sacrificial victims (e.g., Coe 1962; Marcus 1973, 1976, 1983; Scott 1978). The Danzantes Wall is the only remaining portion of a facade revetment wall belonging to the earliest known phase of Building L. This structure was a large pyramidal platform with high talud-sloping walls formed of monumental stones. However, I believe that iconographic inconsistencies here suggest that the carvings are in reused context although the wall supplies the earliest in situ date (Monte Albán Ia) for this class of carved monument (see Orr 1997).

Ceramic and small greenstone depictions of these figures are also known from the period (see Caso 1947:Figures 39, 40a and 40b; Caso et al. 1967; Scott 1978:Figures 11 and 28;).

6. Because this monument was not discovered in primary context (see Urcid Serrano 1992; Cahn and Winter 1993; cf. also Flannery and Marcus 1983:57, 1990), but was used for a building dedication event (e.g., Masson and Orr 1998), the date of its execution has been a point of contention—with arguments ranging from the Rosario Phase (Flannery and Marcus 1983:57) to Monte Albán I (Urcid Serrano 1992) and Period II (Cahn and Winter 1993).

The monument is located between two principal structures at the top of Mound 1. This 15-meter-high pyramid became the focus of civic/ceremonial life at San José Mogote during the Rosario Phase (ca. 700–500 BC). A remarkable Period II cache of ceramic effigies excavated at this mound exhibit ritual impersonation of Cociyo; the principal actor lies on his belly in some replication of that deity's traits (see Masson 1994; Taube 1996; Orr 1997).

7. I have suggested that these stylistic variations are not arbitrary, but refer to specific moments or events (Orr 1997).

Sacred Geography at Izapa and the Performance of Rulership

JULIA GUERNSEY KAPPELMAN

Characterized by monuments that unravel rich narratives throughout carefully delineated ceremonial spaces, the site of Izapa offers a unique glimpse into the organization of sacred space during the Late Formative period (300 BC–200 AD).[1] The carved monuments reveal the rituals performed by Late Formative rulers, whereas the architectural space in which they are contained manifests the primordial landscape of creation. A veritable web of politics and cosmogenesis was woven through the sculptural and architectural programs at Izapa, and Late Formative rulers inserted themselves and their actions into this space, creating a conjunction between myth, political narrative, and individual action. This conjunction between actor and structuring narrative, as discussed in the first chapter of this volume, is at the heart of Sahlins's (1985:xiv) concept of the "structure of conjuncture," which seeks to reveal the nature of power through an analysis of just such interplay. An examination of the conjunction—or sublime merger—of space, architecture, sculpture, mythic narrative, and human action at Izapa provides a lens through which the discourse of rulership, power, and cosmology during the Late Formative period is also revealed.

Izapa is located in the Pacific coastal piedmont of Chiapas, Mexico, which during the Late Formative period was a strategic crossroads that linked Mayan- and Mixe-Zoquean-speaking regions (Figure 4.1). The sculptural vehicle of choice at the site was the stela-altar format, which paired erect, carved stone stelae with low, carved stone altars. These monuments, strategically placed throughout the site core and framed against pyramidal mounds, literally punctuated space with their mes-

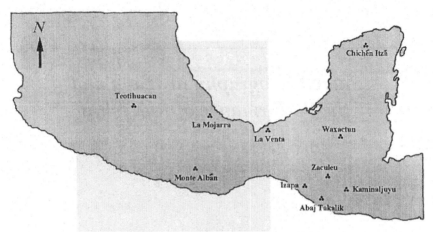

Figure 4.1   Map of Mesoamerica

sages. Together with the architecture, they served to demarcate the boundaries of the sacred landscape and invest it with powerful imagery that defined Izapa's place within the natural world as well as the supernatural sphere.

The stela format was also an effective tool for creating a permanent record of a ruler's ritual performances and contact with the supernatural realm, themes that are paramount within the corpus of Izapa monuments. Moreover, the vivid images of trance journeys that are found on the Izapa monuments testify to the shamanic ideology that underpinned a ruler's political authority, a phenomenon well documented during the Middle Formative period. As Frank Reilly (1994) demonstrated, the carved monuments that were erected by the Olmec in their ceremonial centers visualized an ideology that mandated supernatural sanctification for rulership.[2] This ideology successfully integrated a shamanic belief system—which included the concept of a multilayered universe that was united by means of a central world axis and the notion of a trance experience in which the soul of a shaman traveled into the supernatural realm—into a complex social and political system. Reilly coined the phrase "institutionalized shamanism" to accommodate this Middle Formative ideological complex whose foundations for power rested upon a shamanic belief system. His work, like that of Caroline Humphrey (1994), provides a model for exploring the interaction between inspirational practices and the dynamics of state formation at specific junctures in time. As Humphrey further observed, approaches such as these enable scholars to re-evaluate shamanism as a discourse rather than as a static event (1994:192–193). These approaches also accommodate the variations that ensue when a shamanic ideology is integrated into a context of power. This concept of an institutionalized shamanism provides not only a model for understanding the nature of Late Formative political authority that is expressed in the corpus of monuments at Izapa but also enables one to reconstruct the rituals that were performed within the precincts of the site.

Throughout this chapter, the stela-altar monuments of Izapa will be considered as part of a powerful exchange—or "conjuncture"—between sculpture, architecture, performance space, and actor within the precincts of the site. This discussion will begin by exploring how the dynamics of this cosmologically charged landscape were orchestrated at Izapa during the Late Formative period and then will focus specifically upon the performance of rulership that was recorded within this sacred geography.

The Landscape of Creation

The plazas of Groups A and B held the highest concentration of carved monuments at Izapa and appear to have been the locus of ritual activity (Figure 4.22) (Lowe et al. 1982). Bisecting them is Group H, which formed the central axis of the site at 21 degrees east of north. Group H is bordered to the north by Mound 25 and to the south by Mound 60, the largest pyramid at the site and the highest in the region.[3] On a clear day, the rationale for this orientation of the site's axis is, quite literally, visible: If one stands on the summit of Mound 60 and looks to the north, Mound 25 is framed against the volcano Tacaná that looms dramatically on the horizon.[4] In fact, Mound 25 appears to have been a two-tiered pyramid that echoed the contours of Tacaná (Lowe et al. 1982:262). Mounds 25 and 60 thus form not only a central backbone of sorts for the site, but they also replicate landmarks of the sacred natural geography on a human scale.

Group H, with its quadrilateral arrangement of mounds around a central plaza, provided an ideal space for performance, and it typifies the organization of space at Izapa. The significance of the Group H plaza, not only as an axially aligned microcosm of the natural world but as a performance space, is inferred through the presence of Mound 46 at the center of the plaza. Such a low mound may have served as a dance platform and stage for public rituals. Standing upon the low platform, a ruler

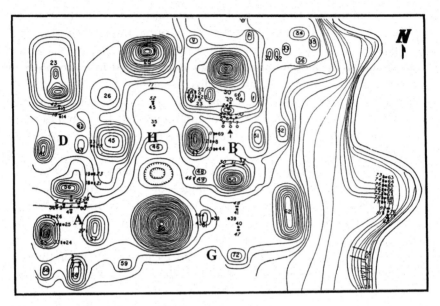

Figure 4.2   Map of central Izapa. After map and topographic survey by Eduardo
Martinez E. in Lowe et al. (1982:end map)

would also have been aligned on a horizontal plane with the central axis
of the site and to Tacaná in the distance.

The Group H plaza and its enormous Mound 60 were also neatly woven into a broader conceptual program that sought to define Izapa as the
center of the world. The space immediately surrounding Mound 60 contained a series of reservoirs, dams, and aqueducts that channeled water
to the Río Izapa, which forms the eastern boundary of the site (Figure 4.3)
(Lowe et al. 1982:263). When Mound 60 was enlarged during the Late
Formative period, its fill was taken from areas surrounding the mound,
which created a reservoir on its north side. This northern reservoir was
aligned on the same axis with Tacaná as Mounds 60 and 25 (Lowe et al.
1982:263). Immediately to the west of Mound 60 was another ancient
reservoir, faced with large stone boulders, and a series of drains that also
date to the Late Formative period.[5]

The reservoir and drainage system at the base of Mound 60 on its north
and west sides created the effect of a body of water surrounding the huge
pyramid at the very heart of the site. These waters most certainly functioned as a symbolic primordial sea, referencing the fertile, first waters of
creation. At the center, Mound 60 rose, replicating the landscape of cre-

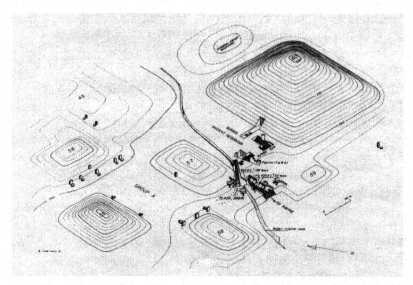

Figure 4.3 Idealized plan of dam and drains surrounding Mound 60.
From Lowe et al. (1982:Figure 8.8).
Courtesy of New World Archaeological Foundation

ation that had been built by Mesoamerican peoples at least since the time of the Olmec and including the mountain of sustenance (where maize was created) rising from the waters of the primordial sea (cf. Freidel et al. 1993:123–172; Reilly 1994:192–233; Schele and Mathews 1998:36–40). For Mesoamericans, this archetypal landscape of creation provided a model for the organization of sacred space that defined each site as the place of creation and the center of the world. It represented—in terms of concrete architectural form and spatial organization—one of the most powerful and fundamental aesthetic tropes in Precolumbian Mesoamerica and provided an enduring structuring principle for the communication of potent messages of cultural identity and political legitimacy (cf. Schapiro 1953; Armstrong 1975). Furthermore, the establishment in the natural landscape of this cosmological archetype provided a theater in which human order and the very foundations of rulership could be dramatized (cf. Wheatley 1971).

In Mesoamerica, these aesthetics of space and form defined each site as a Tollan, or "place of the reeds," where civilization, arts, and government flourished and where the right to rule was divinely sanctioned.[6] Within this paradigm, the mountain of sustenance was conceptually joined with another mountain, Coatépec, or "Snake Mountain," that was associated with the original divine mandate to perform war and make sacrifice. It was defined by a ballcourt at its base that contained a "Well of Water," making the surrounding landscape fertile (see Tezozomoc 1975, 1980). Through this conceptual union, the mountain at the center of the primordial sea was both the place of creation and the place of sacrifice, and it symbolized this duality inherent to a Mesoamerican worldview. The enormous time depth of this paradigm for the organization of sacred space throughout Mesoamerica has been well documented from the Middle Formative through the Terminal and Postclassic periods at sites like La Venta, Waxaktun, Tikal, Chichén Itzá, El Tajín, and Tenochtitlán.[7]

It appears that the Izapans, like their Mesoamerican counterparts through time, defined their site as a Tollan and erected Mound 60 as their own version of Coatépec. Although no architectural or sculptural features survive that explicitly identify Mound 60 as Snake Mountain, its context within the landscape of creation clearly defines it as such. Not only did the Mound 60 pyramid rise above the primordial sea, but its base was marked by a ballcourt (Figure 4.4). As Gareth Lowe et al. (1982:254) observed, low pyramidal Mounds 48 and 49—placed at the junction of space between Mounds 50, 60, and the reservoir—are suggestive of a ballcourt yet are very small for this purpose. Nonetheless, the two mounds probably functioned as an effigy ballcourt whose role, although perhaps not functional, was critical to defining the landscape of creation where they occupied a position on the edge of the primordial sea that surrounded the base of Coatépec.[8] This effigy ballcourt also occupied a strategic location within the site's overall organization: at the juncture of plaza groups H, G, and B, where much of the carved sculpture at the site was concentrated. In fact, its location may have marked one of the major processional routes through the site that directed people through the sacred geography of creation.

One of the primary points of entry to Izapa may have been the banks of the Río Izapa, which winds along the eastern periphery of the site to the southeast of Group G (Figure 4.4). There, as Lowe et al. (1982:257–259) observed, a terrace was constructed along the western bank of the river just south of a group of nineteen rough boulder stelae that were placed in a line, along with accompanying altars, in a bend of the river. A stone-paved ramp led down to the river bank, where a carved stone basin, or fountain stone, was found *in situ* beneath a spring on the river bank.[9] Lowe et al. (1982:259) noted that the paved ramp not only provided convenient access to the river and spring-fed fountains but also

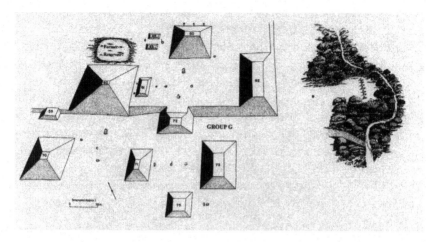

Figure 4.4   Plan showing location of
Mounds 48 and 49 and paved ramp to Rio Izapa
After Lowe et al. (1982:Figure 14.1)

must have served a ceremonial purpose. They suggested that the paved ramp might have supported ritual processions to the spring-fed water that was gathered in the stone basins and may also have "served as a formal entranceway into Izapa for visiting delegations arriving from the east" (Lowe et al. 1982:81). Such a point of entry would have led directly to the ceremonial core of the site and formed a symbolic conduit between the sacred waters of Mound 60 and the Río Izapa itself.[10]

Confirming the significance of this ceremonial path and point of entry is small Mound 61 that sits adjacent to Mound 60 on its eastern side (Figure 4.4). Lowe et al. (1982:254) noted that Mound 61 was an exceptionally well-constructed building with plaster floors and cut-stone walls dating to the Late Formative Guillen phase. Such fine construction was anomalous at Izapa, where the vast majority of architecture was characterized by riverstone platforms. The Mound 61 structure, at the base of Coatépec and facing the ramp that led down to the Río Izapa, thus probably served an important function on ritual circuits to and from the site. As visitors made their way up the paved ramp from the river and slowly ascended the raised courtyard of Group G on their way to the heart of the site, they would have been greeted by this exceptional structure, framed as it were against the enormous Izapa version of Coatépec. Upon reaching the low platform of Mound 61, visitors would have been afforded a dramatic view of the waters of creation that flowed to the north of Mound 60 and the effigy ballcourt that emerged along the water's banks, defining the space as a place of sacrifice and rebirth.

Izapa declared itself to be the center of the world, a Tollan, and a place of creation through both a dialogue with the natural environment and the incorporation of a pan-Mesoamerican aesthetic vocabulary that structured and clearly communicated the sacred nature of the site. Furthermore, this human-built environment provided a dramatic setting in which demonstrations of rulership and power, in both this world and the other, could be performed. Fortunately, the monuments placed within this environment provide detailed documentation of the ceremonies enacted within its confines. Their imagery also gives voice to the potent political messages that were intricately woven into, and legitimated by, this cosmological context.

The Performance of Rulership:
Plaza Group A

Plaza Group A (Figure 4.5) is located to the west of Mound 60 and forms the western boundary of the ceremonial precinct of Izapa. Together with Group B, it held the majority of sculpture at the site and was a locus for ritual activity during the Late Formative florescence of the site.[11] Group A was also physically and conceptually linked to the sacred geography of the site core. Lowe et al. (1982:171) observed that an inlet drain formed of large flat stones at the southeast corner of Mound 57 served as a plaza drain for Group A. This drain emptied the waters from the Group A plaza and delivered them to the reservoir on the west side of Mound 60, or the primordial sea at the base of Coatépec. This Late Formative system of channels at Izapa followed in the same vein as the aqueducts in the sacred precincts at such Olmec sites as San Lorenzo, La Venta, and Teopantecuanitlan and foreshadowed similar systems at various sites across Mesoamerica through the Postclassic period.[12]

Deftly inserted into this sacred geography were stela-altar pairs that carried powerful propagandistic messages. Their primary message was the cosmological and shamanic foundations for rulership and their performance within the sacred landscape (Guernsey 1995; Kappelman 1997). For example, at the center of the group of stelae that abut Mound 56, recessed slightly further than its counterparts, is Stela 4. Stela 4 (Figure 4.6) depicts a ruler standing on a ground line in a dynamic posture and wearing the costume of a bird. He wields an ax of some sort in his left hand while carrying another object at his side in his right. From his forearms

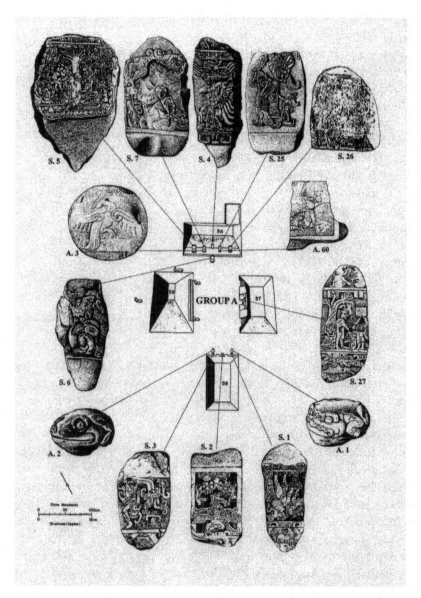

Figure 4.5   Plan of Group A showing locations of major monuments.
After Lowe et al. (1982:Figure 8.1)

dangle long feathers attached with a large knot to his wrists. He also wears a long-beaked headdress that is distinctly avian.

Hovering above the central figure on Stela 4 is a second, winged being who descends from the celestial sphere. His wings are spread in flight, and he wears a very similar beaked headdress to that of the figure below him. The wings of this descending figure are marked with glyphic elements that correspond to hieroglyphs in the epi-Olmec script on Late Formative La Mojarra Stela 1 (Figure 4.7) (Anderson 1993; Kaufman, personal communication 1995).[13] According to John Justeson and Terrence Kaufman's analysis of the La Mojarra text (1993), the epi-Olmec glyph on the right wing of the Izapa figure reads *'owa*, or "macaw." Hence, the costume of the flying figure on Stela 4 appears to be explicitly labeled as that of a macaw.

Monuments that depict rulers in bird costumes date back at least to

Figure 4.6   Izapa Stela 4. From Norman (1976:Figure 3.5).
Courtesy of New World
Archaeological Foundation

Olmec times and have been identified as images of transformation in which a ruler is engaged in shamanic flight or a journey to the cosmic realm (Furst 1968; Reilly 1994).[14] As Reilly (1994:5) argued, these performances of the shamanic journey were an aspect of an institutionalized shamanism that incorporated the tenets of a shamanic belief system as the ideological foundation for political power. In other words, a ruler needed not only to demonstrate his prowess in the social and political spheres of the natural world but also to demonstrate his ability to communicate with—and manifest the powers of—the supernatural realm of the Otherworld. The vivid imagery of Middle Formative monuments records such publicly staged transformation rituals and, perhaps even more significantly, testifies to the highly performance-oriented nature of rulership (Reilly 1994).

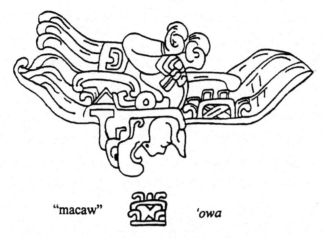

"macaw"   'owa

**Figure 4.7   Detail of flying figure from Izapa Stela 4
and comparison of wing markings to "macaw"
glyph from La Mojarra Stela 1.**
Drawing by Kappelman

The dynamic pose of the ruler on Izapa Stela 4 clearly indicates some sort of performance. In fact, the imagery appears to represent a scene of ritual transformation expressed as a simultaneous vision: Below, the ruler performs in the costume of the bird in the earthly realm, while above he is envisioned as a transformed bird. The scene on Izapa Stela 4 thus conflates the ruler's earthly performance and his otherworldly flight. Importantly, in his transformed persona, the ruler has been endowed with characteristics of the Principal Bird Deity, a macaw who, in the *Popol Vuh* of the Quiche Maya, was one of the primary deities of the last creation (Tedlock 1985; Cortez 1986; Kappelman 1997).

The Principal Bird Deity was central to the display and legitimization of rulership during the Late Formative period, as monuments from Izapa, Kaminaljuyu, Abaj Takalik, and Zaculeu attest (Kappelman 1997). The cosmological foundations for this phenomenon can be traced to the myth of the shamanic relationship between the Maya deity Itzamna and the Principal Bird Deity, who was called Itzam-yeh during the Classic period (Schele 1992; Freidel et al. 1993). The bird Itzam-yeh was the *nagual*, or animal spirit companion, of the primordial shaman Itzamna.[15] Itzamna, labeled God D in the Postclassic codices by Paul Schellhas (1904), was an old god who was integral to the acts of creation (Freidel et al. 1993). Classic period vessels represent Itzamna as an artist, sage, or *itz'at* and refer-

Figure 4.8   Esperanza-phase stuccoed vessel from Kaminalijuyu Tomb B-II.
Drawing by Constance Cortez after Kidder et al. (1946:Figure 207e)

ence his role as one of the modelers of the sky during creation or portray him as an enthroned king presiding over rituals. The name Itzamna literally means "one who does *itz*" (Freidel et al. 1993). In Yucatec Maya, *itz* refers to milk; nectar; dew; juice; and bodily fluids such as sweat, semen, and tears. *Itz* is also "a morpheme whose significance is related to ideas of knowledge, magic, [and] occult power" (Barrera Vásquez 1980:272). As David Freidel et al. (1993:412) noted, the term *itzam* also designates shamans or individuals who had access to the supernatural world and who could manipulate the *itz*, or cosmic substance of the Otherworld. Hence, when a shaman contacted the Otherworld, that shaman was the earthly analogue to Itzamna, the primordial shaman.

A stuccoed vessel from Kaminaljuyu depicts Itzamna transforming into his avian *nagual* Itzam-yeh (Figure 4.8) (Kappelman 1997).[16] All four figures wear the regalia associated with the bird and Itzamna, yet the features change from individual to individual, moving from the anthropomorphic features of Itzamna to the curved beak of the Principal Bird Deity Itzam-yeh. Such imagery evoked Itzamna's role as the primordial shaman and documented his transformation into his avian counterpart. As the *nagual* of Itzamna, the Principal Bird Deity functioned as a highly potent symbol of this shamanic journey.

In accordance with their Middle Formative antecedents, Izapa Stela 4 and similar monuments from other Late Formative sites depicted rulers transforming into the bird in validation of their abilities to perform the shamanic journey and contact the Otherworld. Through such an act of transformation, a ruler became the earthly analogue to the primordial shaman Itzamna and the heir to his shamanic powers. The importance of this declaration is dramatized through the prominent placement of Stela 4 in Group A at Izapa: It literally forms the conceptual pivot for the remainder of the monuments in the group.

Figure 4.9 Izapa Stela 2.
From Norman (1976:Figure 3.3).
Courtesy of New World
Archaeological Foundation

Directly across the plaza from Stela 4, and aligned with it to Tacaná, is Stela 2 (Figure 4.9) (Norman 1980). Stela 2 reiterates the theme of avian transformation but couches it within the mythological tradition of the *Popol Vuh*. Stela 2 depicts a winged figure with a clearly human face descending into the parted branches of a fruit-laden tree with a crocodilian base. The winged figure is very clearly wearing the costume of the Principal Bird Deity identified on Izapa Stela 4 and represents another version of the Izapa ruler transforming into the avian deity. The position of the two small figures that flank the tree suggests that they are Late Formative prototypes for the Hero Twins of the *Popol Vuh*, Hunahpu and Xbalanque (Cortez 1986:88–89). Interestingly, one episode from the *Popol Vuh* recounts a battle between the Hero Twins and the Principal Bird Deity (called Seven Macaw) who ruled in the era of the past creation and claimed to serve as its celestial light (Tedlock 1985). Offended by the arrogant pretense of the bird, the Hero Twins shot him down from his perch in a tree. [17] As Seven Macaw landed on the ground, however, he managed to seize the arm of Hunahpu and tear it out of him. Nevertheless, the actions of the Hero Twins ultimately prevailed and served to terminate the bird's reign in the precreation era.

The imagery of Izapa Stela 25 (Figure 2.10) references this battle between the bird and the Hero Twins even more explicitly. Constance Cortez (1986:67) identified the bird in the tree on Stela 25 as a Late Formative prototype for Seven Macaw of the *Popol Vuh*. She also noted that the Hero Twin who stands beneath the bird was missing his arm and related this to the *Popol Vuh* narrative in which the Hero Twin lost his arm in the skirmish with the bird.[18] Rather than a depiction of Seven Macaw's destruction, however, the image portrays the bird perched in glory on top of the staff, adjacent to a crocodilian version of the World Tree.[19]

**Figure 4.10   Izapa Stela 25. From Norman
(1976:Figure 3.26).**
Courtesy of New World Archaeological Foundation

Moreover, Stela 25 depicts the bird as the manipulator of a serpent cord, or metaphorical cosmic umbilicus, that connected the natural world to the supernatural realm.[20]

The cosmic umbilicus that is dangled by the bird from its perch atop the World Tree provides a critical clue to understanding the role of the bird within this episode of the creation story. It is not a scene of the bird's defeat or death; rather, it is an image of the bird as a conduit to and denizen of the supernatural realm. Such a representation is in accordance with the bird's role as a symbol of shamanic passage into the mythic time and realm of the Otherworld. One of the basic tenets of shamanic transformation is a ritual death or dismemberment that leads to a reconstitution or rebirth (Eliade 1964). The shooting of Itzam-yeh by the Hero Twins thus represents symbolic transformation through death and is conceptually parallel to the act of a ruler undergoing bloodletting or a hallucinogenic trance that induced a death-like state (Guernsey 1995; Kappelman 1997).

Izapa Stela 2 features an Izapan ruler as the protagonist within this same mythic cycle, performing in the guise of the Principal Bird Deity. In fact, the imagery of Stela 2 strongly suggests that Late Formative rulers not only adopted the garb of the bird while performing shamanic feats but actually performed certain passages from the creation story in the persona of the avian deity. By transforming into the bird, as on Stelae 2 and 4, rulers demonstrated their abilities to perform the shamanic journey and grounded them within a mythological framework. These acts confirmed their identity as the analogues in the natural world to the primordial shaman Itzamna and were equated with the generative acts performed by Itzamna at the time of creation. Moreover, the acts of avian transformation performed by Izapa rulers and memorialized on their monuments attest that the foundations of rulership during the Late Formative period were firmly rooted in a shamanic belief system.

This message dominated the thematic programming of Group A. Stelae that depicted avian transformations were centered at the southern and northern boundaries of the plaza and were axially aligned to the volcano Tacaná in the distance. This theme was reiterated on Stela 25 as well as on Altar 3, just to the west of Stela 4, which depicted a ruler garbed once again as the avian deity and hovering above a terrestrial band. Even more important, these carved monuments chronicled the types of rituals actually performed within the confines of the Group A plaza.

Whereas the rituals that inspired these monuments can be inferred by the Izapa imagery, the hieroglyphic text of Late Formative La Mojarra Stela 1 (Figure 4.11) appears to record such a performance. According to Justeson and Kaufman's (1993) analysis of the La Mojarra text, the inscription offers explicit documentation of a ruler's charismatic performance that was enacted within the context of a series of rituals that celebrated his accession, reign, and victorious battles. Most significant, the text of La Mojarra Stela 1 narrates the transformation of the ruler into a bird as part of a public performance during which he declared his rulership.

According to Justeson and Kaufman's translation of the inscription (1993; personal communication 1995, 1996, 1997), one important passage

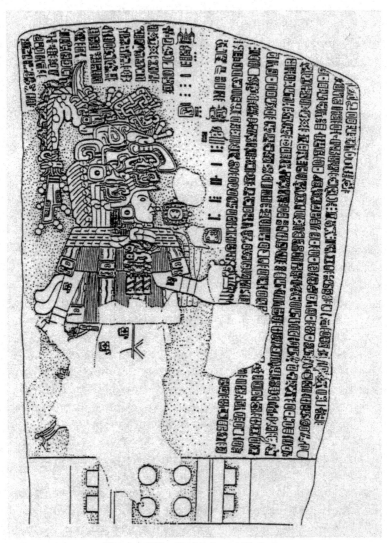

Figure 4.11   La Mojarra Stela 1.
Drawing by George Stuart

within the text records the paraphernalia that was taken by the La Mojarra ruler, Harvest Mountain Lord, during a public ceremony.[21] Of the objects taken, one was a "macaw bundle" or "macaw lashing." Importantly, the "macaw" glyph used to describe this bundle is the same glyph that appears on the wings of the flying figure on Izapa Stela 4 (Figure 4.12).

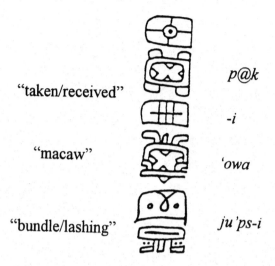

"taken/received"   p@k

                                 -i

"macaw"   'owa

"bundle/lashing"   ju'ps-i

Figure 4.12   Excerpt from text of La Mojarra Stela 1.
Drawing by Kappelman

The inscription then continues and includes the description of a bloodletting ritual performed by the ruler. After describing this bloodletting
event, the text states that the protagonist was "arrayed" as a macaw and
named as a "co-essence" or "shape-shifter" (Justeson and Kaufman, personal communication 1998). The text then states that the ruler, in the persona of the macaw, declared his rulership. In other words, the ruler appears to have let blood as the means to enable his trance journey, after
which he donned the costume of the macaw and began his transformation into the bird, culminating in his public declaration of rulership.[22]
The imagery of La Mojarra Stela 1 provides a visual complement to this
narrative, as it depicts the ruler garbed in the elaborate costume of the
Principal Bird Deity.

La Mojarra Stela 1, although dating from several hundred years later
than the Izapa stelae, provides a Late Formative hieroglyphic text that
appears to narrate the imagery depicted on the nontextual Izapa monuments (Kappelman 1997). The inscription features the avian transformation of the ruler as one of the defining moments in his public declaration
of rulership, much as the Izapa monuments showcase the avian transformation rituals of rulers within the sacred precincts of the site. Furthermore, the inscription of La Mojarra Stela 1 provides unique textual documentation of the role of the Principal Bird Deity within the vocabulary of
rulership during the Late Formative period.

Figure 4.13   Izapa Stela 5.
Drawing by Kappelman after Norman (1973:Plate 10)

Other monuments within Group A provide further context for the performance of rulership.[23] Punctuating the western end of the row of stelae
in front of Mound 56 is Stela 5, with the most complicated and dense imagery of all the Izapa monuments (Figure 4.13). An enormous World
Tree, or *axis mundi*, bisects the central image of Stela 5, connecting the levels of the universe and marking the center of the world. The roots of the
tree rest on a ground line that is marked by pyramidal shapes containing
double merlons, signs which have Middle Formative precedents and sig-
nify the terrestrial sphere or openings into the earth (Reilly 1994:226). Below the earth band is a series of curly volutes denoting the primordial
waters of creation that flow beneath the terrestrial layer. Above, the tree's

branches reach up to a sky band whose symbols recall the celestial bands on stelae and altars from La Venta (Stirling 1943; Quirarte 1973). The watery basal band of Stela 5 may be a direct reference to the waters of the adjacent reservoir that originated in Group A. In fact, the image on Stela 5 may be a cosmic map of sorts that charted sacred space at Izapa and defined the site as the central axis of the universe.[24]

On either side of the Stela 5 composition are two enormous, arching serpentine creatures who literally burp out the characters within the image: Their presence defines the scene as sacred, or supernaturally sanctified. Within their confines, a series of figures perform ritual activities. In the lower right corner, shaded by an umbrella held by an attendant, sits a figure who wears the Jester God headband of rulership and may represent an Izapa ruler. On the opposite side of the tree, two seated figures face each other over a brazier and perform some sort of offering. Above, supernatural figures, birds, and fish cavort amidst the branches of the tree and volutes of the framing serpents. In effect, Stela 5 can be understood as a quasi-historical scene that framed the activities of elite ritual practitioners within the cosmic landscape of creation.

Centering Rulership in the Cosmic Environment: Plaza Group B

Group B is dominated by the large Mound 30 platform that supports eight secondary structures (Figure 4.14). Lowe et al. (1982:184) dated the final platform modifications to the late Guillen phase, although the Mound 30 pyramid itself may have had some Early Classic modifications.[25] In front of the Mound 30 platform are three monumental stone pillars, each with a carved stone sphere on top (Figure 4.15). The pillars, which range from 115 to 135 centimeters in height, formed a triangular arrangement. As Karl Taube (1998) noted, this triadic arrangement is found throughout the Classic Maya realm in monumental and domestic architecture and references the three-stone hearth, a symbol that marked the heart, or center, of the universe.[26] As a metaphor for the cosmic hearth, the monumental pillars constitute yet another powerful aesthetic trope that provided the fundamental structuring principle and contextual environment for the monuments and ritual performances contained within Group B.

A Classic period text on Quiriguá Stela C records one of the initial acts of creation that entailed setting three throne stones in order to form a great cosmic hearth and lay the foundation for the present universe

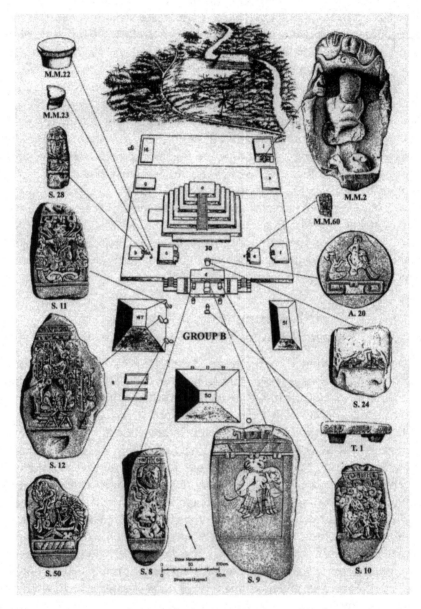

Figure 4.14   Plan of Group B showing locations of major monuments.
After Lowe et al. (1982:Figure 9.1)

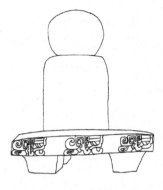

**Figure 4.15   Stone pillar with sphere
(Miscellaneous Monuments 5 and 6)
behind Throne 1.**
Drawing by Kappelman after Norman
(1976:Figure 5.32)

(Schele 1992:122–126; Freidel et al. 1993:79–84; Looper 1995a:156–165, 1995b). In astronomical terms, this hearth referred to three stars in the constellation Orion that were perceived as riding the back of a turtle and that marked the location of the Maize God's rebirth (Schele 1992:134; Looper 1995b). Accordingly, the triadic arrangement of stone-capped pillars in Group B at Izapa referenced the setting of the celestial hearth. The pillars also declared, in powerful cosmological terms, that Izapa was the center of the universe and the place where the acts of creation were performed. Important, too, this theme of the three stones afforded continuity with the ideological program of Group A, as it was the deity Itzamna who set the third stone of creation and was one of the protagonists within this creation event.[27]

The politics of rulership were also eloquently inserted into this cosmological schema. Throne 1 (Figure 4.15) is located directly in front of the center pillar of the three stones of creation in Group B. When seated there, literally at the pivot of the cosmic hearth, the enthroned ruler not only commanded the political landscape but symbolically reenacted the founding events of the present creation. In effect, his rule was equated with the acts of Itzamna and the other gods that were visible in the night sky and that enabled the very existence of the universe. Moreover, the throne itself reiterated the metaphorical nature of the *stones* of creation as the *thrones* of creation, in which the seat of rulership was given cosmological legitimacy. The sculptural programming of Group B, by invoking the fundamental aesthetic trope of the three stones of creation, provided a dramatic cosmological context for political display.

The incised designs of Throne 1 reiterated the cosmic nature of the ruler's role as he sat on the throne at the center of creation (Kappelman 1997). The top of Throne 1 (Figure 4.16) bears a cartouche with scalloped

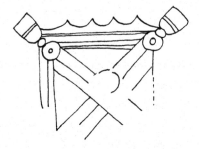

Figure 4.16   Cartouche on top of Throne 1.
Drawing by Kappelman after Norman (1973:Plate 63)

edges and centrally infixed crossed bands that mark a portal to the Otherworld. When seated upon the throne, the Izapa ruler literally became the conduit that linked the earthly world to the supernatural realm. Confirmation of this exists on Izapa Stela 8 (Figure 4.17), which stood at one corner of the small platform that abutted Mound 30.[28] The ruler on Stela 8 is seated on a throne within a quatrefoil cartouche that marks the back of an enormous zoomorph. Significantly, the profile of the throne pictured on Stela 8 exactly reproduces that of Throne 1. Directly above the quatrefoil on Stela 8 is a crenellated portal that corresponds to the portal on Throne 1. In effect, Stela 8 visually recorded the actions performed by the Izapa ruler as he sat on Throne 1, passed through the cosmic portal, and conjured the powers of the universe.

The carvings on the sides of Throne 1 also echo this theme (Figure 4.15). The sides are incised with personification heads that can be identified as versions of the personified *sak nik*, or "white flower," which typically marked the end of supernatural conduits during the Late Formative period. The *sak nik* symbol carried a range of meanings that referenced the mythic origins of fertility and life, or the vital life forces which were transmitted to this world from the supernatural realm.[29] When seated upon Throne 1, with the personified *sak nik* heads dangling at his feet, the ruler became the conduit of this vital life force: He literally channeled cosmic power. In this role he was also analogous to the Principal Bird Deity who had manipulated the cosmic serpent conduit from the supernatural world on Stela 25 in Group A.

Ritual Circuits and the Choreography of Creation

Having examined the articulation of sacred space within the central precinct of Izapa, it becomes possible to reconstruct the types of rituals

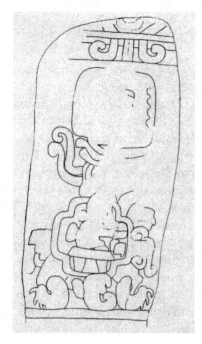

Figure 4.17 Izapa Stela 8.
From Norman (1976:Figure 3.8).
Courtesy of New World
Archaeological Foundation

performed within that space and the paths that they would have followed. As discussed, the paved ramp off the Río Izapa may have provided one of the most important points of entrance into the site. Ascending the path to the Group G plaza, one would have been greeted by the finely constructed Mound 61 building, framed against the enormous contours of Izapa's version of Coatépec. The message would have been clear: With each step, the landscape of creation was dramatically unfolding. The reservoirs around Mound 60 would have been understood as the primordial sea of creation that encircled the base of Snake Mountain, and the effigy ballcourt formed by Mounds 48 and 49 would not only have confirmed this identification but alluded to the political contests and cosmogonic feats performed there as well.

Perhaps from there the ritual circuit would have continued into the wide plaza of Group B, whose thematic programming centered around the fundamental aesthetic trope of the three stones of creation. The trope functioned as the general structure—ideological, spatial, and sculptural—in which performances of rulership and reenactments of events from creation were contextualized and given meaning. That such events took place is verified by the imagery of Stela 8 (Figure 4.17), which presents a snapshot of sorts of just such ritual activity. The Izapa ruler would have enthroned himself at the central pivot of this landscape and become the cosmic conduit that united the natural world to the supernatural realm. In so doing, he would have drawn a powerful analogy between his acts of rulership and the very first acts of creation in which the three hearthstones were set.

Leaving the Group B plaza, one would have emerged into the enormous Group H plaza, with its vista of Coatépec and the primordial sea to the south and the volcano Tacaná to the north. Low Mound 46, located on the banks of the reservoir, may have functioned as a dance platform where the ruler continued his ritual performance, framed once more against the backdrop of creation.

Skirting the waters of the primordial sea, the procession may have ended in Group A. There, the imagery of the monuments suggests that the plaza space was ignited by the shamanic transformations of the Izapa ruler into his animal spirit companion, the Principal Bird Deity. This space must surely have been a place of conjuring, a place where the shamanic journey was performed. Moreover, as a place of magic where the ruler defined himself as the analogue to the primordial shaman and prototypical ruler Itzamna, Group A literally gave tangible form to the shamanic foundations for Late Formative rulership.

In conclusion, the open plazas, architecture, sculpture, ritual circuits, and recorded narratives at Izapa formed part of a greater cultural structure, or poetics, that sought to define the nature of Late Preclassic rulership. The conjunction of these various elements—some tangible, others more elusive—reveals a public discourse that visualized and defined human order and legitimized the power of the Late Formative ruling elite. When viewed as part of a cohesive, coherent, and cleverly articulated program, the messages encoded at Izapa become charged with an ancient vitality.

References

Anderson, Lloyd B.
   1993 *The Writing System of La Mojarra and Associated Monuments.* Washington, D.C.: Ecological Linguistics.
Armstrong, Robert Plant.
   1975 *Wellspring: On the Myth and Source of Culture.* Berkeley: University of California Press.
Barba de Piña Chan, Beatriz.
   1990 Buscando Raíces de Mitos Mayas en Izapa. *Historia de la religión en Mesoamérica y áreas afines.* México, D.F.: UNAM Instituto de Investigaciones Antropológicas.
Bardawil, Lawrence W.
   1976 The Principal Bird Deity in Maya Art—An Iconographic Study of Form and Meaning. *The Art, Iconography and Dynastic History of Palenque, Part III.* Edited by Merle Greene Robertson. Proceedings of the Segunda Mesa Redonda de Palenque, 1974. Pebble Beach, CA: The Robert Louis Stevenson School. 195–209.
Barrera Vásquez, Alfredo.
   1980 *Diccionario Maya Cordemex: Maya-Español, Español-Maya.* Mérida, Mexico: Ediciones Cordemex.

Carrasco, David.
  1982   *Quetzalcoatl and the Irony of Empire*. Chicago: University of Chicago
          Press.
Coe, Michael D., and Richard A. Diehl.
  1980   *In the Land of the Olmec: The Archaeology of San Lorenzo Tenochtitlán*.
          Austin, Tex.: University of Texas Press.
Cortez, Constance.
  1986   *The Principal Bird Deity in Late Preclassic and Early Classic Maya Art*. M.A.
          thesis, University of Texas at Austin.
Ekholm, Susanna M.
  1969   *Mound 30a and the Early Preclassic Ceramic Sequence at Izapa, Chiapas,
          Mexico*. Papers of the New World Archaeological Foundation 25. Provo,
          Utah: New World Archaeological Foundation.
Eliade, Mircea.
  1964   *Shamanism: Archaic Techniques of Ecstasy*. Translated by Willard R. Trask.
          Princeton: Princeton University Press.
Florescano, Enrique.
  1994   *Memoria Mexicana*. México, D.F.: Fondo de Cultura Económica.
Foucault, M.
  1972   *The Archaeology of Knowledge and the Discourse on Language*. New York:
          Pantheon.
Freidel, David A., Linda Schele, and Joy Parker.
  1993   *Maya Cosmos: Three Thousand Years on the Shaman's Path*. New York:
          William Morrow.
Furst, Peter T.
  1968   The Olmec Were-Jaguar Motif in the Light of Ethnographic Reality.
          Dumbarton Oaks Conference on the Olmec. Edited by Elizabeth P. Benson.
          Washington, D.C.: Dumbarton Oaks. 143–178.
  1981   Jaguar Baby or Toad Mother: A New Look at an Old Problem in Olmec
          Iconography. *The Olmec and Their Neighbors: Essays in Memory of
          Matthew W. Stirling*. Edited by Elizabeth P. Benson. Washington, D.C.:
          Dumbarton Oaks. 149–162.
Girard, Rafael.
  1966   *Los Mayas: Su civilización, su historia, sus vinculaciones continentales*. Méx-
          ico, D.F.: Libro Méxicano Editores.
Grove, David C.
  1970   The Olmec Paintings of Oxtotitlan Cave, Guerrero, Mexico. *Studies in
          Pre-Columbian Art and Archaeology 6*. Washington, D.C.: Dumbarton
          Oaks.
Grube, Nikolai, and Werner Nahm.
  1994   A Census of Xibalba: A Complete Inventory of *Way* Characters on
          Maya Ceramics. *The Maya Vase Book: A Corpus of Rollout Photographs of
          Maya Vases, Volume 4*. Edited by Barbara Kerr and Justin Kerr. New
          York: Kerr Associates. 686–714.
Guernsey, Julia.
  1995   Stelae-Altars at Izapa: Cult or Political Ideology? Paper presented at
          the 94th Annual Meeting of the American Anthropological Association,
          Washington, D.C.

Hellmuth, Nicholas M.
1986   *The Surface of the Underwaterworld: Iconography of Maya Deities of Early Classic Art in Peten, Guatemala*. Ph.D. dissertation, Institute of Art History, Karl-Franzens-Universität, Graz.
1987   *Monster und Menschen in der Maya-Kunst*. Graz, Germany: Akademische Druk u. Verlagsanstalt.
Houston, Stephen, and David Stuart.
1989   The *Way* Glyph: Evidence for "Co-essences" Among the Classic Maya. *Research Reports on Ancient Maya Writing* 30. Washington, D.C.: Center for Maya Research.
1996   Of Gods, Glyphs and Kings: Divinity and Rulership Among the Classic Maya. *Antiquity* 70:289–231.
Humphrey, Caroline H.
1994   Shamanic Practices and the State in Northern Asia: Views from the Center and Periphery. *Shamanism, History, and the State*. Edited by Nicholas Thomas and Caroline Humphrey. Ann Arbor, Mich.: University of Michigan Press. 191–228.
Justeson, John S., and Terrence Kaufman.
1993   A Decipherment of Epi-Olmec Hieroglyphic Writing. *Science* 259:1703–1711.
1996   Un desciframiento de la escritura epi-olmeca. *Arqueología* 8:10–25.
Kappelman, Julia Guernsey.
1997   *Of Macaw and Men: Late Preclassic Cosmology an Political Ideology in Izapan-Style Monuments*. Ph.D. dissertation, University of Texas at Austin.
Kidder, Alfred V., Jesse D. Jennings, and Edwin M. Shook.
1946   *Excavations at Kaminaljuyu, Guatemala*. Originally published as Carnegie Institution of Washington Publication 561. University Park, Pa.: Pennsylvania State University Press.
Koontz, Rex A.
1994   *The Iconography of El Tajín, Veracruz, Mexico*. Ph.D. dissertation, University of Texas at Austin.
Lipp, Frank J.
1991   The Mixe of Oaxaca: Religion, Ritual, and Healing. Austin, Tex.: University of Texas Press.
Looper, Matthew G.
1995a *The Sculpture Programs of Butz'-Tiliw, an Eighth-Century Maya King of Quiriguá, Guatemala*. Ph.D. dissertation, University of Texas at Austin.
1995b The Three Stones of Maya Creation Mythology at Quiriguá. *Mexicon* 27(2):24–30.
Looper, Matthew G., and Julia Guernsey Kappelman.
1999   *The Celestial Umbilicus in Mesoamerica: A Floral Metaphor for the Source of Life*. Manuscript on file, Department of Art and Art History, California State University, Chico.
Lowe, Gareth W., Thomas A. Lee Jr., and Eduardo Martinez Espinosa.
1982   *Izapa: An Introduction to the Ruins and Monuments*. Papers of the New World Archaeological Foundation 31. Provo, Utah: New World Archaeological Foundation.

Martínez Donjuan, Guadalupe.
1982   Teopantecuanitlan, Guerrero: un sitio olmeca. *Revista Mexicana de Estudios Antropológicos* 28:128–132. México, D.F.: Instituto Nacional de Antropologia y Historia.
Matos Moctezuma, Eduardo.
1987   The Templo Mayor of Tenochtitlán: History and Interpretation. *The Great Temple of Tenochtitlán: Center and Periphery in the Aztec World*. Edited by Johanna Broda, David Carrasco, and Eduardo Matos Moctezuma. Berkeley: University of California Press. 15–60.
Miller, Arthur G.
1974   The Iconography of the Painting in the Temple of the Diving God, Tulum, Quintana Roo, Mexico: The Twisted Cords. *Mesoamerican Archaeology: New Approaches*. Edited by Norman Hammond. London: Duckworth. 167–186.
Norman, V. Garth.
1973   *Izapa Sculpture, Part 1*. Papers of the New World Archaeological Foundation 30. Provo, Utah: New World Archaeological Foundation.
1976   *Izapa Sculpture, Part 2*. Papers of the New World Archaeological Foundation 30. Provo, Utah: New World Archaeological Foundation.
1980   *Astronomical Orientations of Izapa Sculptures*. M.A. thesis, Brigham Young University.
Pearson, Michael Parker, and Colin Richards.
1994   Ordering the World: Perceptions of Architecture, Space, and Time. *Architecture and Order: Approaches to Social Space*. Edited by Michael Parker Pearson and Colin Richards. London: Routledge. 1–37.
Princeton, Art Museum.
1995   *The Olmec World: Ritual and Rulership*. Princeton: Art Museum, Princeton University.
Quirarte, Jacinto.
1973   Izapan-Style Art: A Study of Its Form and Meaning. *Studies in Pre-Columbian Art and Archaeology* 10. Washington, D.C.: Dumbarton Oaks.
Reilly, Frank Kent, III.
1989   The Shaman in Transformation Pose: A Study of the Theme of Rulership in Olmec Art. *Record of the Art Museum, Princeton University* 48(2):4–21.
1994   *Visions to Another World: Art, Shamanism, and Political Power in Middle Formative Mesoamerica*. Ph.D. dissertation, University of Texas at Austin.
Sahlins, Marshall.
1985   *Islands of History*. Chicago: University of Chicago Press.
Schapiro, Meyer.
1953   Style. *Anthropology Today*. Edited by A. L. Kroeber. Chicago: University of Chicago. 287–312.
Schele, Linda.
1992   *Notebook for the XVIth Maya Hieroglyphic Workshop at Texas*. Austin, Tex.: University of Texas.

Schele, Linda, and Matthew Looper.
  1996   *Notebook for the XXth Maya Hieroglyphic Forum.* Austin, Tex.: University
         of Texas.
Schele, Linda, and Peter Mathews.
  1998   *The Code of Kings: The Language of Seven Sacred Maya Temples and Tombs.*
         New York: Scribner's.
Schellhas, Paul.
  1904   Representation of Deities of the Maya Manuscripts. *Papers of the
         Peabody Museum of American Archaeology and Ethnology* 4(1).
Shook, Edwin M., and Alfred V. Kidder.
  1952   *Mound E-III-3, Kaminaljuyu, Guatemala.* Contributions to American An-
         thropology and History 53, Carnegie Institution of Washington Publi-
         cation 596. Washington, D.C.: Carnegie Institution.
Stirling, Matthew W.
  1943   Stone Monuments of Southern Mexico. *Bureau of American Ethnology
         Bulletin* 138. Washington, D.C.: Carnegie Institution.
Taube, Karl.
  1992   The Major Gods of Ancient Yucatan. *Studies in Pre-Columbian Art and
         Archaeology* 82. Washington, D.C.: Dumbarton Oaks.
  1994   The Birth Vase: Natal Imagery in Ancient Maya Myth and Ritual. *The
         Maya Vase Book: A Corpus of Rollout Photographs of Maya Vases, volume 4.*
         Edited by Justin Kerr. New York: Kerr and Associates. 652–685.
  1998   The Jade Hearth: Centrality, Rulership and the Classic Maya Temple.
         Function and Meaning in Classic Maya Architecture. Edited by Stephen D.
         Houston. Washington, D.C.: Dumbarton Oaks. 427–478.
Tedlock, Dennis.
  1985   *Popol Vuh: The Definitive Edition of the Mayan Book of the Dawn of Life and
         the Glories of Gods and Kings.* New York: Simon and Schuster.
Tezozomoc, Alvarado.
  1975   *Crónica Mexicana.* México, D.F.: Editorial Porrúa.
  1980   *Crónica Mexicayotl.* México, D.F.: Editorial Porrúa.
Wheatley, Paul.
  1971   *The Pivot of the Four Corners.* Chicago: Aldine.

Notes

1. The pertinent cultural phases for this period at Izapa include Frontera (ca. 450–300 BC), Guillen (ca. 300–50 BC), Hato (ca. 50 BC–100 AD), and Itstapa (100–250 AD). According to Lowe et al. (1982:23), the vast majority of monuments at Izapa were carved and placed in their present positions during the Guillen phase.

2. For comparative discussions of the intricate relationships between rulership, divinity, and access to the supernatural for the Classic Maya, see Freidel et al. (1993); Grube and Nahm (1994); and Houston and Stuart (1996).

3. Lowe et al. (1982:254) dated the upper portion of the Mound 60 pyramid to the late Guillen phase. They suggested that Mound 25 was built entirely during the Frontera and Guillen phases, or roughly 500–0 BC (Lowe et al. 1982:263).

4. See Norman (1980) for a discussion of the astronomical orientations of the sculpture and architecture at Izapa.

5. Lowe et al. (1982:171) suggested that this reservoir on the western side of Mound 60 may have been paved over by the end of the Guillen phase. Mound 60 may have been enlarged again at this point in time.

6. Numerous scholars have discussed the concept of Tollan in a Mesoamerican world view, including Carrasco (1982); Matos Moctezuma (1987); Florescano (1994); Koontz (1994); and Schele and Mathews (1998).

7. See Matos Moctezuma (1987); Koontz (1994); Reilly (1994); Schele and Mathews (1998:36–40, 197–255); and Schele and Kappelman, chapter 2 in this volume.

8. Lowe et al. noted that "some drainage system almost surely passes between the tiny Mound 49 and the huge Mound 60 pyramid" (1982:254), which suggests that the two parallel mounds were conceptually linked to the orchestration of sacred space around Mound 60. Mounds 48 and 49 follow in a tradition of effigy ballcourts that dates back to the Middle Formative at sites like Teopantecuanitlan (Logan Wagner, personal communication 1997; see also Martínez Donjuan 1982 and Reilly 1994).

9. This basin, Miscellaneous Monument 55, is accompanied slightly further downstream by Miscellaneous Monument 56, another carved stone basin. Details preserved on Miscellaneous Monument 56 include transverse lip grooves that allowed water to flow in and out through the basin (Lowe et al. 1982:281).

10. An entrance on the eastern side of Izapa would have provided a logical point of entry for communication with sites such as Abaj Takalik, located only about 50 kilometers to the southeast of Izapa in the Pacific coastal piedmont of Guatemala. The Río Izapa, although relatively small, is a tributary of the Río Suchiate, which empties into the Pacific Ocean and is the largest river in the Soconusco.

11. As Lowe et al. demonstrated, Group A was "the result of a long progression of Guillen-phase sculptural and construction activity. All the monuments here must have been in contemporaneous use or veneration as presently arranged, although they may have been sculpted over many years" (1982:159).

12. See, for example, Coe and Diehl (1980:118–126); Koontz (1994:97); and Princeton (1995:99).

13. La Mojarra Stela 1 was pulled from the Acula River at the village of La Mojarra in Veracruz, Mexico. It bears Long Count dates of 143 and 156 AD, although Justeson and Kaufman (1996) placed its actual date at approximately 157 AD. For a discussion of the epi-Olmec script on the monument, which embodies texts in a pre–proto-Zoquean language, see Justeson and Kaufman (1993, 1996).

14. See, for instance, Oxtotitlan Mural 1 (Grove 1970) and La Venta Altar 4 (Reilly 1994).

15. For the history of this argument, see Bardawil (1976); Hellmuth (1986, 1987); and Taube (in Houston and Stuart 1989:note 7).

16. This Esperanza-phase cylindrical tripod was part of an assemblage of grave goods found in Kaminaljuyu Tomb B-II (Kidder et al. 1946). Cortez (1986:46–49) identified the avian figures on this vessel as part of the Principal Bird Deity complex.

17. Interestingly, Lipp (1991:75) recounted a similar version of this myth in Mixe folklore, which suggests that the story was part of a pan-Mesoamerican creation account.

18. Barba de Piña Chan (1990) further noted that the appendage that hangs from the rear underbelly of the bird on Stela 25 is the disembodied arm of Hunahpu. Izapa Stela 25 thus provides a Late Formative period prototype for the Classic period stucco from Toniná that not only depicts the same battle between the bird and Hunahpu but includes a hieroglyphic text that reads *k'ak u k'ab*, "chopped off his arm" (Schele and Looper 1996:20).

19. Schele (1992); Freidel et al. (1993); and Looper (1995) discussed the astronomical symbolism of the creation story in which narratives are visually played out in the movements of the Milky Way, constellations, and planets in the night sky. One of the critical conformations of the Milky Way, known as the "Crocodile Tree," references that portion of the creation story in which the Principal Bird Deity was defeated by the Hero Twin.

20. For a discussion of the metaphorical symbolism of serpent cords and umbilici, see Miller (1974); Freidel et al. (1993); Taube (1994); Looper (1995); Kappelman (1997); and Looper and Kappelman (n.d.).

21. The word *ken-e*, "seen, visible, in plain sight," is included in the text, indicating the public nature of this event (Justeson and Kaufman, personal communication 1997).

22. It is important to note here that there is Late Formative period archaeological evidence for bird costuming. In the Tomb II royal burial in Kaminaljuyu Mound E-III-3 was a bird mask that had been assembled from thirty-one greenstone pieces that were attached to an organic backing of some sort (Shook and Kidder 1952:115). A ruler wears a bird mask much like that found in the Tomb II burial on Kaminaljuyu Stela 11, which confirms that these masks were actually worn by rulers during ritual performances recorded on stela monuments.

23. For instance, Stela 6, located at the base of Mound 56 directly in front of Stela 4, depicts an enormous *Bufo marinus* toad identifiable by the pitted parotid glands on its shoulders. Another *Bufo marinus* is represented by boulder Altar 2. Furst (1981) and Reilly (1989) discussed the hallucinogenic properties of the venom of the *Bufo marinus* and its association with the iconography of transformation during the Middle Formative period. The juxtaposition of Stelae 6 and 4 may allude to the means by which the ruler performed the trance journey. It is also interesting that Stelae 2, 4, and 6—with their themes of rulership, transformation, and the shamanic journey—create the central axis of Group A and align directly with the volcano Tacaná in the distance (cf. Norman 1980).

24. The primordial waters of creation were also referenced in the imagery of Stelae 1 and 3, which flanked Stela 2 in front of Mound 58, just south of the plaza drain that channeled the waters into the Mound 60 reservoir. Stela 1 appears to be a Late Formative version of the Maya deity Chak, the god of rain and lightning (Girard 1966:40; Norman 1976:87; Taube 1992:22), whereas the deity represented on Stela 3 possesses attributes of both Chak and God K of the Maya. These two stelae in Group A depict gods closely associated with rain and water, appropriate references for their placement adjacent to the channeled waters.

25. The earliest known construction of the Mound 30a pyramid dates to the Duende phase, sometime before 600 BC (Ekholm 1969; Lowe et al. 1982:184). A Late Formative burial beneath the Mound 30e platform contained an offering of jade beads and is indicative of the significance this group held as the location of the earliest ritual activity at the site. The paired stairways on the southern edge of the platform also suggest a ceremonial or processional function (Lowe et al. 1982:184).

26. See also Pearson and Richards (1994) for a discussion of the symbolism of the domestic hearth at the world center.

27. The text of Quiriguá Stela C records that the third stone of creation, a water throne, was set by Itzamna (Schele 1992:125; Looper 1995b).

28. Norman (1976:105) noted the parallels between Izapa Throne 1 and Stela 8, as did Taube (1998), who compared Throne 1 to an altar from El Perú that also depicts a ruler enthroned within a cartouche. The text on the El Perú altar describes the cartouche as *tu yol ak*, "in the portal of the turtle," thereby placing the vision of the enthroned ruler within the context of the Maize God's rebirth.

29. See Freidel et al. (1993:183–185); Looper (1995:131–134); Kappelman (1997:77–132), and Looper and Kappelman (n.d.) for more complete discussions of the symbolism of the *sak nik* form.

Dance Performances at Quiriguá

MATTHEW G. LOOPER

Since the time that European visitors to Mesoamerica first saw the ancient cities of the Maya, explorers assumed that the grand architectural spaces of these cities were originally sites of pageants or spectacles. In the sixteenth-century report of Diego García de Palacio to the king of Spain, for example, the writer suggested that certain platforms at Copán were used for *mitotes*, or dances, similar to those performed by the contemporary Maya of Yucatán and Guatemala (Palacio 1985). In addition, modern scholars have used an ethnographic analogy with contemporary Maya dances to propose that dance performances took place in the central zones of various Maya cities (Schele and Freidel 1990:103–129; Schele and Grube 1990; Freidel et al. 1993:257–292). Nevertheless, the precise characterization of dance movements has eluded scholars, nor have they been able to place specific dance movements in their architectural contexts. A detailed study of the relations of space and performance among the ancient Maya has been lacking.

To begin to address this issue, it is useful to consider another Mesoamerican culture, the Aztecs, for whom both ethnohistorical and archaeological evidence is available. For the Aztecs, the most important space in the empire was the central ceremonial precinct of Tenochtitlán with its epicenter, the Templo Mayor (Matos Moctezuma 1988). Part of the significance of this space is owed to its location, at the center of the Aztec capital city on a site chosen for them by the gods. In addition, the space was empowered by its manner of construction. The various buildings were conceived as embodiments of core myths of the Aztecs, having to do with their migrations through various sacred locations where important supernatural events occurred. The space was also embellished with elaborate sculpted and painted programs, which communicated these mythic associations. Art itself, as well as multiple layers of construction with associated offerings, imbued the space with supernatural energy. Further, the space was laid out according to alignments with celestial bodies, thereby assuring the integration of site with natural environment.

In addition to its constructed meanings, which were relatively stable or accrued over time, the ceremonial precinct of Tenochtitlán also had numerous ritual meanings—transient meanings that were determined by performance. The very presence of priests, rulers, and other powerful figures in and near the central precinct imbued the space with sacred qualities, as did the creation and housing of deity images that were housed within its walls. The significance of the space was also intermittently manifested through various ritual and dance ceremonies performed in its confines. One of the most important of these dances was performed during the Izcalli festival, a commemoration of the five "empty days" that preceded the Aztec new year, was celebrated every fourth year. Described by Fray Sahagún (1951–70, Volume 2:151–152), the "Lordly Dance" performed on this occasion by Moctezuma in the company of the highest Aztec lords consisted of the fourfold circling of the principal ritual plaza of Tenochtitlán, in front of the Templo Mayor. As interpreted by R. F. Townsend (1979:47), this ritual movement within the cosmologically defined space adjacent to the Templo Mayor purified both city and empire in preparation for the ceremonies of yearly renewal. The functions of the main plaza of Tenochtitlán illustrate vividly how cultural meanings of space are determined through performance (see Reese-Taylor and Koontz, chapter 1 in this volume). In addition, the Izcalli festival exemplifies the political functions of performance. The deep meanings imbued in the sacred precinct over time rendered it qualitatively different from other spaces; thus, actions performed in this microcosmic space had profound implications for the macrocosm.

In analyzing the meanings of this performance, the particular form of the Lordly Dance deserves special notice. Although little is mentioned of the fine details, the circling motion of the procession is extremely important, for it is semantically loaded. In short, it is a cosmic diagram, based on the perceived movement of the sun around the Earth that orders both space and time from the epicenter of a ceremonial precinct. Another well-known manifestation of this pattern is seen in the great Calendar Stone, in which day names are arranged in a ring, inscribed within the cosmological structure of the solar disk. Many other examples of this pattern or aesthetic trope of circular space-time could be cited throughout

Mesoamerican history (see Reese-Taylor and Koontz, chapter 1 in this volume). In contemporary Chamula, for example, a similar performance is conducted during the Festival of Games, a calendrical ceremonial cycle during which the moral Tzotzil Maya world is ritually destroyed and recreated (Gossen 1986). At the climax of the festival, the principal performers, or Passions, who are charged with caring for the head of the Sun/Christ, run into the ceremonial center and circle it counterclockwise three times. This motion has clear cosmological significance, as it maps out the movement of the sun on a horizontal plane.[1] Following this performance, the performers conduct a fire walk, which represents the ascent of the Sun/Christ into the heavens and the reordering of the cosmos. At Chamula as well as Tenochtitlán, circular performances established the cosmological significance of calendar ceremony through a patterning of human movements and timing onto a sacred landscape.

In the present chapter, I propose a reconstruction of the dance performances that took place at the Classic Maya city of Quiriguá (Izabál, Guatemala), in association with a large platform designated 1A-1. Using spatial analysis and the iconography and programming patterns of public sculpture associated with this platform, I will suggest that the platform and its sculpture program provided a setting for dance performances that took place during the festivals of period ending the Classic Maya anniversary of the ritual calendar. Further, I will suggest that these festivals featured a circular counterclockwise dance that was symbolically associated with the renewal of cyclical temporal periods in Mesoamerican ritual, analogous to the Lordly Dance of the Aztecs. The performances that took place in the context of this platform support the identification of circular space-time as an important Mesoamerican aesthetic trope.

Ancient Maya Dance Performance

Before considering the nature of dances associated with Platform 1A-1 at Quiriguá, it is useful to review the cultural significance of Maya dance performance. Elsewhere, I argued that ancient and modern Maya dance constitutes a continuous cultural tradition (Looper 1991). Of course, contact with European culture has substantially changed forms and meanings of Maya ritual (Bricker 1981). However, pre-Hispanic and contemporary dance share a number of general characteristics. Dance may be considered a type of performance, functioning within both ancient and modern Maya society as an important medium through which basic cultural principles are forged and communicated (Looper 1991; Freidel et al.

1993:257–292). Generally speaking, Maya ceremonial dance may be characterized as the formalized rhythmic movement of costumed people performed to musical accompaniment before an audience (Looper 1991:11). In addition, the social functions of dance are encoded in the very term used to refer to the activity. Terms for dance among the modern Maya have various roots and derivations. In K'ichean languages, the term is a cognate of *xajoj*, which is related to the word for sandal. Speakers of Yucatecan and Ch'olan, the languages most closely related to the ancient Maya script, use a cognate of *ak'ot*, which is derived from the root *ak'*, "give, offer," plus a passive suffix *-ot* (Martha Macri 1997, personal communication). N. Grube (1992) identified the glyphic expressions for dance in the Classic inscriptions, assigning the stem a value of AHK'OT. Although affixation patterns may indicate a slightly different reading, it is clear that the Classic period word for dance was derived from the term for making an offering. In fact, some Classic period texts use the same main sign to compose words for both "dance" and "offer."[2] This linguistic connection firmly established the sacrificial connotations of dance among the Maya.

Both ancient dances and the traditional dances of the modern Maya serve important social and political functions (Looper 1991:20–24). Central to Maya dance performance is the generation of a context for supernatural contact through the wearing of sacred costume, the manipulation of holy objects, the execution of certain steps, and the trance states induced by rhythmic music and movement as well as the consumption of intoxicants. Ethnohistorical and ethnographic evidence demonstrates that Maya sacrificial rituals often took the form of a dance, serving to open the paths between the worlds of humans and the gods that allowed for the bestowal of divine blessings on society (Looper 1991:17–20).

The Maya interpretation of dance costumes and implements as the vessels for divine power also bestowed upon the wearer a certain prestige. In many cases, especially for the ancient Maya, this prestige was translated into political currency, and the dancer was guaranteed social status. In a similar manner, prestige accrued for the performer when ancient Maya performance represented important historical or mythological actions. Such pageants associated the performer with great events. An additional political implication of communal Maya dance performance, however, is the reinforcement of horizontal social relationships through the representation of communal and ethnic history or myth. Such performances are powerful means of generating community cohesion and identity.

Figure 5.1   Bonampak Temple 1, Room 1, south wall mural,
detail of lower register. Drawing by Linda Schele

Because the focus of Classic Maya art is on the representation of elite or supernatural subjects, there is insufficient evidence to document community participation in dances. Ancient Maya dance was usually represented as a solo royal performance or as a small elite ensemble, as in the dance scene from Room 1 of Structure 1 at Bonampak (Figure 5.1) (Houston 1984). In fact, the texts that accompany the three dancing figures in this scene include not only the verb for dance but also various elite titles, such as *ch'ok* "prince", *ajaw* "lord", and *k'uhul ajaw* "holy/god lord" (see Houston 1984; Grube 1992). In other instances in which there is no textual reference to dance, such as a panel from Palenque in the Dumbarton Oaks collection, artists depicted figures with the heel of one foot raised in order to indicate a dance ritual (Coe and Benson 1966:16). The appearance of the dance glyph in association with the figure of the Yaxchilán ruler in the heel-raised posture on a panel from the Yaxchilán region (Figure 5.2) confirms this posture as an iconographic indicator of dance (Grube 1992). Dancing supernatural beings also comprise an important genre of Maya representation and are often shown in the heel-raised posture. For example, the Maize God is often shown in Maya ceramics as a dancer (Figure 5.3) (Looper 1991; Freidel et al. 1993:276–284).

Although the heel-raised posture allows an identification of certain figures in Maya art as dancers, it is unlikely that this is a literal depiction of a dance position in which the feet are turned outward. It seems likely that this position is meant to represent the weight-shift that results from forward movement through space. The image results from the convention of representing legs in profile rather than frontally. The posture may also represent a "stomp step," in which the ball of the foot is pounded on the ground with the other foot remaining in place (Kathryn Reese-Taylor

Figure 5.2   Lintel from Yaxchilán region.
Drawing by Nikolai Grube

1991, personal communication). Either way, the heel-raised posture is clearly a conventional reference to dancing motion that is not specific to particular dances. Often, artists elected to exclude even the minimal dynamism of the heel-raised posture in representations of dance. For instance, on Yaxchilán Lintel 53, the text indicates that the king is dancing, yet the royal figure is rendered in a highly rigid pose. An important implication of this representation from Yaxchilán is that many of the static images of kings on stelae could connote dance performances, represent-

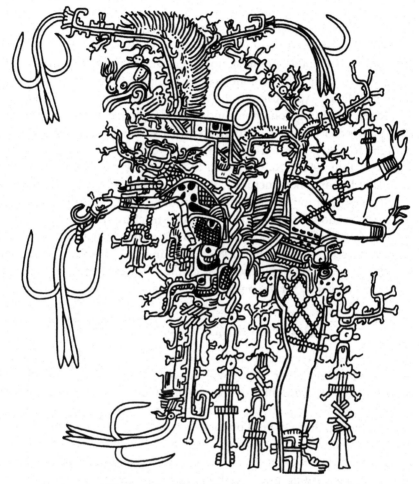

Figure 5.3   Maize God as a dancer.
Drawing by Looper after a polychrome vessel

ing them in a nonliteral fashion that preserves the static monumentality of the royal portrait.

Even though most Maya art is not concerned with the literal depiction of the motions of historical dances, there are a few salient exceptions that should be mentioned. One example appears on a vase that shows warriors leading a captive to sacrifice (see Schele and Miller 1986:232, 233). The artist who decorated this vase painted the figures marching continuously around the vessel so that, as the vase is held in the hand and rotated, the viewer's impression is of a circular procession. Exactly this sort of procession, in which captives are paraded by captors in a circular route, is described in early ethnohistorical sources as a dance (Tozzer 1941:117–118). Another possible movement that may be reconstructed directly from ancient representations is the spinning or twirling motion of a sacrificial dance. Appearing in the art of several sites near the Usumacinta River, including Bonampak and Yaxchilán, this motion is implied by long panels that project from dancers' waists, as if sustained by the centrifugal forces generated by a spinning dancer (Schele and Miller 1986:193; Tate 1992:228). Owing to the elaborate representation in the murals of Bonampak Structure 1, Room 3, we are able to reconstruct the specific architectural context for the spinning dance. In this image, the dancers are shown arrayed on a stepped structure that is apparently a representation of the terraced hillside upon which Structure 1 was built (Ruppert et al. 1955; Miller 1986). The unusual images of dance at Bonampak are strong evidence that certain Maya architectural settings served as the venue for the presentation of dances.

Dance Iconography at Quiriguá

In contrast to the complex panoramic and narrative compositions found at Bonampak and other sites, royal imagery at Quiriguá conforms to a narrow range of representation that is relatively formalized and confined to monumental sculpture. At Quiriguá, such imagery was concentrated in a ceremonial precinct built on the banks of the Motagua River in a program associated with Platform 1A-1. One of the most important complexes of monumental art and architecture known from the ancient Maya world, the 1A-1 program was commissioned by the prominent Late Classic king of Quiriguá, K'ak Tiliw Chan Yoat, or K'ak Tiliw for short (Looper 1995a). The Platform 1A-1 program of K'ak Tiliw is particularly relevant to this study because it remains intact. Thus, the program's visual and spatial dimensions remain assessable *in situ*, a valuable asset in the reconstruction of its functions in the context of performance. The program consists of five large stelae and one ceremonial throne erected between 761–780 AD in a quadrilateral formation, facing southward, atop a broad, low platform (approximately 100 x 85 x 0.5 meters) (Figure 5.4). Stelae D, E, and F mark three of the corners of this quadrilateral, whereas the triad of Stelae A and C and Zoomorph B marks the fourth (Looper 1995b). A seventh monument, Zoomorph G, is located adjacent to Stelae

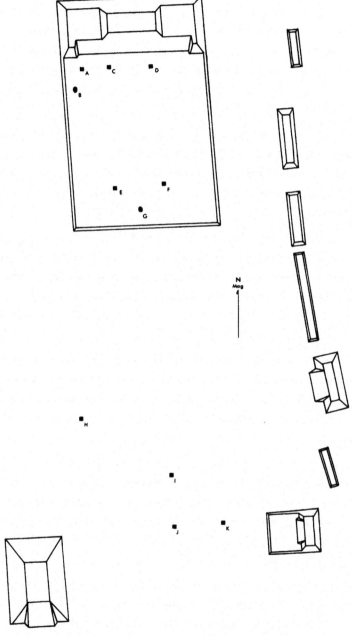

Figure 5.4   Plan of Quiriguá Great Plaza.
Modified after Jones et al. (1983:28).

E and F, but because this monument was placed after the death of K'ak Tiliw, it is not considered to be part of the program.

The northern end of the 1A-1 platform is defined by a tall structure, 1A-3, which originally featured a broad stairway that extended along most of its south face (Coe and Sharer 1979:15). The stelae in this group (Stelae F, D, E, C and A) display texts on their east and west faces and royal portraits on their south faces. Their north faces feature either additional royal portraits or, as in the cases of Stelae A and C, supernatural beings. Zoomorph B represents a supernatural polymorph (the "Cosmic Monster"), which faces southward and is adorned on its east, north, and west sides with hieroglyphic texts (Stone 1983). Each monument of the Platform 1A1 program commemorates the ending of a *ho'tun* (five x 360-day year) period, an anniversary of the ordering of the cosmos that occurred in the remote past.

In each monument of the Platform 1A-1 program, the figures of the king are rendered in rigid, frontal poses, with only the king's arms and the objects he holds breaking the strict bilateral symmetry of the compositions (Figure 5.5). Thus, the reconstruction of ancient dances at Quiriguá must be based on information other than figural composition or posture. Of particular importance in this regard are various costume elements that appear in the stela compositions that are elsewhere associated with dance. Seen at Bonampak, Yaxchilán, and elsewhere, the features prominent in Maya dance representation include frontal pose, relative isolation in the composition, elaborate feather headdresses and back racks, and the manipulation of objects (see Grube 1992). At Quiriguá, each royal image of the Platform 1A-1 stelae is rendered with stacked feathered headdresses and ceremonial objects in the hands, as seen on Yaxchilán Lintel 53. On Stelae D (Figure 5.5) and E, south and north faces, each image of the king is shown holding a shield and God K scepter. The two objects correspond to dance implements shown on other Maya monuments in which the king is clearly shown in a dance posture, as on Tzum Stela 3. On Yaxchilán Lintel 53, the dance glyph accompanies a scene of the king performing with the same God K and shield.

Another feature of the Quiriguá Platform 1A-1 stela portraits that indicates dance ritual is the set of shell tinklers worn dangling from the heavy belt. Such tinklers would have generated percussive rhythms as the king danced and are also worn by the dancer shown on Tzum Stela 3. The elaborate high-backed sandals worn by K'ak Tiliw in the Quiriguá representations may also be associated with the dance because they are not a part of

everyday royal attire as represented in ancient Maya art. Such
sandals appear in many images
that have been identified as dance
ritual, such as Tzum Stela 3, Yaxchilán Stela 11 and Lintel 5, and
the Palenque House D piers (see
Freidel et al. 1993:269, 272, 274).

Whereas the dance costumes of
the king shown on Quiriguá Stelae D and E are represented
widely in Maya art and may not
be associated with a specific ceremonial occasion, the imagery of
Stelae F, C, and A evokes a dance
performance that concerned the
theme of cosmogenesis (Looper
1995a). Such a "Dance of Creation" is also suggested in the
polychrome vases that show the
Maize God in the guise known as
the Holmul Dancer (Figure 5.3)
(see Taube 1985; Freidel et al.
1993:274–286). As noted by various scholars, these images show
the Maize God dancing with a
cosmological back rack. Usually,
the central icon of this back rack is
a throne constructed of bones,
upon which is seated one of several animals: jaguar, reptile, or
monkey. These thrones seem to
correspond to three thrones that
were set under the authority of the
Maize God on 13.0.0.0.0 4 Ajaw 8
Kumk'u (13 August 3114 BC), according to the text of Quiriguá
Stela C (Schele 1992:121–150).

The key images associated with
this dance as it took place at

**Figure 5.5 Quiriguá Stela D,
north face.** Drawing by Looper

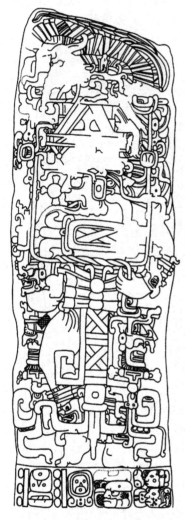

Figure 5.6
Quiriguá Stelae C, north face.
Drawing by Looper

Quiriguá appear on Stelae A and C north (Figure 5.6). Each of these images features a supernatural being shown with the heel-raised posture widely associated with dance (Kubler 1969:17). Nikolai Grube (1996, personal communication) identified the Stela A figure as a jaguar god named Ik' Hun or Ik' Hunal ("Black Headband"), who is named on the west text of the same stela. The Stela C figure is the patron of the *hab'* period Pax. The two figures are adorned with the triple knots associated with blood sacrifice, and they grasp twisted cords that descend from a celestial register marked by a sky band and Celestial Bird. The flower symbols and terminal heads of these cords reveal their identity as *sak nik*, or "white flower," a metaphor for the Maya breath (Freidel et al. 1993:99–106, 182–184; Looper 1995a:131–134). In Maya cosmology, the white flower cords functioned as a "cosmic umbilicus," which the gods caused to descend from the sky at the dawn of Creation and through which gods were continually reborn into the world (Schele and Looper 1996:93). In astronomical terms, the sky umbilicus was conceived as the pathway of the ecliptic, which, emerging from the zenith, stretched toward the east and west. It was through this celestial umbilicus that the planets, sun, and moon were born and died. On Quiriguá Stelae A and C, the white flower cords actually fall toward the east and west due to the orientation of the monument. In sum, the imagery of these stelae refers to a supernatural dance associated with the period ending, during which sacrifice brings forth the emergence of white flower cords of birth, a potent event central to cosmogenesis.

The south faces of these two monuments also show events related to Creation, but in this case, the actor is the ruler, K'ak Tiliw, instead of a supernatural being (Figure 5.7) (Looper 1995b). On each of the monuments, the ruler is shown holding a throne constructed of jaguar pelt and crossed bones. The Stela C throne is adorned with jaguar heads, whereas snake heads terminate that of Stela A. These heads identify the thrones as the first two thrones set by the gods in primordial times. Thus, the programming of Stelae A and C contrasts imagery of royal and divine performances that represent key moments in the narrative of cosmogenesis. The placement of these images on period-ending stelae served to explicate the significance of the period ending as a reenactment of the creation of the cosmos.

Stela F, the initial monument of the 1A-1 program, explores the same theme as Stelae A and C, although it presents the king as the sole actor. On the south face (Figure 5.8), the king is shown holding a double-headed serpent, which stretches from the apex of the monument marked by Celestial Bird. This double-headed serpent is iden-

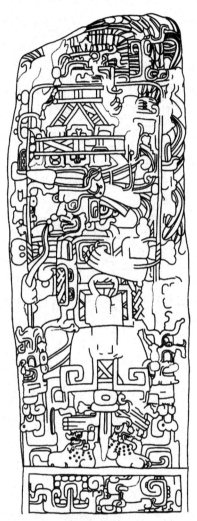

Figure 5.7
Quiriguá Stelae A, south face.
Drawing by Looper

tified as yet another representation of the sky umbilicus, not only because the umbilicus is commonly represented as a snake, but because on Stela F it stretches from the celestial realm toward the east and west, like the ecliptic. In addition, on Stela F south, the body of the snake is composed of linked earflare assemblages. In Maya iconography, the earflare is often represented as a flower or with floral attributes, and

**Figure 5.8 Quiriguá Stela F,
south face (partial).**
Drawing by Looper

many actual earflares are fashioned in the shape of flowers. Further, in contemporary Maya cosmology, the ecliptic is sometimes called a "path of flowers" (Holland 1963:77), firmly associating the representation of Stela F with the imagery seen on Stelae A and C.

Although the southern royal image of Stela F casts the king as a creator deity, manifesting the ecliptic-umbilicus in the sky, the north face of the monument displays the king in a contrasting guise (Figure 5.9). Here, the king's headdress is adorned with vertically oriented water bands (marked with doubled disks and dots), which are gripped by personified waterlilies. The north face of Stela F, then, places the king in the watery Underworld, out of which life springs and into which the dead fall. The two faces of Stela F commemorate royal dances in contrasting heavenly and underworldly guises that dramatized the king as a world-creator. The adornment of a period-ending monument with such imagery reinforced the significance of the festival as a celebration of cosmogenesis. On Stela F, as in Stelae A and C, the royal images preserve and document the performances that transformed myth into history and sanctified the festival celebration.

Platform 1A-1 as a Performance Space

Whereas the imagery of the Platform 1A-1 monuments allows the identification of the dances that were performed in their midst, the structure of the platform space itself may be analyzed to determine its ritual function.

The prototype for the Platform 1A-1 program at Quiriguá is found in the early Classic foundations of the city, around the early fifth century AD. In emulation of the larger centers of Tikal and especially Copán, to which early Quiriguá was subordinate, the provincial center was fitted with raised platforms supporting small superstructures and accented with carved stelae. Two of these complexes have been identified—one located on a hilltop west of the current floodplain center, designated Locus 002, or Group A, and another, Group 3C-7, located in the floodplain, north of the current site core (Morley 1935:49; Ashmore 1980, 1981; Ashmore et al. 1983:58–60; Sharer et al. 1983:43). The low, broad stone-faced earthen platforms typical of this period served as the foci for public ritual, apparently providing an elevated stage for performances. The texts and imagery of the stelae that were probably placed in front of these complexes (Stela U and Monument 26) specified the ceremonial significance of the architecture. Their modestly scaled royal portraits show the king in a state of communication with the supernatural world, making permanent the periodic rituals that took place on the platforms (Looper 1995a:33–54).

Figure 5.9   Quiriguá Stela F, north face (partial).
Drawing by Looper

Following the abandonment of the Early Classic floodplain center and a Middle Classic hiatus, Quiriguá's architectural and monumental traditions were revived in the eighth century, shortly after the accession of K'ak Tiliw in 724 AD. By the 750s, K'ak Tiliw had rejuvenated the stela tradition of the city by specifically copying the iconographic, stylistic, and textual modes of the local Early Classic monumental tradition (Looper 1995a:90–124). The architectural context for the king's first three stelae (H, J, and probably S), however, differs from the Early Classic model. Instead of positioning stelae in front of platforms and thereby subordinating them to architecture, the ruler displayed his elaborate monuments in a spacious plaza north of the newly renovated acropolis, demarcated on the west by the Motagua River and on the east by a series of low mounds (Figure 5.4). The large open space of the Great Plaza had a distinctly public character, having been visible from the river, with at least one dock allowing for the mooring of canoes (Ashmore et al. 1983:56). The Great Plaza could easily have held the entire projected population of the Quiriguá area, and its scale suggests that the plaza may have been designed to accommodate people from distant regions (see Schortman 1993:201). In fact, archaeological evidence does attest to the presence of such crowds in the Great Plaza, for ceramic fragments were found ground into the plaza surface (Jones et al. 1983:10).

As a setting for mass spectacle, this new monumental locus at Quiriguá seems to have been inspired specifically by the earlier sculpture program of the king 18 Rabbit (Waxaklajun Ub'ah K'awil) at Copán. Here, K'ak Tiliw's former overlord constructed a large open plaza, accented by monumental sculptures that have been interpreted as processional markers and pilgrimage shrines (Newsome 1991). As with the 18 Rabbit's program at Copán, the open space of the Quiriguá Great Plaza set off K'ak Tiliw's monuments as independent sculptures, emphasizing their likely role as the focal points of processions. Quiriguá Stela H, in particular, seems to have served as a processional marker, as it was erected near a canoe dock at the entrance to the Great Plaza. The symbolism of stelae as pathways of supernatural communication strongly supports the interpretation of these monuments as loci for sacrifice and prayer. Indeed, the quantities of modeled effigy censer fragments found in the Great Plaza, often in association with the monuments, lend support to this hypothesis because incense was a standard offering to the Maya gods (Benyo 1979:565; Ashmore 1981).

K'ak Tiliw's Platform 1A-1 program, which was initiated in 761 AD, north of the Great Plaza monuments, represented a return to the Early Classic local tradition of monumental placement. The new program, however, was far grander than anything that had been attempted before and was richer in performance possibilities than its antecedents. Of particular importance in establishing a theatrical nature for the 1A-1 program was its architectural backdrop, Structure 1A-3. This structure bounded the stage visually, providing a field of reference for viewing the monuments placed atop the platform as well as performers. The six monoliths themselves seem to have served as stage properties, taking an active role in the generation of the theatrical environment. Notably, the diminished size of the monuments nearest to Structure 1A-3 (Stelae A, C, and D and Zoomorph B) relative to the two stelae near the platform edge (E and F), generates a false perspective that enhances the sense of depth of the platform space when viewed from the front (south). Ample space for the audience was provided on the south, east, and west sides of the platform, bounded by low mounds on the east and the river on the west. Viewers may also have been positioned on the stairway of Structure 1A-3, looking down upon the platform. The resulting frontal stage configuration recalls the raised, covered stages mentioned in sixteenth- and seventeenth-century reports of Maya dances (Ponce 1932:328; Tovilla 1960:183; Estrada Monroy 1979:168).

In addition to its function as a frontal stage, however, K'ak Tiliw's platform provided ample space in both south-north and east-west axes to support a full range of movement. The quadrilateral arrangement of monuments on Platform 1A-1, as well as their squared cross-sections, are crucial in defining the rectilinear planar quality of this space. Indeed, just as the imagery of the monuments in this group defines the period ending as a replay of creation through royal agency, the symbolic associations of the square, cardinally oriented figure amplified the significance of the period-ending rituals. The cosmic symbolism derived from the movement of the sun throughout the year, from rising and setting points on the southern horizon during the winter solstice, to stations on the northern horizon during the summer solstice. Rafael Girard (1962:45) documented the marking of these solstitial points with stones by the Ch'orti' Maya and interpreted it as a fundamental definition of the cosmos. This definition of the cosmos by four directional markers is documented for postconquest Maya and other Mesoamerican groups (see Thompson 1970:194–196, 331–373). It seems likely that the quadrilateral grouping of monuments on Platform 1A-1 relates to a Classic period cognate of these concepts, representing an abstract map of the cosmos. Each monument set up by K'ak Tiliw for a period ending dramatized the creation of the cosmos that the festival celebrated and thereby enhanced the mythos of the king as a creator god.

Apart from its symbolic import, the distribution of monuments atop Platform 1A-1 generates a spatial matrix strongly suggestive of particular movement patterns. The twinned southern stelae, E and F, function formally as a gateway, implying that the passage between them served as a processional entryway. The placement of Zoomorph G directly on this pathway is particularly telling in this respect, for the monument served as the death memorial for the great king. The Maya frequently placed such funerary monuments in principal entryways of architectural groups in order to "terminate" the spaces within (Schele and Miller 1986:74). For example, Palenque Temple 14 was constructed upon the death of the king Kan B'alam to block the principal entry to the Cross Group, for which Kan B'alam was the patron (Schele and Miller 1986:65, 74).

Sophisticated new approaches to programming of monumental texts and images atop Platform 1A-1 complemented K'ak Tiliw's overwhelming new setting for narrative performance at Quiriguá. Beginning with Stela F, the texts of K'ak Tiliw's monuments are structured around the comparison of the current monument dedication event with supernatural period-ending events in the extremely ancient past. Reading sequentially from east to west sides, the texts of Stelae D, E, and F state the current dedication date, provide a paradigmatic supernatural period-ending event, and then recount selected historical events up to a restatement of the current period ending. The climax of the program, comprised of the texts of the twin stelae A and C that occupy the northwest corner of the platform, also focuses the narrative on historical and mythological period endings but reorders the sequence and inserts an account of cosmogenesis. On each monument of the Platform 1A-1 program, the texts conform to a reading order of east to west, generating an organic unity for the program. Although the hieroglyphic narrative patterns of K'ak Tiliw's Platform 1A-1 were inspired by certain texts of the earlier ruler of Copán, 18 Rabbit, K'ak Tiliw's texts represent a simplification of previous models. Eschewing nearly all dynastic information, these texts promulgate a supernatural persona of the ruler, who is capable of directly tapping spiritual energies.

Like the monuments' texts, the images of the 1A-1 stelae may be read in a specific sequence, from south to north, generating patterns of cause and effect and complementation (Looper 1995a). The figures that adorn the south and north faces of K'ak Tiliw's monuments atop Platform 1A-1 proclaim the supernatural charter of the king's authority. These images place the king in contrasting supernatural or earthly realms, as in Stelae D and E, or show him invested with the trappings of a deity who presided over cosmic creation, as in Stela F, C, and A and Zoomorph B. Although the basic two-faced figural composition of these monuments may have been inspired by earlier models at Copán, its specific implementation at Quiriguá was innovative and served to reinforce the narrative content of the texts.

In sum, the squared shapes of the monuments themselves, with figures and texts oriented systematically to the four cardinal directions, reinforces the formal quality of the Platform 1A-1 space as a bounded envelope with movements directed inward and across the stage, from left to right. These qualities of the monuments, in addition to their placement in a rough quadrilateral at the four corners of the platform, may suggest that the kind of movement that took place among them was circular. The initiation of the monumental program on the platform with Stela F implies that the circuit was begun with a right-hand turn upon entering the platform space in order to pass this monument first. The placement of texts on Zoomorphs B and G reinforces this pattern because a counterclockwise movement around the monuments is required to read them. Such movements may have been manifested as pilgrimage routes or circular dances akin to the *Kolomche'* documented in the sixteenth-century Yucatán (Tozzer 1941:93–94) or the sacrificial dances described by other early chroniclers (Villagutierre y Soto-Mayor 1983:302; Palacio 1985:40).

As in the Aztec new year ceremonies and the Chamula Festival of Games, the monumental program at Quiriguá commemorated the rebirth of the cosmos. A circular dance within its confines would have enhanced the symbolic import of the program, drawing attention to the quadrilateral arrangement of monuments and characterizing the platform space as a cosmogram. Not only does the imagery of the Platform 1A-1 monuments derive from dance costume, but the sculptures also define performance spaces through their formal qualities and integration with the architecture. In this setting, the sculptures memorialize the public dances and pageants that took place in the spaces surrounding them. The monuments' imagery and arrangement evoke important aspects of the period-ending festival's symbolic significance as a celebration of cosmic renewal, as well as create a venue for the dramatic presentation of this festival.

At Quiriguá, the portrayal of the king on the stelae as a dancer served to integrate the king into this nexus of power. Maya royal portraiture was conceived not as mere abstraction but as an embodiment of the persona of the ruler (Stuart 1996). Thus, the monuments' imagery and placement may be characterized as a surrogate royal performance, frozen in the medium of stone. The monuments represent the Quiriguá king as an active performer, not only through his costume but by the monuments' positions, which mark key body positions in the space of the platform. As with the monuments' texts and images, in which the king wields the powers of creation, the program memorializes performances in which he constructed cosmic space. The Platform 1A-1 program is a remarkable testament to the poetics by which Maya rulers personalized space and mythology as a means of supporting their sovereignty.

References

Ashmore, W.
   1980   Discovering Early Classic Quiriguá. *Expedition* 23(3):35–44.
   1981   *Settlement at Quiriguá, Guatemala: A Functional Definition of the Site and a Taxonomy of Maya Settlement Units*. Ph.D. dissertation, University of Pennsylvania, Philadelphia.
Ashmore, W., E. M. Schortman, and R. J. Sharer.
   1983   The Quiriguá Project: 1979 Season. *Quiriguá Reports, Volume 2*. Edited by E. M. Schortman and P. A. Urban. Philadelphia: University Museum, University of Pennsylvania. 55–78.
Benyo, J.
   1979   *The Pottery Censers of Quiriguá, Izabal, Guatemala*. M.A. thesis, State University of New York, Albany.
Bricker, V. R.
   1981   *The Indian Christ, The Indian King: The Historical Substrate of Maya Myth and Ritual*. Austin, Tex.: The University of Texas Press.
Coe, M. D., and E. P. Benson.
   1966   *Three Maya Relief Panels at Dumbarton Oaks*. Studies in Pre-Columbian Art and Archaeology 2. Washington, D.C.: Dumbarton Oaks.
Coe, W. R., and R. J. Sharer.
   1979   The Quiriguá Project: 1975 Season. *Quiriguá Reports, Volume 1*. Edited by W. Ashmore. Philadelphia: University Museum, University of Pennsylvania. 13–32.
Estrada Monroy, A.
   1979   *El Mundo K'ekchi' de la Vera-Paz*. Guatemala City, Guatemala: Editorial del Ejército.
Freidel, D., L. Schele, and J. Parker.
   1993   *Maya Cosmos: Three Thousand Years on the Shaman's Path*. New York: William Morrow.
García de Palacio, Diego.
   1985   *Letter to the King of Spain*. Translated by E. G. Squier. Culver City, Calif.: Labyrinthos.
Girard, R.
   1962   *Los Mayas Eternos*. México, D.F.: Antigua Librería Robredo.
Gossen, G.
   1986   The Chamula Festival of Games: Native Macroanalysis and Social Commentary in a Maya Carnival. *Symbol and Meaning Beyond the Closed Community: Essays in Mesoamerican Ideas*. Edited by G. Gossen. Studies on Culture and Society 1. Albany: Institute for Mesoamerican Studies, State University of New York. 227–254.

Grube, N.
    1992   Classic Maya Dance: Evidence from Hieroglyphs and Iconography. *Ancient Mesoamerica* 3:201–218.
Holland, W. R.
    1963   Medicina Maya en los Altos de Chiapas: Un estudio del cambio sociocultural. México, D.F.: Instituto Nacional Indigenista.
Houston, S. D.
    1984   A Quetzal Feather Dance at Bonampak, Chiapas, Mexico. *Journal de la Société des Américanistes* 70:127–137.
Jones, C., W. Ashmore, and R. J. Sharer.
    1983   The Quiriguá Project: 1977 Season. *Quiriguá Reports, Volume 2.* Edited by E. M. Schortman and P. A. Urban. Philadelphia: University Museum, University of Pennsylvania. 1–38.
Kubler, George.
    1969   Studies in Classic Maya Iconography. *Memoirs of the Connecticut Academy of Arts & Sciences* 18. New Haven, Conn: Connecticut Academy of Arts & Sciences.
Looper, M. G.
    1991   *The Dances of the Classic Maya Deities Chak and Hun Nal Ye.* M.A. thesis, Department of Art, University of Texas at Austin.
    1995a   *The Sculpture Programs of Butz'-Tiliw, an Eighth-Century Maya King of Quiriguá, Guatemala.* Ph.D. dissertation, Department of Art, University of Texas at Austin.
    1995b   The Three Stones of Maya Creation Mythology at Quiriguá. *Mexicon* 17(2):24–30.
Mace, C. E.
    1984   *Two Spanish-Quiché Dance-Dramas of Rabinal.* Tulane Studies in Romance Languages and Literatures 3. New Orleans, La.: Tulane University.
Matos Moctezuma, E.
    1988   *The Great Temple of the Aztecs: Treasures of Tenochtitlán.* London: Thames and Hudson.
Miller, M. E.
    1986   *The Murals of Bonampak.* Princeton: Princeton University Press.
Morley, S. G.
    1935   *Guide Book to the Ruins of Quiriguá.* Supplementary Publication 16. Washington, D.C.: Carnegie Institution of Washington.
Newsome, E.
    1991   The Trees of Paradise and Pillars of the World: Vision Quest and Creation in the Stelae Cycle of 18 Rabbit-God K, Copán, Honduras. Ph.D. dissertation, Department of Art, University of Texas at Austin.
Ponce, Fray A.
    1932   *Fray Alonso Ponce in Yucatán 1588.* Middle American Research Series Publication 4. New Orleans: Tulane University.
Ruppert, K., J. E. S. Thompson, and T. Proskouriakoff.
    1955   *Bonampak, Chiapas, Mexico.* Publication 602. Washington D.C.: Carnegie Institution of Washington.

Sahagún, Fray B. de.
   1951–1970   *The Florentine Codex*. Translated by A. J. O. Anderson and C. E. Dibble. Santa Fe, N.Mex.: Monographs of the School of American Research.
Schele, L.
   1992   *Notebook for the XVIth Maya Hieroglyphic Workshop at Texas*. Austin, Tex.: University of Texas Press.
Schele, L., and D. Freidel.
   1990   *A Forest of Kings: The Untold Story of the Ancient Maya*. New York: William Morrow.
Schele, L., and M. E. Miller.
   1986   *The Blood of Kings: Dynasty and Ritual in Maya Art*. Fort Worth, Tex.: Kimbell Art Museum.
Schele, L., and M. G. Looper.
   1996   *Notebook for the XXth Maya Hieroglyphic Forum at Texas*. Austin, Tex.: University of Texas Press.
Schele, L., and N. Grube.
   1990   The Glyph for Plaza or Court. *Copán Note 86*. Honduras: Copán Mosaics Project and the Instituto Hondureño de Antropología e Historia.
Schortman, E. M.
   1993   *Archaeological Investigations in the Lower Motagua Valley, Izabal, Guatemala: A Study in Monumental Site Function and Interaction. Quiriguá Reports, Volume 3*. Edited by R. J. Sharer. Philadelphia: University Museum, University of Pennsylvania.
Sharer, R. J., C. Jones, W. Ashmore, and E. M. Schortman.
   1979   The Quiriguá Project: 1976 Season. *Quiriguá Reports, Volume 1*. Edited by W. Ashmore. Philadelphia: University Museum, University of Pennsylvania. 45–73.
Sharer, R. J., W. Ashmore, E. M. Schortman, P. A. Urban, J. L. Seidel, and D. W. Sedat.
   1983   The Quiriguá Project: 1978 Season. *Quiriguá Reports, Volume 2*. Edited by E. M. Schortman and P. A. Urban. Philadelphia: University Museum, University of Pennsylvania. 39–54.
Stone, A.
   1983   *The Zoomorphs of Quiriguá*. Ph.D. dissertation, Department of Art, University of Texas at Austin.
Stuart, D.
   1996   Kings of Stone: A Consideration of Stelae in Ancient Maya Ritual and Representation. *RES* 29/30:149–171.
Tate, C.
   1992   *Yaxchilan: The Design of a Maya Ceremonial City*. Austin, Tex.: University of Texas Press.
Taube, K. A.
   1985   The Classic Maya Maize God: A Reappraisal. *Fifth Palenque Round Table, 1983*. Edited by V. M. Fields. San Francisco: Pre-Columbian Art Research Institute. 171–181.

Thompson, J. E. S.
  1970   *Maya History and Religion.* Norman, Okla.: University of Oklahoma Press.
Tovilla, M. A.
  1960   *Relaciones histórico-descriptivas de la Verapaz, el Manche y Lacandon, en Guatemala.* Guatemala City, Guatemala: Editorial Universitaria.
Townsend, R. F.
  1979   *State and Cosmos in the Art of Tenochtitlán.* Washington, D.C.: Dumbarton Oaks.
Tozzer, A. M.
  1941   *Landa's Relación de las Cosas de Yucatán.* Papers of the Peabody Museum of American Archaeology and Ethnology 18. Cambridge, Mass.: Peabody Museum of Archaeology and Ethnology, Harvard University.
Villagutierre y Soto-Mayor, J. de.
  1983   *History of the Conquest of the Province of the Itza: Subjugation and Events of the Lacandon and Other Nations of Uncivilized Indians in the Lands from the Kingdom of Guatemala to the Provinces of Yucatán in North America.* Translated by R. D. Wood. Culver City, Calif.: Labyrinthos.
Watanabe, J. M.
  1983   In the World of the Sun: A Cognitive Model of Mayan Cosmology. *Man* (n.s.) 18:710–728.

Notes

1. Similar concepts are documented in Mam (Mayan) grammar, in which space and world directions are modeled on the circular movement of the sun (Watanabe 1983).

2. See Palenque Temple of inscriptions, West panel, J9; Copán Stela E altar, Cp2. The glyph used to spell the root of *yak'aw* "he gives," is the same glyph (T516) as that used in the "dance" expressions. I suspect that T516 is simply AK', rather than AK'TA (or AHK'OT) because a ta syllable seems to be required when the stem for "dance" [a(h)k'ta] is intended. There is only one clear example (Copán Temple 18) where the ta syllable seems to have been deleted.

6

The Poetics of Power
and Knowledge at La Venta

CAROLYN E. TATE

Around 900 BC, a group of people living near the Gulf of Mexico began intensively to construct a ritual center on a strip of high ground oriented roughly north-south. On this site, they built an enormous earthen mound that today measures 33 meters high. To secure the materials for a series of earth sculptures and freestanding stone sculptures, they journeyed hundreds of kilometers to the mountainous southern edge of their world, as well as to volcanoes to the west and southeast. The extreme acts of transporting materials for La Venta's big mound, of finding and transporting the basalt boulders for its colossal heads, of hauling tons of serpentine from over the mountains, and other more ephemeral acts can be considered to have constituted vast performances that instilled power into the city's ceremonial zone. This chapter brings several kinds of evidence to bear on the question of how La Ventans defined power. It examines the region from where the La Ventans procured their building and sculptural materials as the likely terrestrial model for the design of the site. It discusses the practices of replication and repetition that the La Ventans used in creating the ritual space and provides analogies with other cultures in which these practices make a place powerful. It explores parallels between contemporary Mixe shamanism and ritual practice and some major features of La Venta. Finally, it considers the importance of the small stone figurines of precious materials cached in the ceremonial court as representations of specific meditative postures. Taken together, each of these culturally "texted" objects and practices point to a recognition of power as having a tangible existence independent of individuals and their interpersonal negotiations.

What were the ways in which the La Ventans conceived power? This chapter contends that the La Ventans and, to some extent, other Middle Formative peoples developed a manifold notion of power that incorporated several aspects not widely familiar in contemporary Western societies. These included the "ritual heat" accrued through performance of the intensive labor and skilled artisanship and travel necessary to transport and construct La Venta; access for certain individuals to specific kinds of knowledge through the will of supernormal patrons of shamanic power frequently depicted in the ritual space; and finally, forms of heightened consciousness gained through deliberate cultivation, or in other words, through disciplined practice of the several meditation postures illustrated in La Venta's sculpture. Such forms of power probably articulated with rulership at some points in La Venta's history. Although the nature of rulership at La Venta remains unclear, this exploration into the varieties of power and knowledge attested to in the site's design may spark future inquiry into how rulers garnered their positions.

I.

After an oil refinery was built about a kilometer southwest of its big mound and most of its monuments were relocated in Villahermosa, La Venta—excavated in the 1940s and 1950s—received little scholarly attention for several decades. Because of its unique massive offerings of hundreds of tons of serpentine blocks and its mosaic pavements, La Venta is arguably one of the most important sites in Mesoamerica, yet it remained poorly published upon. Since 1981, however, it has been the subject of excavations directed by Rebecca González-Lauck under the auspices of the Instituto Nacional de Antropología e Historia. Also, Latin Americanist Frank Kent Reilly has devoted several articles and chapters to the iconography of La Venta's sculpture and architecture. I have built on their discoveries in several papers, and I will summarize some basic information and relatively new concepts regarding La Venta's ideology here.

Among the ceremonial cities (Tate 1992:25–28) in Mesoamerica constructed between 1200 and 400 BC (Heizer 1971:52), La Venta is remarkable for its very early large earthen mound construction (Complex C), its nearly 80 monumental sculptures, and for the fact that many intensively crafted artworks were cached underground in ancient times and thereafter never seen but only known to exist (Figure 6.1). Physically, La Venta dominates a long, narrow salt dome near the Bay of Campeche amid an alluvial plain. The La Ventans seem to have selected this high ground for

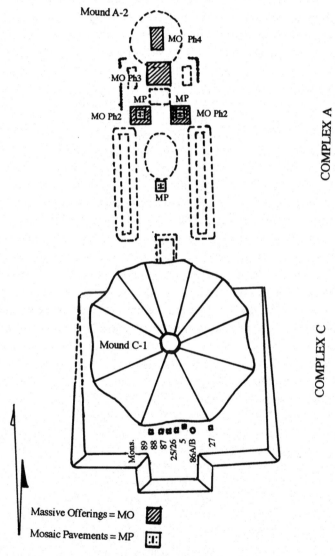

Figure 6.1 Plan of Complex A and C at La Venta.
After Gonzalez Lauck 1990, 1997

its north-south orientation because an 8 degrees west-of-north axis dominates the placement and shape of all the visible structures of La Venta, as
well as the offerings buried deep under the surface below many layers of
carefully sorted colored clays.

In addition to its early large mound construction or mountain effigy,
La Ventans also deposited tons of cut serpentine blocks, imported from a
source of stone hundreds of kilometers away, in pits up to 20-by-20 meters square and 4 meters deep. Reilly (1994) suggested that if Complex C,
the mound, represented a mountain or volcano, as proposed by Robert
Heizer (1971), then the La Venta earth sculptors completed a conceptual
cosmogram by digging huge pits for the deposition of green serpentine
blocks (the massive offerings), which represented the waters of the Underworld. Over two of the massive offerings, but still buried underground, was a layer or pavement of the same cut serpentine blocks
arranged into a mosaic pattern. The two consecutive plazas, one north of
the other, in which the massive offerings and mosaic pavements (along
with many other buried objects) were located are called Complex A.

Reilly (1994:132) convincingly argued that the design of the mosaic
pavements incorporated three elements. The double merlon (or double-
step design) at the northern end symbolized the entrance to the Underworld. The bar and four elements that comprised the large central portion of each Mosaic Pavement at once referred to the place of La Venta as
proposed by E. P. Benson (1971:29) and to P. D. Joralemon's God I, the
"Olmec Dragon," which represented the earth and its fertility (Joralemon
1976:45–52). The fringed diamonds represented *nymphaea ampla*, the waterlily that grows in the swamps surrounding La Venta, and in its entirety, the mosaic pavement design represented the plant-choked surface
of La Venta as an entrance to the Underworld. Thus, according to Reilly,
Complexes A and C at La Venta were a deliberately created diagram of
the levels of the shamanic cosmos: the mountain that reached into the
sky, the surface of the earth and its bounty, and the watery Underworld.

In a recent paper I amplified Reilly's interpretations of La Venta using
two principal lines of evidence: the specific terrain of the Isthmus of
Tehuantepec and the beliefs of the twentieth-century Mixe, descendants
of the Olmec. I proposed that La Venta replicated the topography of its
makers' known world and that the massive offerings and mosaic pavements represented, respectively, a female water supernatural being and a
female earth-surface supernatural being who, along with the male thunder being, functioned at La Venta as sources of shamanic political power
(Tate 2000).

Because it is still necessary to defend the use of ethnography in interpreting ancient cultures, I will explain why I do so. After several years of studying the art and culture of the complex societies of Formative period Mexico, commonly called Olmec, I concluded that the initial iconographic interpretations, which were not tied to a specific ethnographic framework, are less than satisfactory. Most scholars accept L. R. Campbell and T. S. Kauffman's argument that the Olmec spoke an ancestral language of the Mixe-Zoque language family and not a Mayan language as had been proposed earlier (Campbell and Kaufman 1976). The few speakers of this once-widespread language family exist today in mostly remote locations in northeastern Oaxaca, where they went when displaced by the Aztecs. Only a few anthropologists have reported on the Mixe (Beals 1945; Miller 1956; Nahmad 1965; Carrasco 1966; Rodríguez E. 1974). Although the issues of ideology and ritual began to be explored by these authors, the data were scant. With the recent publication of a carefully written volume on the religion, ritual, and healing of the Mixe, a society of about 76,000 individuals who are the linguistic and cultural descendants of the Olmec (Lipp 1991), I felt it was essential to see how the beliefs of the Mixe compared to the material evidence of Olmec culture.

I must say that the first few times I studied Frank Lipp's book I could see little connection to what I had read of the Olmecs. After several years of rereading it, suddenly many parallels emerged. I realized that the contemporary view of Olmec civilization created in the 75 years since the discovery of La Venta was not based on comprehensive analyses of iconography and the performative creation of single sites but was conceived as a generalized Olmec symbol system, the interpretation of which was unconnected with the actual beliefs and practices of a closely related people. Several of my publications since then have focused on La Venta, examining groups of objects (the stone figurines, the massive offerings) as expressive forms related to their performance spaces. The resulting concepts about La Venta, and by implication about other Gulf Coast Olmec peoples, are significantly different from what has preceded them. They offer an ethnographically based paradigm for La Venta. It may be difficult to understand because doing so requires discarding much of what has been learned about Olmec symbolism. Rather than jumping into the ethnographically based analogical interpretations, the first new material this chapter presents is a consideration of the design of the ritual spaces of La Venta and its relationship to the La Ventans' known world.

II.

A prominent aesthetic feature of La Venta's mounds and the plazas they define is that they conformed to an 8 degrees west-of-north orientation. The central axis that bisected Complexes A and C possessed this orientation. From the top of Mound C, if one sights along this axis, one sees the closest mountain south of La Venta (Figure 6.2). The stretch of high ground on which the site was built points to this mountain. This 1243-meter-high peak rises about 100 kilometers away, and I think it is likely that the relationship between this prominent feature on the horizon and the north-south strip of high ground determined the orientation of the site.

North of Mound C, in Complex A, the site's designers oriented the three mosaic pavements such that the central bar precisely paralleled the central axis of La Venta (Figure 6.3). The four elements or dots were distributed at the intercardinal points, or where the sun rises and sets on the solstices. Many contemporary and ancient Mesoamerican peoples organize space by the solstitial sunrise and set points on the horizon, as do the Mixe (Lipp 1991:30).[1] Simply put, this design diagrams the north-south island as the surface of the earth acted upon by the sun.[2] Several authors have investigated the bar-and-four-dots motif.[3] It has been called a La Venta place-name and a symbol for a crocodilian earth dragon. I accept these readings, but Mixe gender concepts and ritual practice suggest a much richer interpretation, one that will be explored later.

Returning to La Venta's mosaic pavements, the northern motif is a double merlon design, interpreted as an entrance into the earth or Underworld by Reilly (1994:131–132). The southern motif consists of four diamond shapes, each with four sprouts, which have been interpreted as waterlilies (Reilly 1994:131–132). These designs seem to refer to regional topography; about 15 kilometers to the north of the site is the Gulf of Mexico, where the watery underworld touches the realm of humans. Surrounding the site were riverine estuaries and swamps choked with waterlilies and other vegetation. Thus, in a sense the mosaic pavements describe the island's form, its interaction with the sun, and the landscape immediately to the north and south of the site. Two of the three are above the massive offerings, which Reilly (1994:131–132) interprets as effigies of seas. The combination of mosaic pavement and massive offerings thus forms an earth-surface diagram above the sea effigy. To initiate each of five construction phases, the La Ventans excavated a huge pit in which to deposit a sea effigy (Figure 6.4) (Drucker et al. 1959:125).

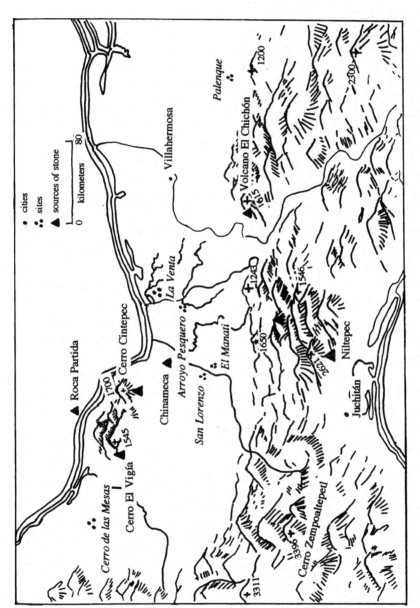

Figure 6.2 Map of La Venta area.
After Stirling (1943:LXXXIV(3)325)

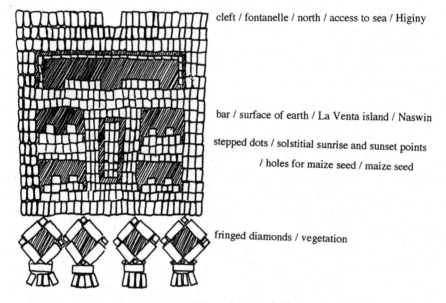

cleft / fontanelle / north / access to sea / Higiny

bar / surface of earth / La Venta island / Naswin

stepped dots / solstitial sunrise and sunset points / holes for maize seed / maize seed

fringed diamonds / vegetation

Figure 6.3   La Venta's Mosaic Pavement

This ceremonial court (Complex A) with its buried sea in the north and its effigy of a volcano in the south replicates the topography of La Venta's region, specifically the Isthmus of Tehuantepec.[4] The sea lies 15 kilometers to the north. To the south, the first major peak, 1219 meters high, is about 100 kilometers away, along a continuation of La Venta's central axis. The active volcano, El Chichón or La Unión, 1615 meters high, lies about 122 kilometers to the southeast of La Venta. Another peak approximately the same height as El Chichón is about the same distance to the southwest, such that the three form a triangle of natural mountains, creating an inverse pattern with the triangular arrangement of Phases II and III earth surface diagrams buried at La Venta.[5]

These mountains are visible today from the top of La Venta's pyramid whenever rains clear the sky of atmospheric haze and the black smoke from the nearby refinery, as is the range of twenty peaks, Cerro Zempoaltepec, that forms the current Mixe homeland. Metamorphic rocks such as the schists, andesites, and diorites used for some monumental sculptures came from these visible mountains. The serpentine used to create the massive offerings and mosaic pavements is thought to come from the flanks of the highest mountain on the Isthmus, the 2621-meter peak near Niltepec (Williams and Heizer 1965:12) not visible from La Venta.

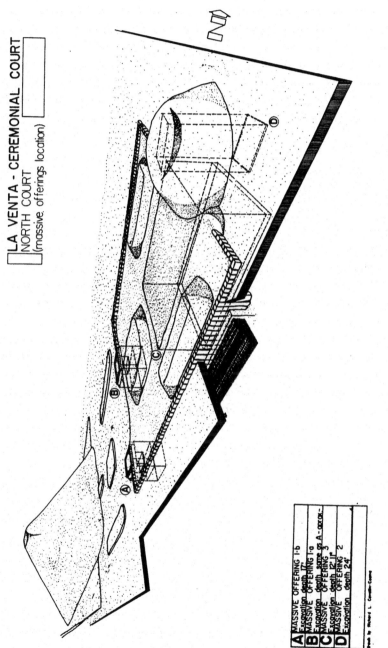

LA VENTA - CEREMONIAL COURT
NORTH COURT
(massive offerings location)

A	MASSIVE OFFERING 1-b
	Excavation depth 17'
B	MASSIVE OFFERING 1-a
	Excavation depth same as A - approx.
C	MASSIVE OFFERING 3
	Excavation depth 12 1/2'
D	MASSIVE OFFERING 2
	Excavation depth 24'

draw by Richard L. Cavallin-Cosma

Figure 6.4   La Venta's Massive Offerings.
Drawing by Richard Cavallin-Cosma, 1997, after Drucker et al. 1959

The remote locations from which the La Venta people procured stone were much more numerous and occupied a much larger area than at any of the other Olmec sites. With the exception of the basalts from the Cerro Cintepec in the Tuxtla range to the west, used as material for some of the large monuments, most of the stones came from the mountains to the south (Williams and Heizer 1965:12). By displaying stone from distant places, the built environment of La Venta demonstrated the inhabitants' intimate knowledge of the face of the earth from Roca Partida, the island in the Bay of Campeche, which is the source of the basalt columns, to El Chichón in the southeast and to Niltepec in the south.

Negotiating the terrain to locate the deposits of desirable stones and negotiating with the peoples and metacosmological (to use terms defined by Pannikar 1987) beings encountered on the journey and at the sought-for location must have made exciting subjects for many tales of exotic experiences and knowledge. Proof that the travelers had acquired such knowledge existed in the form of the materials they had acquired. Teams of people returning with loads of stone must have occasioned some sort of festivity. Digging the pits and depositing the serpentines prior to further modification of the ceremonial court also must have called for a ritual performance, possibly accompanied by narratives regarding the heroic adventures of negotiating the terrain and its dangers, natural and supernatural. These deeds responded to challenges beyond providing props for storytelling, however. The ultimate task was to define the known world, to model the terrestrial plane as well as the domains of above- and below-ground supernormal influences. In this way, ritual practitioners demonstrated their knowledge of these worlds and circumscribed spaces in which ritual practices aimed at supernatural knowledge and political control could be enacted.

The decision to depict the actual terrain with a shift in scale and complexity contained artistic, devotional, and political dimensions. Of necessity, the La Ventans made the mountain and sea effigies smaller than the actual objects but larger than previously had been attempted in Mesoamerica. Similarly, the La Ventans executed colossal heads, thrones, and stelae in the largest possible scale. In this emphasis on scale, the La Ventans followed the lead of their predecessors at San Lorenzo, whose monuments date several hundred years earlier. Large scale public works with ritual and political functions must have been a means by which the La Ventans demonstrated their knowledge of and mastery over the environment, their ability to organize labor to transport the material, and the skill of carvers. The power manifested by these acts related to skilled transport and crafting, arcane knowledge of distant realms, and expertise in negotiation with humans and supernatural forces.

The entire process of exploration, negotiation, returning home with information, setting out with crews, quarrying stone, carrying it back, and then fashioning sculptures or massive offerings with the stone, linked each feature of La Venta with a distant location, a series of events, and a temporal coordinate. Such focus enhanced the status of both the distant location and its replica at the ceremonial site. It is likely that once the stone had been transported to La Venta, carving it engaged another kind of power by attracting the presence of supernormal entities. Although few colonial or modern commentaries exist on the process of art- or architecture-making in Mesoamerica, Diego de Landa recounted some of the rituals involved in an annual renewal of wooden sculptures of the ancestors in sixteenth-century Yucatán. I discussed it at length in my work on Yaxchilán (Tate 1992:30–31).

Basically, patrons negotiated with potential carvers, who refused to accept the responsibility of carving because of the recognition by all involved that making images of powerful beings demanded the handling of spiritual energies, which were unpredictable and could cause harm to the carver or his family if the spiritual beings were displeased with any element of the performance of the carving process. Community elders were obliged to intercede and promised to accompany the carvers in the preparatory purification and fasting rites as well as during the period of seclusion in the month of Mol, during which the objects were manufactured. During the next twenty-day month, priests brought the sculptures into the community and the spirit of that ancestor was installed. The sculpture began its life as a vessel of spiritual energy. Given the likelihood that La Ventans designed their site as a cosmogram, it is also likely that they intended to activate spiritually the components of its design. Installing what Robert Plant Armstrong (1981) called "affecting presence" in ritual spaces and objects is common in many societies; it was accomplished through specific spiritual practices. George Michel wrote about the personal spiritual preparation for construction of a Hindu temple. The role of the artist, he said, was not self-expression, but

... to give visible form to the values of his society rather than to communicate a personal interpretation of those values ... That the artist thought of his work as a means of access to the divine is demonstrated in the large amount of literature that describes the mental preparation and ritual purification that he is to undergo before commending the work. Only in this way can the artist identify himself with the transcendental principles to which he attempts to give visible form (Michel 1977:54).

This comparison suggests that in addition to any economic value the stockpiling of stone might have had at La Venta, it is highly likely that the processes involved were considered sacred. As a result, the focus of spiritual energy on the Ceremonial Court imbued the place with a form of power important to the La Ventans. To explain how continuing ritual performance augments sacredness and accrues spiritual power in some societies, I offer another example from Hindu India:

> ... the Hindu sensibility appreciates the intensity of devotion brought to a place by the crowds of worshippers. As Ram Shankar Tripathi, one of the governing priests of Vishvanatha [Shiva, as "lord of all", in Benares] today, explained, 'Countless people have come here with worshipful hearts and have centered their devotion here at Vishveshvara for hundreds of years. By virtue of that history, this place is special. There is a saying, "Pilgrims make the *tirtha* [place of pilgrimage]" (Eck 1982:123).

Although Euramerican thinking considers repetition and redundancy as boring practices to be avoided, among the contemporary Maya they are employed poetically to generate "heat" in the heart of the speaker and in any ritual situation. Ritual heat causes one to be more sun-like, which is the ideal state (Gossen 1974:37). La Venta exhibits considerable redundancy in its design, as do Maya sites. Its builders initiated five phases of construction with the deposition of a massive offering, each of which consisted of thousands of nearly identical-shaped serpentine blocks. Similarly, there are three known mosaic pavements (Figure 6.5). Four colossal heads straddled the central axis north of Mound A-2. Seven large thrones exist. Hundreds of jade celts were counted and placed into the ground along the center line and above the mosaic pavements. Ten stelae were erected, five at the foot of Mound C (and four of these were nearly identical). Three giant fetus effigies (Tate and Bendersky 1999) marked the southern extent of the ritual architecture along the central axis. The repetitive tasks of building the site and its monuments likely proved, as Mary Helms (1993) has said in reference to other material, that the energizing link between society and its cosmological realm in which ancestors and the creative power reside was still active. The ability of La

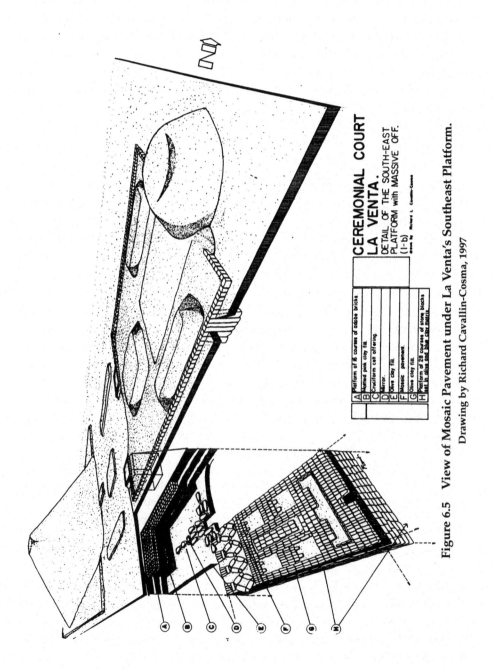

Figure 6.5   View of Mosaic Pavement under La Venta's Southeast Platform.

Drawing by Richard Cavallin-Cosma, 1997

Venta sculptors to create a likeness of a ruler and to represent a sacred, concealed, state of rapid transformation from one state of being to another, that of the fetus, proved the supernatural capabilities of the artists to access other realms of knowledge.

Thus, the site, its materials, and its monuments represented several forms of knowledge and power. La Venta demonstrated its inhabitants' knowledge of the Isthmus and the power to replicate it, which opened the energizing link between humans and supernatural powers. It also exhibited their knowledge of the skills of exploration, transport, trade, negotiation, and carving, each of which required supernatural sanction, and the power to manifest images reflecting those supernaturally controlled skills. I think that by comparing the ritual practices evident at La Venta with those of their descendants, the Mixe, it is possible to suggest more specifically the identity of some of those supernaturals whose sanction the people sought.

III.

Among the contemporary Mixe, the numinous beings, which ethnographer Frank Lipp calls "supernatural reality configurations" (1991) manifest as either male/female pairs or female pairs. Embodying the wind and thunder is a male/female pair (but considered generally as male) called *'Ene*, who I (Tate 2000) proposed is the contemporary descendent of the ubiquitous, anthropomorphic, almond-eyed Olmec supernatural. The earth's surface is a supernatural reality configuration that consists of a female dyad called *Na swi n*. Manifestations of life, growth, seas, lakes, and rivers is another female dyad called *Higiny*. These are the most important of several such beings.

Na swi n seems to be closely related to the symbolism of La Venta's mosaic pavements. She is the earth's surface and is called Mother Earth, the ". . . all-knowing of human affairs and the maternal repository of primordial wisdom" (Lipp 1991:30–31). She is associated with the north and with the color dark green. Her calendar name is One World. She is alive, and trees, water, plants, and mountain, and all the sustenance of humankind issue from her. As Lipp describes her: "The world and all it encompasses—trees, water, forests, mountains—is to the Mixe alive, and since it gives them their entire sustenance, they cannot exist without her" (1991:30–31). Thus far, the mosaic pavements have been interpreted as representations of the earth's surface and sprout vegetation.[6] They were made of green stone and were in the north relative to the mountain/pyra-

mid. In a previous paper (Tate 2000), I presented arguments that Joralemon's (1976:37) Olmec Dragon or God I and the four-nub headband worn
by humans and the almond-eyed supernatural are zoomorphic and regalia versions, respectively, of the bar-and-four-dots earth surface design
and are related to the Mixe's *Na swi n*.

The other Mixe female supernatural, *Higiny*, is the water goddess. She
presides over human birth and fishing. She reigns over springs, rivers,
and streams and is present in the veins of the male member. She has a
strong relationship with the day sign *Huginy*, meaning "Fontanelle" (Lipp
1991:68). I proposed that the La Venta Olmec conceived of springs, rivers,
streams, and the like as female and represented this concept with the cleft,
the opening between the human and supernatural realms, that can appear
on any supernatural being or important parts of the human body.[7]

Whereas *Na swi n* embodies the terrestrial aspects of earth, *Higiny* rules
over the bodies of water. If a dual concept of feminine supernatural reality configurations existed at La Venta, then the massive offerings of tons
of green serpentine dug into pits as large as 20-by-20 meters were probably related to a water goddess such as *Higiny* who controlled the riverine
and marine resources on which they depended heavily. The massive offerings may have symbolized the generation of human life attributed to
Higiny whereas the mosaic pavements represented an earth-surface female, from whom came all vegetation. Mound C, the mountain effigy,
probably represented the abode of '*Ene*. Four stelae depicting him stood
at the southern foot of Mound C, facing what may have been the actual
'*Ene* mountain on the horizon to the south (Figure 6.6).

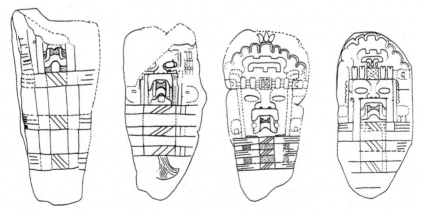

**Figure 6.6   The four "Thunder wearing Earth regalia" stelae at the foot of
Mound C. From left to right (east to west): Monuments 89, 88, 25/26, 27**

**Figure 6.7   Figurine from Arroyo Pesquero
(Dumbarton Oaks; height = 16.3 centimeters)**

Among the contemporary Mixe, *Na swi n* is the source of shamanic
healing power who calls men and women to serve as shamans. Being
called by *Na swi n* while under the influence of hallucinogenic mush-
rooms is one of two patterns of shamanic initiation among the Mixe. A
shaman called by *Na swi n* excels in knowledge of medicinal plants and
clairvoyance. Because the four-seed headband is a wearable version of
the bar-and-four-dots design, figures wearing either symbol probably
proclaimed their affiliation with *Na swi n* as a source of shamanic power
(Figure 6.7). The principal figure on La Venta Stela 2 exhibited a bar-and-
four-dots design in his headdress.

The other general type of shamanic initiation comes through a series of
dreams and involves interactions with *'Ene*, the thunder-rain deity. This
shaman literally travels to other villages to learn curing rituals and also
travels in dreams and visions to other shamanic cosmic levels (Lipp
1991:150–154). Did the Olmec conceive of a thunder-rain supernatural?
Most scholars (Reilly 1994:147; Joralemon 1996:56) think that the almond-
eyed supernatural with the four-seed headband represented a thunder-
rain deity except K. Taube (1996), who interprets it as maize. Furthermore,
Reilly (1994) proposed that the almond-eyed supernatural had a shamanic
function as a conduit for power, its image controlled by shamans.

I have proposed that the almond-eyed supernatural corresponds to
'Ene as a patron of shamanic power. Many Olmec personages wear a
headdress plaque depicting *'Ene*, such as the frontal figure on La Venta
Altar 5 and Monument 1 of San Martin Pajapan, a sculpture nearly iden-

tical to La Venta Monument 44, which also displays this plaque as an emblem of the personage's shamanic patron. *'Ene* himself can wear the *Na swi n* headband, which suggests to me that the earth was seen as the greatest power, sought as a patron even by *'Ene*. Some La Venta sculptures exhibited emblems of both *Na swi n* and *'Ene*. Of the four stelae depicting the almond-eyed supernatural at the southern foot of Mound C, assembled by González-Lauck (1997), two of the *'Ene* figures wore the earth-power headband. The other two probably did also, but we cannot be certain until the upper portions of those broken stelae are located. The jade figurine from Arroyo Pesquero, which I think was La Venta's sacred spring, wears his own *Na swi n* headband, plus a headdress plaque depicting *'Ene* wearing the same headband. On the back of the figure's head is a bar-and-four-dots *Na swi n* design as well (Figure 6.8).

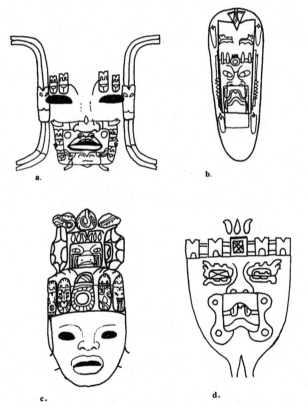

Figure 6.8   The maize seed headband (a) from the Las Limas figure; (b) celt from Arroyo Pesquero; (c) head of figurine from Arroyo Pesquero; (d) design on jade face from Las Tuxtlas

The Mixe call their vast assemblage of ritual procedures *Naswinmituni* or "work of the earth." The rules governing specific ceremonies are lengthy and specific, but generally, ritual practice involves creating a sacred space by placing offerings of pine bundles, each with a significant numerical count, and other items on the earth. In the dual-phase rituals, first resinous pine bundles are burned with other offerings to establish an exchange of sacred energy between the petitioners and *Na swi n*. (Figure 6.9). After this sacrifice, some green pine bundles are offered with other

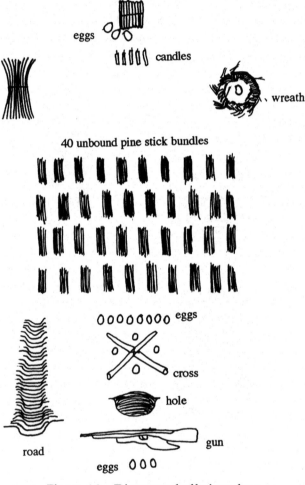

**Figure 6.9   Diagram of offerings for a
Mixe hunting ritual.**
After Lipp 1991:97

objects for the well-being and forgiveness of the earth and as advance thanks for that which the person asks. Sometimes the pine bundles represent a pine tree and sometimes (when in conjunction with circular pine wreaths) they are referred to as the "male member" (Lipp 1991:81–88).

This seems to be a continuation of the practice of placing many skillfully crafted green stone celts above the mosaic pavements at La Venta. In the Formative period, hard jade and green stones, imported from distant places and crafted into celts shaped like corn ears or male members, seem to have been the most valuable material offerings that could be made. Over each massive offering and its accompanying earth design pavement, the La Ventans deposited such celts in two kinds of arrangements. One consisted of numbers of celts laid in layers. Associated with the twin Phase II Mosaic Pavements was a cruciform arrangement, recently interpreted by Reilly (1994) as the world tree and cosmic axis.

The mosaic pavements may persist in Mixe ritual practice. As Lipp (1991) explained it, contemporary Mixe ritual practice includes those in which stars or constellations are petitioned for protection for an individual, which might include gaining wealth or knowledge or enhancing a close relationship with the powers of *Na swi n*. On the date set for the ceremony, the petitioner performs purifying practices including bathing in the river; wearing white clothing; and obtaining white or virgin beeswax, chickens, and candles. At night the petitioner's party journeys to the mountain. Table-like altars of boughs are set up and oriented toward specific astral bodies. Below the tables, five holes are dug to form a quincunx in the surface of the earth. Feathers from fowl to be sacrificed are placed in the holes, and eventually, blood from the birds drips into these holes in a specific sequence, followed, after prayer, by mescal. This constitutes an offering to the spirits of the deceased and as an invocation to the supernatural reality configurations to join and to partake of the offering.

When the quincunx design is used as part of a marriage ritual in western Mixe villages, the holes represent the bride, her mother, the groom, and his father. These individuals place four tamales in the holes near the end of a fifteen-day, postnuptial liminal period as offerings to the Christian holy beings, the Mixe supernaturals, the winds, and their ancestors. The quincunx is also used in a village protection rite, accompanied by the offerings of prepared food and sacrificed turkeys. The same quincunx design forms the pattern for maize seed divination. Although at various times the five holes may represent members of society involved in a specific ritual or celestial bodies petitioned by a shaman for success in his or her efforts, they simultaneously form receptacles for sacrifices to *Na swi n*. The quincunx and its antecedent at La Venta—the bar-and-four-dots design, which formed the major element on the mosaic pavements and also was worn as a headdress ornament by shamans—related to the power of the all-knowing, sacred, female earth and to the shamanic power she grants to some individuals.

IV.

A third way in which the La Ventans expressed their concepts of power was through their selection of a subject for portable sculpture: that of human bodies engaged in spiritual practices with the intention of cultivating knowledge unbounded by the limitations of the human mind. Over their massive offerings, La Ventans cached figurines and other objects carved of precious stone. Although the monuments may represent specific individuals, such those portrayed in the colossal heads, the figurines' significance seems to lie in their representation of a specific pose. Seldom do modern researchers focus on culturally accepted postures— that is, on specific positions that can be held comfortably for some time. This situation is rapidly changing as the body becomes recognized by contemporary thinkers as subject to political contestation. In a recent book, Maxine Sheets-Johnstone points out that in Western theory, language has been the primary, if not the sole, establisher of meaning. In ignoring posture and other spatio-kinetic behaviors,

> Our intercorporeal semantics and its rich and complex archetypal forms in turn disappear without a trace . . . Were we to turn as intensively toward the body as we have toward language, we would find that the corporeal turn would yield insights no less extraordinary than those of any kind of linguistic turn (Sheets-Johnstone 1994:111–112).

The ancient makers of the stone figurines must have intended to use posture as a means to communicate information beyond linguistic boundaries because similar figurines were buried at sites across southern Mesoamerica. It is obvious that posture was a primary bearer of meaning, for the subjects of most Olmec stone figurines do not include regalia or ritual objects that are so evident on monumental sculpture. Some have argued that the figurines may have been dressed. Before leaping to that conclusion, we should consider them as they were found and note that the human figure was restricted to a small set of specific postures with a few variations. Through an examination of several hundred Olmec stone figurines, I determined that there were only four basic postures: standing in a flexed-knee pose with evenly distributed weight, seated cross-legged with a straight back, a transitional pose in which one knee or calf touches the ground and the other leg is poised for action (known as the shamanic transformation pose (Reilly 1989), and a contortionist's backbend in which the feet rest on the head (Tate 1998). In stone figurines, humans were portrayed as adults, as children, as fetuses, in transformation to an animal alter ego, and as dwarfs or hunchbacks. Restriction to four may seem insignificant, except when one considers that a study of posture in art traditions and cultural habits around the world found about 1,000 distinct, codified postures (Hewes 1955).

Perhaps the lack of written documentation or verbal testimony regarding the intended meaning of the postures has dissuaded most researchers from investigating posture in three-dimensional art. However, direct corporeal knowledge may be called upon to reveal their significance. In certain Eastern traditions, it is assumed that corporeal knowledge exists and that it is the result of a establishing a disciplined link between body and mind. Charged by vital energy, such a link also has the potential to allow perception of realities beyond the mundane. Three of the four postures in which Olmec carvers rendered their subjects are specific, well-known postures of meditation. Because I have dealt with this at length elsewhere (Tate 1998), suffice it to say here that the twenty-four standing adult figures excavated at La Venta are carved without clothing or regalia (except the occasional loin cover) and consistently stand with flexed knees, straight back, evenly distributed weight, and arms either relaxed by their sides or bent with hands at the midsection. This posture is fundamental to meditation in several traditions, notably Chinese T'ai Chi and Hatha Yoga. Such a parallel does not presuppose a direct historical connection. It does reflect that each culture sought a means of cultivating a mind/body connection, probably independently. The feasibility of a mind/body connection is impossible to prove intellectually because it cannot be perceived intellectually.

The point has been made repeatedly since the time of Dögon, the 12th-century Japanese monk, or even much earlier in the Indian Vedas that one cannot understand the goal of meditation through purely intellectual means but only through practice (cultivation) and intention (Yuasa 1987:115). At La Venta, meditation postures were portrayed, and therefore, certain individuals must have engaged in meditation practices. This statement does not imply a specific spiritual goal for the meditation practice. That Mesoamerican peoples believed that the body had links with vital energies outside of itself is stressed by Alfredo López-Austin in his work on the body in Aztec ideology: "There is nothing in Mesoamerican thought to authorize our believing there existed a body-soul dichotomy. To the contrary, according to indigenous thought, the embodiment of psychic entities is quite apparent" (López-Austin 1980). Whether they subscribed to the Hindu concept of vital energy as absolute consciousness to the contemporary health practitioner Dean Ornish, M.D.'s, goal of focused stillness, or to some other objective is not clear. But they apparently engaged in meditation techniques for some purpose likely connected with knowledge of a reality beyond that perceived solely by the mind.

In a book comparing Eastern and Western approaches to a mind-body theory, Yasuo Yuasa found that most Western thinkers dismiss the possibility of an "achieved mind-body unity" (1987:4). Western intellectual and scientific methodologies

> ... assume ... that the connection between mind and body must be constant (not developed) and universal (not variable among different people). Since they do not consider exceptional personal achievements, the body-mind unity remains for them a theoretical possibility rather than a state actualized by exemplary individuals such as religious and artistic masters (Kasulis 1987:2–3).

Because the state of mind-body unity must be achieved, it is not a constant awareness that is either "on" or "off." It exists in degrees and is augmented through the process of cultivation or practice, which is precisely what the Olmec stone figurines illustrate. They could have been buried at the site to charge the energizing link between the community the supernormal forces.

During La Venta's Phase III, the sixteen standing meditation figurines of Offering 4 were cached just east of the edge of the buried Massive Offering 3 (Figure 6.10). In the northeast platform (a meter east of Offering 4), during the same phase, La Ventans cached Offerings 5 and 6, both consisting of jade earspools, a stone maskette/headdress ornament representing 'Ene, and a string of beads. These items were laid on a bed of cinnabar. Offering 7 had similar contents but may have been deposited in an earlier phase (Drucker et al. 1959:152–174). The close spatial association of the regalia of shamans, perhaps shamanic rulers, and the meditation figures suggests a link between the practitioners of meditation and the shamanic rulers. Either the three rulers whose regalia was deposited there also sought supernormal awareness through meditation, or they valued counsel from such individuals. Because standing meditation figures have been found from all regions of Middle Formative Mesoamerica, including Chiapas, Guerrero, Chalcatzingo, Puebla, and of course Tabasco, the figurines could have been used by spiritual practitioners to illustrate precisely the poses of meditation to others speaking a different language. The teacher also would have demonstrated some sort of breathing technique. As Yuasa (1987:4) points out, the first step in establishing a connection between mind and body is to decide with the available mind to place the body in a special form or posture, then to establish the link through the breath because it can be controlled autonomically or consciously.

Although Yuasa found that in modern neurophysiology, psychoanalysis, and philosophy, nothing specifically contradicts the concept of achieved mind/body unity, and that some Western thinkers devote research to abnormal states, they usually investigate pathological or sub-

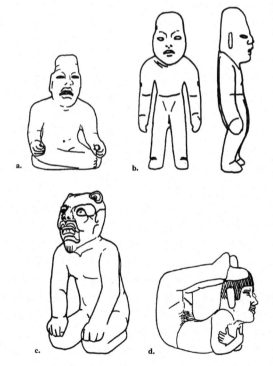

Figure 6.10 Jade figurines from La Venta

normal states rather than the supernormal. Whether or not readers accept for themselves that a mind/body unity can be cultivated, they
should certainly not expect the ancient Olmecs to conform to a contemporary Western rational belief system.

In Eastern traditions of spiritual practice, once one attains a consistently high level of awareness beyond the rational, powers accrue, such
as clairvoyance, control over pain, and so forth. In Vedanta philosophy,
these are not the goal of meditation practice but merely a by-product.
Such powers could have been considered desirable in the shamanic
worldview at La Venta, or mental clarity; physical well-being; or enlight-
enment, that is, the perception that the individual is one with absolute
consciousness and its energy, may have been their goal. In any case, these
figurines (found at La Venta and throughout Middle Formative
Mesoamerica) demonstrate that meditation practices existed, likely
aimed at achieving a supernormal state equated with some sort of spiritual power. Based on the paucity of their portrayal in the art of later cultures, these practices apparently did not persist widely into the Classic
period. Sitting cross-legged with an upright back remained a posture of
authority, however, illustrated in Maya, Zapotec, and Teotihuacan ceramic figurines and occasionally jades and other mediums.

V.

In the first chapter of this volume, the editors addressed "the poetical
questions of what makes a proper or powerful text." To me, this raised
the issue of how the La Ventans conceived power. It appears that for the
La Ventans, as Michel Foucault suggested, ". . . power and knowledge directly imply one another . . . " (1977:27). However, contrary to Foucault's
assertion, we may be able to distinguish in the ritual and spiritual practices at La Venta a kind of knowledge that does not "presuppose and constitute at the same time power relations" (Foucault 1977:27).

Three complexes of objects and the performances that the society enacted in creating and using them have been explored in this chapter. The
first section discussed broad concepts of knowledge and power residing in
metacosmological beings that were activated by creative acts including
travel, trade, and art-making. In complex, performative aesthetic acts, the
builders of La Venta embodied these in their ritual space, thereby centering
power there. Individuals acquired, on behalf of the community, knowledge
of distant realms and peoples. Through coordinated effort, La Ventans
gathered into the heart of their realm proof of this knowledge in the form

of materials. Further testifying to their cognizance of distant places and peoples, they replicated the two most powerful surrounding features of the landscape, the mountain and the sea, and carved in several thrones images of the caves they had explored. Their skill at crafting, transport, trade, and negotiations with human and supernatural forces was manifested in the visible sculptures. The art-making process itself, if it was similar to that of the Maya, probably involved petitioning, sacrificing to, spiritual oneness with, and installation of powerful forces or beings in the sculptures.

Several aesthetic choices were emphasized in "Olmec art" (to use two Western terms). Makers derived forms from actual observations of topography, of ritual actions, of specific events and individuals. The Olmec tendency toward three-dimensionality in sculpture and architecture makes sense when such replication was their goal. I have argued elsewhere that Olmec art is to a significant degree stylized (Tate 1995), not "realistic" as others assert. Although the subject matter is based on the things and beings the Olmec observed (some through nonrational means), the forms are always simplified to emphasize a particular aspect of the object; for example, the standing figures omit anatomical detail to emphasize pose. This distinction is important because whereas realism is faithful to the outward appearance of a thing, stylization seeks patterns and inner character, and I think the Olmecs engaged in the latter practice. Possibly the process of conceptualization of a sculpture or architectural form was similar to what art historian Ananda Coomaraswamy described for Indian art:

> . . . rarely if ever have Indian artists drawn with a model before them, and the image proper is at all times, from first to last, obtained by a process of mental visualisation . . . Thus the form is always reached by a process of synthesis and abstraction, rather than by observation, and is always in the last analysis a memory image. When we perceived increased reality or truth, we must ascribe this, not to a change of habit but to heightened consciousness, a more complete identification of consciousness with the theme itself,—in other words, to a more profound empathy (Coomaraswamy 1965).

In such a manner, the design decisions the La Ventans made, notably replication of geographic features and of powerful individuals, the emphasis on grand scale, and the insistent repetition, conceptually linked the processes of making the work with the forces it invoked, and thereby "constituted a powerful or proper text" (Coomaraswamy 1965).

In the second section, the chapter correlated La Venta's principal constructions—Mound C, the massive offerings, and the mosaic pavements—with analogous contemporary Mixe supernaturals '*Ene* (thunder-rain); *Higiny* (a female ruling bodies of water, childbirth, fishing); and *Na swi n* (the all-knowing earth mother, who judges human behavior). These effigies of the metacosmological and metameteorological supernaturals probably served as the most potent available spaces for the practice of rituals directed at least in part to these very powers. The mosaic pavements, consisting of precious material and covering layers of colored clays and offerings of celts, served as offerings to *Na swi n*. Groups may have ascended Mound C at night to make earth altars and supplicate the forces embodied as stars for successful shamanic practice or political endeavors. The effort of building sea effigies may have been intended to honor *Higiny* for her assistance in childbirth and fishing. Several parallels between the evidence for ritual practice at La Venta and that of the Mixe today were explored. These included the prominent use of quincunx earth-altar designs, the structurally similar practices of placing green pine bundles and caching green celts on the earth as offerings to her. If the analogy between La Venta and Mixe ritual practices is viable, shamans called by *Na swi n* were clairvoyant and learned to cure with medicinal plants. Those called by '*Ene* practiced divination with maize seeds, saw powerful designs revealed in dreams (which they probably painted on their bodies, forming the prototypes for the designs incised on so many Olmec figures), and flew to other realms to acquire esoteric knowledge with which they could cure or harm others and control situations. Shamans likely assisted in the grand rituals accompanying the placement of the massive offerings and mosaic pavements, perhaps placing the layers of jade celts, figurines, effigies of sea creatures and other crafted offerings into the altar of the earth. Through ritual performances, the La Ventans encoded shamanic power associated with metameteorological and metacosmological beings into their sacred spaces.

Finally, hidden below the surface of the earth were the things apparently considered to embody knowledge of the most distant realms and power of the most potent supernaturals and humans. The sources of Olmec jade, from which a few of the standing and seated meditation figures, as well as celts, headdress "maskettes" representing '*Ene*, earspools, beads, and so on were carved, are so difficult to find that with one exception, they remain unknown today. La Ventans located and imported from the other side of the Isthmus, across the mountains, the serpentines that constitute the massive offerings and other objects. It seems that the greater the knowledge and energy required to obtain or accomplish something, the more potent the La Ventans considered it to be. This idea is true of the quest for their goal in meditation as well, which demanded focus, intention, and assiduous practice. Seeing potency as distant and difficult to attain does not mean conceiving power as something separate from oneself.

Most Mesoamericanists seem to agree with Foucault that all power is relationally constituted relative to a body of knowledge. A similar approach to power has been discussed by practice theorists, such as Marshall Sahlins, Sherry B. Ortner, and Pierre Bourdieu:

> ... the dynamic intrinsic to how people do things in culturally effective ways ha[s] delineated a surer focus on the expedient and negotiated dimensions of human activity or, in other words, the play of power in the micropolitics of all social action. In this context, power refers less to physical control of people than to social prestige or the concern to secure the dominance of models of reality that render one's world coherent and viable (Bell 1998:206).

The process of creating a ceremonial center surely aimed at securing a dominant model of reality. Certainly political struggles and micropolitical negotiations over gender issues, household economy, and the like occurred at La Venta. However, these ideas still situate power in negotiations among individuals and do not acknowledge beliefs such as those of the Maya and Zapotec that all individual power is a manifestation of a cosmic vital energy.

Power, in the form of the life-principle (the Tzotzil *ch'ulel* or Zapotec *pèe*) existed independently but flowed through humans as well as other things. The Tzotzil Mayan word *ch'ulel* refers to an inner vital energy that permeates living things, sacred places, time, materials, and meteorological forces (Freidel et al. 1993:182). As ethnographer Evon Vogt explained, "The most important interaction in the universe is not between persons and objects, but among the inner souls of persons and material objects" (1976:18–19). Similarly, the Zapotec term *pèe* refers to wind, breath, and spirit. It animates things such as clouds, wind, lightning, time, the heart and blood of a person or animal, and the life forces of plants (Marcus and Flannery 1996:19). We are still unaware of Mixe-Zoquean terms for power and knowledge. However, it seems highly likely that Middle Formative period ideology centered around a layered, animated universe in which the more challenging the aesthetic task; the greater movement,

knowledge, and time devoted to replicating the sacred; the more inex-
orable the meteorological or cosmological force one petitioned, then the
greater the power that accrued to the community and its individuals. At
least this overarching concept of power—that which animates all things,
generates life, and regenerates life—is not subject to human micropoli-
tics, but it can be cultivated. Mesoamerican peoples did engage in negotiation with the many manifestations of vital energy—with rain-thunder
and earth beings, with ancestors, with their own and others' animal
souls—through ritual. Performance of ritual acknowledged and honored
the existence of power and aimed to unite external power with the body
and consciousness of the performers. Indulging in political negotiation
and forgetting one's identity with the community and cosmos via the energizing link erodes one's ability to focus on such spiritual power. By
centralizing knowledge and power in a ritual space through multiple
means, La Ventans created a place in which these energies were tangible
through spiritual practices. As a poetic statement about the impregnation
of architectural spaces and crafted objects with power, the text which the
La Ventans created did not depend on the rational vision of the spectator
(because the most sacred parts could not be seen) but on the conceptual
knowledge and ritual practice of the participants.

References

Armstrong, R. P.
   1981   *The Powers of Presence: Consciousness, Myth, and Affecting Presence.*
          Philadelphia: University of Pennsylvania Press.
Beals, R. L.
   1945   *Ethnology of the Western Mixe.* Berkeley: University of California Press.
Bell, C.
   1998   Performance. *Critical Terms for Religious Studies.* Edited by M. C. Taylor.
          Chicago: University of Chicago Press. 205–224.
Benson, E. P.
   1971   *An Olmec Figure at Dumbarton Oaks.* Studies in Pre-Columbian Art and
          Archaeology 8. Washington, D.C.: Dumbarton Oaks.
Campbell, L. R., and T. S. Kaufman.
   1976   A Linguistic Look at the Olmec. *American Antiquity* 41:80–89.
Carrasco, P.
   1966   Ceremonias publicas paganas entre los Mixes de Tamazulapam. *Summa*
          antropologica en homenaje a Roberto J. Weitlaner. Edited by A. Pompa y
          Pompa. México, D.F.: Instituto Nacional de Antropología e Historia.
          309–312.
Coomaraswamy, A. K.
   1965   *History of Indian and Indonesian Art.* 2nd ed. New York: Dover Publica-
          tions. 35.

Covarrubias, M.
   1946   El Arte "Olmeca" o de La Venta. *Cuadernos Americanos* 24(4):153–179.
Drucker, P., R. F. Heizer, and R. J. Squier.
   1959   *Excavations at La Venta, Tabasco, 1955.* Bureau of American Ethnology Bulletin 170. Washington, D.C.: Smithsonian Institution.
Eck, D. L.
   1982   *Banaras, City of Light.* Princeton: Princeton University Press.
Foucault, Michel.
   1977   *Discipline and Punish: The Birth of the Prison.* Translated by Alan Sheridan. New York: Pantheon Books.
Freidel, D. A., L. Schele, and J. Parker.
   1993   *Maya Cosmos: Three Thousand Years on the Shaman's Path.* New York: William Morrow.
González-Lauck, R. B.
   1994   La antigua ciudad olmeca en La Venta, Tabasco. *Los Olmecas en Mesoamerica.* Edited by J. E. Clark. México, D.F.: El Equilibrista/Turner Libros/CITIBANK/MEXICO. 93–112.
   1997   Acerca de pirámides de tierra y seres sobrenaturales: observaciones preliminares en torno al Edificio C-1. La Venta, Tabasco. *Arqueologia* 17(Enero-Junio):79–98.
Gossen, G. H.
   1974   *Chamulas in the World of the Sun: Time and Space in a Maya Oral Tradition.* Prospect Heights, Ill.: Waveland Press.
Heizer, R. E.
   1971   Commentary on: "The Olmec Region—Oaxaca." *Contributions of the University of California Archaeological Research Facility* 11:51–69.
Helms, M. W.
   1993   *Craft and the Kingly Ideal: Art, Trade, and Power.* Austin, Tex.: University of Texas Press.
Hewes, G. W.
   1955   World Distribution of Certain Postural Habits. *American Anthropologist* (n.s.) 57(2):231–244.
Joralemon, P. D.
   1976   The Olmec Dragon: A Study in Precolumbian Iconography. *Origins of Religious Art and Iconography in Preclassic Mesoamerica.* Edited by H. B. Nicholson. Los Angeles: UCLA Latin American Center. 27–72.
   1996   In Search of the Olmec Cosmos: Reconstructing the World View of Mexico's First Civilization. *Olmec Art of Ancient Mexico.* Edited by E. P. Benson and B. d. l. Fuente. Washington, D.C.: National Gallery of Art. 51–60.
Kasulis, T. P.
   1987   Editor's Introduction. *The Body: Toward an Eastern Mind-Body Theory.* By Yasuo Yuasa. Edited by T. P. Kasulis. Translated by Shigenori Nagatomo and Thomas P. Kasulis. Albany, N.Y.: State University of New York Press.

Lipp, F. J.
  1991   *The Mixe of Oaxaca: Religion, Ritual and Healing*. Austin, Tex.: University of Texas Press.
López-Austin, A.
  1980   *The Human Body and Ideology: Concepts of the Ancient Nahuas*. Translated by T. Ortíz de Montellano and B. Ortíz de Montellano. Salt Lake City: University of Utah Press. 2–3.
Marcus, J., and K. V. Flannery.
  1996   *Zapotec Civilization: How Urban Society Evolved in Mexico's Oaxaca Valley. New Aspects of Antiquity*. London: Thames and Hudson.
Michel, G.
  1977   *The Hindu Temple*. New York: Harper & Row.
Miller, W. S.
  1956   *Cuentos Mixes*. Biblioteca de Folklore Indígena. México, D.F.: Instituto Nacional Indigenista.
Nahmad, S.
  1965   *Los Mixes: estudio social y cultural de la región del Zempoaltepetl y del Istmo de Tehuantepec*. Memoria del Instituto Nacional Indigenista XI. Mexico, D.F.: Instituto Nacional Indiginista.
Pannikar, R.
  1987   Deity. *The Encyclopedia of Religion, Volume 4*. Edited by Charles J. Adams. New York: Macmillan.
Parsons, E. C.
  1936   *Mitla: Town of Souls and Other Zapotec-Speaking Pueblos of Oaxaca, Mexico*. Chicago: University of Chicago Press.
Reilly, F. K., III.
  1989   The Shaman in Transformation Pose: A Study of the Theme of Rulership in Olmec Art. *Record of the Art Museum, Princeton University* 48(2):4–21.
  1994   Enclosed Ritual Spaces and the Watery Underworld in Formative Period Architecture: New Observations on the Function of La Venta Complex A. *Seventh Palenque Round Table, 1989*. Edited by M. G. Robertson and V. M. Fields. San Francisco: Pre-Columbian Art Research Institute. 125–136.
Rodríguez E., M. a. L. B. R.
  1974   *La cultura Mixe: simbologia de un humanismo*. México, D.F.: Editorial Jus, S. A.
Sheets-Johnstone, M.
  1994   *The Roots of Power: Animate Form and Gendered Bodies*. Chicago: Open Court.
Stirling, Matthew W.
  1943   La Venta's Green Stone Tigers. *National Geographic* 84(3):321–332.
Tate, C.
  1992   *Yaxchilan: The Design of a Maya Ceremonial City*. Austin, Tex.: University of Texas Press.

1995   Art in Olmec Culture. *The Olmec World: Ritual and Rulership.* Edited by
        J. Guthrie. Princeton: Art Museum, Princeton University/Harry N.
        Abrams. 47–68.

1998   La Venta's Stone Figurines and the Olmec Body Politic. *Memorias del
        Tercer Simposio Internacional de Mayistas.* México, D.F.: Instituto de In-
        vestigaciones Filológicas, Universidad Nacional Autonóma de México.
        335–358.

2000   Patrons of Shamanic Power: La Venta's Supernatural Entities in Light
        of Mixe Beliefs. *Ancient Mesoamerica* 10(2):169–188).

Tate, C. E., and G. Bendersky.

1999   Olmec Sculptures of the Human Fetus. *Perspectives in Biology and Medi-
        cine* (Spring).

Taube, K.

1996   The Olmec Maize God: The Face of Corn in Formative Mesoamerica.
        RES 29/30:39–81.

Vogt, E. Z.

1976   *Tortillas for the Gods: A Symbolic Analysis of Zinacanteco Rituals.* Cam-
        bridge, Mass.: Harvard University Press.

Williams, H., and R. R. Heizer.

1965   Sources of Rocks Used in Olmec Monuments. *Sources of Stones Used in
        Prehistoric Mesoamerica.* Contributions of the University of California
        Archaeological Research Facility 1. Berkeley: University of California
        Archaeological Research Facility. 1–40.

Yuasa, Yasuo

1987   *The Body: Toward an Eastern Mind-Body Theory.* Edited by Thomas P. Ka-
        sulis. Translated by Nagatomo Shigenori and Thomas P. Kasulis. SUNY
        Series in Buddhist Studies. Albany, N.Y.: State University of New York
        Press.

Notes

1. The ancient Maya, certain Olmec groups such as the people at Teopantecuanitlan, and the contemporary Maya and Mixe all organize space according to
solstitial rise and set points.

2. Elsie Parsons (Parsons 1936) suggested that the bar and four dots represents
the world quarters or four corners of the earth. Here I modify her observation by
referring specifically to the solstitial sunrise and -set points, marked by the Olmec
at other sites, such as by the monoliths at Teopantecuanitlan's sunken court (Martinez Donjuan 1995:106).

3. The bar-and-four-dots has been regarded as a place name for La Venta (Benson 1971:29) and alternatively as an indicator of God Number One, referred to as
a dragon, in a scheme of ten Olmec gods proposed by David Joralemon (1976:21)
but not universally accepted. The "dragon" is a zoomorphic character with ser-
rated eyebrows who frequently sprouts vegetation and has been further identified as a crocodilian, the source of vegetative fertility, by Reilly (1994:15, 133).

4. As do most pyramids in Mesoamerica, this mound probably represents a mountain or volcano despite the fact that its shape was a stepped pyramid (González-Lauck 1994).

5. Today's archaeologists consider problematic the phase assignments made by the Smithsonian archaeologists.

6. This powerful supernatural reality configuration regulates human behavior in the agricultural fields and countryside, both of which are sacred to her. Entering the agricultural field, one honors its sacred nature by wearing clean clothes. Likewise, when returning home, one washes hands and feet before entering. In the countryside, the Mixe must control their anger and sexual desire lest they arouse the wrath of Naswin, who can penalize a family for years for wrongful actions.

7. The cleft has been interpreted as ". . . the symbol of contact between divinity and man by way of the crown or pineal gland . . . " (Covarrubias 1946) and as a signifier of "jaguar power," used to protect various parts of the body (Benson 1971) and as the portal in the earth to the Otherworld (Freidel et al. 1993: 429, n.21).

Merging Myth and Politics:
The Three Temple Complex
at Teotihuacan

Annabeth Headrick

The scholarship on the site of Teotihuacan has suffered because of comparison. The Maya created stelae, large, elaborately carved monuments with clearly depicted images of kings. By comparison, the Teotihuacanos left us only with murals that have a repetitive, cookie cutter–like nature. The same personages are stamped out over and over again, seemingly denying their individualism. The Maya had a sophisticated writing system with which they recorded the birthdays, anniversaries, accessions, and deaths of their kings. They placed these carved records in their main plazas, very much in the public view. In contrast, glyphs may appear only rarely at Teotihuacan. When they do appear, complex syntax is largely missing. The glyphs seem to be nouns, labels to identify an individual name or a corporate entity. Instead of appearing in highly visible public locations, the limited writing occurs on pottery or murals in residential structures. The settlement pattern of Maya cites has an organic quality. Radiating roads, much like an octopus with fluctuating tendrils, connect the ceremonial center to clusters of residential structures. In opposition, Teotihuacan has a rigid, planned, grid-like organization. Families may have been assigned a square plot of land, oriented to the main avenue, and they and their descendants lived within this allotted box for hundreds of years.

In short, scholars have often highlighted what is different about Teotihuacan.[1] They have compared it to the famous Maya, and seeing differences, they have sometimes ostracized it from the Mesoamerican tradition. Ironically, the comparison that has so differentiated Teotihuacan can also serve to reincorporate the site back into the Mesoamerican tradition. Teotihuacan need not be dealt with in isolation, for comparison can offer new insight into the iconography and political structure of this decidedly individual but nevertheless Mesoamerican site.

This chapter follows the premise that there are fundamental Mesoamerican beliefs that transcend the various cultural and temporal boundaries in Mesoamerica. I am not proposing that Mesoamerican religion did not change over its 4,000-year history, but I do suggest that we can identify core Mesoamerican myths that withstood the tests of time. Furthermore, key images in these myths were based on Mesoamerican aesthetic tropes that formed the scaffolding for the narrative. Much like variations on a theme, these myths were elaborated upon, manipulated, and differently stressed, but nevertheless, the basic aesthetic trope survived.

The examination of one core Mesoamerican myth, the myth of the three stones of creation, will illustrate this. David Freidel et al. (1993) have shown that this myth appears in several Mesoamerican cultural groups. I hope to demonstrate that it also appears at Teotihuacan and that the particular triadic, aesthetic trope regulated other expressions of power and legitimacy at the site. This exercise will demonstrate that Teotihuacan did participate in the Mesoamerican tradition, and as a nice bonus, it will reveal a possible political structure of this well-known, but little understood, site.

Mesoamerica and the Myth of the Three Stones of Creation

In Maya versions of this myth, creator deities placed three stones at the beginning of time. Stela C from the Maya site of Quiriguá records this event in a hieroglyphic text. It reads:

On the date 4 Ahaw 8 Kumk'u
The three stones were set.
The Jaguar Paddler and the Stingray Paddler seated a stone.
It happened at the First-Five-Sky-Place, the Jaguar-throne-stone.
The Black-House-Red-God seated a stone.
It happened at the Earth Partition Place, the Snake-throne-stone.
Itzamna seated the Waterlily-throne-stone.
It happened at the Lying-down-sky place, the First-three-stone place
(Freidel et al. 1993:66–67; Schele and Looper 1996:92).

This is just one of several accounts of the three throne stones that were placed by the gods at the time of creation. After this act, the gods separated the sky from the earth and erected the world tree at the center of the universe.

Freidel et al. (1993) highlighted the central importance of this myth. They recognized that the act of placing the three stones of creation served to center the cosmos. With a center, the sky could be lifted from the waters of the earth. In addition, they identified a Maya constellation of three stars arranged in a triangular pattern as the three stones of creation. However, the three stones did not exist just in the sky, for every Maya had a symbolic reproduction of the three stones in her house. Even today, people in Mesoamerica make their hearths by placing three stones in a triangular fashion and balance their griddle on these stones. Just as the three stars in the sky served to center the cosmos, these three hearth stones provide a center for the modern Maya household. In other words, the three stones exist in the heavens and on earth. Both the heavens and the earth have a center, and the Maya symbolically lived, and still live, at that center.[2]

Once the myth was revealed through textual analysis, it was apparent that the three stones of creation had always been in the art of the Maya, just waiting to be discovered. In the *Madrid Codex*, a turtle, identified as a nearby constellation, has the three stones on its back (Figure 7.1), yet such images did not begin with the Maya. On a celt from the earlier Olmec (Figure 7.2), a hand appears to set the three stones (Reilly 1994). An eye near the stones is a standard symbol for a star, indicating that the event transpired in the sky. Just as in the Maya text, the Olmec hand sets the three stones in the sky at the time of creation. The Postclassic Mixtec also included pictures of the three stones in their painted manuscripts. In the *Selden Codex*, three stones appear underneath the world tree (Figure 7.3). This directly matches the Maya myth in which the gods place the three stones and then erect the world tree. The myth even survived among the Aztec of postconquest times. In the *Codex Chimalpopoca*, the mythical ancestors of the Aztec are told to shoot arrows in the cardinal directions. The text then reads:

> And when you have shot your arrows
> place them in the hands of Xiuhtecutli,
> the God of Fire, the Old God
> the three who are to guard him—
> Mixcoatl, Tozpan, and Ihuitl
> these are the names of the three hearth
> stones (Knab and Sullivan 1994:63).

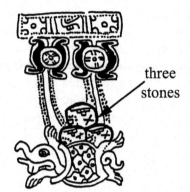

three
stones

**Figure 7.1 Turtle with
three stones on its back,**
Madrid Codex

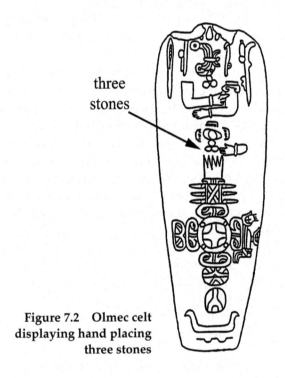

three
stones

**Figure 7.2 Olmec celt
displaying hand placing
three stones**

Once again, the concept of the three stones is connected with mythical time and the concept of the hearth.

These examples demonstrate that the concept of the three stones was a core component of Mesoamerican myth. I want to stress that this is Mesoamerican myth. It is not an idea limited to one of the many cultures of Mesoamerica, for it appears, at the very least, among the Olmec,

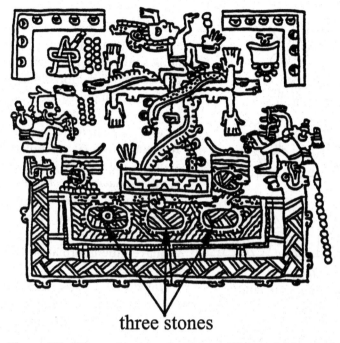

three stones

Figure 7.3 Three stones under the world tree, *Selden Codex*

Maya, Mixtec, and Aztec. In addition, the myth does not seem to have a temporal limitation among the urban cultures of Mesoamerica. The Olmec celt dates to the Late Formative period (500 BC–200 AD), suggesting that the myth enjoyed a livelihood of approximately 2,000 years in ancient Mesoamerican art and texts, and the myth of the three hearth stones still survives in modern-day Maya communities. Both the longevity and multicultural nature of the myth indicate that all Mesoamericans held some concept of the three stones of creation, placed by the gods at the beginning of time.

Teotihuacan and the Three Mountains

So, we turn to Teotihuacan. Contemporary with the Maya, and fast on the heels of the Olmec, we would expect to see evidence of the myth of the three stones of creation at this very prominent Mesoamerican site. In fact, we do, but I would argue that it appears not in the form of three stones

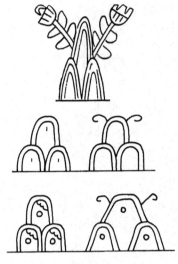

Figure 7.4
Three mountain motif

but in the ubiquitous three mountain motif (Figure 7.4). Drawn as three simple U-shaped forms, the mountains sometimes have snow-capped peaks or flowers growing from them, further securing their identification as mountains. This motif has long been an accepted standard symbol in the Teotihuacan visual vocabulary. Scholars have recognized it as a common motif and have suggested that it is associated with water, vegetation, and fertility, a common iconographic identification for imagery of which we have little information (von Winning 1987:11–12).

However, if we approach Teotihuacan from a Mesoamerican perspective, it is tempting to view the three mountain motif as an adaptation of the myth of the three stones of creation. Tempting as this is, the tertiary nature and the fact that mountains have a conceptual similarity to stones is not enough to secure an identification. The identification requires some explanation for the transformation of the myth. Most likely, the transformation resulted from the Teotihuacanos' need to adopt a metaphor that fit the reality of their daily existence. That daily existence included a valley with three prominent mountains.

Teotihuacan sits in a broad basin ringed by a series of mountain ranges. Out of these mountain ranges, three mountains can easily be chosen as the three most visually striking. These are Cerro Gordo in the north, Cerro Patlachique in the south, and Cerro Malinalco in the west (Figures 7.5–7.7). The prominence of these mountains is so apparent that Manuel Gamio (1979:8–14) highlighted them in his comprehensive study of the valley's geography. Unaware of their connection to the mountain motif, he published photographs and included detailed descriptions of these three mountains. However, a secure connection between these mountains and the motif requires proof of the importance of these mountains to the ancient Teotihuacanos. It must be shown that the Teotihuacanos distinguished these three mountains from all the other mountains around Teotihuacan and recognized them as special.

Figure 7.5   Cerro Gordo and the Moon Pyramid

The initial evidence that the Teotihuacanos distinguished these three mountains comes from the integration of the architecture with the environment. The Avenue of the Dead leads visitors from south to north, with the huge mountain of Cerro Gordo functioning as the visual climax of the procession (Figure 7.5). The enormous Moon Pyramid sits in front of Cerro Gordo, with the real mountain framing the humanmade mountain, forming a bond between the two that is both visual and symbolic (Linné 1934:32–33; Tobriner 1972:104).

Cerro Gordo is an extinct volcano, and the remains of the crater form a cleft that was highly symbolic for the ancient Mesoamericans. In Mesoamerican myth, the cleft mountain was the source of the most important food of all, maize. In the central Mexican version, Quetzalcoatl changed into an ant, burrowed into the mountain, and retrieved the four colors of maize. In the Maya version of this myth, the maize god, assisted by his sons, sprouted out of the crack in the earth (Taube 1985, 1986; Freidel et al. 1993:281).

Cerro Gordo was not only the symbolic source of maize, but it was also the source of the other most valuable substance, water. Teotihuacan's fields were irrigated by a series of natural springs found in the valley, but tradition holds that the source of the spring water was Cerro Gordo.

Cerro Gordo was envisioned like an inverted pottery vessel, a clay pot filled with water. Reportedly, up on the mountain there are special locations where one can even hear the water inside the mountain. Deep lava tubes produce a sound that is eerily like the sound of water sloshing in a vessel (Nuttall 1926: 76; Tobriner 1972:110–111; Taube 1986:52). Thus, Cerro Gordo was the mountain of sustenance, the cleft mountain that provided the corn and water that sustained the people. The Moon Pyramid mimicked the shape of the actual mountain, reproducing the volcano in adobe and stone, thereby appropriating the symbolism of Cerro Gordo. As one walks up the Avenue of the Dead, Cerro Gordo eventually disappears from view, completely replaced by the Moon Pyramid. The pyramid and the mountain are one and the same.

If the location of the Moon Pyramid was based on Cerro Gordo, then the location of the Sun Pyramid was probably influenced by a sacred cave found underneath this pyramid (Heyden 1981). The entrance to the cave lies just below the stairs of the largest pyramid at the site, and the petalled cave sits approximately under the center of the pyramid. Although integration with underworld symbolism seemingly influenced the immediate location, the design of the pyramid carefully incorporated the surrounding mountains of the terrestrial and celestial realm. Standing in the north and looking to the south, the profile of the Sun Pyramid exactly duplicates the natural profile of the mountain called Patlachique (Figure 7.6). Both the pyramid and the mountain descend to the right in a series of sloped steps.

Ascending to the top of the Sun Pyramid affords an unobstructed view of the entire valley and exposes the third mountain recognized by the Teotihuacanos. Across the valley from the Sun Pyramid is Cerro Malinalco (Figure 7.7). Initially disturbing is the fact that Cerro Malinalco sits to the north of the Sun Pyramid's east-west axis. Directly across from the Sun Pyramid is Cerro Colorado, but the visual prominence of Cerro Malinalco makes it the stronger candidate for the third mountain. Even modern-day Mexicans recognize the isolated prominence of this mountain, for a huge Mexican flag flies from the top of this sequestered mountain.

In truth, a low ridge connects Cerro Malinalco and Cerro Colorado, and it is possible that the Teotihuacanos conceptually linked these two peaks. Astronomical associations of the Sun Pyramid make this a distinct possibility. The spot where the Pleiades set on the day of solar zenith passage is on the slopes of Cerro Colorado (Aveni 1980:222–226). Although it would have been a much more tidy package if the Pleiades had set upon the crest of Cerro Malinalco, it is also true that the merging of myth with

Figure 7.6   Cerro Patlachicque and the Sun Pyramid

**Figure 7.7   View west from the Sun Pyramid with
Cerro Colorado on the left and Cerro Malinalco on the right**

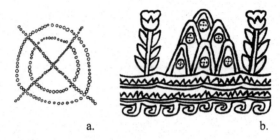

a.   b.

**Figure 7.8   (a) Pecked cross from Cerro Gordo
(adapted from Aveni 1980:223); (b) Teotihuacan
vessel with mountain motif**

the reality of the physical world is often an approximation. The signs of
the gods are fortuitous but a bit imprecise as well.

On the slope of Cerro Colorado, archaeologists found a pecked cross
chipped into a rock outcropping, and similar pecked crosses have been
found on Cerro Gordo (Figure 7.8a). Even though unconfirmed by archaeologists, climbers have reported petroglyphs of concentric circles on
Patlachique. These pecked crosses are not particular to the mountains
under discussion, for they appear on mountains throughout the valley,
within the city itself near the Sun Pyramid and dozens of other places in
the city, and in Mesoamerica from the state of Zacatecas to Uaxactun in
Guatemala (Aveni and Hartung 1982). Some of the pecked crosses may
have marked sight lines for important astronomical events. The mountains, therefore, would not only carry the symbolism of the three stones,
but they also record the order of the heavens. The Maya recognized the
stones on the earth as their hearths and in the sky as a constellation. Likewise, the Teotihuacanos probably saw the celestial aspects of their earthly
but lofty mountains. Such beliefs interweave heaven and earth, which
creates a connection between the human and supernatural realms.

Interestingly, many mountain motifs at Teotihuacan include small circles on their summit (Figure 7.4). On one vessel the five dots of a quincunx
decorate the center of each circle (Figure 7.8b). The quincunx signifies the
five cardinal directions, a symbol related to the carefully pecked dots com-
posing the pecked crosses. I suggest that these circles on the mountain
motif represent the pecked crosses found on the mountains around Teotihuacan. The artists may have included the circles to emphasize the role of
mountains as astronomical markers. This identification also provides additional evidence that the mountain motif is indeed a mountain.

The vase with the quincunx circles on the mountains raises another issue, for it has six rather than three mountains. In truth, the mountain motif does appear in several multiples, but this does not discredit the present hypothesis. Although mountains may appear in a variety of numbers, by far the most common quantity of mountains grouped for the motif is three. Whereas the Teotihuacanos emphasized the importance of three mountains in their symbolism, it did not blind them to the fact that there were other mountains. Mountains other than Cerro Gordo, Cerro Patlachique, and Cerro Malinalco held sacred symbolism to the Teotihuacanos, yet as a unit, these three mountains probably held a special significance.

The Teotihuacanos did not limit themselves only to recognizing the sacredness of mountains in their immediate surroundings. The site of Chalcatzingo is quite a distance away, but Teotihuacan-style paintings in the site's caves suggest that Chalcatzingo was a pilgrimage destination.[3] One such painting provides evidence that the Teotihuacanos did connect numerical concepts of mountains with a sense of place (Figure 7.9). The painting includes two mountains around an opening with the features of a mouth. The painter positioned the mountains asymmetrically, which is not typical in Teotihuacan-style painting. David Grove (1987:191–193) noted this asymmetry and took special care to look for the third mountain. He noted that the third mountain could have weathered away but argued that two may represent the original number. As he suggested, anyone who has visited Chalcatzingo can easily surmise why there would only be two mountains. The major en-

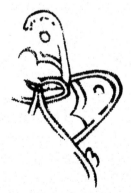

vironmental aspect of the site is the two mountains that project out of the plain in a startlingly abrupt manner. Chalcatzingo, most assuredly, is a two mountain place, and the Teotihuacanos might have branded it as such with their painting.

At Teotihuacan the integration of the architecture with the natural mountains, the astronomical markers, and the visual prominence of particular mountains indicate that Cerro Gordo, Cerro Patlachique, and Cerro Malinalco were singled out as the three prominent mountains in the

Figure 7.9 Teotihuacan-style painting of two mountain motif from Cave 19, Chalcatzingo (adapted from Grove 1987:192)

Teotihuacan Valley. These three mountains surely correspond to the three mountain motif and function as the Teotihuacan version of the three stones of creation. We can assume that the official Teotihuacan doctrine was that these three mountains were the first three stones placed at the time of creation. Proceeding from this doctrine, the Teotihuacanos would have held that they lived at the site of creation, and thus their city was positioned at the center of the cosmos. This need to live at the center is fully consistent with Doris Heyden's (1981) proposal that the Teotihuacanos and other Mesoamericans practiced a form of geomancy whereby the physical environment as it reflected mythological constructs served as a guide to the foundation and planning of settlements and cities.

Earlier, I argued that the Moon Pyramid functioned as a humanmade reproduction of Cerro Gordo, that is, the pyramid was a symbolic mountain. This belief was not restricted to Teotihuacan, for all Mesoamericans conceptually linked their pyramids to mountains. Maya hieroglyphic inscriptions refer to the pyramids as *witz*, the Maya word for mountain. At the Maya site of Palenque, pyramids physically made a link with mountains. The Temple of the Inscriptions was built into the side of a sacred mountain, and the Maya built the Temple of the Cross over a natural mountain (González 1993:39). At the Terminal Classic site of El Tajín, an actual mountain frames the Pyramid of the Niches, again symbolically binding the constructed with the natural. Much later in the Postclassic period, the Aztec referred to their Templo Mayor as *Coatepec*, the Snake Mountain where their culture hero Huitzilopochtli was born and defeated his sister Coyolxauhqui. In this volume, Kathryn Reese-Taylor and Rex Koontz argue that El Tajín's Pyramid of the Niches was an earlier version of this Coatepec, further connecting this pyramid with a mountain (see chapter 1). In short, it is a fundamental principle in Mesoamerica that pyramids symbolize mountains from mythology.

The Three Temple Complex

At Teotihuacan, the symbolism of the three mountain/stones of creation was further elaborated upon within the city. The major pyramids do not stand in isolation; they are accompanied by pairs of pyramids. The Sun Pyramid provides the archetypal case (Figure 7.10). In front of the pyramid are two smaller structures forming a triad with an altar at the center. If pyramids were metaphorical mountains, a triad of pyramids would symbolize the three mountain/stones of creation. In other words, originally there was the myth of the three stones of creation; the Teotihuacanos may have then taken this myth and promoted the belief that the three mountains of their valley were the three stones of creation, and then they built symbolic reproductions of the three mountains within the city with their pyramids.

This triadic arrangement of structures seen in the Sun Pyramid may have served as the model for many other temple structures within the city. Throughout the city of Teotihuacan are the well-known three temple complexes. As the name suggests, these are arrangements of three temples around a patio, with an altar at the center (Wallrath 1966; Angulo Villaseñor 1987). Although precise dating requires

Figure 7.10   The Sun Pyramid with altar and two accompanying temples (adapted from Millon 1993:19)

the excavation of many more temple complexes, Matthew Wallrath (1966:116), George Cowgill (1974:388), and Evelyn Childs Rattray (1992:4–6) positioned them in the Tzacualli phase, although work by Patricia Plunket and Gabriela Uruñuela (1998) demonstrates that the origins of the three temple arrangement dates back at least as far as the Preclassic period.[4] The Teotihuacan Mapping Project found more than twenty free-standing three temple complexes in their extensive survey of the city (Cowgill 1974:388).

The Teotihuacanos built their three temple complexes in a variety of sizes. In their largest form, they incorporated the grandest structures at the site, including both the Moon and Sun Pyramids (Millon 1992:390; Pasztory 1992:296). These giant triadic arrangements formed community-level three temple complexes. The enormous plazas and towering temples would have provided adequate space for participation of the entire population and any visitors to the city. Rituals in such imposing three temple complexes could have offered communal cohesion and reinforced the state religion.

Another group of three temple complexes have an intermediate size. This group is distinct from the apartment compounds but not directly along the Avenue of the Dead; René Millon (1973:40; 1981:212–213) argued for the existence of *barrio* temples at Teotihuacan that played an administrative role.[5] *Barrio*-level three temple complexes probably were the location of neighborhood rituals. *Barrio* rituals reinforced the bonds of neighborhoods within the vast city and would have been a useful means of political control through civic and religious obligations and participation.

In an even smaller format, the Teotihuacanos constructed household-level three temple complexes. By the Tlamimilolpa phase (200–400 AD), the majority of Teotihuacanos seem to have lived in structures commonly referred to as apartment compounds. These are dwellings that were roughly rectangular or square; one-story in height; and bounded by high, windowless walls (Séjourné 1959, 1966b; Millon 1973, 1976, 1981, 1993; Manzanilla 1993:92). Although appearing in many variations, the internal space of each of the apartment compounds included a maze of habitational rooms arranged around open patios. In most of the apartment compounds, one of the largest of these open patios takes the form of a small-scale three temple complex with an altar in the center.[6] The altars, the open nature of the patios, and the artifacts recovered from the patios indicate that these served as areas for ritual activities. Therefore, these domestic-level three temple complexes probably served as the ritual area for the extended family living within each compound (Manzanilla 1991). Thus, from the ceremonial center to the neighborhood to the household, the three temple complexes seem to reproduce the mythological three stones of creation. A possible state doctrine that Teotihuacan was located at the exact location of creation may have started with the natural environment, may have been elaborated upon with civic structures, and may have even infiltrated the home in the form of apartment compound three temple complexes.

The Three Temples of Atetelco

A set of murals in one apartment compound three temple complex provides insight into how the intensive reproduction of this myth merged with the political structure of Teotihuacan. The murals appear in the apartment compound called Atetelco. Atetelco lies in the northwest quadrant of the city and seems to have been the residence of a fairly prosperous lineage. The ritual patio is called the White Patio and dates to approximately 300–400 AD (Cabrera 1995:206) (Figure 7.11). The three temples of the White Patio have open porticos, and the walls of these porticos are decorated with murals painted in red and white.

Each of the porticos has the same basic compositional elements, even though several iconographic motifs substitute for each of those elements.

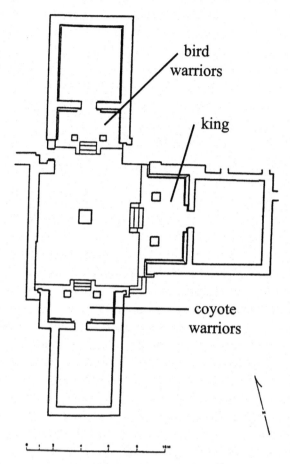

Figure 7.11   **Plan of the White Patio,**
Atetelco (adapted from Miller 1973:158)

For instance, the upper walls of each portico consist of a net-like grid with a particular individual repeated in each of the diamond-shaped openings of the grid; however, the individual changes between each of the porticos. The central portico in the east depicts numerous images of an individual that Linda Schele (1995) has identified as the king (Figure 7.12a). One basis for her argument is that many Mesoamerican kings dressed themselves in the accoutrements of the primary deity. In the case of the Maya, rulers often wore the costume of the maize god, thereby associating themselves with the preeminent god of their pantheon. Likewise, the individual in the central temple of the White Patio has characteristics of that city's primary deity, the Great Goddess. Specifically, he wears the fanged nose plaque and bird-festooned headdress of the Great Goddess. Other characteristics of his position include his staff of office and the conch shell trumpet he holds at his waist. The staff is very similar to the royal staff wielded by a Zapotec ruler on Monolith 1c from Monte Albán (Figure 7.13) that Marcus Winter (1990:131–132) identified as a staff of office and a symbol of power for the Zapotec. Oaxaca also provides evidence that the possession of the conch shell trumpet is a royal prerogative. Ten conch shell effigies found inside the elaborate Period I Tomb 43 at Monte Albán led Kent Flannery and Joyce Marcus to argue that conch shell trumpets were associated with public office among the Zapotec (Flannery 1976:335; Flannery and Marcus 1983:90). Thus, thematically, the central temple seems to be associated with the office of the king.

As for the flanking porticos, each of these temples is dedicated to the imagery of a particular warrior order associated with an animal. In the diamond-shaped spaces of these murals, members of a coyote warrior order appear in the south temple (Figure 7.12b), and bird warriors appear in the north temple (Figure 7.12c, 7.12d). The rationale for the animal associations of the military orders lies with observations Freidel et al. (1993) made about Maya soldiers. Building on the extensive evidence for a belief in nawalism—or a belief that humans not only have but can change into an animal companion—the authors suggest that ancient Maya soldiers went into battle transformed into their animal counterparts. The murals of Atetelco would suggest that the Teotihuacanos shared this common Mesoamerican belief.

The most convincing evidence of this assertion comes from the north temple, which features members of the bird warrior order. On the two side walls of the portico, the principal image is a typical Teotihuacan warrior wearing a year sign headdress and carrying a bundle of three atlatl darts (Figure 7.12c). In his other hand is a stick or baton with which he strikes a bird whose head spurts droplets of blood. The result of this violence or sacrifice appears on the rear wall of this same portico. Here, the repeated individual is a composite bird human (Figure 7.12d). The figure still sports a year sign headdress and carries the atlatl darts, but he now grips the actual atlatl. While the left hand holding the darts is human, the claws poking through the atlatl indicate that the other hand has the form of a bird. Likewise, bird claws emerge from the straps of his human sandals, and he has a tail, feathers covering his body, and a beaked bird face.

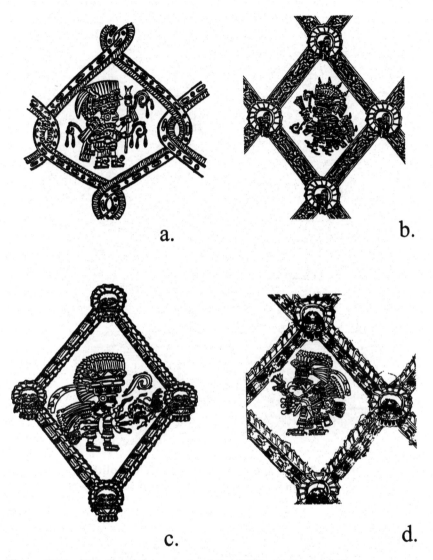

Figure 7.12   Details of the murals of the White Patio, Atetelco,
Teotihuacan: (a) east portico depicting the Teotihuacan king (adapted
from von Winning 1987:104); (b) south portico depicting a coyote warrior
(adapted from Villagra Caleti 1971:Figure 17); (c) side wall of the north
portico depicting a warrior hitting a bird (adapted from Pasztory
1974:Figure 15); (d) rear wall of the north portico depicting a bird warrior
(adapted from von Winning 1987:95; Villagra Caleti 1971:Figure 21)

**Figure 7.13   Zapotec ruler with staff, Monolith 1c,
Monte Albán (adapted from Marcus 1983:Figure 5.8)**

Were it not for the upright stance and the obvious human clothing, the figure could be said to be more bird than human. Indeed, I would argue that this is a human, but a human who has transformed into his animal companion via the violent ritual shown on the side walls. That is, the north portico seems to show a vision of cause and effect, telling the audience just how the transformation transpires. Thus, on the side walls the warrior sacrifices a bird, which results in the imagery of the rear wall: the warrior's ability to transform into a supernatural bird. Although the south portico only shows fully transformed coyote warriors (Figure

7.12b), its close proximity to the north portico suggests similar activities. The figures depicted in these diamond spaces also wear the year sign headdress and carry an atlatl and atlatl darts. They, too, walk like humans even though they have claws, fur, and coyote snouts and teeth. The individuals associated with this portico seem to transform into coyotes when they go into war.

Even though the imagery of the murals provides a wealth of information about religious rituals and belief systems, in their simplest form each of the porticos is dedicated to one thematic element, specifically the office of the king and two military orders (Figure 7.11). What is interesting about the murals is how the physical placement of each thematic concept seems to suggest the relationship of the actual political bodies. The imagery of the king appears in the central temple. This temple is larger, has a floor that is elevated above the other two, and probably had a higher roof. All of these elements indicate that this structure was the most important structure in the group. Certainly it is fitting that imagery of the highest political office appears in the most important temple. Accordingly, the flanking structures have secondary status; ritual activities in these two temples probably supplemented the primary rituals in the central temple. It therefore follows that the imagery in these two temples represents political institutions of secondary importance to the office of the king. The king may have needed the orders of the bird and coyote warriors for support and legitimization, but nevertheless, the king held the supreme position of power. I am suggesting that the physical arrangement of the murals may reflect the actual political structure of Teotihuacan. The politics of Teotihuacan may have been envisioned as a triadic structure. The primary governing bodies may have been the king and the military orders of the bird and coyote warriors.

Support for such a political structure comes from the later Aztec. Underneath the Aztec king and his cabinet were the powerful military orders of the eagle and jaguar knights. At the Aztec site of Malinalco, eagle and jaguar thrones decorate a room used for the installation of provincial rulers (Townsend 1992:37). The thrones indicate the powerful role played by the military orders. In the *Florentine Codex*, Fray Bernardino de Sahagún repeatedly ties the office of the king to the eagle and jaguar knights. Describing a creature called a *chimalcoatl* or shield-serpent, Sahagún relates that a person who saw the snake ". . . gains merit: he merits the eagle mat, the ocelot [jaguar] mat; it is said that he merits the estate of ruling general, of general" (Sahagún 1950–1969, Volume XI:81). The mention of the mat is particularly interesting, as it is a well-established sym-

bol of rulership throughout Mesoamerica. In fact, the passage harkens
back to the throne room of Malinalco, for the eagle and jaguar thrones
were equivalents of the eagle and jaguar mats. Sahagún's association of
the eagle and jaguar with the mat closely connects concepts of power to
the military orders.

Sahagún (1950–1969, Volume VI:23–26) also records that the status of
the ruler directly affected the members of the eagle and jaguar orders.
When the ruler abused his position, the eagle and jaguar knights were
troubled and wept. Likewise, so intimately was their well-being tied to
the ruler that when the ruler died, the knights professed their desire to
die. Although such statements reflect the exaggeration of public displays,
it is notable for the purposes at hand that it is the eagle and jaguar
knights who are specifically mentioned as being linked to the ruler. A
symbiotic relationship of power seems to have existed between the king
and the military orders. The structural relationship between the murals
of the White Patio suggests that a similar codependency may have characterized the political structure of Teotihuacan.

Political Structure and
the Three Stones of Creation

Thematically, I have suggested, each of the porticos of the White Patio features a different political entity. The king, the bird warriors, and the coyote warriors each commandeer one of these spaces to celebrate the nature
and insignia of their respective offices (Figure 7.11). The physical isolation
of the three political bodies in their own temples recognizes their independence, even while the temples form one architectural space that reveals the hierarchical relationship between them. The ruler is in the center,
towering over all other political bodies, yet this pinnacle needs its base of
support that appears in the White Patio as the bird and coyote warriors. I
have argued that Teotihuacan had a triadic political structure much like
that recorded for the Aztec, and that the physical arrangement of thematic
motifs in the White Patio reflects an actual political structure. However,
the murals of the White Patio convey an even richer message, for they integrate political structure with cosmological mythology.

In an ingenious conflation, the murals of the White Patio merge the political structure of Teotihuacan with the creation myth. If the three temple
complexes symbolically represented the three stones of creation, then the
designer of the White Patio purposefully overlaid the political structure
onto this mythical event of genesis. Each political body is associated with

one of the temples; therefore, each political body is associated with one of the three stones of creation. An analogy was made between the act of the gods at creation and the political institutions subsequently created by the humans living at Teotihuacan. The political institutions of the king and the orders of the bird and coyote warriors were conceptually linked to the three stones of creation. It is as if the gods ordained that the city should be governed by a triadic political system. These human constructs were legitimated by their comparison to this core myth. The political structure seems preordained from the beginning of time.

One might wonder why the ritual space of an apartment compound would concern itself with the political structure of the city as a whole. Much is missing in this puzzle, for there is little evidence as to who lived at Atetelco. Residents of the compound may have had strong lineage ties to the king, but there is little to suggest this. More likely, the inhabitants of Atetelco were members of military orders, perhaps even the bird and coyote orders, and they chose this decorative program to emphasize the ruler's reliance on their political support. The strong martial themes throughout the White Patio are in accord with such an idea, as are other murals at Atetelco. Just north of the White Patio are rooms with murals depicting war shields. Decorative motifs from construction that post-dates the White Patio continue to feature the bird and coyote. One such patio north of the White Patio has coyotes emerging from bowls, and the later Painted Patio included terra-cottas of birds and coyotes (Armillas 1950:57; Cabrera 1992). Atetelco's preoccupation with these two military motifs indicates that its residents could have been members of these elite political bodies and therefore had reason to glorify their close relationship with the ruler.

Sahagún (1950–1969, Volume IV:91) provided some rationale for why members of the military would choose to support the ruler. He explained that before an official installation, a newly elected Aztec ruler needed to conduct a war to obtain captives for the inaugural ceremonies. A successful war necessitated the support of the military who would fight and bring home these captives. The ruler gained the support of the military through incentive. Warriors who brought back a captive were rewarded with elevated status. The bond between the king and the military was one of mutual dependence. Each profited by the other's success. Perhaps members of the military lived within the apartment compound of Atetelco and commissioned these murals to emphasize their connection with the most important political office in the city, the basis for much of their social status.

The political themes in the private context of the White Patio may also stem from the Teotihuacan state's desire to integrate the periphery with the center. In a variety of sizes, the Teotihuacanos replicated the three temple complex within the city. From the most public triadic groupings such as the Sun Pyramid to the three temple complexes in the *barrios* and apartment compounds, the same arrangement of ritual structures suggests a uniformity to ritual and belief. State rituals in public spaces may have been replicated in more domestic spaces, thereby reinforcing the ideals of the state. It would seem that the invasive finger of the state entered even the private arenas of Teotihuacan life.

Thus, from the ceremonial center to the *barrio* to the household, the three temple complexes reproduced the mythological three stones of creation. The state doctrine that Teotihuacan was located at the exact location of creation started with the natural environment, was elaborated upon with civic structures, and even infiltrated the home in the form of apartment compound three temple complexes. Specifically in the White Patio, the building of the three temple complex at Atetelco brought with it not just the mythological doctrine of the center but also the political structure. The creation of the world, the setting of the three stones, may have explained just why the ruler and two warrior orders governed Teotihuacan. Teotihuacan's elite compared their power structure to the act of the gods.

In concluding this discussion, I have to say that I am not fully convinced that this triadic political system remained intact throughout the approximately 700-year span of Teotihuacan. There is clear evidence that there were other military orders besides the bird and coyote orders. These other orders may have competed for power with the bird and coyote orders, even displacing the bird and coyote orders for long periods. Surely the rise and fall of individual fortunes or the charisma of a particular leader led to modifications and manipulations of the system. Nevertheless, I do strongly maintain that the White Patio offers a view of the political agenda of the residents of one apartment compound at one moment in Teotihuacan's history. For one reason or another, the residents of Atetelco chose to promote a political structure that integrated political institutions with the fundamental mythological belief of the city. Even though Teotihuacan has long kept its political structure secret from modern scholars, the White Patio provides a glimpse of the strategic positioning of one group of individuals who lived together inside the walls of Atetelco. It tells us how the Teotihuacanos strove to integrate their temples with the natural environment, and it tells us how the city and its political institutions must reflect the order established by the gods at the time of creation.

Acknowledgments

My sincerest thanks to George Cowgill, Linda Schele, Karl Taube, Kathryn Reese-Taylor, and Rex Koontz, who all read and commented on various versions of this paper.

References

Angulo Villaseñor, Jorge.
  1987 Nuevas consideraciones sobre Tetitla y los llamados conjuntos departamentales. *Teotihuacan: Nuevos datos, nuevas síntesis, nuevos problemas.* Edited by Emily McClung de Tapia and Evelyn Childs Rattray. México, D.F.: UNAM. 275–315.
Armillas, Pedro.
  1950 Teotihuacan, Tula y los Toltecas. *RUNA* 3:37–70.
Aveni, Anthony F.
  1980 *Skywatchers of Ancient Mexico.* Austin, Tex.: University of Texas Press.
Aveni, Anthony F., and Horst Hartung.
  1982 New Observations of the Pecked Cross Petroglyph. *Space and Time in the Cosmovision of Mesoamerica.* Edited by Franz Tichy. Lateinamerika Studien 10. Munich, Germany: Wilhelm Fink Verlag. 25–41.
Cabrera, Rubén.
  1992 A Survey of Recently Excavated Murals at Teotihuacan. *Art, Ideology, and the City of Teotihuacan.* Edited by Janet Catherine Berlo. Washington, D.C.: Dumbarton Oaks. 113–128.
  1995 Atetelco. *La Pintura Mural Prehispánica en México, I, Teotihuacan.* Edited by Beatriz de la Fuente. México, D.F.: UNAM and Instituto de Investigaciones Estéticas. 202–257.
Cowgill, George L.
  1974 Quantitative Studies of Urbanization at Teotihuacan. *Mesoamerican Archaeology: New Approaches.* Edited by Norman Hammond. Austin, Tex.: University of Texas Press. 363–396.
  1993 What We Still Don't Know about Teotihuacan. *Teotihuacan: Art from the City of the Gods.* Edited by Kathleen Berrin and Esther Pasztory. San Francisco: Thames and Hudson and The Fine Arts Museum of San Francisco. 117–125.
Flannery, Kent V.
  1976 Contextual Analysis of Ritual Paraphernalia from Formative Oaxaca. *The Early Mesoamerican Village.* Edited by Kent V. Flannery. New York: Academic Press. 333–345.

Flannery, Kent V., and Joyce Marcus.
  1983 The Earliest Public Buildings, Tombs, and Monuments at Monte Albán, with Notes on the Internal Chronology of Period I. *The Cloud People: Divergent Evolution of the Zapotec and Mixtec Civilizations.* Edited by Kent V. Flannery and Joyce Marcus. New York: Academic Press. 87–91.

Freidel, David, Linda Schele, and Joy Parker.
  1993 *Maya Cosmos: Three Thousand Years on the Shaman's Path.* New York: William Morrow.

Gamio, Manuel.
  1979 *La población del Valle de Teotihuacan.* México, D.F.: Instituto Nacional Indigenista.

González, Arnoldo.
  1993 El Templo de la Cruz. *Arqueología Mexicana* 1(2):39–41.

Grove, David C.
  1987 *Ancient Chalcatzingo.* Austin, Tex.: University of Texas Press.

Headrick, Annabeth.
  1996 *The Teotihuacan Trinity: unMASKing the Political Structure.* Ph.D. dissertation, University of Texas at Austin.

Heyden, Doris.
  1981 Caves, Gods, and Myths: World-View and Planning in Teotihuacan. *Mesoamerican Sites and World-Views.* Edited by Elizabeth P. Benson. Washington, D.C.: Dumbarton Oaks. 1–39.

Joralemon, Peter David.
  1971 A Study of Olmec Iconography. *Studies in Pre-Columbian Art and Archaeology 7.* Edited by Elizabeth P. Benson. Washington, D.C.: Dumbarton Oaks.

Knab, T. J., and Thelma D. Sullivan.
  1994 *A Scattering of Jades: Stories, Poems, and Prayers of the Aztecs.* New York: Simon and Schuster.

Kubler, George.
  1967 *The Iconography of the Art of Teotihuacan.* Washington, D.C.: Dumbarton Oaks.

Linné, S.
  1934 *Archaeological Researches at Teotihuacan, Mexico.* Stockholm, Sweden: The Ethnographical Museum of Sweden.

Manzanilla, Linda.
  1991 Arquitectura doméstica y actividades en Teotihuacan. *Cuadernos de Arquitectura Mesoamericana* 13:7–10.
  1993 Daily Life in the Teotihuacan Apartment Compounds. *Teotihuacan: Art from the City of the Gods.* Edited by Kathleen Berrin and Esther Pasztory. San Francisco: Thames and Hudson and The Fine Arts Museum of San Francisco. 91–99.

Marcus, Joyce.
  1983 Stone Monuments and Tomb Murals of Monte Albán IIIa. *The Cloud People: Divergent Evolution of the Zapotec and Mixtec Civilizations.* Edited by Kent V. Flannery and Joyce Marcus. New York: Academic Press. 137–143.

Miller, Arthur G.
1973   *The Mural Painting of Teotihuacán.* Washington, D.C.: Dumbarton Oaks.
Millon, René.
1973   *Urbanization at Teotihuacan, Mexico: The Teotihuacan Map, Volume 1.* Austin, Tex.: University of Texas Press.
1976   Social Relations in Ancient Teotihuacán. *The Valley of Mexico: Studies in Pre-Hispanic Ecology and Society.* Edited by Eric R. Wolf. Albuquerque, N.Mex.: University of New Mexico Press. 205–248.
1981   Teotihuacan: City, State, and Civilization. *Handbook of Middle American Indians, Supplement, Volume 1.* Edited by Victoria R. Bricker. Austin, Tex.: University of Texas Press. 198–243.
1992   Teotihuacan Studies: From 1950 to 1990 and Beyond. *Art, Ideology, and the City of Teotihuacan.* Edited by Janet Catherine Berlo. Washington, D.C.: Dumbarton Oaks. 281–320.
1993   The Place Where Time Began: An Archaeologist's Interpretation of What Happened in Teotihuacan History. *Teotihuacan: Art from the City of the Gods.* Edited by Kathleen Berrin and Esther Pastory. San Francisco: Thames and Hudson and The Fine Arts Museum of San Francisco. 17–43.
Nuttall, Zelia.
1926   Official Reports on the Towns of Tequizistlan, Tepechpan, Acolman, and San Juan Teotihuacan Sent by Francisco de Castaneda to His Majesty, Philip II, and the Council of the Indies in 1580. *Papers of the Peabody Museum of Archaeology and Ethnology* 11 (2): 45–84.
Pasztory, Esther.
1974   *The Iconography of the Teotihuacan Tlaloc.* Washington, D.C.: Dumbarton Oaks.
1988   A Reinterpretation of Teotihuacan and Its Mural Painting Tradition. *Feathered Serpents and Flowering Trees: Reconstructing the Murals of Teotihuacan.* Edited by Kathleen Berrin. San Francisco: The Fine Arts Museum of San Francisco. 45–77.
1992   Abstraction and the Rise of a Utopian State at Teotihuacan. *Art, Ideology, and the City of Teotihuacan.* Edited by Janet Catherine Berlo. Washington, D.C.: Dumbarton Oaks.
1997   *Teotihuacan: An Experiment in Living.* Norman, Okla.: University of Oklahoma Press.
Plunket, Patricia, and Gabriela Uruñuela.
1998   Preclassic Household Patterns Preserved Under Volcanic Ash at Tetimpa, Puebla, Mexico. *Latin American Antiquity* 9(4):287–309.
Rattray, Evelyn Childs.
1992   *The Teotihuacan Burials and Offerings: A Commentary and Inventory.* Nashville, Tenn.: Vanderbilt University Publications in Anthropology.
Reilly, F. Kent, III.
1994   *Visions to Another World: Art Shamanism, and Political Power in Middle Formative Mesoamerica.* Ph.D. dissertation, University of Texas at Austin.

Sahagún, Fray Bernardino de.
  1950–1969   *Florentine Codex: General History of the Things of New Spain.*
                Translated by Charles E. Dibble and Arthur J. O. Anderson. Books 1–13.
                Monographs of The School of American Research and The Museum of
                New Mexico. Santa Fe, N.Mex.: School of American Research and the
                University of Utah.
Schele, Linda.
  1995   The Olmec Mountain and the Tree of Creation in Mesoamerican Cos-
                mology. *The Olmec World: Ritual and Rulership: Essays by Michael D. Coe
                et al.* Princeton: The Art Museum, Princeton University, and Harry N.
                Abrams. 105–117.
Schele, Linda, and Matthew Looper.
  1996   *Notebook for the XXth Maya Hieroglyphic Forum at Texas.* Austin, Tex.:
                University of Texas Press.
Séjourné, Laurette.
  1959   *Un palacio en la ciudad de los dioses: Teotihuacan.* Mexico, D.F.: Instituto
                Nacional de Antropología e Historía.
  1966a   *Arqueologia de Teotihuacan: La Ceramica.* México, D.F.: Fondao de Cultura
                Economica.
  1966b   *Arquitectura y pintura en Teotihuacan.* México, D.F.: Siglo XXI.
Taube, Karl A.
  1985   The Classic Maya Maize God: A Reappraisal. *Fifth Palenque Round Table,
                1983.* Edited by Merle Greene Robertson. San Francisco: Pre-
                Columbian Art Research Institute. 171–181.
  1986   The Teotihuacan Cave of Origin. *RES* 12:51–82.
Tobriner, Stephen.
  1972   The Fertile Ground: An Investigation of Cerro Gordo's Importance to
                the Town Plan and Iconography of Teotihuacan. *Teotihuacan: XI Mesa
                Redonda.* México, D.F.: Sociedad Mexicana de Antropología. 103–115.
Townsend, Richard F.
  1992   Landscape and Symbol. *The Ancient Americas: Art from Sacred Land-
                scapes.* Edited by Richard F. Townsend. Chicago: Art Institute of
                Chicago. 29–47.
Villagra Caleti, Agustín.
  1971   Mural Painting in Central Mexico. *Handbook of Middle American Indians,
                Volume 10.* Edited by Robert Wauchope, Gordon Ekholm, and Ignacio
                Bernal. Austin, Tex.: University of Texas Press. 135–156.
Vogt, Evon Z.
  1976   *Tortillas for the Gods: A Symbolic Analysis of Zinacanteco Rituals.* Norman,
                Okla.: University of Oklahoma Press.
von Winning, Haso.
  1987   *La Iconografia de Teotihuacan.* Mexico, D.F.: Instutio de Investigaciones
                Esteticas.
Wallrath, Matthew.
  1966   The Calle de los Muertos Complex: A Possible Macrocomplex of Struc-
                tures Near the Center of Teotihuacan. *Teotihuacan: Onceava Mesa Re-
                donda.* Mexico, D.F.: Sociedad Mexicana de Antropologia. 113–122.

Winter, Marcus.
    1990   Monte Albán: Hilltop Capital in Oaxaca. *Mexico: Splendors of Thirty Cen-turies*. Edited by John P. O'Neill. New York: Metropolitan Museum of Art. 115–134.

Notes

1. For pivotal examples of this tradition, see Kubler 1967; Pasztory 1988, 1992, 1997; and Millon 1992.

2. For the seminal work concerning Mesoamerican concepts of living at the center, see Vogt 1976.

3. Pilgrimage to mountain tops is an established Mesoamerican practice. Sahagún (1950–1969 II:27) recorded that naked priests carried branches to the surrounding mountains at midnight in the month of Panquetzaliztli. Vogt's (1976:183–184) work proved that such rituals continue today amongst the Zinacantecos. As part of year renewal rituals, shamans and their helpers visit mountain shrines to pray and place bundles of red geraniums.

4. Cowgill (personal communication 1996) related that recent ceramic analysis by Annick Daneels in the Group 5–prime three temple complex suggests that these complexes may be no earlier than Miccaotli.

5. It is still unclear whether these midsized temples represent barrios. As Cowgill (1993:123) noted, some of these pyramids seem too large to function as such and seem somewhat isolated from their supposed barrio. Likewise, he emphasized that they do not fit the expected pattern for an administrative network because they are too concentrated in some areas and too sparse in others.

6. For a fuller discussion on three temple complexes in apartment compounds, see Headrick 1996 .

8

A Model for Late Classic Community Structure at Copán, Honduras

Jeffrey A. Stomper

The study of Classic Maya material remains is characterized by a fascination with the inscribed stone monuments, architecture, and exquisite portable works of art, which are among the ancient Maya civilization's principal legacy. Many of these investigations attempt to delve beyond surface appearances in order to discern the cultural systems in which these works were constructed—one example of this approach is the study of the architecture at the site of Copán in Western Honduras. Specifically, the examination of the iconography and site planning associated with Structure 22A, supported by archaeological and ethnographic evidence, provides a means to explore a specific moment in Copán's history and the response of its elite to a time of political turmoil.

In 1985, the Copán Mosaics Project was established to investigate the wealth of information contained in the piles of inscribed stone that tumbled from building facades centuries earlier. The central focus of this project was to examine the ideological adaptations and political strategies of the eighth- and early ninth-century Copán rulers with respect to the demands of an increasing population, expanding elite system and political instability.

The piles of unprovenienced sculpture located about the site provided an insufficient basis for the reconstruction and subsequent interpretation of the sculpted facades. Because researchers realized these limitations, extensive excavations were undertaken in the main group of ruins as part of the Copán Acropolis Archaeological Project. Beginning in 1986, several buildings in the Main Group of ruins came under intense scrutiny—including Structure 22A, the focus of this chapter.

The excavations of Structure 22A, located on the northwest edge of Copán's Main Acropolis (Figure 8.1), were conducted in 1988 and 1990 by me along with Sheree Lane and Barbara Fash. The purpose of these investigations was to test Fash's hypothesis that the woven mat symbol still *in situ* on the east facade of the building indicated that Structure 22A was the mat house, or *Popol Na* (B. Fash and W. Fash 1991; B. Fash et al. 1992). In many Maya languages *pop* means woven mat—a symbol of authority—whereas *na* is translated as house.

In the sixteenth-century colonial Yucatec accounts of the Motul (Martinez Hernández 1929) and San Francisco (1870)dictionaries, a *Popol Na* is referred to as the "council house" or "community house." These readings are reiterated in the early seventeenth-century Cholti Maya dictionary by Pedro Morán, in which the term for Mat House—the *Popol Otot*—is translated as the "community house." Based upon these translations and additional ethnographic evidence, mat houses are believed to represent the place where the community elders and lineage heads met to discuss issues concerning the populace, to conduct ceremonies, and to teach and perform ritual dances (Stomper 1996a).

Sculptural Analysis

When sculptural adornments remain *in situ* on a building facade, they provide an ideal situation that further excavations serve to enhance. A recognized motif, its method of articulation and position upon a building, furnishes the research team with invaluable advance knowledge and a keener awareness of what to look for during the excavation process. The existing mat motif on the eastern side of Structure 22A was the key to reconstructing the other mat sculptures that fell around the perimeter of the building when it collapsed (Figure 8.2). The somewhat tedious task of plotting the fallen positions of each sculpted mat motif, many of which were still in a semiarticulated state, enabled the project almost to reconstruct fully the ten mat designs as they originally appeared upon the building (Figure 8.3).

The analysis of the fall patterns of these mat motifs indicate that large, sculpted mats were placed over all three doorways on the south facade and in three corresponding positions on the back side of the building. Two additional mats were placed on each of the east and west facades.

Along with the mat motif, another important clue for reconstructing the facade came in the form of a large sculpted glyph that fell directly in front of the west column on the front side of the building. This hiero-

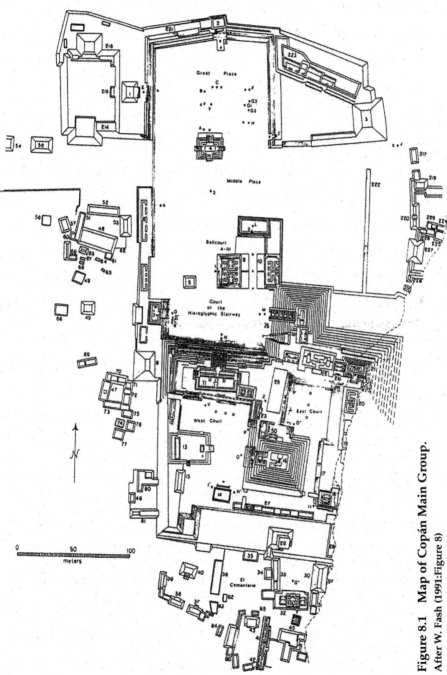

Figure 8.1 Map of Copán Main Group.
After W. Fash (1991:Figure 8)

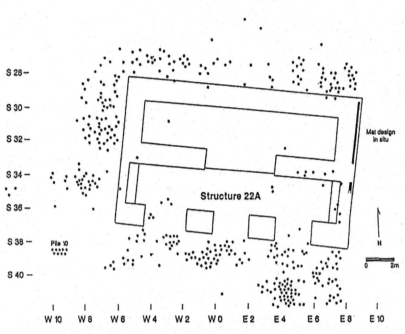

Figure 8.2   10L-22A mat motif fall pattern map.
After Fash et al. (1992:Figure 11)

glyph was found next to its companion mat design. Again, through careful plotting, excavation, and extensive search through the piles of sculpture at the site, a total of nine hieroglyphs were found to have adorned the structure—one on the west facade, two on the north, two on south, and one glyph on each corner (Figure 8.4).

Associated with each of these nine hieroglyphs were parts of sculpted bodies and headdresses (Figure 8.5). Although no complete figure was excavated, the numerous fragments of limbs, loincloths, and headdress feathers were matched with bodies found scattered about the site. From the fall patterns of the sculptures, we know that these human figures were seated in niches above the hieroglyphs. In addition, pieces of sculpture from a single large figure were found throughout the excavation of the structure. These pieces are part of a roof comb that held an image of the ruler sitting atop a double-headed jaguar throne.

The iconography of this structure provides an emic view of how the Copán Maya structured their community. It illustrates how the commu-

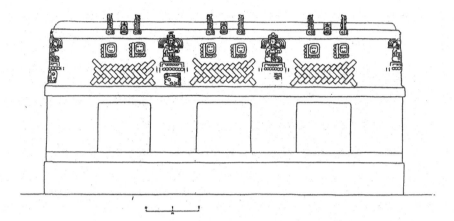

Figure 8.3 Drawing of Structure 10L-22A reconstruction.
After W. Fash (1991:Figure 85)

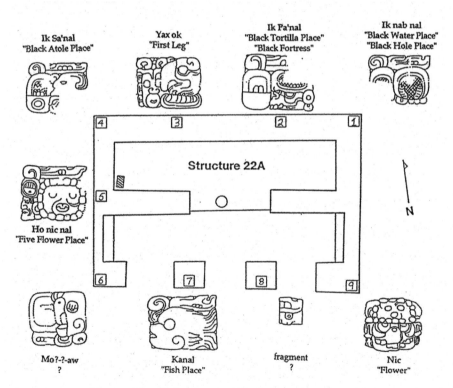

Figure 8.4 Toponyms and locations on 10L-22A.
Drawing by Barbara Fash with additions by Elizabeth Pope

**Figure 8.5   10L-22A niche
figure (front facade).**
Drawing by Barbara Fash

nity was organized in relation to the physical geography of the valley and how the Copán Maya understood their place in the greater Maya cosmos. To understand the extent and meaning of the artwork on the facade, a review/overview of other models of Maya community structure is necessary before presenting my model of the Copán community based on Structure 10L-22A.

Maya Community Structure

An analysis of the function and meaning of Structure 10L-22A provides the basis for a model of community structure at Copán. The model draws upon previous work concerning social and political organization by researchers, such as Edward Kurjack, Michael Coe, and William Fash. Although space does not permit a complete analysis of each scholar's work, a brief summary of each is needed in order to provide a foundation for my present study.

The excavation of a single structure often does not provide sufficient data to make broad inferences about cultural behavior, yet the case of Structure 10L-22A is different. The combination of settlement pattern data, along with archaeological and ethnographic data, provides the basis for creating a model of ancient Maya community structure for Copán during the Late Classic period.

Several scholars have attempted to create models of Lowland Maya community structure with varying degrees of success. Their success was often limited by the nature of the data, and with the addition of more information, the models become more robust. Copán, with more than a century of archaeological research, provides an opportunity to create one of the most dynamic models yet. In order to create this model, an examination of earlier attempts to describe ancient Maya community structure is necessary. What follows is not a comprehensive review of all scholarship on Maya community organization but rather a selection of models that are pertinent to this study.

Concentric Ring Mode
of Community Structure

Bishop Diego de Landa, writing in the fifteenth century, was probably the first scholar to write about Maya social organization and community structure. He stated that the Maya:

> . . . lived together in towns in a very civilized fashion. They kept the land well cleared and free from weeds, and planted good trees. Their dwelling place was as follows: in the middle of the town were their temples with beautiful plazas, and all around the temples stood the houses of the lords and the priests, and [those of] the most important people. Thus came the houses of the richest and those who were held in the highest estimation nearest these, and at the outskirts of the town were the houses of the lower class (Tozzer 1941:62).

This statement indicates that proximity to the site center equaled power and probably wealth. Thus, the community could be divided into concentric zones, with power and prestige emanating from the center out. William Sanders and Barbara Price noted that there is a tendency for all preindustrial urban centers to exhibit this pattern (1968:147–148). Bishop Landa's observations provide a testable hypothesis concerning the post-Conquest Maya that can be examined against archaeological evidence obtained from the Maya of the Classic period.

Landa's model was tested and confirmed by Edward Kurjack's work at Dzibilchaltun (Kurjack 1974; Kurjack and Andrews 1976; Kurjack and Garza 1981). Kurjack discovered that the building complexes with the most vaulted architecture clustered near the center of the site, defining the core area. He argued that the vaulted masonry structures were more expensive than thatched roofed structures and thus were occupied by those with wealth and status, confirming Landa's observations (Kurjack 1974).

According to Kurjack, Dzibilchaltun was divided into three concentric areas (Figure 8.6):

1. The central group consisted of a heavy concentration of vaulted architecture in a small (.25 km^2) area surrounding the Cenote Xlacah.
2. The central aggregate contained a clustering of vaulted ruins in an elongated area of over 3 km surrounding the central group.

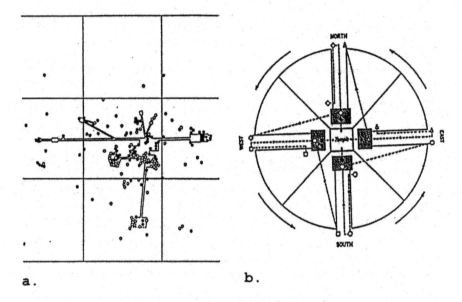

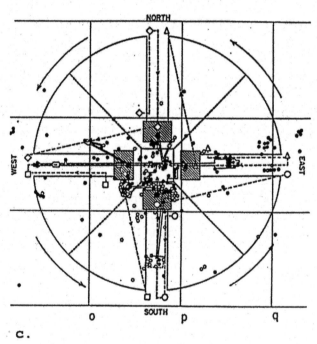

Figure 8.6 (a) Map of Dzibilchaltun core area.
After Kurjack (1974:Figure 24); (b) Coe's quadripartite division of the community.
After Coe (1965:Figure 1); (c) Overlay of Coe's model on Dzibilchaltun

3. The peripheral sphere was the area where small groups of vaulted ruins are widely-scattered (1974:93–94).

In addition, the masonry structures of the core area were built on low platforms, with some degree of order and planning in their layout. Surrounding these platforms were small, less well-constructed buildings that were scattered in a seemingly random fashion. Kurjack stated that these clusters were neighborhoods and that, ". . . clusters of buildings almost certainly housed members of some form of social group" (1974:93). He was less certain if they were kin groups due to the fact that the boundaries between groups of buildings within the clusters were stronger than the boundaries between the clusters themselves.

Kurjack's reconstruction of Dzibilchaltun community structure is directly in correspondence with Bishop Landa's sixteenth-century observations. The concentric concentration of wealth/status/power occurred on several levels. At the site level, the vaulted masonry buildings tended to cluster near the center of the site. These vaulted masonry buildings, constructed atop the platforms, were the centers around which the smaller structures revolve. Finally, in the peripheral area, causeways linked otherwise strongly demarcated building complexes to each other, as well as to the site core (Kurjack and Garza 1981:308). The use of causeways as a sort of umbilical cord to attach remote areas to the site core was evidenced by the clustering of vaulted architecture around the causeways. On an even larger scale, the causeway systems of other sites (such as the Coba-Yaxuna, Uci-Cansahcab, and the Izamal-Ake) served to connect distant satellite communities and distinct sites together. Certainly, these causeways were used for transport, but their underlying purpose was to unite symbolically two or more communities. Even though their distance from the dominant site would place them far from the concentric ring that possessed the highest degree of wealth/status/power, the causeway enabled the satellite communities to be directly connected closer to the center.

Due to its large size and tropical forest locale, settlement data from Tikal have been difficult to synthesize. William Haviland and other scholars, such as Marshall Becker, Peter Harrison, and Dennis Puleston, have focused their studies on settlement patterns at the site (Haviland 1968, 1972, 1982, 1985, 1992; Harrison 1970; Becker 1982, 1986; Puleston 1983). These examinations provide a model of community organization similar to that proposed by Kurjack for Dzibilchaltun. Wendy Ashmore recently examined the architectural layout of Twin Pyramid groups with regard to cosmology and directionality (1991).

According to these scholars, there was a clustering of major palaces near the core of the site. Although they were not confined to the central area, they were far more prominent in the core than elsewhere in the site (Puleston 1983). Haviland argued that the very heart of the city was the Central Acropolis, in which the ruling family probably lived, and farther from the center of the site there were fewer and fewer major palace complexes (1992:51). This layout is consistent with Kurjack's reconstruction of concentric rings of vaulted architecture at Dzibilchaltun.

As in Dzibilchaltun, Tikal palace structures were surrounded by and associated with smaller buildings. These concentrations of structures represented residence by clans or "localized lineages" (Haviland 1972:5). In addition, causeways cut through swampy lands to connect key locations of the site core, providing a practical physical connection in this swampy area while symbolically connecting important locales and defining the nucleus of the site. Furthermore, defensive constructions in the forms of low walls were found, possibly defining the maximum extent of the core area. Again, this pattern is the same one (except for the defensive walls) exhibited by Dzibilchaltun and discussed by Landa.

Several other sites, such as Becan, Cuca, Dzonote Ake, and Muralla de Leon contain walls/defensive works that served to define the core area. Cuca, for example, had both an inner and an outer wall. The inner wall surrounded the ceremonial heart of the city and elite residences, whereas the area enclosed by the outer wall was densely settled with additional elite and other types of residential structures (Webster 1976). Those living outside the walls could flee into the inner areas during short periods of conflict, while those who permanently resided inside the walls (along with the most sacred structures of the site) were always protected. Therefore, the walls served an obvious defensive nature but can also be understood as visible markers for the differentiation of levels of wealth, status, and power.

There are several common features presented in the above models on community structure. First and foremost, proximity was proportional to status, wealth, and power, creating a pattern of concentric rings emanating out from the site core. Due to certain topographic concerns (such as *cenotes, bajos,* and so forth) these rings are never exact, but the clustering of elite and sacred structures near the core is evident. Second, the relationship between proximity and power/wealth/status was reflected on every level from the house level, to the cluster or complex level, to the intrasite and intersite level. Third, the clusters of residential units served as the loci for clans, localized lineages (Tikal), or social groups (Dzibilchaltun). Finally, the causeway served as a symbolic unifier of disparate areas, in addition to being a means of transportation and communication.

Four Quarters Model
of Community Structure

One of the most important works on ancient Maya community structure was published in 1965 by Michael Coe. Using ethnohistorical documents, mainly the native *Book of Chilam Balam of Chumayel* and Bishop Landa's accounts, Coe proposed a model of Maya community structure different from, yet complementary to, that described above. Instead of concentric rings of occupation emanating out from the site core, Coe's model resulted in a quadripartite division of the site/community (Coe 1965) (Figure 8.6b).

His interpretation came from a careful reading of the Uayeb Rites discussed in Landa's *Relación de las Cosas de Yucatán* (Tozzer 1941:135–150). The Uayeb Rites involved ritual feasting, dancing, and the movement of idols from rock piles located at the community entrances to structures in the center of the city and back again to the entrances. These rock piles, and the entrances that they flanked, were often located on the cardinal points of the compass (Coe 1965:100).

The idols resided at times in the house of a *principal,* located in the center of the city where feasting and dancing took place. Each year a different *principal* would host these rituals. Coe argued that the *principal* resided in one of the four quadrants of the city, and the rituals rotated yearly among the *principales* and therefore among the quadrants. Coe also argued that it is possible that communal authority was transferred from one quadrant to the next on a cyclical basis, mirroring the shift of authority from one principal to the next (Coe 1965:110).

The *principales* that Coe referred to above were probably the *ah holpop*—literally "he (those) at the head of the mat." The *holpop* was described by Alfredo Barrera Vasquez as, ". . . príncipe del convite; el casero dueño de las casa llamada *popol na,* donde se juntan a tratar cosas de republica y enseñarese a bailar para los fiestas del pueblo; tenía a su cargo los edificios municipales" (1981:345).[1] Roys stated that the *holpop*:

> . . . were like *regidors* or captains, and through them the people negotiated with the lord for whatever they desired. These and no others, consulted with the lord on matters and embassies from outside. The term, holpop, is found only in the sources concerning the Yucatán (Roys 1943:64).

The lord mentioned in the above quotation was the *halach uinic*, the "real man"(Roys 1943:59) who served as the ruler of the town or the province. In addition to acting as the head of the town (which was also was the provincial capital), the *halach uinic* formulated foreign policy and directed the government of his province through local town leaders called *batabs*, many of whom were related to him. The position of *halach uinic* was hereditary, and he usually ruled for life (Roys 1943).

The *halach uinic* and his *batabs* were advised by the *holpop* in each town. In addition to acting as councilors to the governors, the *holpop* served as chief singer and organizer of festival dances that often took place at the *Popol Na*. Roys mentioned another type of councilor, the *ah cuch cab*, who served under the *batab* and ". . . had his vote like a *regidor* in the *cabildo* (municipal government), and without his vote nothing could be done" (1939:43). The *ah cuch cab* also served as the head of the *parcilidad* or sub-division of the town and may have functioned as a lineage head and been part of the town council (Tozzer 1941:63).

Returning to the functions of the *holpop*, an additional responsibility of this group was to provide food for the festivals—each *holpop* was ac-countable for certain provisions (*Relaciones de Yucatán*:90, 96). The *ah cuch cab* and the *holpop* also shared many of the same social functions; I would argue that they may have been the same office, yet they operated at dif-ferent governmental levels or areas. References to the *holpop* are associ-ated with the *halach uinic* (the level of provincial government), whereas mentions of the *ah cuch cab* are related to the *batabs* (the level of local/town government). Another possibility, using a modern analogy, is that the *ah cuch cab* and the *holpop* were somewhat like the U.S. Senate and House of Representatives: They both had similar functions, prestige and power, but they were different in the way they operated and who they represented.

As indicated in the aforementioned dictionary entries, the *holpop* and the *ah cuch cab* were both councilors and high ranking members of their lineage. They played substantial roles in community festivals and gather-ings, important responsibilities in relation to the present examination the function and significance of Structure 10L-22A at Copán. In addition to proposing a quadripartite division of the community, Coe also specu-lated on the roles various social groups may have had in the sociopoliti-cal makeup of a pre-Columbian Maya community. Coe's views on the *ha-lach uinic, ah cuch cab*, and *holpop* are similar to those expressed by me elsewhere (Stomper 1996a, 1996b). Coe argued that the *holpop* was a rep-resentative from an outstanding lineage who resided in one of the city's quarters. These quarters were highly endogamous wards that, like the *calpulli* of the more conservative settlements of the contemporary Tzotzil and Tzeltal Maya of Chiapas, were made up of exogamous patrilineages (Coe 1965:106).

The models of community structure discussed above are not diametrically opposed and even share some common elements. Kurjack, along with Haviland and Coe, agree that the residents of the cities lived in kin and social groups (Coe 1965; Haviland 1968, 1972, 1982; Kurjack 1974; Kurjack and Garza 1981). Looking at a map of Dzibilchaltun (Figure 8.6c), Coe's quadripartite division is reflected in the layout of the main causeways, which are generally oriented to the cardinal directions. It is also possible that the principal residences of the elite were located within one of the innermost concentric rings of power/wealth/status and within one of the four quadrants of the site. Using elements from the work of Kurjack and Coe as a foundation, I will attempt to construct a model of Maya community structure for Late Classic period Copán.

A Model of Late Classic Community Structure for Copán

Kurjack relied primarily on settlement pattern data and Coe on ethnohistorical documents for their respective models of community structure. This present model for Copán uses additional information not accessible to the aforementioned scholars—the excavation of Structure 10L-22A, Copán's *Popol Na* or community house. The iconography and archaeology of the *Popol Na* provide the opportunity to form a more accurate model for Copán, as it offers an emic view of how the community was organized. Copán's Structure 10L-22A represents the physical manifestation of how the Maya perceived the structure of their own community.

As part of Proyecto Arqueológico Copán (PAC) Phases I and II, a detailed map of a 24 km² area of the Copán Valley was created. This map provided the foundation for the settlement pattern studies of the area, as well as for future work on community organization. In the process of creating the map, a multilevel, hierarchic classification of structures was created based on size, the number of structures, and the presence or absence of vaulted stones or sculpture (Willey et al. 1978; Leventhal 1979; Willey and Leventhal 1979). A. Freter (1988) later modified this system (see Table 8.1; Figure 8.7).

Thousands of structures were mapped and classified using this schema (W. Fash 1983a; W. Fash and Long 1983). Nearly all of the Type 3 and 4 groups were found in the immediate vicinity of the Main Group. Of the Type 4 sites, four were located in Las Sepulturas, six in the El Bosque re-

Table 8.1 : Copán Site Typology

Site Type	Description
Non mound	Surface concentration of artifacts with no associated building debris
Single mound	Isolated mound
Aggregate mound	2–3 mounds with no formal courtyard; structures less than 1m in height; earth or cobble construction
Type 1	3–5 mounds with 1 structure less than 1 m in height; cobble or masonry construction
Type 2	6–8 mounds with 1–2 courtyards; mounds less than 3 m in height; cobble or masonry construction
Type 3	6–10 mounds with 1–3 courtyards; mounds less than 5 m in height; some vaulted structures
Type 4	8–100 mounds with multiple courtyards; some mounds greater than 5 m in height; increased number of vaulted structures; sculpture
Type 5	Main Group complex

gion, two each in Salamar/Comendero, and El Pueblo (now the modern town of Copán Ruinas) and one in Ostuman (in the far western end of the valley). The Type 3 sites were somewhat more widely scattered but were concentrated in the regions mentioned above. Most of the Type 3 and 4 sites were located within a 1-kilometer radius of the main group, often along one of the two causeways emanating from the site (Figure 8.8).

In 1983, William Fash made an initial attempt at creating a model of community structure at Copán (1983a). He relied heavily on the ethnographic data of Charles Wisdom (1940) obtained from the Chorti in nearby Guatemala. Based on Wisdom's research, Fash postulated that the architectural groups (Type 1 through Type 4) were the functional equivalent of the Chorti *sian otot* or aldeas. According to Wisdom, the *sian otot* were made up of a number of single-household families (sometimes multiple-household) containing the family of a headman and the subsidiary households of his married sons and daughters who remained in his family group (Wisdom 1940:18). In addition, each *sian otot* occupied a single geographic area whose boundaries, although not marked, were known to those in the surrounding area (Wisdom 1940:218).

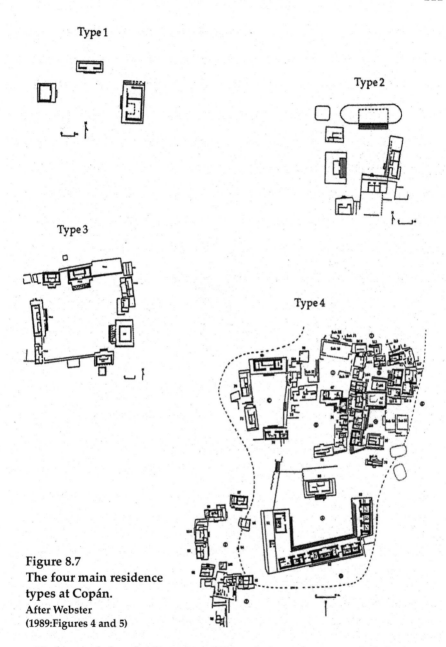

Figure 8.7
The four main residence
types at Copán.
After Webster
(1989:Figures 4 and 5)

Fash noted that the Type 3 and Type 4 sites often occupied distinct areas (although this is less apparent in the densely settled Las Sepulturas and El Bosque areas). Because of this fact, Copán's Type 3 and Type 4 sites could have served a similar function as Kurjack's neighborhoods and Haviland's clusters (W. Fash 1983a:271). In addition, Fash (1983a:284)

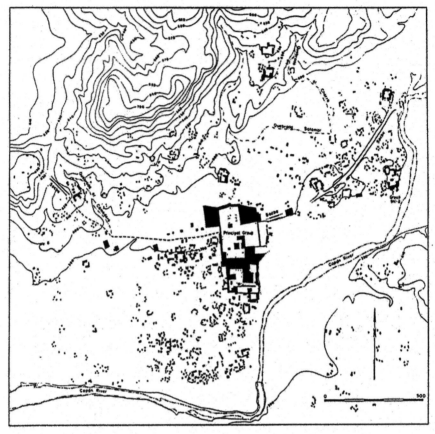

Figure 8.8   Map of Copán Valley.
After W. Fash (1991:Figure 96)

also mentioned that some of these sites are paired, such as two Type 3 sites in the Mesa de Petapilla region or a Type 3 and a Type 4 site in the Ostuman region (Figure 8.9a and.9b). Wisdom mentions that marriages often occurred between two families in a *sian otot* and that usually only two families intermarry, the children of one tending to marry the children of the same generational level of the other (Wisdom 1940:253). Thus, the pairing of the larger Type 3 and Type 4 sites may be indicative of this marriage pattern.

I have focused on the larger Type 3 and 4 sites because I believe that these sites served as the locus for elite activity in their respective areas. Excavations of Group 9N-8 in Sepulturas has demonstrated that this was probably the case (W. Fash 1983b; Sanders 1989; Webster 1989). Fash concluded that the residential compounds within a 1-kilometer radius of the

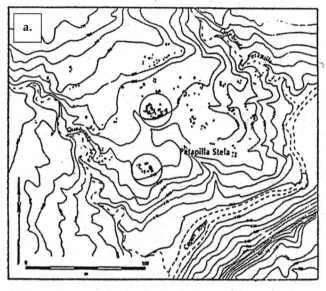

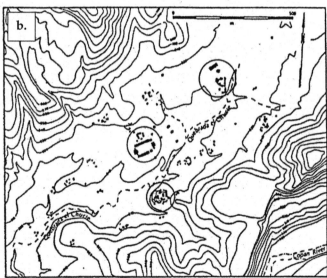

Figures 8.9 a and b

(a) Paired residences in Petapilla.
After W. Fash (1983b:Figure 7.3);

(b) Paired residences in Ostuman.
After W. Fash (1983b:Figure 7.5)

site core were probably the settlements of some of the earliest subjects of the Copán polity. Their size and proximity to the main group indicate that these were the houses of the more powerful elite of the Copán Valley. Causeways extending east and west from the main group were bordered by many of the largest residential compounds, thereby linking the elite lineages to the core.

It is important to note that both causeways terminate approximately 1 kilometer from the center of the main group (Figure 8.8). Also, approximately 1 kilometer due north of the main group is a large residential compound—the only one of its kind in the immediate vicinity. Located 1 kilometer south is the Río Copán, which is bordered by numerous clusters of residential ruins. Fash stated, "It would appear that the Maya again have provided us with an 'emic' definition of the maximum extent of their 'core' area, one kilometer from the geographic (and perhaps ritual) center of the Main Group" (W. Fash 1983a:294).

Fash's model of community structure for Copán contained elements of Dzibilchaltun's concentric zones and Coe's quadripartite division of community. As mentioned previously, most of the Type 3 and Type 4 sites were within the 1-kilometer zone that was demarcated by the causeways. This zone is also the most densely settled region of the Copán Valley. The east-west orientation of the causeways and the north-south orientation of the main group with the presence of large residential compounds 1 kilometer to its north and south divided the area into four parts. Due to the topography of the valley (it is much broader east-west than it is north-south), these divisions and concentrations were not physically uniform. The causeways tended to curve north, following the shape of the Copán Valley, and there was little settlement to the north of the main group due to the encroaching mountains and the use of the area as a quarry for much of the valley's building stone. Although topography alters the geometry of the layout, symbolically and conceptually the Copánecs divided their region into quarters, which radiated out from the site core of the Main Plaza.

The core area was clearly defined by the extent and density of the settlement, as well as the construction of the causeways that terminated at large residential groups. The causeways clearly defined the north and south halves of the area, while the main group served as the divider between east and west. Structure 10L-22A served the people who inhabited this area. Further analysis of the function and purpose of this building must be related to the archaeological, iconographic, and epigraphic data uncovered within both the main group structures and the core area.

Structure 10L-22A and
Late Classic Community Structure

The iconography of Structure 10L-22A provides an emic view of how the Copán Maya structured their community. This structure not only illustrates how the community was organized in relation to the physical geography of the valley, but it also demonstrates how they viewed their place in the greater Maya cosmos. This idea will be made readily apparent in the analysis below. The mat was the dominant motif of Structure 10L-22A. This motif, coupled with the linguistic evidence for the readings of *pop* as mat and *na* or *otot* as house (Stomper 1996a) and the evidence provided by the previously mentioned colonial sources (the San Francisco and Motul dictionaries), clearly shows that buildings referred to as *mat houses* served as the council house—the locus for the community activities of the leaders of the Maya lineages.

The theory that Structure 10L-22A was the community or council house for eighth-century Copán is further augmented by the set of nine glyphs that appear upon the building's facade (Figure 8.4). As discussed previously, six of these nine glyphs have a particular postfix, read as *nal*, that indicates that the glyph is a toponym, or the name of a location. The toponyms that appear upon the facade of Copán's *Popol Na* include the "Black Water" or "Black Hole Place" (*Ik nab nal*); the "Black Tortilla" or "Black Fortress Place" (*Ik pa'nal*); the "First Leg/First Foot" (*Yax ok* or *Yaxo'ok*); the "Black Atole Place" (*Ik sa'nal*); the "Five Flower Place" (*Ho nic nal*); the "Fish Place" (*Kanal*); and "Flower" (*Nic*). The two remaining glyphs are incomplete and cannot be fully deciphered.

Archaeological and epigraphic work conducted outside the Copán Acropolis provides evidence to support the view that these glyphs represent toponyms. One example of this is the glyph upon Structure 10L-22A, at Position 7, read as *Kanal* and translated as the "Fish Place." Andrews, in his excavations of Group 10L-2 just to the south of the Copán Acropolis, recovered a similar glyph within the fill of a collapsed building that was once part of a residential compound (B. Fash 1992; Fash and Andrews 1992; Andrews personal communication 1999) (Figure 8.10a). In addition, a similar fish motif also decorated other buildings of Group 10L-2.

A second region in the Copán Valley is associated with one of the glyphs recorded on Structure 10L-22A. This glyph, at Position 1, signifies the *Ik nab nal* or "Black Water" or "Black Hole Place" (Figure 8.10b). The figure that sits atop this toponym on Structure 10L-22A wears a pendant of tied cords around his neck. Recently, Pennsylvania State excavations in the Sepulturas area (Group 8N-11) recovered a figure from the facade of one of the structures that has this motif as his pectoral—perhaps indicating the place from which the figure came. The identification of this area as the "Black Water" or "Black Hole Place" is further supported by the numerous small reservoirs that dot the Sepulturas area.

Ik nab nal ("Black Water" or "Black Hole Place") is also found on Quiriguá Stelae H and J. On these stelae, the Quiriguá ruler Cauac Sky referred to himself as a "Black Copán Ahau" (Figure 8.11). The *Ik nab nal*

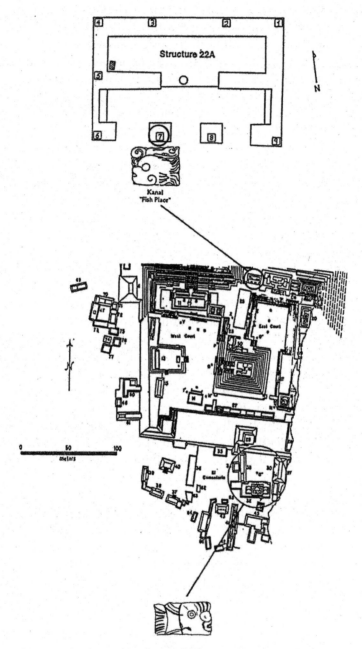

Figure 8.10 Location of *Kanal* glyph on 10L-22A
and location Group 10L-2 with fish glyph.
Top: drawing by Barbara Fash; Middle: after W. Fash
(1991:Figure 8); bottom: after B. Fash (1992:Figure 10c)

toponym or the other two toponyms that refer to black (*ik pa'nal* and *ik sa'nal*) may be in reference to Quiriguá or the Quiriguá rulers. This would not be unexpected because the two sites had strong historical ties. The "Black Hole Place" place-name also occurs on Stela 10, located in the west end of the Copán Valley.

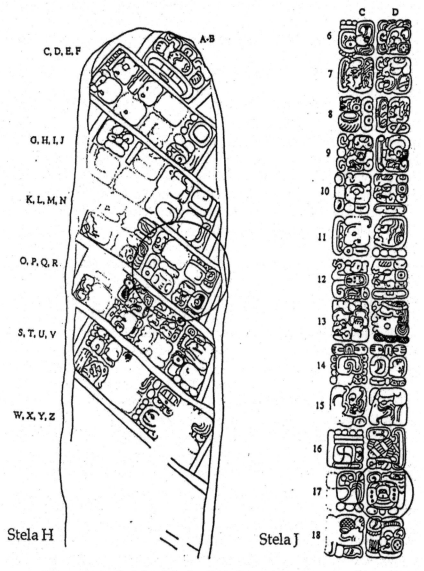

Figure 8.11 Quiriguá Stelae H and J. Left: Quiriguá Stela H.
After Looper (1995:Figure 4.12); right: Quiriguá Stela J.
After Looper (1995:Figure 4.18c)

Although these are the only direct links between the toponyms depicted upon Structure 10L-22A and sites that may have been part of the Copán polity proposed thus far, further research may reveal additional associations. An indication of where these other sites may be located is suggested by the positional correlation between the location of the glyphs on the building and the actual area of the valley that they represent. For example, the *Kanal* toponym, positioned upon the south facade of Structure 10L-22A, corresponds to the location of Group 10L-2, due south of the Acropolis. Furthermore, the *Ik nab nal* toponym is located on the northwest corner of Structure 10L-22A, whereas the Sepulturas building decorated with the chords is located to the northwest of the Copán Main Group.

Considering the positional arrangement of the nine glyphs upon Structure 10L-22A, these toponyms, and the localities to which they refer, may indicate the internal division of the valley by lineage or ward. Another possibility is that the toponyms refer to areas in the valley considered sacred to the Copán Maya. The association of the Structure 10L-22A glyphs with Maya cosmological concepts, such as those concerning the division of the Middleworld by the cardinal directions (indicated in the previous discussion of the quartering of communities), is reiterated by the mythological connotation of some of the toponyms. For example, upon the Yaxchilán Hieroglyphic Stairway David Stuart and Stephen Houston (1994) have found reference to a "Black Hole" in association with a ball game that took place in mythological times (Figure 8.12a). Likewise, these scholars link the toponym for the "Five Flower Place" that appears on Structure 10L-22A with a mythological text on Copán Stela C (Figure 8.12b).

Although some scholars may find it difficult to reconcile the mythological interpretation of these toponyms with the concept of a secular council house, Structure 10L-22A suggests a closer association between actual and supernatural places than commonly recognized for the ancient Maya. These relationships suggest that certain locations or lineages within the Copán Valley were identified with mythologically significant realms, at the very least through the use of a similar name, thereby emphasizing a direct link between the different realms of the Maya cosmos. In addition to understanding the toponyms, an analysis of the figures that sit atop them aid in defining the function that Structure 10L-22A in eighth-century Copán. The figures are distinguished in their dress and have a variety of accoutrements, such as pendants and headdress ornaments, that individualize them. They probably depict actual representa-

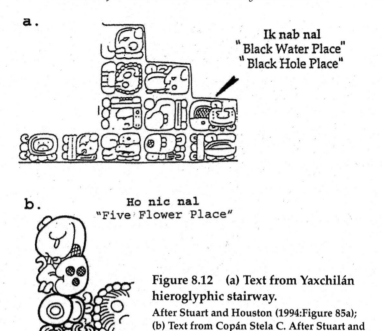

a.

Ik nab nal
" Black Water Place"
" Black Hole Place"

b.   Ho nic nal
"Five Flower Place"

Figure 8.12   (a) Text from Yaxchilán
hieroglyphic stairway.
After Stuart and Houston (1994:Figure 85a);
(b) Text from Copán Stela C. After Stuart and
Houston (1994:Figure 92c)

tives of the localities or lineages indicated by the toponyms. Who were
these figures, and what did they do at the "mat house"? In order to further elucidate these questions, it is necessary to return to an evaluation of
the ethnohistorical sources.

Although these figures could represent the *ahauob* (nobles) or *sahals* (regional governors) who are mentioned frequently within Classic period
inscriptions, it is most likely that they are holders of the office of *holpop*—
a title translated as "he at the head of the mat." As discussed previously,
the importance of this title, and of buildings known as the *Popol Na* in
which *holpop* held their council, are clarified within the colonial-period
documents. For example, in his book *The Titles of Ebtun*, Ralph Roys
stated, "*ah holpop* means he who is at the head of the mat ... This lord
(the *Ah Holpop*) governed and ruled his people in this province with his
caciques, whom they called *holpop*"(1939:43). Roys further stated, "They
were governed formerly by their *caciques*, whom they called *holpop*
... these and no others, consulted with the lord on matters and em-
bassies from outside"(1943:64). Susanna Miles (1957), in her study of the
Pokom Maya of Highland Guatemala, stated that the councillors came
from and represented the various lineages of the town. Furthermore,

these lineages resided in distinct areas, opening the possibility that their lineage affiliation could be referred to by toponym.

The characteristics of the *holpop* provide an analogy for interpreting the function of the individuals represented on Structure 10L-22A. The figures upon this facade (Figure 8.3) are seated at the head (the end) of sculpted mats, the primary symbol of legitimacy and political authority among the Maya. Clearly, these figures depict the lords who "governed and ruled his people in this province" mentioned in Roys. This reiterates the interpretation of the *Popol Na* as a house of council.

Social, Political and Cosmological Implications of the *Popol Na*

Although ethnographic analogy provides a guide for reconstructing Classic period social institutions, other evidence is needed in order to understand fully the functions of the *Popol Na*. This evidence is provided through an examination of the temporal, physical, and cosmological factors involved with the construction, design, and decoration of Structure 10L-22A at Copán.

From the moment of his accession to the throne in 695 AD, the thirteenth ruler of Copán, 18 Rabbit, was a dominant force in the Copán Acropolis and throughout the surrounding valley. Not only was he responsible for a large number of public art projects, including most of the stelae in the Main Plaza, the final version of the ballcourt, and Structure 10L-22, 18 Rabbit also expanded the hegemony of Copán. The iconography and positioning of his monuments place the ruler at the center of the cosmos and are visual testaments to his divine status. In 738 AD, just a few days after dedicating the final version of the ballcourt, 18 Rabbit was captured and later beheaded by Cauac Sky, a rival lord from Quiriguá. The capture and death of Copán's powerful king caused a political crisis within the city.

Just thirty-one days after the death of 18 Rabbit, a little-known figure named in the inscriptions as Smoke Monkey was quickly installed as the fourteenth ruler of Copán. Based on evidence from the excavations and imagery of Structure 10L-22A, the dedication of this building dates to 9.15.15.0.0 9 Ahau 18 Xul (June 4, 746), a time squarely in the reign of Smoke Monkey[2]. Because of the timing of its construction, the *Popol Na* must be understood as part of Copán's reaction to the political crisis caused by the unexpected and humiliating loss of their powerful leader.

The untimely death of 18 Rabbit was a blow to Copánec civic pride, but it also served notice that the ruler (i.e., the central authority) was vulnerable. Structure 10L-22A was clearly a response to this vulnerability, but there are several possible hypotheses concerning the underlying reasons for its construction. The first hypothesis is that the *Popol Na* construction was an expression of power by the elite lineages of the valley, an attempt by them to proclaim physically their power and prestige in Late Classic period Copán. By constructing the *Popol Na* in a prominent location of the Acropolis, the elite invades the sacred space of the East Court, once the exclusive domain of the king. The fourteenth ruler, Smoke Monkey may have attempted to solidify his power base among the elite by including the *Popol Na* among the collection of buildings in the Acropolis.

It is important to note that in the monuments recovered thus far, Smoke Monkey does not make any declaration of a genealogical link to 18 Rabbit nor to his tie to the continuous legacy of the Copán kings. These facts suggest that perhaps, at the time of 18 Rabbit's death, there was no direct heir to the throne, and rulership passed to Smoke Monkey, possibly a more distant relative. If this theory illustrates the actual circumstances surrounding Smoke Monkey's accession, it would further explain his need to incorporate the *holpop*—the lineage heads—upon the facade of Structure 10L-22A and into the new king's political circle (Figure 8.13).

Figure 8.13   Sketch of 10L-22A.
After B. Fash et al. (1992:Figure 15)

In states where lineage membership determines social status (segmentary states), power, wealth, and prestige are continually shifting. In order to attain his position as the Copánec ruler, it is possible that Smoke Monkey (and possibly his lineage) may have had to concede some of his power and prestige to the elite lineages in exchange for their support. Furthermore, due to Smoke Monkey's lack of association with 18 Rabbit, it is entirely possible that he was not of the royal lineage but rather was a member of another elite lineage. With a marginal political base, the support of the valley elite would be essential, and the *Popol Na* an ideal means of expressing it.

The second theory pertaining to the reasons for the construction of Copán's *Popol Na* addresses concepts of elite councils, kinship, and consensus. The *Popol Na* can be viewed as a monument signifying the unity of Copán's elite with the Copán central authority. With the image of the king surrounded by his provincial leaders, the iconography of the *Popol Na* visually proclaimed (by placing him at the very head of the mat) the rule of Smoke Monkey along with the support he received from the most powerful elite. In addition, by placing the lineage heads and their associated toponyms so prominently upon this public building, the unity of Copán's polity was emphasized in a manner not evident before this time.

The serpent, *sac*, and *ahau* motifs on Structure 10L-22A may indicate that this structure was also a symbolic *sac nic te'il na* or "white flower house" (Figure 8.3). This imagery was also present on the facade of Structure 9N-82 at Sepulturas, a building that served as the lineage house or, at least, the locus for lineage activity. If Structure 10L-22A was considered a lineage house, then, based on the presence of the numerous representatives and toponyms depicted on the facade, it was the lineage house for the entire Copán polity.

The reason why the *Popol Na* served as a symbol of unity can be answered by examining the role of elite councils. Elite councils strove to maintain a front of consensus when faced with a decision or crisis. Because of their kinship ties to the ruler and their high status in the community, it was in their best interest to present a united front in the face of political crisis and to maintain the authority of the king. The success or failure of the central authority greatly affected their own social, economic, and political standing (Stomper 1996a).

A final theory concerning the intentions behind the construction of Structure 10L-22A concerns Maya religion and cosmology, which were often used as a social unifying force, especially during times of political crisis. The placement and the iconography of Structure 10L-22A emphasized the cosmological ordering of the Maya world. Structure 10L-22A was located in the sacred realm of the East Court, whose final version took shape during 18 Rabbit's reign. During the time of its construction, 18 Rabbit filled his private court with numerous structures that visually asserted his tie to the cosmos, such as Structure 10L-20, the Bat House (B. Fash 1989); and Structure 10L-22, the Witz Mountain (Freidel et al. 1993). Given its association with the cosmologically dominated East Court, the *Popol Na* can be viewed as a means for the Late Classic period Copánecs to represent the extent and location of the Copán community in the physical as well as supernatural world.

These worlds are centered on Smoke Monkey, whose large figure sits atop a double-headed jaguar throne. As detailed in the text of Stelae C at Quiriguá, the first of the three hearthstones of creation is named the Jaguar Stone Throne, whose placement in the sky initiates a series of actions leading to the creation of the world and of time itself (Freidel et al. 1993:66–67; Looper 1995). Therefore, by situating himself on this jaguar throne, Smoke Monkey places himself at the center of the universe, surrounded by his primary councilors.

The cosmological associations of Structure 10L-22A are even more evident when this structure is examined in relation to the East Court as a whole (Figure 8.14). The false ballcourt (Miller 1988) at the base of the Jaguar Stairway indicates that the floor of the court is the realm of the Underworld. At the top of the Venus-Jaguar Stairway, the Venus god emerges from the mouth of an ecliptic snake (Freidel et al. 1993). The top of the stairway represents the horizon, the point of transition between the Underworld and the Middleworld, and Venus is just beginning to rise above it. On the north side of the court stands Structure 10L-22, which represents the Witz Mountain, the place signifying the First Mountain of Creation (Freidel et al. 1993:149). This building served to place the king (18 Rabbit) at the center of the world as the *axis mundi*. By constructing Structure 10L-22A adjacent to Structure 10L-22, Smoke Monkey and his councils infiltrated this sacred realm. Smoke Monkey further reiterated his cosmological status by placing himself upon the double-headed jaguar throne atop the roof comb of the *Popol Na* for all to see. The *Popol Na* was a three-dimensional cosmogram that displayed how the Copán Maya world was ordered and the place of the king and his councilors in the physical and cosmic worlds.

In conclusion, the hypotheses presented above must be viewed in light of the archaeological and epigraphic evidence found in the main group and in the valley. The population of Copán in Late Classic period times

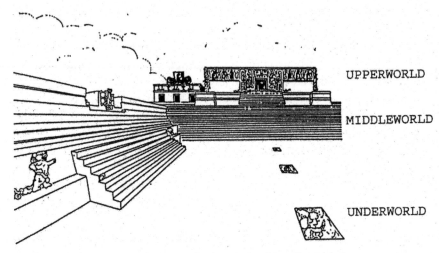

UPPERWORLD

MIDDLEWORLD

UNDERWORLD

Figure 8.14   Isometric drawing of Copán East Court.
After Freidel et al. (1993:Figure 3.23)

greatly exceeded the carrying capacity of the valley; therefore, an ecological and economic disaster was threatening (Sanders 1989). 18 Rabbit was
certainly aware of the social and political ramifications of these pressures, and his extensive construction projects in the main group and
monuments to his divine status may have been a response to them. After
18 Rabbit's death, his two successors, Smoke Monkey and Smoke Shell,
dramatically reduced the number of new constructions in the main
group (although the effort to construct the Hieroglyphic Stairway with
more than 2,000 glyphs may account for this). This suggests that their
power base and ability to organize the labor needed for major construction projects was curtailed. In this light, the construction of the *Popol Na*
(a permanent structure in a highly visible and sacred locale) can be seen
as a monument to the new powers and prestige held by the elite at a time
of changing political and economic circumstances.

   Additional evidence from the reign of the last ruler of Copán, Yax Pas,
also tends to support this theory. Yax Pas, the sixteenth ruler; his half
brother, Yahau Chan Ah Bac; and a relative, Yax Kamlay, are named as
the protagonists on the throne located inside Structure 10L–22A. Yax Pas
is also mentioned with these individuals on Altars G1, T, and U. In addition, he participated in numerous house dedications at elite residences
throughout the valley (W. Fash and Schele 1986; Grube and Schele 1987;
W. Fash 1988, 1991; Webster 1989; Fash and Stuart 1991). This power/

prestige-sharing may be evidence of growing restrictions on the power of the Copán ruler and the development of new strategies to address political and economic changes in the Late Classic period. The presence of other royal names on some of Yax Pas's monuments, coupled with his presence at house dedications of elite residences and ever-increasing population pressures indicates that Yax Pas needed to expend a considerably greater amount of time and energy maintaining and publicly demonstrating his elite power base than did his royal predecessors.

The evidence presented thus far indicates that the construction of Structure 10L-22A was a demonstration that the elite had gained power and prestige during a time of political and economic upheaval. Further, this interpretation most accurately reflects the archaeological and epigraphic data from Late Classic period Copán. However, the religious and cosmological connotations of the structure should not be completely discarded, for the messages communicated through the iconography of the building is highly complex, and it likely possesses multiple levels of meanings. Symbolic language is highly interpretive and depends greatly on the intended audience and the context in which it is presented.

In sum, the evidence presented in this chapter indicates that Structure 10L-22A served as Copán's *Popol Na*, its community house, and its construction must be understood as a reaction to the changing social and political circumstances following the death of the ruler 18 Rabbit. The epigraphic and archaeological data from the main group and throughout the valley during the Late Classic period suggest that there were great social, political, and ecological pressures on the community structure. The construction of the *Popol Na* was a direct result of these pressures and reflects an active attempt by the new king and his elite supporters to manipulate traditional political and ideological systems within a changing world.

References

Ashmore, Wendy.
    1991   Site-Planning Principles and Concepts of Directionality Among the Ancient Maya. *Latin American Antiquity* 2(3):199–226.
Barrera Vasquez, Alfredo.
    1980   *Diccionario Maya Cordemex, Maya-Espanol, Espanol-Maya*. Mérida, Mexico: Ediciones Cordemex.
Becker, Marshall J.
    1982   Ancient Maya Houses and Their Identification: An Evaluation of Architectural Groups at Tikal and Inferences Regarding Their Functions. *Revista Espanola de Antropología Americana* 12:111–129.

1986   Household Shrines at Tikal, Guatemala: Size as a Reflection of Economic Status. *Revista Espanola de Antropología Americana* 14:81–85.

Coe, Michael D.
1965   A Model of Ancient Maya Community Structure in the Maya Lowlands. *Southwestern Journal of Anthropology* 21:97–114.

Fash, Barbara.
1989   Temple 20 and the House of Bats. Paper presented at the Seventh Round Table of Palenque, Palenque, Chiapas, Mexico.
1992   Late Classic Sculptural Themes in Copán. *Ancient Mesoamerica* 3:89–104.

Fash, Barbara, and William Fash.
1991   "He at the head of the mat": Archeological Evidence of a Classic Maya Council House from Copán, Honduras. Paper presented at the 90th Annual Meeting of the American Anthropological Association.

Fash, Barbara, William L. Fash, Sheree Lane, Rudy Larios, Linda Schele, Jeffrey Stomper, and David Stuart.
1992   Classic Maya Community Houses and Political Evolution: Investigations of Copán Structure 22A. *Journal of Field Archaeology* 19(4):419–442.

Fash, William L.
1983a   *Classic Maya State Formation: A Case Study and Its Implications.* Ph.D. dissertation, Harvard University.
1983b   Deducing Social Organization from Classic Maya Settlement Patterns: A Case Study from the Copán Valley. *Civilization in the Ancient Americas: Essays in Honor of Gordon R. Willey.* Edited by Richard M. Levanthal and Alan L. Kolata. Albuquerque, N.Mex.: University of New Mexico Press, and Cambridge, Mass.: Peabody Museum of Archaeology and Ethnology, Harvard University. 261–288.
1988   A New Look at Maya Statecraft from Copán, Honduras. *Antiquity* 62:157–159.
1991   *Scribes Warriors and Kings: The City of Copán and the Ancient Maya.* London: Thames and Hudson.

Fash, William L., and David Stuart.
1991   Dynastic History and Cultural Evolution at Copán, Honduras. *Classic Maya Political History: Archaeological and Hieroglyphic Evidence.* Edited by T. Patrick Culbert. A School of American Research Book. Cambridge: Cambridge University Press. 147–179.

Fash, William L., and Kurt Z. Long.
1983   El mapa arqueologia del Valle de Copán. *Introduccion a la arqueologia de Copán, Volume 3.* Edited by Claude F. Baudez. Tegucigalpa, Honduras: Secretaria de Estado en el Depacho de Cultura y Turismo.

Fash, William L., and Linda Schele.
1986   The Inscriptions of Copán and the Dissolution of Centralized Rule. Paper presented at the 51st Meeting of the Society of American Archaeology, New Orleans.

Freidel, David, Linda Schele, and Joy Parker.
1993   *Maya Cosmos: Three Thousand Years on the Shaman's Path.* New York: William Morrow.

Freter, A.
1988 *The Classic Maya Collapse at Copán, Honduras: A Regional Settlement Perspective.* Ph.D. dissertation, Pennsylvania State University.

Grube, Nikolai, and Linda Schele.
1987 The Date on the Bench from Structure 9N-82, Sepulturas, Copán, Honduras. *Copán Note 23.* Copán, Honduras: Copán Mosaics Project and the Instituto Hondureño de Antropología e Historia.

Harrison, Peter.
1970 *The Central Acropolis, Tikal, Guatemala: A Preliminary Study of the Functions of Its Structural Components During the late Classic Period.* Ph.D. dissertation, University of Pennsylvania.

Haviland, William A.
1968 Ancient Lowland Maya Social Organization. *Archaeological Studies in Middle America.* Middle American Research Institute Publication 26. New Orleans: Tulane University. 93–117.
1972 A New Look at Classic Maya Social Organization at Tikal. *Ceramica de Cultura Maya* 8:1–16.
1982 Where the Rich Folks Lived: Deranging Factors in the Statistical Analysis of Tikal Settlement. *American Antiquity* 47(2):427–429.
1985 Population and Social Dynamics: The Dynasties and Social Structure of Tikal. *Expedition* 27(3):34–41.
1992 Distinguishing the High and Mighty from the Hoi Polloi at Tikal, Guatemala. *Mesoamerican Elites: An Archaeological Assessment.* Edited by Diane Chase and Arlen Chase. Norman, Okla.: University of Oklahoma Press. 50–60.

Kurjack, Edward B.
1974 *Prehistoric Lowland Maya Community and Social Organization: A Case Study at Dzibilchaltun, Yucatán, Mexico.* Middle American Research Institute, Tulane University Publication 38. New Orleans: Tulane University.

Kurjack, Edward B., and E. Wyllys Andrews V.
1976 Early Boundary Maintenance in Northwest Yucatán, Mexico. *American Antiquity* 41:318–325.

Kurjack, Edward B., and Silvia Garza T.
1981 Pre-Columbian Community Form and Distribution in the Northern Maya Area. *Lowland Maya Settlement Patterns.* Edited by W. Ashmore. A School of American Research Book. Albuquerque, N.Mex.: University of New Mexico Press. 287–309.

Leventhal, Richard.
1979 *Settlement Patterns at Copán, Honduras.* Ph.D. dissertation, Harvard University.

Looper, Matthew.
1995 *The Sculpture Program of Butz-Tiliw, an Eighth-Century Maya King of Quiriguá, Guatemala.* Ph.D. dissertation, University of Texas at Austin.

Martinez Hernández, Juan.
1929 *Diccionario de Motul.* Mérida, Mexico: Compania Tipografica Yucateca.

Miles, Susanna.
  1957   The Sixteenth-Century Pokom Maya: A Documentary Analysis of So-
         cial Structure and Archaeological Setting. *Transactions of the American
         Philosophical Society* 47:731–781.
Miller, Mary E.
  1988   The Meaning and Function of the Main Acropolis, Copán. *The Southeast
         Maya Zone*. Edited by Elizabeth Boone and Gordon Willey. Washington,
         D.C.: Dumbarton Oaks. 149–194.
Morán, Pedro.
  1935   *Arte y diccionario en lengua Choltí* (manuscript copied from the Libro of
         Fray Pedro Morán of about 1625). Baltimore: Maya Society.
Puleston, Dennis.
  1983   *The Settlement Survey of Tikal*. Tikal Reports 13. Philadelphia: University
         Museum of the University of Pennsylvania.
Relaciones de Yucatán.
  1898–1900   *Colección de documentos inéditos relativos al descubrimiento, con-
         quista y organización de las antiguas posesiones Españoles de Ultramar, 2nd
         series, Volumes 11 and 13*. Madrid, Spain: Ministero de Ultramar.
Roys, Ralph L.
  1939   *The Titles of Ebtún*. Carnegie Institution of Washington Publication 505.
         Washington, D.C.: Carnegie Institution.
  1943   *The Indian Background of Colonial Yucatán*. Carnegie Institution of Wash-
         ington Publication 548. Washington, D.C.: Carnegie Institution.
Sanders William T.
  1989   Household, Lineage and State at Eighth Century Copán, Honduras.
         The House of the Bacabs, Copán, Honduras. Edited by David Webster.
         Washington, D.C.: Dumbarton Oaks. 89–105.
Sanders, William T., and Barbara Price.
  1968   *Mesoamerica: The Evolution of a Civilization*. New York: Random House.
San Francisco Dictionary.
  1870   *Diccionario Maya-Español y Español-Maya de convenio de San Francisco en
         Mérida*. Mérida, Mexico: Copiado por C. Hermann Berendt, M.D.
Stomper, Jeffrey.
  1996a *The Popol Na: A Model for Late Classic Community Structure at Copán,
         Honduras*. Ph.D. dissertation, Yale University.
  1996b A Model for Late Classic Community Structure at Copán, Honduras.
         Paper presented at the 61st Annual Meeting of the Society for American
         Archaeology Annual Meetings, New Orleans.
Stuart, David, and Stephen Houston.
  1994   Classic Maya Place Names. *Research Reports on Ancient Maya Writing* 33.
         Washington, D.C.: Center for Maya Research.
Tozzer, Alfred M.
  1941   *Landa's Relación de las Cosas de Yucatán: A Translation*. Papers of the
         Peabody Museum of American Archaeology and Ethnology, Harvard
         University, Volume XVIII. Reprinted with permission of the original
         publishers by Kraus Reprint Corporation, New York, 1966.

Webster, David.
  1976   *Defensive Earthworks at Becan, Campeche, Mexico: Implications for Maya Warfare.* Middle American Research Institute Publication 41. New Orleans: Tulane University.
Webster, David, editor.
  1989   *The House of the Bacabs, Copán, Honduras.* Studies in Pre-Columbian Art and Archaeology 29. Washington, D.C.: Dumbarton Oaks.
Willey, Gordon, and Richard Leventhal.
  1979   Prehistoric Settlement at Copán. *Maya Archaeology and Ethnohistory.* Edited by Norman Hammond and Gordon R. Willey. Austin, Tex.: University of Texas Press. 75–102.
Willey, Gordon, Richard Leventhal, and William Fash.
  1978   *Ceramics and Artifacts from Excavations in the Copán Residential Zone.* Papers of the Peabody Museum of Archaeology and Ethnology Volume 80. Cambridge, Mass.: Harvard University.
Wisdom, Charles.
  1940   *The Chorti Indians of Guatemala.* Chicago: University of Chicago Press.

Notes

1. English translation: "... prince of the banquet; landlord (owner) of the house called the *popol na,* where they gather to deal with matters of the republic and teach dance for the town festivals."

2. Structure 10L–22A postdates Structure 10L–22 and predates the construction of 10L–230. Structure 10L–22 contains a date celebrating the 1 katun anniversary of 18 Rabbit's accession (9.14.3.6.8 [715 AD]). Structure 10L–230 was added after the dedication of the Hieroglyphic Stairway at 9.16.5.0.0 (756 AD). A date of 9.15.15.0.0 9 Ahau 18 Xul (746 AD) is the most likely (Stomper 1996a:135–137).

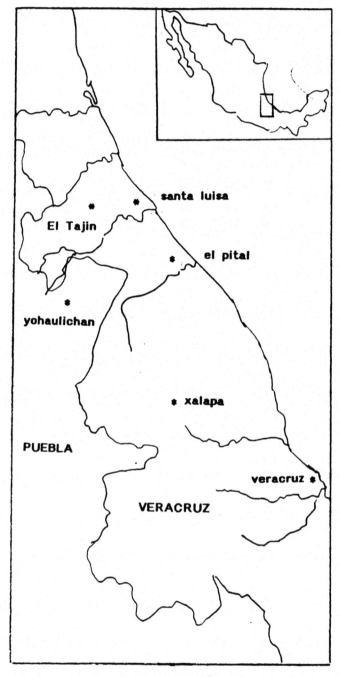

Figure 9.1   The Central Gulf Coast.
Drawing by Sarro after Brüggemann et al. 1992:18.

The Form of Power:
The Architectural Meaning
of Building A of El Tajín

Patricia Joan Sarro

El Tajín was the largest and most important city on the Gulf Coast of Mexico during the Late Classic and Early Postclassic periods. Located in the modern state of Veracruz, it enjoyed a strategic location for trade and cultural interaction with both the Maya to the south and east and central Mexican cities to the west (Figure 9.1). Its participation in the pan-Mesoamerican ball game cult is well recognized, and it has even been suggested that El Tajín may have been a center for the game and its rituals within the region and beyond (Miller 1996:94).

Seventeen ballcourts have now been mapped, and many of the buildings in the lower sector of the city are physically or formally related to one of these courts. There are ball game-related images on the walls of the courts themselves and on other structures far removed from the locus of the game. Such widespread use of these images attests to the game's importance to the life of the city, and these scenes clearly illustrate that the playing of the ball game was only one event in a cycle that included warfare and human sacrifice. They also show that this complex was created under the direct control of the ruling elite, its purpose to secure the favor of the gods.

In this chapter I contend that Building A, located in Tajín Chico, the city's most elevated and privatized zone, although physically separated from the locale of such public rituals, narrates this same drama through architectural form. Such nonfigurative cues as building plan, access, and ornamentation serve to connect this restricted space and therefore the elites of the city, with the rites that take place in the temples and ballcourts below. In doing so, they serve to ground the power of the elite in the power of the sacred.

El Tajín in Time and Space

The first written reference to El Tajín appeared in an article published in 1785, relating how a government inspector came upon a structure the local Totonac people called *Tajín*, meaning "lightning" or "thunder" (Ruiz 1785). Explorers followed in the nineteenth century, and the city has been the subject of archaeological study since the early twentieth century. Its central civic and ceremonial area has been mapped and several of its buildings excavated. Yet many questions basic to the understanding of the city's history remain unanswered or the subject of scholarly debate.

The city's builders, once thought to be the ancestors of the Totonacs who now inhabit the area, are now believed by most scholars to have been the Huastecs, who inhabit a large area of eastern Mesoamerica that includes northern Veracruz.[1] Chronology is also debated. Two contrasting timelines for the city now appear in the literature, and each presents a radically different view of the city's history.[2] José García Payón (1957), whose work at El Tajín began in the 1930s and continued until the 1970s, and other scholars such as S. Jeffrey K. Wilkerson (1973) and Paula and Ramón Krotser (1973), concluded that the city began as a village in the first century AD and flourished until the twelfth century. Jürgen Brüggemann (1992a:65, 1992b:54–59) and members of his team, who conducted excavations and ceramic studies from 1983 to 1992, and some of whom continue to work at the site, propose instead that the history's rise and fall occurred within a period of only three hundred years (850–1150 AD).

Although presenting different views of the city's development, and therefore of its possible interactions with other Mesoamerican cultures, both timelines do agree that El Tajín's major building phase occurred during the Terminal Classic and early Postclassic periods. Flourishing during this time, El Tajín was one of a number of Mesoamerican cities that rose to prominence following the demise of the great central Mexican city of Teotihuacan. At the same time, several lowland Maya cities were experiencing a sharp decline. Each of the emerging cities was faced with the problem of establishing a power base and communicating that power within and beyond its boundaries. In many cases, art served as the conveyer of that message. Debra Nagao (1989) has convincingly shown that the central Mexican cities of Cacaxtla and Xochicalco used selected elements of both Teotihuacan and Maya iconography to achieve this end, each reconfiguring them in a unique manner. Visual associations with such undeniably powerful cities and cultures spoke of participation in a cultural continuance while establishing new, local orders.

The power of El Tajín is also expressed through its art and architecture. Here, however, the encoded message is not one of association with the great cities of another time or place. It is instead a message of cosmic connections: The connections made between men and gods through the ritual ball game cycle and the connection between the power of this cycle and that of the ruling elite who controlled it.[3]

Reading the Visual Text

Many of the sources of information that exist for other areas of ancient Mesoamerica are not available for the study of El Tajín. The city's demise predates the Spanish Conquest by at least three hundred years, and the only written record yet discovered is in the form of a few calendrical name glyphs found in the reliefs of the Building of the Columns. Ethnographic and historical studies are hampered by the questions concerning the ethnicity of the city's builders. Much of our interpretation of the meaning of the iconography of El Tajín must, therefore, draw on analogies to what is known of the art, life, and beliefs of Mesoamerican cultures for which richer databases exist.

Although aspects of El Tajín's art, iconography, and, arguably, its system of beliefs are unique, they clearly fall within a pan-Mesoamerican system of beliefs and modes of artistic expression. Evidence of the 260-day calendar in the few surviving glyphs, the use of bar-and-dot notation, and the playing of the ball game all suggest this, and archaeological evidence confirms trade connections with central Mexico and the Maya area. These similarities and connections argue for analysis through cautious and rational analogies. The art and culture of Teotihuacan, the Maya, and the Aztecs, for which we have the most physical and textual evidence, provide the richest sources for such interpretations.

El Tajín's connections with the cities of central Mexico and the lowland Maya region were direct, but it was separated from the Postclassic Aztec by both distance and time. Since George Kubler's seminal paper (1961) on the subject asserted a disjunction between forms and their meanings over time, it has been recognized that wholesale assumptions of continuity cannot be made. However, arguments for methods of iconographic analyses that cautiously employ cross-cultural and cross-temporal comparisons between Mesoamerican cultures appear in the most current literature, and many more studies employ such a methodology.[4] Many scholars now feel that there is a solid middle ground between continuity and disjunction and that "we may use such a view not to discount the uniqueness of particular societies, but as a way to approach understandings of the rich variety of cultures within the context of shared features and traditions" (Quilter 1996:313).

The Ritual Ball Game Cycle: Warfare, Sacrifice, and Rulership

We know that at the time of the Spanish Conquest the Aztecs played the ball game for a number of reasons, ranging from pure sport to the reenactment of cosmic myth and ritual. Chroniclers tell us that there were two courts in the sacred precinct of Tenochtitlán, the Aztec capital, and that one was described as being for the use of men, the other for the use of the gods, implying that there were both sacred and secular versions of the game. Many scholars suggest that the same was probably true in Mesoamerica during the Classic period as well (see, for example, Miller and Houston 1987:48). The Hero Twins of the Quiche Maya Book of the Dead, the *Popol Vuh*, played for sport before they were made to play for their lives against the gods of the underworld (Tedlock 1985). Given the range of ballcourt

Figure 9.2   South Ballcourt, northwest panel (Kampen 1972:Figure 22)

shapes and sizes across Mesoamerica and throughout time, it is quite possible that there were variations in the form of play as well.[5]

The known imagery of the art of both the Aztec and the Maya illustrate the game only in its ritual context.[6] Our knowledge of other forms of the game comes from native or Spanish texts. For El Tajín, the art and architecture are our only text, and, not surprisingly, these elite structures and objects tell us only of the game as it was played in myth and reenacted in ritual.

The actual playing of the ball game is never illustrated in the art of El Tajín, but the six stone relief panels from the city's South Ballcourt depict a number of associated rituals. In two of these, the narrative occurs in an open area defined by two parallel sloping walls, the configuration of the Mesoamerican ballcourt. In one of these scenes, the rubber ball used in the game is shown set on the ground between the two figures, and both are dressed in the ballplayer's regalia of yoke, *palma*, and protective kneepads (Figure 9.2). The pair appears to be conversing on the ballcourt, perhaps awaiting the start of the game. Their elaborate headdresses indicate their elite status.

The other panel depicts a scene of sacrifice. Again, the central figures wear elite headdresses and protective ball game gear (Figure 9.3). Sacrifice is integral to this ritual game, as shown here and elsewhere. That the two are closely linked in Mesoamerican thought and practice is evident from the skull racks placed conveniently close to ballcourts in Aztec Tenochtitlán and Maya Chichén Itzá. Scenes of sacrifice by decapitation involving figures in ballcourt dress appear in the ballcourts of Chichén Itzá, Aparicio, and Santa Luisa Cotzumalhuapa, as well as El Tajín.

The other four scenes depicted on the South Ballcourt are not shown as taking place on the ballcourt, but their location on the walls of the court clearly connects their events with the game played there. In one, a figure is being outfitted not for the game, but for war; in another, musicians play as an eagle-costumed dancer gestures over a prone figure, accompanied by musicians (Kampen 1972:Figures 49, 51). Temporal order is not indicated in these panels, but a number of possible sequences have been suggested (see, for example, Kampen 1972; Wilkerson 1987; Koontz 1994). What is clear is the unification of the ball game, warfare, and sacrifice in their imagery and placement. These actions draw the attention and participation of members of the supernatural world.

Each scene is bounded on one side by a skeletal figure who looks on from a watery realm. A grotesque face hovers over the scene in which the warrior is dressed, and at the moment of sacrifice another skeletal super-

Figure 9.3   South Ballcourt, northeast panel (Kampen 1972:Figure 23)

natural reaches down from above to receive the offering of human life. In the two central panels, human and otherworldly figures appear together in a watery underworld, a locale often depicted in the art of El Tajín (Figure 9.4). In these images, sacrifice is extended to the realm of the gods, and divine auto-sacrifice is performed in return for human. The central panels and other relief images from El Tajín also indicate that ball game-related sacrifice was believed to result in communication with the gods and with rewards of agricultural fertility and prosperity. They depict trees and plants, including locally grown corn and maguey from the highlands, springing from the bodies of victims and growing up around scenes of sacrifice (See, for example, Kampen 1972:33a). "Even a superficial analysis of the iconographic contexts at Chichén, Bilbao and Tajín suggest the aim of the ball game sacrifice was the rejuvenation of agricultural fertility" (Pasztory 1972:444).

The ball game cycle is again portrayed in one of the relief compositions of the Building of the Columns on Tajín Chico's highest terrace. These sculptures contain the city's only known glyphic inscriptions, many of

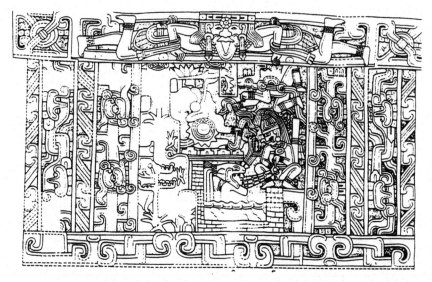

Figure 9.4   South Ballcourt, southcentral panel (Kampen 1972:Figure 24)

which identify a single figure, 13 Rabbit, sometimes shown as the principal figure, sometimes as one participant among many. In one scene, this lordly personage is shown personally directing all stages of ball game-related ritual (Figure 9.5). He is here depicted twice: as the central, seated figure who receives the captives of war, and as one of those leading captives before him (Koontz 1994:127–128). In the central image, 13 Rabbit sits surrounded with signs of other events of the ritual complex. The game's rubber ball and the head of an already-sacrificed victim lie at his feet. To his left, the divine reward of abundant vegetation grows from the victim's corpse. In this single image, as in the six panels of the South Ballcourt, the full ritual cycle of warfare, ball game, sacrifice, and divine reward is depicted.[7]

Tajín Chico:
An Elite Acropolis

The ballcourts of El Tajín, like those of many other Mesoamerican cities, are set in the heart of the city, amidst temples, palaces, and plazas.[8] At El Tajín, this is the lower area of a city center that is divided into two major sectors. Although their construction periods overlap, at least the outermost, final phases of the buildings of Tajín Chico postdate the majority of

Figure 9.5   Column fragment, Building of the Columns.
Drawing by Sarro after Wilkerson 1990:Figure 80,
with additional data from Wilkerson 1987.

those of the lower area (Figure 9.6).[9] This lower area is also the more public and accessible. Its many temples, plazas, and ballcourts identify it as a
place of gathering and ritual. In contrast, there are no ballcourts and only
one structure (not yet excavated) that may have served as a temple in
Tajín Chico (Figure 9.6T). The large-scale Building of the Columns, the
city's largest construction and one of its last, once stood on the highest
ridge. From here all of El Tajín is visible. It is generally believed that the
many platforms and multiroomed structures of Tajín Chico were dedicated to the activities of city and regional government and to the residence of the most elite (García Payón 1965:22, Brüggemann 1991a:100).
    I would argue, however, that Tajín Chico was a zone of ritual as well as
residence, albeit a more private and restricted one than that below. A similar division of ritual space into public and private areas occurs elsewhere in Mesoamerica. At Copán, the Hieroglyphic Stairway and the
steps leading to Building 10L-11 separate the public northern plazas from
the smaller, enclosed East and West Plazas (Fash 1991:Figures 8, 16).[10]
Cynthia Kristan-Graham (chapter 12 in this volume) describes another
separation of public and private ritual space at Chichén Itzá.

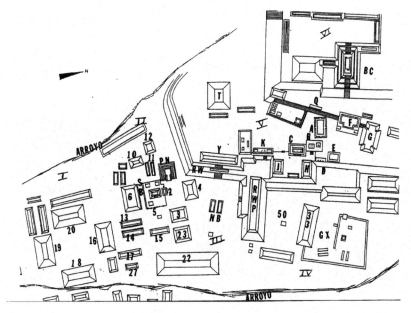

Figure 9.6   Plan of El Tajín.
Drawing by Sarro after Wilkerson 1987.

Tajín Chico and lower Tajín are physically separated both by elevation and the architectonic barrier of the Retaining Wall that supports the terraces above (Figure 9.7). Its two wide staircases lead only to a narrow ridge and provide no direct access to the buildings above. Beyond this level, the path leading to the buildings and plazas of Tajín Chico grows increasingly narrow, restricted, and indirect.

Nearly all the buildings that line the outer rim of Tajín Chico have porticoes or three-sided rooms, which open visually onto this lower space (Figure 9.8). This configuration, like the wall's broad staircases, suggests welcome and access, yet this visual path is matched by true access only in the case of Building Y. Early excavations suggest that one can pass through this building into the area around Temple T, and thus it may have served as a point of both access and control. Other plazas of Tajín Chico, and the Building of the Columns above them, can be entered only by an increasingly narrow and restricted series of staircases and passageways. To enter the seemingly welcoming outer rim buildings, one must circle around them to their true entrances, which are on the sides that face away from the Retaining Wall. To gain access to these buildings, one must already have passed through a series of staircases and passages to

Figure 9.7   The Retaining Wall with the North Ballcourt

the inner plazas of Tajín Chico. The wide Retaining Wall steps and the open-sided structures above serve then to create a visual rather than an actual direct connection between the public and restricted zones of the city. It is in this way they unite Tajín Chico and its elite functions and residents with the people and rituals below.

The Retaining Wall forms two sides of the Plaza of the North Ballcourt, one of the largest open spaces in the city. The wide steps and three-sided buildings above may indeed have served a practical function as viewing stands for the events of the ball game complex. They may also have extended those events into Tajín Chico, acting as places of ritual display, perhaps even of sacrifice. Such possible uses aside, the physical proximity of the Retaining Wall to the ballcourt and the apparent openness of the buildings above visually link Tajín Chico with the ritual court and plaza. By extension, all of Tajín Chico is connected with the city's lower area and thus the ruling elite with the ball game and other sacred rites.

Reading the Forms of
Mesoamerican Architecture

Unlike the open-sided buildings of the outermost ridge, those of Tajín Chico's inner plazas are not easily visible from below the Retaining Wall.

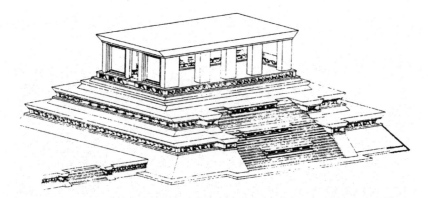

Figure 9.8 Building C reconstruction (Wilkerson 1987:39)

In these, the connection with lower Tajín is expressed through formal quotations rather than visual access. This is most evident in the form of Building A, a multiroomed structure set strategically at the base of the broad staircase that leads to the Building of the Columns (Figure 9.9). Small mural fragments have been recovered that suggest that at least some of Building A's walls once were decorated with painted scenes of ritual activity, but too little has survived for us to reconstruct anything approaching a full iconographic program. Yet, even without direct depictions of the game or related events, the form of Building A alone serves as a text that relates the final stage in the ball game drama: the reemergence of life from the underworld.

The reading of meaning in architectural form is well established in Mesoamerican studies. Kubler's analysis of the talud/tablero profile drew on form and the pattern of its use to conclude that the profile indicated or imparted sacredness to structure and space (Kubler 1973, 1985:354). Others have found iconographic meaning in urban plans or have included iconographic information in the analyses of form and placement. Wendy Ashmore's model for the cosmic significance of spatial manipulation in Maya lowland cities is based on the analysis of city plans, together with information on the Maya view of the cosmos (Ashmore 1991). Richard Townsend (1979, 1987) and others draw on their knowledge of Aztec cosmology and ritual as well as the analysis of built form to conclude that the Templo Mayor complex of Tenochtitlán embodies and encodes the myth of Huitzilapochtli and relates the power of that deity to the Aztec ruler. Saburo Sugiyama (1993) includes information from other Mesoamerican cultures in his interpretation of the cosmic and

**Figure 9.9   Building A below the Building of the Columns,
during excavations, 1993**

calendrical significance of the Pyramid of the Feathered Serpent in Teotihuacan. My approach is similar to that of these authors in interpreting
the associational meaning of Tajín Chico from both the formal elements
of structure and space and from iconographic information found in both
the art of El Tajín and that of the wider Mesoamerican area.

Building A:
A Cosmic Map

Entrance to Building A is through a narrow set of recessed steps cut into
the south side of its solid base (Figures 9.10–9.12). This tunnel-like passage is set into an ornamental framework stuccoed and painted to mimic
a shallow staircase.[11] The balustrades of this false staircase are decorated
with step frets and topped by niches, a configuration closely matching
that of the actual staircase of the Pyramid of the Niches and other of the
lower sector's temple platforms (Figure 9.13).[12]

Whatever the specific function of Building A, this replication of a temple facade declares the structure's sacred nature in a formal language
specific to El Tajín. The quotation of architectural form as decorative mo-

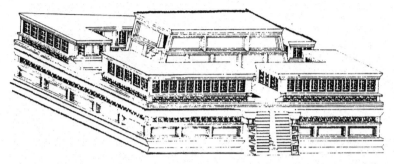

Figure 9.10   Building A reconstruction (Wilkerson 1987:49)

Figure 9.11   Building A's entrance

tif is well documented elsewhere in Mesoamerica. One example is Structure 1 of the Maya site of Xpuhil (Heyden and Gendrop 1988:Plate 168). The three temple platforms that soar above its low facade are entirely false, their steps unclimbable, the temple forms above unenterable solid masses. These are decorative elements, not architectural forms, that serve to associate Structure 1 with the temples of the powerful cities of the Peten, such as Tikal. In its false staircase facade, Building A is similarly

Figure 9.12   Building A's entrance from above

Figure 9.13   The Pyramid of the Niches

identified with sacred temple space, but in this instance the reference is local, and the sacred space that of El Tajín itself.

The form of Building A suggests associations with the ball game and its rituals even more powerfully. Its formal relationships to ballcourts and pyramids serve as signs of the cosmic cycle and elite ritual. Ceremonies related to the four quarters of the universe and the three cosmic levels of earth, heavens, and underworld are here made timeless and are concretized in space. The three levels and four-part plan of Building A symbolize nothing less than the three-tiered universe and four quarters of the earthly realm that were the Mesoamerican cosmic map.

The lowest level of Building A is a rectangle of solid fill. Above it, a smaller solid base with sloped sides once supported a single room that formed the third level (García Vega 1936, 1937). This smaller base is framed by four L-shaped suites of two rooms each. Each of these suites rounds one of the four corners, the aisles between them forming a cross. The plan of the second level of Building A thus fits the pan-Mesoamerican construct of the universe as comprised of four quarters associated with the four cardinal directions.[13] In this worldview, a fifth, vertical line is shared by the three realms of the heavens, earth, and underworld. The three levels of Building A can be seen as representing these. The lowest is solid fill, the dense, impenetrable mass of the underworld. The second level, with its four aisles, is the earth, inhabited by humanity and divided into four quarters. The third, temple-like room above a sloped base represents the celestial.

The four aisles of upper Building A are in the form of mini-ballcourts. They duplicate, on a small scale, the sloped-sided type that is now known to be the dominant one at the site (Figure 9.14). The side walls of these aisles, like those of many of El Tajín's courts, are formed of a low banquette topped by a widely sloping wall. On the ballcourts, porticoes or open-sided rooms above serve as protected viewing spaces. On Building A, these are indicated by shallow niches, which may have served a practical purpose as benches.

False ballcourts are known from the Maya region of Mesoamerica. Both the East and West Courts of the Copán Acropolis have been identified as such, as indicated by the three stone ball game markers set into each court's floor and other sculptural iconography (Miller 1988:181; Freidel, Schele, and Parker 1993:352–353). Only at Building A, however, is the architectural form of a ballcourt exactly replicated. The second level of Building A can be read as the four quarters of the earth defined as the ballcourts of El Tajín. The tunnel-like entrance is then analogous to

Figure 9.14   Ballcourt 11, with Temple 12 in the distance

the passage between the earth and the underworld, a passage created through the activities of the ball game cult as depicted in the relief sculptures of the South Ballcourt.[14]

Emergence from a hidden realm to the light above is like the rising of the sun after its nightly journey through the darkness of the underworld. Walter Krickeberg (1966), using primarily Aztec myth and imagery, describes the ball game as a metaphor for the sun's journey across the heavens, into the underworld—symbolized by the ballcourt—and its return. Esther Pasztory summarizes the cosmological basis for the game in Mesoamerica as follows:

> The ballgame symbolizes the disappearance of the sun into the underworld. The sun meets his death during a ballgame waged by him and his brother (the planet Venus) against the gods of death and night. The underworld, a watery land of night, is the domain of the earth-moon goddess who becomes the bride of the night sun. Subsequently, the earth goddess gives birth to the young god of maize (who is actually the sun reborn) and he and Venus defeat the powers of darkness (1972:445).

Thus, the earth itself is defined in terms of the ballcourt, and the ballcourt serves as the link between the earth and the underworld, the place of emergence both in myth and in the architectural form of Building A.

The cross that represents the four quarters of the earth is also formally linked to the quatrefoil cartouche that from Preclassic Olmec times depicted the connection between the earth and the underworld (Schele and Freidel 1991:308; Reilly 1996:35). This liminal space is a place of great power, one also associated with rulership. Dorie Reents-Budet (2001) has noted that the quatrefoil marked with crossed bands is one of a limited number of motifs that appear on the piers of court buildings depicted on Maya painted vessels.

The image of a powerful figure set within this cross-shaped passage is found throughout Mesoamerica. On the rock carving known as El Rey at the Olmec site of Chalcatzingo, a deity or ruler sits within a cave shown in cross-section as two-thirds of the quatrefoil cartouche.[15] The form here is clearly seen as being the earth monster, the cave its mouth. In El Rey, the result of the ruler's communication between the earth and the underworld is fertility: Winds blow from the mouth of the cave, phallic raindrops fall to earth, and plants spring up. The Classic Maya used this same form to frame the images of ancestors and, on the early ballcourt markers of Copán, show humans and underworld deities united in the ballgame (Fash 1991:Figure 69). In Building A, the living elite actually stand within the cross or quatrefoil space, having passed first through the "maw" of the tunnel entrance.

This representation of the opening between the earth and the underworld in the form of a cross was used again at El Tajín in the murals of Building J (Figure 9.15).[16] Here a series of figures, elaborately garbed in feathered headdress and jade necklaces, are depicted in a horizontal band on a bench that frames three sides of what appears to be a throne room. Each figure is framed by the cross-shaped entrance to some undes-

Figure 9.15   Mural fragment from Building J (drawing by Sarro)

ignated interior space. It is impossible to say if these figures are gods or if they represent people from El Tajín's historical or legendary past. The murals are very small scale (the entire bench structure is less than a meter high), and the three examples of the figure now visible are all greatly ruined in the facial area.

The headdressed figure framed in each cross-shaped cartouche appears in an active position, as though involved in ritual dance. His locale within the cross-shaped space suggests that his dance connects him with the underworld. Linda Schele (1988) has demonstrated that the Palenque rulers shown dancing in the Dumbarton Oaks Panel and a number of other images from that city are depicted at the moment of apotheosis. Having overcome death, they are dancing out of Xibalba, the Maya underworld. These Maya reliefs are narrative, each showing the ruler full length and in the presence of one or both long-deceased parents (Schele 1988:Figures 10.4, 10.9). The mural figures of Building J are visible only from the hips up and are framed within the cross without any narrative context indicated. Yet their arm positions and the vegetal forms emerging from their mouths suggest that they too are dancing out of the underworld. Schele (1988:315) believes that the dance of these Maya rulers may be related to that of the Hero Twins of the *Popol Vuh*, who danced to celebrate their triumph over the Lords of the Underworld in the ball game.

As rulers, sacrificed ball players, or mythological figures, the dancing lords of Building J may indeed celebrate in dance the triumph over death, and their triumph may also be due to the rites of the ball game complex. The court is often depicted as the connecting point between the earth and the underworld in the art of the Maya. Writing about Maya ballcourts, Mary Ellen Gutierrez (1993) points out the relationship between the ballcourt profile and the cleft in the *tun witz*, the first true mountain of creation; the quatrefoil cartouches of Copán were set along the axis of the ballcourt floor. Building A images the four quarters of the earth and the entire cosmos in terms of the ritual ball game complex—its events and its locale. What is depicted in the murals of Building J may have been reenacted in ritual at Building A.

Building A:
Ritual Reference or Ceremonial Space?

The representation of the cosmic map in the form, ornamentation, and arrangement of architecture has parallels in the architecture of other Mesoamerican cities. Buildings 10L-11 and 10L-22 of the Late Classic city of Copán, like Building A, are set in a restricted area, elevated above a ballcourt plaza. Each has a doorway surrounded with sculptural elements that form cosmograms. As at Building A, to enter one must literally pass through the levels of the cosmos. The Templo Mayor of the Aztec capital city of Tenochtitlán is a particularly well-studied example of architecture as cosmic image. Like Temple A, this most important of Aztec temples represents the four quarters of the earthly realm and the three levels of the cosmos (Townsend 1979:37–39; Matos Moctezuma 1987). Beyond the imaging of universal space, the Templo Mayor also depicts time, specifically the mythic time of creation. This myth is stated in both architecture and sculpture and was reenacted in ceremony. Such specifics of belief and ritual at El Tajín are unknown to us. It is also unclear how Building A was actually used. We know from conquest-era texts that the Templo Mayor was just that, a major temple set within a clearly defined sacred precinct, devoted to ritual and closely associated with rulership.

Building A does not resemble any Mesoamerican temple, and its locale is far from the structures of El Tajín that do. Mesoamerican palaces are far more varied in form, and, indeed, the term is used to describe almost any relatively large structure of fine workmanship that is not obviously a temple. But Building A's base and the configuration of its rooms imply more than space for residence or government, the usual functions of a palace. It may be possible that it is ritual in more than reference, although the nature of that ritual is not clear. Formal and iconographic references are to the ball game cycle, but it is clear that the ball game was not played here; the court-like aisles are far too small and inaccessible. Nor is there space at the top of the staircase for temple rituals to be performed. Yet Building A's tunnel-like entrance and opening onto the upper level do suggest a possible theater for ceremony.

At the small, mostly unexcavated Classic site of Morelos Paxil, Veracruz, another building with a tunnel-like entrance has been discovered (García Payón 1939, 1940). This low pyramid platform, that site's Building A, has no staircase on the side facing its plaza and can be entered only by climbing a staircase accessed from the opposite side. Passing through the body of the platform, the climber emerges onto the surface on the plaza side. It would have been possible for a ritual participant to appear (or disappear) via this hidden staircase during ceremonies.

David Freidel and Charles Suhler (1999) have recently discovered two Late Preclassic platforms with trapdoor access from hidden corridors below at the northern Maya site of Yaxuná. They have concluded that these may have been dance platforms used in a ritual much like that performed by the Quiche Maya and described by a sixteenth-century Spanish observer. In this ritual, two dancers, representing the Hero Twins in the underworld, first disappear and then reappear in a cloud of smoke, using a trap door (Coe 1989:161–162).

Building A faces onto two large plazas. Many of the structures to the southwest, the side of its tunnel entrance, have been excavated. They are multiroomed structures, one with a true second story (Building B). A number of these include rooms lined with benches, and, like Building J, these may have served as places of elite residence and gathering. The plaza to the northeast has never been fully excavated, and its buildings, although mapped, remain to be explored. On this side of Building A, directly opposite the tunnel entrance and below one of the ballcourt-shaped aisles, is a shallow niche bordered on the left and right by narrow panels of geometric decoration. This configuration in stucco can be compared to the formal arrangement of entrance and balustrade, and thus forms a second entrance to the building, a "face" to this plaza. The evidence of Yaxuná's tunneled structures and Building A of Morelos Paxil suggests that Building A also may have been used in a ceremony of emergence. It may be that the ruler entered Building A's southwest tunnel, to emerge onto its ballcourt-like surface, and appear on the opposite side. Given the building's formal references to the ball game cycle and the cosmic map, this ceremony would have been one somehow connected with the game and its rituals and the power they conferred, one reenacting a mythic emergence from the underworld. Such ceremonial use would not preclude Building A's having had residence or government as its primary function. Such a function could only have increased the prestige of the building, its residents, and those favored with viewing such an event in this elevated, restricted area of the city.

In their art, the elite of El Tajín chose to state their power not through lineage, as did the classic Maya, but through elite control over ritual. In narrative images, acts of warfare and interaction with the gods are portrayed in relationship to the ballgame, the central core of the city's belief and worship, and it is the elite who are shown to direct and guide these actions. Tajín Chico's embracing of the plaza of the North Ballcourt, and the visual connection between those separate spaces, announces both connection and control. Building A, and the ceremonies that took place there, claims the full ball game ritual cycle and its sacred power for the rulers of the city. Its narration of the ball game myth and significance in this restricted, elite locale declares the right of rulership in Tajín Chico to be grounded in the rites of the ballgame.

Acknowledgments

This project began as a section of my doctoral dissertation, and Esther Pasztory, my academic advisor, gave generously of her time and support at every stage. Several colleagues in Mexico were of great assistance, providing access to materials and data, and sharing their ideas on El Tajín with me. Among these, S. Jeffrey K. Wilkerson, Jürgen Brüggemann, Mario Navarrete Hernandéz, Sara Ladrón de Guevarra, and Doris Heyden merit particular thanks. Rex Koontz continues to be a true colleague; our discussions about the city have greatly expanded my views on the life and art of El Tajín.

References

Ashmore, Wendy.
  1991   Site-Planning Principles and Concepts of Directionality among the Ancient Maya. *Latin American Antiquity* 2(3):199–226.
Brüggemann, Jürgen K.
  1991a   Analysis urbano del sitio arqueológico del Tajín. *Proyecto Tajín, Volume 2*. Edited by K. Jürgen Brüggemann. México, D.F.: Instituto Nacional de Antropología e Historia. 81–126.
  1991b   Otra vez la cuestión totonaca. *Informes, Proyecto Tajín 1991, Volume 1*. México, D.F.: Archivo Técnico, Instituto Nacional de Antropología e Historia.
  1992a   Arquitectura y urbanismo. *Tajín*. Edited by Jürgen K. Brüggemann, Sara Ladrón de Guevarra, and Sánchez Bonilla. México, D.F.: CITIBANK. 55–83.
  1992b   La ciudad y la sociedad. *Tajín*. Edited by Jürgen K. Brüggemann, Sara Ladrón de Guevarra, and Sánchez Bonilla. Xalapa, Veracruz: Gobierno del Estado de Veracruz. 52–77.
Brüggemann, Jürgen K., Sara Ladrón de Guevarra, and Sánchez Bonilla.
  1992   *Tajín*. Xalapa: Gobierno del Estado de Veracruz.
  1992   *Tajín*. México, D.F.: CITIBANK.
Coe, Michael D.
  1989   The Hero Twins: Myth and Image. *The Maya Vase Book, Volume 1*. Edited by Justin Kerr. New York: Kerr Associates. 161–184.
Fash, William L.
  1991   *Scribes, Warriors and Kings*. London: Thames and Hudson.
Freidel, David, and Charles Suhler.
  1999   The Path of Life: Toward a Functional Analysis of Ancient Maya Architecture. *Mesoamerican Architecture as a Cultural Symbol*. Edited by Jeff Karl Kowalski. New York: Oxford University Press. 274–297.
Friedel, David, Linda Schele, and Joy Parker.
  1993   *Maya Cosmos: Three Thousand Years on the Shaman's Path*. New York: William Morrow.

García Payón, José.
1939 Exploraciones en el Totonacapan Septentrional y Meridional (en El Tajín y Misantla), temporada de 1939. *Informes CXXVI, Estado de Veracruz, Tajín Volume 2, 1936–1940.* México, D.F.: Archivo Técnoco, Instituto Nacional de Antropología e Historia. 944–945.
1940 Exploraciones en la zona arqueológico del Tajín, de Municipio de Papantla, Veracruz, 1939–40. *Informes CXXVI, Estado de Veracruz, Tajín, Volume 2, 1936–1940.* México, D.F.: Archivo Técnico, Instituto Nacional de Antropología e Historia. 945–946.
1957 *El Tajín, Official Guide.* México, D.F.: Instituto Nacional de Antropología e Historia.
1962 Exploraciones arqueológicos en El Tajín, durante la temporada de 1961–1962. *Informes CXXX, Estado d Veracruz, Tajín, Volume 6, 1959–1962.* México, D.F.: Archivo Técnico, Instituto Nacional de Antropología e Historia. 958–963.
1965 La ciudad arqueológica del Tajín. *Revista Jarocha* 34–35:21–25.
García Vega, Agustín.
1936 Informe de los trabajos de exploración de las ruinas del Tajín. *Informes CXXVI, Estado de Veracruz, Tajín, Volume 2, 1936–1940.* México, D.F.: Archivo Técnico, Instituto Nacional de Antropología e Historia. 941–942.
1937 Informe de los trabajos ejecutatos en la zona del Tajín. *Informes CXXVI, Estado de Veracruz, Tajín, Volume 2, 1936–1940.* México, D.F.: Archivo Técnico, Instituto Nacional de Antropología e Historia. 943–944.
Gutierrez, Mary Ellen.
1993 Ballcourts: The Chasms of Creation. Texas Notes on Precolumbian Art, Writing, and Culture 53. Austin, Tex.: University of Texas Press.
Heyden, Doris, and Paul Gendrop.
1988 *Pre-Columbian Architecture of Mesoamerica.* New York: Electra/Rizzoli.
Kampen, Michael E.
1972 *The Sculptures of El Tajín, Veracruz, Mexico.* Gainesville, Fla.: University of Florida Press.
Koontz, Rex.
1994 *The Iconography of El Tajín, Veracruz, Mexico.* Ph.D. dissertation, University of Texas at Austin.
Krickeberg, Walter.
1966 El juego de pelota Mesoamericano y su simbolismo religioso. *Traducciones Mesoamericanistas, Volume 1.* Edited by Paul Kirchoff. México, D.F.: Sociedad Mexicana de Antropología. 191–313.
Krotser, Paula H., and Ramón Krotser.
1973 Topographía y cerámica de el Tajín, Veracruz. *Anales* 7(3):177–221.
Kubler, George.
1961 On the Colonial Extinction of the Motifs of Pre-Columbian Art. *Essays in Pre-Columbian Art and Archaeology.* Edited by Samuel Lothrop. Cambridge, Mass.: Harvard University Press. 14–34.
1973 Iconographic Aspects of Architectural Profiles at Teotihuacan and in Mesoamerica. *The Iconography of Middle American Sculpture.* New York: Metropolitan Museum of Art. 24–39.

1985 Renascence and Disjunction in the Art of Mesoamerican Antiquity. *Studies in Ancient American and European Art: The Collected Essays of George Kubler*. Edited by Thomas Reese. New Haven: Yale University Press. 351–359.

Ladrón de Guevarra, Sara.

1992 Pintura y Escultura. *Tajín*. Edited by Jürgen K. Brüggemann, Sara Ladrón de Guevarra, and Sánchez Bonilla. México, D.F.: CITIBANK. 99–132.

Leyenaar, Ted J. J., and Lee A. Parsons.

1988 *Ulama: The Ballgame of the Mayas and the Aztecs*. Leiden: Spruyt, Van Mantgem, and De Does bv.

Matos Moctezuma, Eduardo.

1987 Symbolism of the Templo Mayor. *The Aztec Templo Mayor*. Edited by Elizabeth Hill Boone. Washington, D.C.: Dumbarton Oaks. 185–209.

Miller, Mary Ellen.

1988 The Meaning and Function of the Main Acropolis, Copán. *The Southeast Classic Maya Zone*. Edited by Elizabeth Hill Boone and Gordon R. Willey. Washington, D.C.: Dumbarton Oaks. 149–194.

1996 *The Art of Mesoamerica, from Olmec to Aztec*. London: Thames and Hudson.

Miller, Mary Ellen, and Stephen Houston.

1987 Stairways and Ballcourt Glyphs: New Perspectives on the Classic Maya Ballgame. *RES* 14:47–66.

Nagao, Debra.

1989 Public Proclamation in the Art of Cacaxtla and Xochicalco. *Mesoamerica After the Decline of Teotihuacan*. Edited by Richard A. Diehl and Janet Berlo. Washington, D.C.: Dumbarton Oaks. 83–104.

Pasztory, Esther.

1972 The Historical and Religious Significance of the Mesoamerican Ballgame. *Religíon en Mesoamerica. XII Mesa Redonda*. Edited by Jaime Litvak King and Noemi Castillo Tejero. México, D.F.: Sociedad Mexicana de Antropología. 441–455.

Quilter, Jeffrey.

1996 Continuity and Disjunction in Pre-Columbian Art. *RES* 29/30:82–101.

Reents-Budet, Dorie.

2001 Classic Maya Conceptualization of the Royal Court: An Analysis of Palace Court Renderings on the Pictorial Ceramics. *The Royal Courts of the Ancient Maya*. Edited by Takeshi Inomata and Stephen Houston. Boulder: Westview Press.

Reilly, Kent F., III.

1996 Art, Ritual, and Rulership. *The Olmec World, Ritual and Rulership*. Edited by Michael D. Coe et al. Princeton: The Art Museum, Princeton University. 27–45.

Ruiz, Diego.

1785 Papantla. *Gazeta de Mexico* 42:347–354.

Sánchez Bonilla, Juan.

1995 Edificio I. El Palacio del Arte en El Tajín. *El Tajín. Estudios Monográficos*. Edited by Héctor Cuevas Férnandez et al. Xalapa: Universidad Veracruzana. 31–65.

Sarro, Patricia Joan.
1995 *The Architectural Meaning of Tajín Chico, the Acropolis of El Tajín, Mexico.* Ph.D. dissertation, Columbia University.
Schele, Linda.
1988 The Xibalba Shuffle: A Dance of Death. *Maya Iconography.* Edited by Elizabeth P. Benson and Gillett G. Griffin. Princeton: Princeton University Press. 294–317.
Schele, Linda, and David Freidel.
1991 The Courts of Creation: Ballcourts, Ballgames, and Portals to the Maya Otherworld. *The Mesoamerican Ballgame.* Edited by V. L. Scarborough and D. R. Wilcox. Tucson, Ariz.: University of Arizona Press. 289–315.
Spinden, Herbert J.
1957 *Maya Art and Civilization.* Indian Hills, Colo.: Falcon's Way Press.
Sugiyama, Saburo.
1993 Worldview Materialized in Teotihuacan, Mexico. *Latin American Antiquity* 4(2):103–129.
Taube, Karl A.
1992 The Temple of Quetzalcoatl and the Cult of Sacred War at Teotihuacan. *RES* 21:53–87.
Tedlock, Dennis, translator.
1985 *The Popol Vuh.* New York: Simon and Schuster.
Townsend, Richard Fraser.
1979 *State and Cosmos in the Art of Tenochtitlán.* Studies in Pre-Columbian Art and Archaeology 20. Washington, D.C.: Dumbarton Oaks.
1987 Coronation at Tenochtitlán. *The Aztec Templo Mayor.* Edited by Elizabeth Hill Boone. Washington, D.C.: Dumbarton Oaks. 411–449.
Wilkerson, S. Jeffrey K.
1973 *Ethnogenesis of the Huastecs and Totonacs: Early Cultures of North-Central Veracruz at Santa Luisa.* Ph.D. dissertation, Tulane University.
1987 *El Tajín, A Guide for Visitors.* Xalapa: Universidad Veracruzana.
1990 El Tajín: Great Center of the Northeast. *Mexico, Splendors of Thirty Centuries.* New York: Metropolitan Museum of Art. 155–181.
1991 The Flute Calls. *The World & I* 6(6):638–651.

Notes

1. Wilkerson 1973. This view is not universally accepted, however. See Brüggemann 1991b.

2. For a discussion of theories concerning the ethnicity of the inhabitants of El Tajín and the city's dates of occupation, see Sarro 1995:3–16.

3. In the past, a number of scholars have argued for direct connections between El Tajín and both Teotihuacan and the Maya region, perceiving a shift from Teotihuacan to Maya style architecture over time (see, for example, Spinden 1957 and Kubler 1985:355).

4. See, for example, Taube 1992.

5. Ballcourts of different shapes and sizes can be found within the same city. El Tajín's many courts vary greatly in size and include examples of both sloped and vertical sides, some with and some without end zones.

6. Parsons believes that a now-lost graffiti from the Maya site of Tikal, Guatemala, may represent a nonritual game, perhaps one played in practice for ritual events (Leyenaar and Parsons 1988:22). However, even these loosely dawn figures wear fairly elaborate headgear, and it is possible that this unofficial image may also depict ritual play.

7. Rex Koontz (1994:127–129) argues convincingly that this and other scenes from El Tajín depict a scaffold-gladiatorial ritual sequence employed to establish authority.

8. See, for example, the plans of Monte Albán and Chichén Itzá and the representation of the Aztec Templo Mayor complex in the early colonial *Primeros Coloniales* (Miller 1996:Figures 62, 146, 163).

9. García Payón believed that the structures he discovered beneath those of Tajín Chico's central plaza were among the city's earliest (Wilkerson 1987).

10. The L-shaped configuration of these staircases, and the way they delineate the Court of the Hieroglyphic Staircase, is quite similar to the relationship of the Retaining Wall to the North Ballcourt Plaza of El Tajín. There are a number of interesting similarities between these two cities that are yet to be examined.

11. The false staircase construction also serves the practical function of buttressing the base of Building A.

12. García Payón and Wilkerson place all of visible Tajín Chico late in the city's history, but Brüggemann believes that the Pyramid of the Niches is one of the city's last constructions. I consider Building A to be later than the Pyramid of the Niches for a number of reasons. First, the argument for a late dating is based only on the building's cramped position within its plaza, which Brüggemann believes indicates that it was the last to be built there. However, without data concerning the depth of each of the plaza's buildings relative to one another, a reliable sequence cannot be determined, making it just as likely that the Pyramid of the Niches was the first to be built, as García Payón and others have said. Second, the close relationship between the false entrance of Building A and the true staircase of the Pyramid of the Niches itself suggests that the pyramid was built first. The false version of Building A has no function other than its form, that of an ornamented staircase. The Pyramid of the Niches has such a staircase, one with balustrades that match the false ones of Building A. It is far more likely that this actual staircase leading to one of the city's most central and important temples was the reference for the shallow, ornamental version than that the opposite were true or that their resemblance be merely coincidental.

13. The actual orientation of Building A and the surrounding structures is not true north but 40⁰ east of north, with the entrance on the southwest side.

14. A connection between Building A and the ball game may also be found in one of the mural fragments from its upper level (Brüggemann et al. 1992:105). It shows two men, one who may be wearing a yoke, positioned to either side of a large red circle. If this is an illustration of the game, it is the only one found thus far in the imagery of El Tajín.

15. David C. Grove, *Chalcatzingo*, Figure 5. New York: Thames and Hudson, 1984.

16. This structure was named Building J by García Payón, but it is called Building I in Brüggemann's more recent maps. It is marked J on the map given here. For analyses of this structure and its murals, see Sánchez Bonilla 1995 and Ladrón de Guevarra 1992.

Political Rhetoric and
the Unification of Natural Geography,
Cosmic Space, and Gender Spheres

LINNEA WREN
KAYLEE SPENCER
KRYSTA HOCHSTETLER

For the peoples of north central Yucatán, Chichén Itzá was simultaneously a formidable militaristic polity, an aggressive trade center, and an
important religious site. The polity self-consciously proclaimed its importance not only by the enormity of its constructions but also by an
imaginative expansion of its visual vocabulary. This expanded vocabulary provided a persuasive form of political rhetoric that asserted the influence of the Itzá across wide geographic regions of Mesoamerica and
that identified the Itzá capital as the geographic site of cosmic creation.
So persuasive was this political rhetoric that it persisted in both Maya
and Mexican cultures long after Chichén Itzá itself was eclipsed.

During the Terminal Classic period, Chichén Itzá emerged as one of
the important polities within a network of politically independent cosmopolitan capitals (Kepecs et al. 1994). The geographic territories under
the direct administrative control of the Itzá probably did not extend outside northern Yucatán. However, the Itzá evidently established a network
of trade and exchange that reached into the southern Maya lowlands and
central Mexico. Moreover, the Itzá apparently converted their economic
and cultural preeminence into claims of military and political hegemony
over much of Mesoamerica.

These claims can be seen in the cist cover (Figure 10.1) from the floor of
the Temple of the Wall Panels (Ruppert 1952). This relief depicts two war

captains who are engaged in a ritual involving a ceremonial offering. The hatch markings suggest that the offering, which is located on the ground between the ritual participants, may be identified as a basket of woven or matted grass. Fragments of several woven baskets with lids have been recovered from the Sacred Cenote at the site (Melford 1992:91, Figure 4.1). Among both the Maya and the Aztecs, woven reed mats were symbols of rulership, and twisted grass cords were implements in auto-sacrifice. Matted grass, or *malinalli*, also suggested a range of additional ritual associations for the Aztecs. It functioned as a metaphorical substitute for the hair and skin of the earth deity, Tlaltecuhtli; it served as an absorbent surface for blood sacrifice; and it was given as an offering to the sun by warriors during battle as a supplication to destroy the enemy (Peterson 1983).

The captains on the cist cover from the Temple of the Wall Panels are encircled by a pair of ascending snakes, consisting of a feathered serpent and a jaguar serpent. The significance of these serpents may be suggested by comparison with the murals at Cacaxtla. In Building II-1, murals painted with serpent and bird imagery flank a doorway that opens to the west from an inner chamber. On the north wall panel (Kubler 1980:Figure 3) a jaguar serpent frames a male figure who is attired in jaguar costume and who holds a ceremonial bar consisting of bundled darts. On the north doorjamb (Kubler 1980:Figure 4) a similarly attired figure is shown

Figure 10.1   Cist Cover from the Temple of the Wall Panels

holding, in his right arm, a vase from which water spills and, in his left hand, a water snake. A flowering corn plant issues from his abdomen. On the south wall panel (Kubler 1980:Figure 6) a feathered serpent frames a male figure who wears black body paint and who holds a ceremonial bar that consists of bundled spears. On the south doorjamb (Kubler 1980:Figure 5) a similarly painted figure is shown holding, in his right arm, a conch shell from which a diminutive human figure emerges. Both in the north and south wall panels and in the north and south doorjambs the compositional formats and the figural poses are closely mirrored, whereas the iconographic complexes are emphatically contrasted.

At Cacaxtla, it is evident that the serpents function as emblems of the two warring parties depicted in the nearby battle murals. The jaguar serpent is accompanied by jaguar warriors whereas the feathered serpent is accompanied by black painted warriors, the more prominent of whom assumes avian markers (Foncerrada de Molina 1978, 1980; Kubler 1980; Quirarte 1983). Karl Taube (1994b) has proposed that the depictions of the jaguar snake and jaguar warriors are characterized by many attributes of Central Mexican ancestry, whereas the depictions of the feathered serpent and bird warrior are replete with many attributes of Maya origin. In Taube's view, the compositions marked with feline attributes denote the western range of highland Mexico while the compositions marked with avian attributes allude to the Maya land of the east.

Taube's association between the paired serpents and the paired geographic regions appears to be confirmed at Chichén Itzá by two exterior reliefs on the Temple of the Wall Panels (Figures 10.2–10.3). Both scenes are organized in three registers. War captains encircled by jaguar and feathered serpents dominate the central axis of the middle registers. Spreading out to each side are landscape scenes. The circular shapes in the north panel may depict barrel cacti (Figure 10.2). Spiny plants with flowers and twisted roots in the murals of Teotihuacan (Berrin 1988:Figure VI.24; de la Fuente 1995:Figures 18–11, 18–16, 18–18) and in the sculpture of Tikal (Jones and Satterthwaite 1982:Figure 69) have been identified by Karl Taube (personal communication 1993) as barrel cacti with exposed roots (Figure 10.4). One plant in the uppermost left hand corner of the north panel of the Temple of the Wall Panels may represent a barrel cactus with roots protruding along its lower circumference. A second plant in the same panel may represent a barrel cactus with flowers blossoming along its upper circumference. The long-tailed birds perching in trees in the south panel may be identified as quetzals (Figure 10.3). The inclusion of flora and fauna typical of different regions suggests that the

Figure 10.2   Temple of the Wall Panels, Chichén Itzá

panels are paired in terms of the geographic regions they represent. The north panel, incorporating barrel cacti, can be understood as an Itzá claim of hegemony over the land of the west, that is, central Mexico. The south panel, incorporating three quetzals, can be understood as an Itzá claim of hegemony over the land of the east, that is, the southern Maya lowlands. The north and south panels can, therefore, both be understood as monumental examples of visual rhetoric. Each panel appears to func-

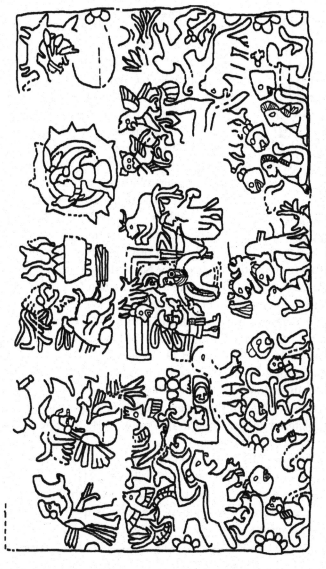

Figure 10.3   Temple of the Wall Panels, Chichén Itzá

tion as part of a propagandistic campaign to magnify the hegemony of the Itzá elite beyond the immediate physical territories within northern Yucatán that were actually controlled by Chichén Itzá.

This assertion of dominion over a large geographic territory was evidently made possible in Itzá political rhetoric by the emergence of Chichén Itzá as the central nexus in a long-distance trade network. Through their advantageous geographic location near the coast of north

Figure 10.4
Barrel cacti

central Yucatán, the Itzá were able to exploit both water and land routes of trade. Itzá merchants reached Veracruz toward their west, around the peninsula to Cozumel toward their east, and Belize and Honduras toward their south (Sabloff and Freidel 1975; Freidel and Sabloff 1984; Krockock 1998). Strategic coastal locations also enabled the Itzá to link their trade routes with important inland sites (Rathje 1975; Sabloff and Rathje 1975; Krochock 1998). Gold and tumbaga objects reached Chichén Itzá from the Pacific coast of Panama and from the Pacific and Caribbean coasts of Costa Rica (Bray 1996). Copper reached Chichén Itzá from Mexico or Honduras (Lothrop 1952). Turquoise reached Chichén Itzá from northern Mexico or New Mexico (Kelley 1980; Harbottle and Weigand 1992). Obsidian reached Chichén Itzá from central Mexico and highland Guatemala (Andrews et al. 1989; Braswell 1997). Tecali reached Chichén Itzá from Puebla and northern Oaxaca (Coggins 1984a). Cotton (Roys 1933; Kepecs and Boucher 1991), *cacao* (Krochock 1998), and salt (Andrews 1983; Andrews et al. 1988; Kepecs et al. 1994; Braswell 1997) were among the most important local products that the Itzá exported from their domain.

This assertion of dominion over a large geographic territory was apparently bolstered and justified in Itzá political rhetoric by the identification of Chichén Itzá as the place of cosmic creation. Because of the religious importance of its Sacred Cenote, Chichén Itzá enjoyed the status of a pilgrimage center (Roys 1933:173–176; Tozzer 1941:109). Sculpture associated with the well suggests that the cenote itself was regarded as a nexus of supernatural power where the cosmos itself had been birthed. This cosmic creation, or birthing, is suggested by the presence at the cenote rim of three monumental frogs. Two of the three frogs carry their offspring on their backs (Ruppert 1952:8). The symbolic importance of frogs in contemporary Yucatecan Maya rainmaking ritual is well documented (Redfield and Villa Rojas 1962:142). The symbolic association of frogs with female sexuality in the ancient cosmologies of Mesoamerica is also documented. Both Maya and Mexican cosmology associated frogs and toads with female sexuality. The up-ended frog birthing glyph of Maya inscriptions is well known. At the Maya site of Balamkú, Campeche, stucco reliefs of the Early Classic period depict full-figure toads (Baudez 1996). The amphibians burp seated lords from their mouths as if metaphorically birthing the kings. In much of Mexico today, the word frog is employed as a term for women's genitalia, and in Aztec speech, the word frog was sometimes used as a name for the Earth Goddess, Tlaltecuhtli (Klein 1988).

The connection between frogs and female procreation as embodied by the Earth Goddess also exists in Chichén Itzá. The Sacred Cenote is connected by a *sacbe* to the Great Plaza and the Great Ball Court. Reliefs and murals in the ballcourt temples include recumbent figures associated with serpents. L. Schele and P. Mathews (1998) have identified these figures as depictions of the jade-skirted Maize God. However, Taube (1994b) has noted the close iconographic similarities between these figures and central Mexican depictions of the Earth Goddess. In both iconography and concept, the long-skirted deity at Chichén Itzá resembles the female earth deity later known to the Aztecs as Tlaltecuhtli. In the North Temple of the Great Ball Court at Chichén Itzá, two columns depict the earth goddess surmounted by trees, the branches of which are interlaced with flowering and fruited vines (Figure 10.5). The balustrades of the

Figure 10.5   Earth Goddess

North Temple depict trees growing from monster heads (Figure 10.6). On the north wall of the North Temple, the earth goddess is shown with a bifurcated serpent emerging from her abdomen. The tongues of the serpent heads are marked as flint blades (Figure 10.7). According to Taube, the motif refers to two related acts of creation, the dismemberment of the Earth Goddess and the raising of the heavens by the cosmic trees.

Like all Maya ballcourts, the Great Ball Court of Chichén Itzá was a supernatural seat associated with cosmic creation. In the iconographic program of the Great Ball Court, the representations of the progenitor of cre-

Figure 10.6 Trees

ation is combined with militaristic subjects. Individual warriors are celebrated in the jambs of the Upper Temple of the Jaguars and on the piers of the South Temple. Acts of military conquest are depicted in the murals of the Upper Temple of the Jaguars while a ritual dance involving an assembly of warriors is shown in the reliefs of the Lower Temple of the Jaguars. Through the rhetorical use of their visual imagery, the Itzá were evidently claiming that they were agents in cosmic creation and that the military conflicts they waged actualized supernatural events in the cosmic realm.

One such supernatural event is the defeat of the Underworld forces of darkness and death. In the exterior reliefs of the Temple of the Wall Panels (Figures 10.2–10.3), the Itzá warlords are set not only in geographic space but also in cosmic space. Jaguars and moan owls, denizens of the Underworld in both Maya and Mexican cosmologies, roam the landscapes of both reliefs. The captives who are seated in the lower register of both reliefs are identified not by rank, ethnic costume, or individual name but instead by their mythic role. A jaguar head emblem floats in front of each captive's face. The back end of each captive's loincloth is lengthened and curved upward so that it forms an animal tail.

K. Ruppert (1952) originally argued that these tails were simian, that the figures represented monkey-people, and that the scenes depicted Maya creation legends. However, comparisons with Maya vase paintings indicate that the animal tails as well as the animal heads associated with the captives are feline. These tails have the thicker dimension of jaguar tails, and they do not display the more pronounced curvilinear shape of monkey tails. Nonetheless, Ruppert's association of these scenes with creation mythology still appears valid. In Maya mythology, jaguars played an important role in the events of the creation epochs preceding the fourth sun, that is, the present era. In the *Popol Vuh*, the epoch of wooden people was ended by monstrous jaguars that came in a black rain and that reduced their victims to bones (Tedlock 1985). Although the *Popol Vuh* relates that the people who escaped became monkeys, a contemporary Lacandon variant of the creation myth identifies an early, failed human race as Jaguar-People (Grove 1972).

In central Mexican mythology, jaguars also played an important role in the events of the creation epochs preceding the fifth sun, that is, the present era. The Aztecs identified the first sun by the calendrical name 4 Ocelotl or 4 Jaguar because the people of the first sun were devoured by ferocious jaguars at the end of this creation era. The second sun, 4 Ehecatl or 4 Wind, was presided over by Quetzalcoatl. At Dos Pilas, La Amelia, and other Maya sites, sculptures depict jaguars beneath the feet of victorious Maya lords. In this compositional format, the jaguar substitutes for the more common motif of the bound and subjugated human captive (Houston 1993:Figures 3–21, 3–24).

The *Popol Vuh* relates a struggle between the destructive Underworld forces and the Hero Twins, Hunahpu and Xbalanque. The Twins had been fathered by a supernatural, Hun Hunahpu, who had been summoned to the underworld, Xibalba. Defeated by the Xibalban lords, Hun Hunahpu had been decapitated. Spittle from the head of Hun Hunahpu in the hand of Xk'ik, the daughter of a lord of Xibalba, had resulted in the conception of the Hero Twins. Like their father, the Twins journeyed to Xibalba where they were challenged to play ball against the lords of death. When they were unvanquished on the playing court, the Twins were subjected to a series of tricks that were designed to defeat and to kill them. But through the assistance of two diviners, Xulu and Pakam, the Twins devised a means of fiery death that would bring them back to life. After the voluntary death of the Twins, the Xibalbans crushed their bones and threw the

Figure 10.7   Serpent heads

powder into a river. Five days later, the Twins reappeared in the guise of fish men. Their subsequent deeds persuaded the Xibalbans to allow themselves to be sacrificed, an act which subdued the forces of death.

In both the north and the south panels of the Temple of the Wall Panels (Figures 10.2–10.3), the defeated enemies of the Itzá are identified as jaguars. The visual imagery may reflect the Itzá identification of their opponents either as an earlier, inferior race from a previous creation or as Underworld beings who had brought destruction to humans during earlier eras. In the north panel (Figure 10.2) the Itzá captain who stands on the western side of the structure on the central axis is depicted as a fish man, a possible reference to the resurrected Hero Twins. Thus, in representing their defeated enemies as jaguars, the Itzá lords may be identifying themselves with supernatural heroes who defeated the destructive underworld forces.

A second cosmic event actualized by the Itzá was the dawning of the new sun. In both Maya and central Mexican cosmology, blood sacrifice was necessary to raise the sun into the heavens and to sustain its journeys. The three faces of the lintel in the Upper Temple of the Jaguars depict the solar deity receiving an offering from a war captain (Figure 10.8). Separating the two seated figures is a skeletal mask with waterlilies. The watery underworld location suggested by this motif is further supported by the placement above the solar deity of a mural band depicting the Earth Goddess (Coggins 1984b).

Around the interior walls of the Upper Temple of the Jaguars are six battle scenes in which prisoners are captured, bound, and stripped for sacrifice (Coggins 1984b:157–165, Figures 17–20; Miller 1977). The reclining figure of an earth goddess is depicted in the upper panel above the west doorway (Coggins 1984:Figure 19; Miller 1977). Above the Earth Goddess, a sacrificial scene of heart excision is portrayed. Only through continuing bloodshed in war and sacrifice could the sun be raised from the Underworld and sustained above the earth. Provided with the necessary blood offerings by the Itzá lords, the solar deity assumes his position in the heavens. In the south panel of the Temple of the Wall Panels (Figure 10.3), the compositional format of the lintels is expanded. The solar deity is shown in the upper register of the panel as he accepts an offering from a war captain encircled by a serpent. Below him are the Itzá lords depicted in poses of conquest. At their feet are the captives of war. Thus, the decorative program of the Upper Temple of the Jaguars offers a cosmic justification for the military campaigns undertaken by the Itzá war captains.

267

Figure 10.8   Solar Deity

Political rhetoric at Chichén Itzá was highly effective because it provided a divine charter not only for justifying military conflicts against other polities but also for promoting social cohesiveness among its own elite. In the inscriptions of Chichén Itzá, the war captains trace their ancestry through their matrilineages. These parentage statements may well reflect the mixed ethnic composition of the people who ruled Chichén Itzá (Grube 1994). The Itzá elite may well have been the sons of nonlocal Maya who are described in ethnohistorical sources as seizing the region of Chichén Itzá. Because these foreigners reportedly entered the region without women, they can be presumed to have married women of local lineages. The choice made by Itzá sons to emphasize their matrilineal descent apparently indicates that their mothers conferred upon them greater social prestige and political legitimacy than did their fathers.

The hieroglyphic texts of Chichén Itzá suggest the importance of the female, as well as the male, gender in determining the divine charter. These texts record numerous individuals as participants of collective rituals, especially fire ceremonies and dedicatory rites. Although biographical events such as births, accessions, and deaths are largely absent, a few parentage statements are included. These statements, which extend to no more than three generations, refer only to matrilineal descent.

Two women are given special prominence as venerated ancestors. A lady who is the possessor of *u wohol*, "her glyphs," is identified as the maternal grandmother of Lady Nik, "flower"(Grube 1994:Figure 14). Lady Ton Ahau, "penis lord," is identified as the mother of Lady K'ayam Ahau (Grube 1994:Figure 13a). Lady K'ayam, in turn, is identified as the mother of K'ak'upacal (Grube 1994:Figure 16b) as well as the mother of K'in Kimi (Grube 1994:Figures 16a–b). As the maternal grandmother of K'ak'upacal, Lady Ton Ahau can be identified as the female ancestral founder of the Itzá elite. The name of this venerable female clearly combines male and female procreative powers. In addition to being the progenitor of the Itzá elite at Chichén Itzá, Lady Ton Ahau may have become the paradigm of the founding ancestor for Postclassic cultures of central Mexico. The Aztec informants of Sahagún reported that the ideal great-grandmother was "the founder, the beginner [of her lineage]" (Anderson and Dibble 1961, Volume 10:5; Nash 1978).

The supernatural progenitor of the Maya, known as Ix Chel, or Goddess O, is depicted in the Lower Temple of the Jaguars on the north entrance column (Figures 10.9–10.10). Like all Mesoamerican deities, Goddess O was multivalent in meaning. She was closely identified with divination, medicine, childbirth, and weaving. In addition to being associated with benevolent forces of creation and healing, Goddess O was also associated with the powers of destruction and death. Among her many aspects, Goddess O was considered to bring storms, rains, and world-destroying floods (Schellhas 1904; Thompson 1939).

In Postclassic depictions, Goddess O often wears a serpent headdress and sometimes holds a serpent in her hands. On the column faces of the Lower Temple of the Jaguars, Goddess O is shown superimposed upon an ascending serpent. In addition to these well-known depictions, another depiction of Goddess O can be recognized in the Lower Temple of the Jaguars in the interior reliefs. These reliefs represent a throng of warriors arranged in five bands. Placed on the central axis in a prominent position is a single female figure wearing a snake skirt (Figure 10.11). She is followed by an assistant who carries a bowl of sacrificial hearts. This figure shares so many of the standard military attributes that Alfred Tozzer (1957, Volume XII:Figure 538) published her as an example of a typical Toltec warrior. However, the clearly outlined breasts below the wide collar indicate that this figure is anything but a typical warrior.

Figure 10.9　Goddess O

This female figure can be identified as the ritual impersonator of a warrior variant of Goddess O. The combination of weaponry and snake attributes shown with this figure confirms the association made by J. E. S. Thompson (1939) between the Maya Goddess O and the Aztec goddess Cihuacoatl. Like Goddess O, Cihuacoatl was regarded as an earth and fertility goddess and was honored as a founding ancestor (Klein 1994). The inclusion of the Warrior/Goddess O impersonator among the Itzá lords can be seen as a rhetorical acknowledgment of the important role that elite women had played in founding and legitimizing Itzá rule.

Like Goddess O, Cihuacoatl was regarded as the patron of midwives and childbirth. She was also considered the protector of warriors. The mar-

Figure 10.10
Goddess O

Figure 10.11
Female wearing snake skirt

tial aspect of the female deity is further revealed by the adoption of the title and costume of Cihuacoatl by the Aztec military leader who was also one of the most trusted advisers to the Aztec king. During its occupancy by the statesman Tlacaelel, the office of Cihuacoatl became especially prominent (Hassig 1988:43, 279). The inclusion of the Warrior/Goddess O impersonator among the Itzá lords is further evidence of the important role that elite women continued to play in maintaining the Itzá polity.

The role played by elite women included childbirth. The Aztecs compared childbirth to a battle, the parturient to a mighty warrior, and newborn infants to captives of their mothers. Women who died in childbirth were described as "suffering manfully" and were accorded an afterlife approximating that of warriors. Warriors who met death in battle or sacrifice were believed to go to a special paradise at the eastern horizon. There they daily escorted the rising sun to its noontime zenith. Women who met death in childbirth were perceived as warriors and were described as if costumed for the battlefield. They were responsible for escorting the sun from its zenith to its disappearance at the western horizon (Klein 1994). Thus, the pairing of eastern and western regions in the Temple of the Wall Panels may allude to the complementarity that the Maya perceived in male and female gender roles (Joyce 1992), as well as to geographic areas and cosmic realms.

The role which elite women played in maintaining the Itzá polity involved economic activities, including spinning and weaving. Cotton was an especially important trade good of northern Yucatán (Kepecs et. al. 1994). Spun and woven into cloth, cotton increased its value as a luxury item. Landa's *relación* reports that woven cloth, in the form of gifts, offerings, and exchanges, were a crucial part of ritual life (Tozzer 1941). It can be assumed that for the Maya, as for the Aztecs, cloth was also a primary means of organizing the flow of goods and services that sustained the state and that cloth served as an idiom of political negotiation. Through their textile production, women advanced men's claims to positions of status and power (Brumfiel 1992). Perhaps because women's activities of spinning and weaving reinforced the state in ways similar to warfare, two-thirds of the spindles and whorls found at Chichén Itzá are decorated with the militaristic emblems of the jaguar and the eagle (Tozzer 1957).

The role that elite women played in maintaining the Itzá polity, in rare instances, may have also included direct participation on the battlefield. Cecilia Klein (1994) cites instances in Aztec mytho-history in which women went to war. She cites one memorable strategy employed by the fifteenth-century ruler of Tlatelolco. When his army of male warriors could not resist the vigorous attacks of the Aztecs, the Tlatelolcan king responded in desperation by ordering women into battle. As one contingent of women flung brooms, cane staves, and weaving implements, a second contingent of women stripped naked, flaunted their genitals, squeezed their breasts, and taunted their foes with charges of cowardice. Even though these women fought in a manner that caricatured male patterns of warfare, other women reputedly adopted masculine military methods. The Aztecs describe Toltec women as having fought valiantly beside their husbands and even as taking prisoners before being killed. The Aztec also described their own women as courageously entering battle against a Tepanec attack in the period prior to the foundation of their capital. One mythic female, Quilaztli, is given special prominence in Aztec accounts. Unwilling to be considered vile, worthless, and of little spirit "like any other woman," Quilaztli is described as dressing herself for battle in order to prove that she was strong and "manly."

These legendary accounts of women warriors may reflect instances in which extraordinary women entered the masculine domain of military action. Recent excavations at Teotihuacan (Sugiyama 1989) have discovered two burial pits of four women who were evidently warriors. Moreover, some women are known from preconquest records to have exercised military and political powers. Such women include Lady Six Monkey, whose deeds are accounted in Mixtec codices, and Lady Wak Chan of Naranjo and Lady Sak Kuk of Palenque (Freidel et al. 1993).

At Chichén Itzá, the Warrior/Goddess O impersonator is placed directly above the dominant male figure who is marked with many symbols of rulership. The appearance of the Warrior/Goddess O impersonator at Chichén Itzá suggests that the political office of Cihuacoatl may have been created in the northern Maya lowlands capital. It further suggests that the origin of this and of many Postclassic concepts of polity and empire may be traced to Chichén Itzá. Finally, it demonstrates the potential of rhetoric to integrate natural geography, sacred space, and even the masculine and feminine spheres into a compelling vision by which contending populations and contentious genders could be unified into polities and inspired into ambitious actions.

Acknowledgments

We would like to thank Peter Schmidt, Saburo Sugiyama, and Karl Taube for the insight and data that they have generously shared with us. We are indebted to Ruth Krochock for her willingness to read early drafts of this paper and to offer advice. Annabeth Headrick, Rex Koontz, and Kathryn Reese-Taylor have provided invaluable suggestions in the development of our ideas.

Finally, we would like to express appreciation for the financial support awarded to us by the Presidential Faculty/Student Collaboration Grant of Gustavus Adolphus College, St. Peter, Minnesota.

References

Anderson, A. J. O., and C. E. Dibble.
   1961   *General History of the Things of New Spain: Florentine Codex.* Santa Fe, N.Mex.: School of American Research.
Andrews, A. P.
   1983   *Maya Salt Production and Trade.* Tucson, Ariz.: University of Arizona Press.
Andrews, A. P., F. Asaro, H. Michel, F. Stross, and P. C. Rivero.
   1989   The Obsidian Trade at Isla Cerritos, Yucatán, Mexico. *Journal of Field Archaeology* 16:355–363.
Andrews, A. P., T. G. Negrón, F. Robles Castellanos, R. Cobos, and P. C. Rivero.
   1988   Isla Cerritos: An Itzá Trading Port on the North Coast of Yucatán, Mexico. *National Geographic Research* 4:196–207.
Baudez, C.
   1996   Balumkú, Campeche. *Arqueología Mexicana* 3(28):26–41.
Berrin, K., editor.
   1988   *Feathered Serpents and Flowering Trees: Reconstructing the Murals of Teotihuacan.* San Francisco: Fine Arts Museum of San Francisco.
Braswell, G.
   1997   El Intercambio Prehispanico en Yucatán, Mexico. *X Simposio de Investigaciones Arqueologicas en Guatemala 1996.* Edited by J. P. Laporte and H. L. Escobedo. Guatemala City: Museo Nacional de Arqueología y Etnología. 545–555.
Bray, W.
   1996   Central American Influences on the Development of Maya Metallurgy. *Los Investigadores de la Cultura Maya 4.* Campeche, Mexico: SEP/FOMES, Univeridad Autonoma de Campeche. 307–329.
Brumfiel, E. M. S.
   1992   Weaving and Cooking: Women's Production in Aztec Mexico. *Engendering Archaeology: Women and Prehistory.* Edited by J. M. Gero and M. W. Conkey. Oxford: Blackwell. 182–204.
Coggins, C. C.
   1984a The Cenote of Sacrifice: Catalogue. *Cenote of Sacrifice: Maya Treasures from the Sacred Well at Chichén Itzá.* Edited by C. C. Coggins and O. C. Shane III. Austin, Tex.: University of Texas Press. 23–166.
   1984b Murals in the Upper Temple of the Jaguars, Chichén Itzá. *Cenote of Sacrifice: Maya Treasures from the Sacred Well at Chichén Itzá.* Edited by C. C.

Coggins and O. C. Shane III. Austin, Tex.: University of Texas Press. 157–165.

Cohodas, M.
1978   *The Great Ball Court at Chichén Itzá, Yucatán, Mexico.* New York: Garland.

Foncerrada de Molina, M.
1978   The Cacaxtla Murals: An Example of Cultural Contact. *Ibero-Amerikanisches Archiv* 4:141–160.
1980   Mural Painting in Cacaxtla and Teotihuacan Cosmopolitanism. *Third Palenque Round Table, 1979, Part 2.* Edited by M. G. Robertson. Austin, Tex.: University of Texas Press. 183–198.

Freidel, D. A., and J. A. Sabloff.
1984   *Cozumel, Late Maya Settlement Patterns.* New York: Academic Press.

Freidel, D. A., L. Schele, and J. Parker.
1993   *Maya Cosmos: Three Thousand Years on the Shaman's Path.* New York: William Morrow.

Fuente, Beatrice, de la.
1995   *La Pintura Mural Prehispanica en Mexico, Volume 1.* México, D.F.: Universidad Nacional Autónoma de Mexico.

Grove, D. C.
1972   Olmec Felines in Highland Central Mexico. *The Cult of the Feline.* Edited by E. P. Benson. Washington, D.C.: Dumbarton Oaks. 183–201.

Grube, N.
1994   Hieroglyphic Sources for the History of Northwest Yucatán. *Hidden Among the Hills: Maya Archaeology of the Northwest Yucatán Peninsula.* Edited by H. J. Prem. Möckmühl, Germany: Acta Mesoamericana 7, Verlag von Flemming. 316–358.

Harbottle, G., and P. C. Weigand.
1992   Turquoise in Pre-Columbian America. *Scientific American* 266(2):78–85.

Hassig, R.
1988   *Aztec Warfare.* Norman, Okla.: University of Oklahoma Press.

Houston, S. D.
1993   *Hieroglyphs and History at Dos Pilas: Dynastic Politics of the Classic Maya.* Austin, Tex.: University of Texas Press.

Jones, C., and L. Satterthwaite Jr.
1982   *Tikal Report No. 33, Part A. The Monuments and Inscriptions of Tikal: The Carved Monuments.* Museum Monograph 44. Philadelphia: University Museum, University of Pennsylvania.

Joyce, R. A.
1992   Images of Gender and Labor Organization. *Exploring Gender Through Archaeology.* Edited by C. Claassen. Madison, Wis.: Prehistory Press. 63–70.

Kelley, J. C.
1980   Rutas de Intercambio en Mesoamerica y el Norte de Mexico. *XVI Reunion de Mesa Redonda, Saltillo, Coahuila, Sept. 9–24, 1979.* Saltillo: Sociedad Mexicana de Antropología.

Kepecs, S. M., G. Feinman, and S. Boucher.
1994   Chichén Itzá and Its Hinterland: World-Systems Perspective. *Ancient Mesoamerica* 5(2):141–158.

Kepecs, S. M., and S. Boucher.
1991   The Prehispanic Cultivation of Rejolladas and Stonelands: New Evidence from Northeast Yucatán. Paper presented at the 47th International Congress of Americanists, New Orleans.
Klein, C. F.
1988   Rethinking Cihuacoatl: Aztec Political Imagery of the Conquered Woman. *Smoke and Mist: Mesoamerican Studies in Memory of Thelma D. Sullivan.* Edited by J. K. Josserand and K. Dakin. BAR International Series 402(i). Oxford: British Archaeological Reports. 237–277.
1994   Fighting with Femininity: Gender and War in Aztec Mexico. *Gendering Rhetorics: Postures of Dominance and Submission in Human History.* Edited by R. C. Trexler. New York: Center for Medieval and Early Renaissance Studies at the State University of New York at Binghamton. 107–146.
Krochock, R. J.
1998   *The Development of Political Rhetoric at Chichén Itzá, Yucatán, Mexico.* Ph.D. Dissertation, University of Texas at Austin.
Kubler, George.
1980   Eclectism at Cacaxtla. *Third Palenque Round Table, 1978, Part 2.* Edited by Merle Greene Robertson. Austin, Tex.: University of Texas Press. 163–172.
Lothrop, S. K.
1952   *Metals from the Cenote of Sacrifice, Chichén Itzá, Yucatán.* Memoirs of the Peabody Museum of American Archaeology and Ethnology Volume X, Number 2. Cambridge, Mass.: Peabody Museum of Archaeology and Ethnology, Harvard University.
Marquina, I.
1951   *Arquitectura Prehispanica.* México, D.F.: Instituto Nacional de Antropología e Historia.
Melford, J. J.
1992   Basketry, Twined Sandal Soles, and Cordage. *Artifacts from the Cenote of Sacrifice.* Edited by C. C. Coggins. Cambridge, Mass.: Peabody Museum of Archaeology and Ethnology, Harvard University. 91–97.
Miller, A. G.
1977   Captains of the Itzá: Unpublished Mural Evidence from Chichén Itzá. *Social Process in Maya Prehistory: Studies in Honour of Sir Eric Thompson.* Edited by Norman Hammond. New York: Academic Press. 197–225.
Nash, J. C.
1978   The Aztecs and the Ideology of Male Dominance. *Signs: Journal of Women in Culture and Society* 4(21):349–362.
Peterson, J. F.
1983   Sacrificial Earth: The Iconography and Function of Malinalli Grass in Aztec Culture. *Flora and Fauna Imagery in Precolumbian Cultures: Iconography and Function.* Edited by J. F. Peterson. BAR International Series 171. Oxford: British Archaeological Reports. 113–148.
Quirarte, J.
1983   Outside Influence at Cacaxtla. *Highland-Lowland Interaction in Mesoamerica: Interdisciplinary Approaches.* Edited by A. G. Miller. Washington, D.C.: Dumbarton Oaks. 201–222.

Rathje, W. L.
1975   The Last Tango in Mayapan: A Tentative Trajectory of Production-Distribution Systems. *Ancient Civilization and Trade*. Edited by J. A. Sabloff and C. C. Lamberg-Karlovsky. Albuquerque, N.Mex.: University of New Mexico Press. 409–448.

Redfield, R., and A. Villa Rojas.
1962   *Chan Kom: A Maya Village*. Chicago: University of Chicago Press.

Roys, R. L., editor and translator.
1933   *The Book of the Chilam Balam of Chumayel*. Carnegie Institution of Washington Publication 438. Washington, D.C.: Carnegie Institute.

Ruppert, K.
1952   *Chichén Itzá: Architectural Notes and Plans*. Carnegie Institution of Washington Publication 595. Washington, D.C.: Carnegie Institute.

Sabloff, J. A., and D. A. Freidel.
1975   A Model of a Pre-Columbian Trading Center. *Ancient Civilization and Trade*. Edited by J. A. Sabloff and C. C. Lamberg-Karlovsky. Albuquerque, N.Mex.: University of New Mexico Press. 369–408.

Sabloff, J. A., and W. L. Rathje.
1975   *A Study of Changing Pre-Columbian Commercial Systems: The 1972–1973 Seasons at Cozumel, Mexico*. Monographs of the Peabody Museum of American Archaeology and Ethnology No. 3. Cambridge, Mass.: Peabody Museum of Archaeology and Ethnology, Harvard University.

Schele, L., and D. A. Freidel.
1990   *A Forest of Kings: The Untold Story of the Ancient Maya*. New York: William Morrow.

Schele, L., and P. Mathews.
1998   *The Code of Kings: The Language of Seven Sacred Maya Temples and Tombs*. New York: Scribner's.

Schellhas, P.
1904   *Representation of Deities of the Maya Manuscripts*. Papers of the Peabody Museum of American Archaeology and Ethnology Volume 4, Number 1. Cambridge, Mass.: Peabody Museum of Archaeology and Ethnology, Harvard University.

Seler, Edward.
1902–1923   *Gesammelte Abhandlungen zur Amerikanischen Sprach und Alterthumskunde*. Berlin, Germany: A. Asher.

Sugiyama, S.
1989   Burials Dedicated to the Old Temple of Quetzalcoatl at Teotihuacan, Mexico. *American Antiquity* 54(1):85–106.

Taube, K. A.
1994a   The Birth Vase: Natal Imagery in Ancient Maya Myth and Ritual. *The Maya Vase Book, Volume 4*. Edited by J. Kerr. New York: Kerr Associates. 652–685.
1994b   The Iconography of Toltec Period Chichén Itzá. *Hidden Among the Hills: Maya Archaeology of the Northwest Yucatán Peninsula*. Edited by H. J. Prem. Möckmühl, Germany: Acta Mesoamericana 7, Verlag von Flemming. 212–246.

Tedlock, D.
 1985 *Popol Vuh: The Definitive Edition of the Mayan Book of the Dawn of Life and the Glories of Gods and Kings.* New York: Simon and Schuster.
Thompson, J. E. S.
 1939 *The Moon Goddess in Middle America with Notes on Related Deities.* Carnegie Institution of Washington Publication 509, Contribution 29. Washington, D.C.: Carnegie Institute.
Tozzer, A. M., editor and translator.
 1941 *Landa's Relacíon de las Cosas de Yucatán: A Translation.* Papers of the Peabody Museum of American Archaeology and Ethnology Volume 10. Cambridge, Mass.: Peabody Museum of Archaeology and Ethnology, Harvard University.
 1957 *Chichén Itzá and Its Cenote of Sacrifice: A Comparative Study of Contemporaneous Maya and Toltec.* Memoirs of the Peabody Museum of American Archaeology and Ethnology Volumes XI and XII. Cambridge, Mass.: Peabody Museum of Archaeology and Ethnology, Harvard University.

Mountain of Heaven, Mountain of Earth: The Great Pyramid of Cholula as Sacred Landscape

Geoffrey G. McCafferty

The pre-Columbian cultures of Mesoamerica practiced a form of geomancy in which elements of the natural environment attained supernatural significance and were used to structure the cultural landscape. Thus caves, springs, mountains, and other natural formations were transformed into "cosmo-magical symbols" (Wheatley 1971) relating to mytho-religious beliefs. Caves and springs served as portals into the Underworld, whereas mountain peaks communicated with the multitiered heavens (Heyden 1981). Incorporating these supernatural phenomena into the cultural landscape served to legitimate the authority of the dominant group while harnessing the symbolic power of the supernatural. The creation of a ceremonial center that drew upon cosmological forces acted to focus supernatural power into the sacred precinct as an *axis mundi*, or pivot for the world dimensions around which all creation revolved (Wheatley 1971). Within the Mesoamerican worldview that recognized a quincunx, or five-directional universe, this pivot included both vertical and horizontal dimensions joined at the center (Carlson 1981).

For the Aztecs of Late Postclassic central Mexico, this worldview was best illustrated through the mythical Coatépec, a portal linking spatial, temporal, and supernatural distance (Reese-Taylor and Koontz, chapter 1 in this volume). Susan Gillespie described the *coatepetl*, or serpent hill, as:

an Aztec Tower of Babel with its base on earth and its summit connecting the earth to the sky. It linked people on the surface of the

earth with the gods in the Upperworld beyond them . . . Coatepec
represents a point of continuity between the terrestrial and celestial
spheres. Finally, the fact that it was a "serpent" hill shows its mediat-
ing qualities, for serpents were viewed as connectors of the vertical
layers of the cosmos throughout Mesoamerica (1989:87).

The Aztecs manifested this mythological concept in the real world by
decorating their pyramids, notably the Templo Mayor of Tenochtitlán,
with serpent imagery. Coatépec, the hill upon which the patron deity
Huitzilopochtli was born and where he defeated the cosmic forces of the
moon (as Coyolxauhqui) and stars, was the *axis mundi* of the Aztec cosmos.

The Pyramid of the Feathered Serpent at Teotihuacan can be interpreted as another serpent hill, dedicated to control over calendrical and
cosmological events (López Austin et al. 1991). The facade of the early
temple is decorated with feathered serpents, each carrying a *cipactli* earth
monster in reference to the mythical creation and ordering of time. The
Feathered Serpent deity, later known as Quetzalcoatl, was an important
mediator between celestial and terrestrial spheres, particularly in its role
of legitimating kingly authority (Gillespie 1989:216) and promoting
priestly knowledge (Nicholson 1971; D. Carrasco 1982).

The tunnel located beneath the Pyramid of the Sun at Teotihuacan (Heyden 1981; Manzanilla et al. 1996) provides further evidence of a geomantic
phenomenon used in site organization. Based on Linda Manzanilla et al.'s
recent reinterpretation, the cave beneath the Pyramid was originally a mi-
neshaft for procuring building materials for pyramid construction. It was
culturally modified into the shape of a four-petaled flower with a long tunnel leading to the west at the same orientation as the Teotihuacan urban
grid. The chamber is remarkably similar to colonial depictions of the
Nahua origin myth for Chicomoztoc (Kirchoff et al. 1976:Folio 16r), and it
has been suggested that Teotihuacan may have served as a prototype for a
related origin myth.[1] While the cave and associated tunnel may have been
abandoned at the end of the Classic period, Teotihuacan remained an important ritual site throughout the Postclassic period, and Aztec artifacts
were discovered within the tunnel (Heyden 1981), suggesting that it may
have been used for oracles or other ceremonies (Manzanilla et al. 1996).

Complementary processes are found at the other great ceremonial center of the central highlands: the Great Pyramid of Cholula. In some ways
the history of Cholula is similar to that of Teotihuacan, although in others
it is quite distinct. Unfortunately, the histories of the two centers have
been so closely linked that the unique characteristics of Cholula have of-

ten been lost in the shadows of its neighbor. *Tlachihualtepetl*, or "man-made mountain" as the Great Pyramid was known at the time of the Spanish Conquest, is by volume the largest construction from pre-Columbian Mesoamerica (Marquina 1970a; McCafferty 1996a). It is also the oldest continuously used ceremonial structure in the Americas, and as such can be viewed as a palimpsest of iconographic information accumulated during a period of 2,500 years.

This paper peels back the layers of meaning in order to reveal the dynamics of socioreligious connotations that have been proclaimed (cf. Nagao 1989) from the Great Pyramid by different peoples and for different purposes. Here I summarize iconographic evidence from the Great Pyramid to interpret the symbolic content of the pyramid and its surrounding ceremonial precinct. Implicit is an assumption that stylistic manipulations were purposeful and relate directly to identity strategies of the elites who directed the monumental construction efforts that resulted in the changing face of the pyramid. These transformations reflect political, ethnic, and religious affiliations, including Cholula's wavering relationship with Teotihuacan, the arrival of ethnic Olmeca-Xicallanca from the Gulf Coast, and the rise of the cult of Quetzalcoatl.

Cholula and the Great Pyramid

Cholula is located in the Puebla/Tlaxcala Valley, east of the Valley of Mexico and about 100 kilometers southeast of Teotihuacan (Figure 11.1). Cholula was famous at the time of the Spanish Conquest as the center for the cult of Ehecatl-Quetzalcoatl (Rojas 1927:160–161; Durán 1971:131; Torquemada 1975–1983, Volume 1:385–387), the Feathered Serpent god associated with the wind; the planet Venus; priestly knowledge; and *pochteca*, long-distance merchants. Dual high priests of the Temple of Quetzalcoatl (the Aquiach and Tlalchiach) presided over a vast religious empire while representing celestial and earthly domains (Rojas 1927; P. Carrasco 1971:21–22). Nobles from central Mexico came to Cholula to offer tribute to these priests and in exchange received legitimation of their authority. *Pochteca* merchants traveled throughout Mesoamerica, making the Cholula marketplace a center for exotic goods (Durán 1971:129) and distributing elaborately decorated and symbolically charged objects in the Mixteca-Puebla stylistic tradition (Nicholson 1982; McCafferty and McCafferty 1994).

The Puebla valley around Cholula was noted as among the most fertile agricultural land in Mexico during the Colonial period, producing boun-

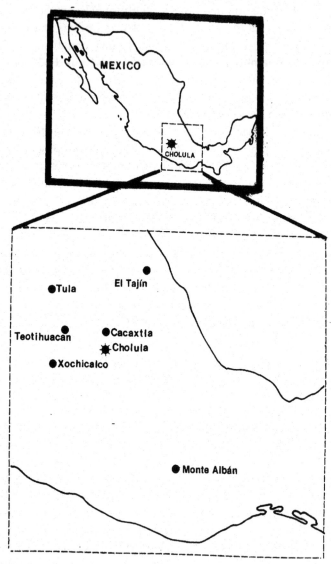

Figure 11.1   Map of Central Mexico, showing Cholula

tiful harvests of corn, beans, maguey, and chilies before the Conquest
(Rojas 1927; Bonfil Batalla 1973; Super 1988). Surrounded by snow-cov-
ered volcanoes, the alluvial valley enjoys an abundance of water resources, permitting irrigation agriculture during the dry season. In the
pre-Hispanic period, several streams converged with the Atoyac River to

form a swampy lake just east of Cholula (Mountjoy and Peterson 1973) where *chinampa* agriculture may have been practiced (Messmacher 1967a). An additional local resource is the clay subsoil that until recently was an excellent material for pottery making (Noguera 1954; Müller 1978). It is still exploited for intensive brick production (Bonfil Batalla 1973).

The Great Pyramid is the principal architectural feature of Cholula (Figure 11.2). It measures more than 400 meters on a side and covers about 16 hectares at its base (Marquina 1970a; McCafferty 1996a). The platform mound measured at least 65 meters in height, but the maximum height is obscured by modifications made in constructing the Colonial period church on its summit. The Great Pyramid was built in a series of four major construction phases spanning a period of about 1,500 years. The earliest evidence for construction dates to the Late Formative period (Noguera 1956; Müller 1973), and active pyramid construction was finally suspended at the end of the Early Postclassic period when an ethnic invasion resulted in the partial abandonment of the ceremonial center and the construction of a "new" Pyramid of Quetzalcoatl in what was to become the plaza of San Pedro Cholula (Olivera de V. and Reyes 1969; *Historia Tolteca-Chichimeca* 1976:Folio 26v–27r; McCafferty 1996b). Ritual use of the Great Pyramid continued during the Late Postclassic period, however, as a shrine to a rain deity, Chiconauquiahuitl, and as the site of ceremonial burials (Lagunas R., Serrano S., and López A. 1976). It continues up to the present when the colonial church dedicated to the Virgin of the Remedies is considered (Olivera de V. 1970).

Figure 11.2 The Great Pyramid of Cholula from the south

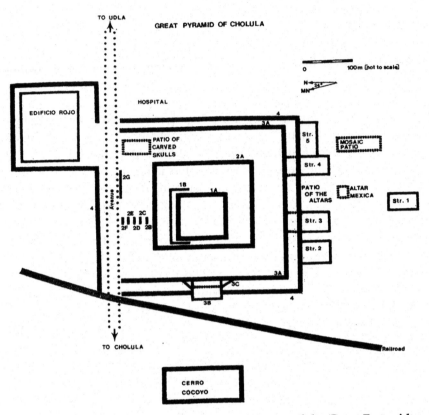

Figure 11.3   Plan of the construction sequence of the Great Pyramid

Archaeological investigations have concentrated on the Great Pyramid since 1931, with several intensive periods of exploration as well as short-term salvage work (Noguera 1937, 1954; Marquina 1939, 1951, 1970b, 1975; Messmacher 1967; Müller 1978; Suárez C. 1985; Paddock 1987; Suárez C. and Martínez A. 1993; summarized in McCafferty 1996a). Because of the enormous size of the pyramid, early phases of construction were explored using tunnels—more than eight kilometers of tunnels expose building facades and follow stairways relating to the major stages of construction and subsequent modification (Figure 11.3). Additional excavations exposed and reconstructed platforms and plazas on the south and west sides of the pyramid, including the Patio of the Altars. As a result of these extensive archaeological investigations, a wide range of information has been recovered. The objective of this study is to weave together archaeological, architectural, art historical, and ethnohistorical data to interpret the meaning content of the Great Pyramid at different stages in its history. Because the existing information is often fragmentary, this chapter can only be a preliminary reading, and as new information becomes available, these interpretations should be critically reevaluated.

Artistic Program of the Great Pyramid

Middle and Late Formative settlement patterns for the Cholula region consisted of a mosaic of small mounded sites at intervals of 5–10 kilometers, including Acatepec, Coronango, Coapan, and Cholula itself (García Cook and Merino Carrión 1987). A settlement survey of Formative Cholula indicated that it may have covered an area of about 2 square kilometers, with monumental architecture in at least three separate areas (McCafferty 1984, 1996b). Eduardo Noguera (1956) discovered Late Formative (El Arbolillo I/Zacatenco I phase) ceramics in the construction fill of the earliest level of the Edificio Rojo, located to the northeast of the Great Pyramid, representing perhaps the earliest construction at the ceremonial center. In fact, the original ground surface beneath the pyramid was littered with Formative period pottery (Noguera 1954:199–200). Mound building ceased at other sites in the immediate vicinity during the Terminal Formative period, suggesting that by about 200 BC Cholula was the predominant center in the valley (García Cook 1981; García Cook and Merino Carrión 1987). At about this time, the first phase of the Great Pyramid was built.

What factors conspired to promote Cholula to preeminence over this nascent kingdom? Why was the Great Pyramid begun at a time when other pyramid mounds were abandoned? Certainly Cholula had a favorable location relative to environmental resources (Mountjoy and Peterson 1973), but other sites had comparable access to fertile farmland and water resources. Instead, Cholula was apparently able to establish the Great Pyramid as an *axis mundi*, a cosmo-magical center connecting the Underworld to the heavens. It was this symbolic resource that distinguished Cholula from its neighbors and eventually enabled it to dominate the region.

The Great Pyramid is located over a spring, which flows from beneath the mound east into the former lake. Thus the Pyramid embodies the concept of *altepetl*, literally a water-mountain, that for later Nahuas was the metaphoric term for "kingdom" (Lockhart 1992).[2] The spring is clearly depicted in the *Historia Tolteca-Chichimeca* (1976:folio 7v) where it is shown

Figure 11.4   The Tlachihualtepetl mound with spring (Kirchoff et al. 1976:Folio 7v)

emerging from a cave beneath the pyramid (Figure 11.4). A modern shrine on the east side of the Pyramid covers a deep well leading down to the spring, which is still a prominent feature of the symbolic landscape.

No actual cave is known from beneath the Great Pyramid, but Bernardino Sahagún (1950–1982, Introductory Volume:48) mentioned caves and tunnels within the Great Pyramid in the Colonial period, and a network of tunnels connecting the pyramid with other pre-Columbian buildings remains part of local oral tradition. Architectural remains of a pre-Columbian corbeled arch were visible until recently in a road-cut on the northeast side of the pyramid as possible evidence for original tunnel construction. The symbolic center of the pyramid may have been discovered during archaeological tunneling in the 1970s (Eduardo Merlo, personal communication 1999). This chamber is now referred to by Cholula residents as the energy center of the pyramid.

One clear distinction between the Great Pyramid and the monumental architecture of Teotihuacan is the orientation. In contrast to the grid alignment of Teotihuacan at 16° east of north, urban Cholula and the

Great Pyramid are oriented at 26° north of west (Marquina 1970a; Tichy 1981:221), where the pyramid faces the sunset on the summer solstice. The distinction in site orientation between the two urban centers suggests that they were not organized around shared cosmological principles. In fact, a geographic boundary based on these site orientations distinguishes Teotihuacan-related sites from what would have been the Cholula kingdom (Tichy 1981).

The contrast between the two sites is more profound than simple orientation, however. Several theories have been proposed to account for the orientation of Teotihuacan, including astronomical observations relating to the Pleiades (Carlson 1981:188; Heyden 1981). With the Great Pyramid of Cholula facing the setting sun on the longest day of the year, the shrine atop the mound would be the last spot illuminated by the dying sun. It is likely, therefore, that the Great Pyramid of Cholula was related to the supernatural sun as well as the calendrical cycle.

The first construction of the Great Pyramid (Stage 1a) measured 120 meters on a side and 17 meters in height (Marquina 1970b). Low walls are preserved from the temple precinct on top of the pyramid, which measured 19 meters on a side. The pyramid facade used a talud/tablero style reminiscent of Teotihuacan, or more locally, Tlalancaleca (García Cook 1981). A series of painted motifs on the tablero of Stage 1b (a minor modification of the original construction) depicts skeletal insects (Figure 11.5), possibly larval butterflies in the process of metamorphosis (Marquina 1970a). The configuration of the frontal face with the body extending out to the side is reminiscent of the Temple of the Feathered Serpents at Teotihuacan.[3] The symbolism of transformation relates to the Mesoamerican concept of cyclical death and rebirth (Klein 1975), whereas the butterfly imagery could relate to the female earth/fertility complex, including its association with the warrior cult (Sullivan 1982; Berlo 1983).

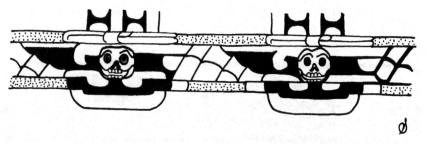

Figure 11.5   Chapulin mural from Stage 1b
(after Marquina 1970b:Lamina I)

The second complete rebuilding of the Great Pyramid (Stage 2a) measured 180 meters on a side and 35 meters in height (Marquina 1970a). The structure was unique in central Mexico because it consisted of stairways on all sides (Margain 1971:69), reminiscent of the *kan witz* four-sided pyramids of the Maya area and notably distinct from contemporary architecture at Teotihuacan. A set of 52 raised stairs on the north side is an obvious reference to the 52-year cycle of the combined solar and 260-day ritual calendars. The calendrical significance provides a further analogy to Teotihuacan's Pyramid of the Feathered Serpent based on the recent interpretation of the Feathered Serpent iconography in relation to Aztec myths of Quetzalcoatl and the creation of the calendar (López Austin et al. 1991).

Several fragmentary building façades represent modifications to the pyramid structure (Stages 2b–2g), particularly on the north side of the mound, perhaps indicating that this was the major axis of ceremonial activity during this time period. The Edificio Rojo is located to the northeast of the Great Pyramid and may represent part of a plaza group with this axis of the pyramid. A set of raised stairs similar to those on Stage 2a of the Great Pyramid occurs on the south facade of the Edificio Rojo, further suggesting that these structures may have been contemporary.[4] The excellent preservation of the Edificio Rojo is a consequence of its having been completely engulfed by a later expansion of the Great Pyramid. The building's name derives from an unpublished account of red painted figures on the tableros of the platform (Sergio Suárez C., personal communication 1999).

Several painted murals have been discovered within the Great Pyramid that relate to Stage 2 facades. One segment depicts two serpents' heads, colored blue with black spots (Figure 11.6; Villagra Caleti 1971:148). Between the serpents is a yellow jaguar with what may be a net over the feline. Although this mural is now badly damaged, the description of the mural by Villagra Caleti recalls the netted jaguars of Teotihuacan. Another mural features a black-on-white checkerboard pat-

Figure 11.6　Mural with jaguars and serpent

tern. This occurs on the west side of the Great Pyramid on what has been called the Edificio Totonaco (Marquina 1970a:41), in part because the checkerboard is reminiscent of the Temple of the Niches at El Tajín. A second example of this pattern is in the Southeast Plaza associated with an early phase of the Patio of the Altars (Acosta 1970a:50).

A third major rebuilding of the Great Pyramid (Stage 3a) is revealed on the west and south sides of the mound. This structure measured approximately 350 meters on a side, with a height of 65 meters (Marquina 1970a). Although it has not been completely documented, this may have been the final complete phase of construction because subsequent evidence for expansion was only in the form of an adobe nucleus that lacked any evidence for finished surfaces. The talud/tablero architecture of Stage 3a is quite similar to that of Teotihuacan and is also found on an early building south of the pyramid. These Teotihuacanoid platforms are associated with an extensive mosaic patio (Acosta 1970d:66), remnants of which have been found in dispersed sections of the ceremonial complex.

Projecting out from the Stage 3a talud/tablero is Stage 3b, which apparently begins at an earlier level of the pyramid construction sequence (Figure 11.7).[5] A hole in the Stage 3a facade reveals evidence of an earlier stairway, suggesting that this may have been a major axis of ritual activ-

Figure 11.7   Stage 3b emerging from Stage 3a

Figure 11.8   Monolith with rectangular hole

ity with considerable time depth. The decorative characteristic of Stage 3b is a carved panel on the tableros in the form of a woven mat. Another mat motif, possibly representing red and blue feathers, appears on a polychrome mural from Phase 3-2 of the Patio of the Altars (Marquina 1970a:Lamina III).

The mat motif is a pan-Mesoamerican symbol for kingship and political authority, with examples from Mixtec, Aztec, and Maya iconography. Napatecuhtli, an avatar of Tlaloc, was the Aztec patron of the mat-makers and was also lord of the four directions (Sahagún 1950–1982, Book 1:45). As an architectural motif, the House of the Mat at Copán is the best comparison, although it is also common in the Yucatán. Translated into Maya as *Popol Na*, the House of the Mat has been interpreted as a political council house (Fash 1991:130–134). In both Mixtec and Aztec representations, rulers are depicted seated on woven mats. The visual impact of ritual performance on an engraved mat panel would have legitimated the action to the audience below.

A crude monolith stands in front of the staircase of Stage 3b (Figure 11.8). It is approximately 4 meters in height, with a rough surface and a rectangular knob on its top surface. The monolith has a rectangular hole through the lower half. A partially excavated stone altar is located near its base. No published account of this feature exists to describe the excavated context of the monolith, but it is possible that it may have functioned as a device for astronomical observations relating to the setting sun at the solstice. For example, a strategically placed vertical rod erected on the Cerro Cocoyo (also known as Cerro Acozoc) mound west of the intervening plaza would cast a shadow through the rectangular hole and onto the horizontal slab/altar at sundown of the solstice.

A subsequent architectural feature (Stage 3c) later removed the front portion of Stage 3b, including the staircase, to cover this west face of the pyramid with a rounded facade made of steep taludes in at least two levels (Figure 11.9). These facades feature jagged stones that project out from the surface beyond the level of the stucco facing, giving the appearance of a "hill of knives" similar to those illustrated in the pre-Columbian Mixtec codices (e.g., *Codex Nuttall* 1975:19). Consolidation and recon-

Figure 11.9   Stage 3c, with Stage 3b in background

struction of Stage 3b resulted in the partial dismantling of this later structure during the *Proyecto Cholula* in the 1960s.

These early stages of the Great Pyramid span a period of more than
1,000 years, with Stage 3a probably dating to the Epiclassic period. During this span, the pyramid's architectural program fluctuated in its similarity to the canons of Teotihuacan (McCafferty 1999b). Following Debra
Nagao's (1989) conception of visual imagery as "public proclamation,"
this suggests shifting claims of affiliation by the Cholula elites as they negotiated their own cultural identity. During the construction of Stage 2,
innovations relating to Gulf Coast style began to appear, possibly indicating the arrival of Olmeca-Xicallanca groups from Veracruz. Although the
chronology of the Pyramid sequence is still poorly defined, this would
suggest that the subsequent construction of the Stage 3a talud/tablero
postdates the fall of Teotihuacan and so may be a statement on the part of
the Cholula elite that they were heirs to the Teotihuacan legacy (even
though for much of the Classic period they denied that relationship). Additional modifications such as the carved mat motif of Stage 3b, however,
relate to the innovative style that later became known as the Mixteca-
Puebla tradition (McCafferty and McCafferty 1994).

The Patio of the Altars Complex

The Patio of the Altars is a large open plaza immediately south of the
Great Pyramid (Acosta 1970a), at the base of what may have been the
main south staircase. The patio is bounded by two long platforms extending south from the base of the pyramid, where they attach to the facade of Stage 3a. The patio was renovated on at least six occasions, but
the format of the ceremonial space remained essentially unchanged as a
three-sided enclosure open to the south with a series of ritual areas, including altars, platforms, and sculpture.

The patio derives its name from two monolithic altars dating to the final phase of the complex. Altar 1, on the east side of the patio, is paired
with a large upright stela to form a stela/altar group (Figure 11.10)
(Acosta 1970b). Altar 2, opposite Altar 1 on the west side of the patio, is
another large horizontal slab (Acosta 1970c) that was placed on an elevated platform so that it was above the level of Altar 1. It was probably
paired with an upright stela to form a complementary stela/altar group.
The base of a stela, designated Altar 3, was found in the fill behind Altar
2, but because the upper portion was located at the base of the staircase
of the pyramid, the stela was reconstructed at the north end of the patio
(Figure 11.11) (Contreras 1970).[6] These two stela/altar groups could have

Figure 11.10   Altar 1

served as thrones for the dual priests of the Olmeca-Xicallanca. They are aligned with the solstitial sunset so that Altar 3 (if placed behind Altar 2) would have cast a shadow onto the stela of Altar 1.[7]

Both the altar and stela of Altar 1, as well as the stela known as Altar 3, were decorated with interlaced volutes around the borders of the large stones. These volutes have been identified as typical of Gulf Coast

Figure 11.11 Altar 3

iconography, such as is found at El Tajín (Acosta 1970b:102).[8] Altar 2 features a more elaborate variation with interlaced serpents in place of volutes (Figure 11.12).

Stylistic similarities between the Epiclassic/Early Postclassic ceremonial center and the Gulf Coast are abundant and indicate strong interaction between Cholula and the Gulf. New pottery types appear at this time that include imitations of Gulf Coast types, even the earliest polychrome types (McCafferty 1996b). Sergio Suárez C. (1985) identified a burial from the Great Pyramid that he interprets as a Maya merchant/priest based on distinctive cranial and dental mutilation and grave goods. The elaborate polychrome murals of Cacaxtla show clear

Figure 11.12 Interlaced serpents on Altar 2

Gulf Coast and Maya influence, and the relationship between Cacaxtla and Cholula has long been argued (McVicker 1985; see also García Cook and Merino Carrión 1990; McCafferty and McCafferty 1994).

The taludes of the pyramid and associated platforms were decorated with a greca pattern of interlocked "T"s (Figure 11.13). This relates to the greca horizon identified for the Epiclassic and Early Postclassic periods from the Gulf Coast, Oaxaca, and Yucatán (Sharp 1978), with its closest parallel with the architectural facade of the Castillo Pyramid at Chichén Itzá. Within the Mixtec tradition of symbolic notation, the greca frieze was interpreted as *ñuu*, signifying metropolis, and was therefore synonymous with the Nahuatl Tollan (Smith 1973:38–39). In Mixtec codices *ñuu* was a common motif on place glyphs involving architectural features. The massive staircase of the Great Pyramid rising above the greca frieze could therefore be perceived as a visual metaphor for *ñuu ndiyo*, "city of the stairs," the Mixtec name for Cholula (Smith 1973:72, n.98; see also McCafferty and McCafferty 1994:58).

A prominent place sign from the Mixtec codices has been glossed as "Cattail Frieze" because it combines both the *ñuu* frieze and the *tule* cattail signs (Smith 1973; Pohl 1994; Jansen 1996). Because one of the prominent acts that occurred at Cattail Frieze was a nose-piercing ceremony (Caso 1966:13), a rite that also occurred at Cholula (Figure 11.14) (Rojas 1927; Kirchoff et al. 1976:Folio 21r), it is plausible that Cattail Frieze was

Figure 11.13   Greca frieze along Patio of the Altars

Figure 11.14   Nose-piercing ceremony at Cholula
(Kirchoff et al. 1976:Folio 21r)

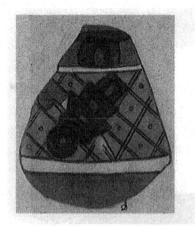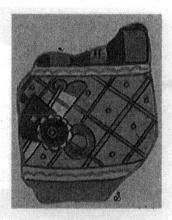

Figure 11.15   Cholula polychrome shards with nose-piercing implements

Figure 11.16   Mural with diagonal bands and stars
(after Marquina 1970b:Lamina II)

an alternative name for Postclassic Cholula that emphasized its multilin-
gual, cosmopolitan nature. Codex-style nose ornaments and bone perfo-
rators appear as decorative elements on Cholula polychrome pottery
(Figure 11.15), further supporting the association.

In addition to the greca pattern on the taludes of the Patio of the Altars,
murals were painted on the tableros. One common motif is of multicol-
ored diagonal bands with star patterns (Figure 11.16). The diagonal motif
is identical to that found in Mixtec iconography to indicate stone/earth
(Smith 1973) and is often incorporated into place glyphs and to indicate
"stone people." In the *Codex Nuttall* (16-I), for example, Lady 3 Flint en-

Figure 11.17   Serpent head from balustrade

ters into a mountain of stone that is further identified by lunar/uterine crescents (Milbrath 1988). The Cholula murals follow this model with the addition of superimposed stars, thus creating a visual metaphor for the Great Pyramid as a "mountain of heaven and mountain of earth/stone."

A polychrome feathered serpent mural associated with an early phase of the Patio of the Altars was found in the southeast plaza (Acosta 1970d:66). This is the clearest reference to Quetzalcoatl at the Great Pyramid, and unfortunately no illustrations of this mural have been published.[9] Other serpent imagery includes the interlaced serpents around Altar 2 and a large stone sculpture in the Patio of the Altars of an open-mouthed serpent with exposed fangs. Another elaborately carved serpent head features a keystone connector that may have made it part of a serpent staircase (Figure 11.17) or even into the wall of a ballcourt similar to the Mixtec *yavui*.

The Postclassic association of Quetzalcoatl with Cholula is clearly established through ethnohistorical accounts (Rojas 1927; Durán 1971; Torquemada 1975–1983, Volume 1:387) and iconography on polychrome ceramics, but it was more explicitly associated with the Pyramid of Quetzalcoatl from the Late Postclassic ceremonial center (Díaz del Castillo 1963:202; Durán 1971:133). According to one mytho-historical account, the fourth pre-Columbian age was dominated by the Toltecs who built a great pyramid at Cholula that was dedicated to Ehecatl-Quetzalcoatl as a deification of the high priest and prophet of the Olmeca-Xicallanca after Cholula and its Great Pyramid were destroyed at the end of the third age (Ixtlilxochitl 1975–1977, Book 1:529–530). Following this mythical association, the significance of Quetzalcoatl at the site would have increased after the abandonment of the Great Pyramid.

The most famous murals of the Cholula ceremonial complex are the so-called *Bebedores*, or drinkers, located on the earliest stage of the Patio of the Altars (Marquina 1971; Müller 1972). The *Bebedores* extend for 60 meters in length along the tablero of the west platform (Structure 31-A) that extends out from the pyramid face. These murals feature a sequence of anthropomorphic figures drinking from cups and bowls while seated around large vessels, presumably containing intoxicating and perhaps hallucinogenic *pulque* (Figure 11.18) (Müller 1972; Kubler 1990:64–5). The figures wear simple loin cloths, but with earplugs and often elaborate turban headdresses. Although some smaller figures stand as servants, the main characters are generally represented as sprawling on a flowered carpet. At least one figure has an animal head representing a bird, and another resembles a monkey; two dogs and a bee are also included in the panel. The weirdly detailed figures suggest

Figure 11.18   Bebedores murals

the act of transformation, perhaps with the inebriated priests changing into their *nagual* animal spirits.

The *Bebedores* murals are poorly understood both in terms of their iconography and their contextual relationship to the ceremonial complex. The ritual use of *pulque* among the Aztecs was closely associated with the goddess Mayahuel, a member of the earth/fertility complex. Florencia Müller (1972) identified parallels between the mural and a *pulque* ceremony recorded in the Mixtec Codex Vindobonensis (J. Furst 1978:202–203; Anders et al. 1992).[10]

The *Bebedores* are unique in Mesoamerican mural art. Some of the human figures resemble Teotihuacanoid figurines, including to some extent the small human figures from the Tlalocan mural of Tepantitla. Stylistically, the Early Postclassic murals from Las Higueras, Veracruz, are the most similar in terms of proportion and costume elements. As a narrative panel of life-size figures, the *Bebedores* resemble the Battle Mural of Cacaxtla (and perhaps the Edificio Rojo), although stylistically they are quite dissimilar.

The Patio of the Altars complex presents an eclectic mix of iconographic styles, including Teotihuacan-style talud/tablero architecture, Gulf Coast volutes, and Mixtec codex-style mural and architectural motifs. It is during this Epiclassic/Early Postclassic period that Cholula became a crucible out of which evolved the Mixteca-Puebla stylistic tradition (McCafferty and McCafferty 1994). The artistic program presented at the Patio of the Altars documents the origins of this development.

The Great Pyramid in the Late Postclassic Period

Violent ethnic change occurred in Cholula with the arrival of Tolteca-Chichimeca groups at the end of the Early Postclassic period (Olivera de V. and Reyes 1969; P. Carrasco 1971; Kirchoff et al. 1976). This is seen archaeologically at the Patio of the Altars, where the megalithic stone stelae were smashed and scattered. At UA-1, located about 1 kilometer east of the Great Pyramid, the Early Postclassic Structure 1 was burned, and a high concentration of projectile points was associated with the living surface, suggesting that the house was destroyed by warfare (McCafferty 1992). This destruction level may therefore relate to the overthrow of the Olmeca-Xicallanca by the Tolteca-Chichimeca, ca. 1200 AD (Olivera de V. and Reyes 1969; McCafferty 1996b, 1999a).

The Great Pyramid itself may have been desecrated. A final building phase (Stage 4) is represented by an adobe brick shell that encased previous construction. No outer facade from this period has been discovered, implying that either this final stage was never completed, or else that the outer layer of stone and stucco was removed for the construction of the new ceremonial center around the Pyramid of Quetzalcoatl. Within the Mesoamerican ideology of warfare and conquest, captives were often depicted nude as a symbol of humiliation (McCafferty and McCafferty 1994). Stripping away the outer facade of the Great Pyramid may therefore have carried symbolic overtones as well as being a practical source for valuable building materials.

The ceremonial center of Cholula was shifted in the Late Postclassic period to what is now the *zócalo* of San Pedro Cholula (P. Carrasco 1971; Kirchoff et al. 1976; Lind 1990). The new Pyramid of Quetzalcoatl was described by the Spanish *conquistadores*, including Bernal Diáz del Castillo (1963:202), who said that it was taller than the Great Temple of Tenochtitlán (see also López de Gómara 1964:130). The pyramid was razed soon after the Spanish Conquest to be replaced by the Cathedral of San Gabriel on the east side of the square (Marquina 1970a:31).

Colonial chroniclers such as Fray Toribio de Benavente Motolinía (1951) and Gabriel de Rojas (1927) provided descriptions of the Great Pyramid as it appeared in the sixteenth century, and as it was perceived in local tradition. Rojas described the Pyramid as a hill made of ancient adobes. Motolinía commented that it was planted in small plots of corn, with rabbits and snakes living on the slopes. On top of the mound was a pre-Columbian shrine dedicated to Chiconauquiahuitl, or 9 Rain (Rojas 1927), a rain deity that in the Mixtec religion was represented as analogous to the Aztec goddess Chalchiuhtlicue (Caso 1979:426). The *Descripción de Cholula* records that children were sacrificed on an altar to bring the rain (Rojas 1927:162–163).

Motolinía (1951) recorded the legend that the Great Pyramid was built by the ancient Cholultecas as a Tower of Babel to reach heaven (see also Durán 1971:257). God stopped them by bringing on a great storm and hurling down a huge stone in the shape of a frog (see also Simons 1968:29). A similar account of the Tower of Babel is still related in San Andrés Cholula, although now the messenger of God is St. Michael, who struck the pyramid with his great sword, shattering the peak to form the smaller pyramids in the surrounding area.

A colossal head found in the Patio of the Altars may correspond to a carved stone frog altar associated with the shrine of 9 Rain (Figure 11.19). The round eyes and thick lipped, toothless mouth is strongly reminiscent of a toad.[11] In this context it is notable that representations of the Great Pyramid in the *Historia Tolteca-Chichimeca* (Kirchoff et al. 1976:Folios 7v,

Figure 11.19   Colossal head from Patio of the Altars

9v–10r, 14r, 26v–27r) consistently depict a large toad atop the pyramid. Toads were symbolically associated with fertility and regeneration in Mesoamerican religion (P. Furst 1981), especially as represented by the earth/fertility goddess complex. Sahagún (1950–1982, Book 2:62) described a ritual in which baked frog effigies were dressed in a woman's skirt and further decorated with blue face paint, in imitation of Chalchiutlicue.[12] Toads were also perceived as heralds for the rain god because in central Mexico toads croak at approaching storms; in this regard they parallel Ehecatl, the wind god, who blows prior to a storm.

The *Historia Tolteca-Chichimeca* (Kirchoff et al. 1976) provides Early Colonial period illustrations of the Great Pyramid as a natural hill covered with grass (Figure 11.20). In addition to the toad perched atop the mound, seven flowers are depicted near the summit, suggesting a calendrical association.[13] The date 7 Flower is somewhat ambiguous: It was the calendrical name for a Mixtec solar god and also for the Nahua deity Xochiquetzal. The Mixtec 7 Flower was analogous to the central Mexican creator god Tonacatecuhtli (Caso 1979:441–442), the male half of the bisexual Ometeotl unity who was linked to fire, maize, and particularly the sun. As the male component of the Ometeotl divine pair, Tonacatecuhtli would have been paired with a female earth/fertility deity such as Chalchiuhtlicue or Xochiquetzal.

**Figure 11.20   Great Pyramid with frog glyph and
7 Flower calendrical name**
(Kirchoff et al. 1976:Folio 14r)

Xochiquetzal was the goddess associated with sexuality and the arts; she also had solar attributes (McCafferty and McCafferty 1999). She was associated with Tonacacihuatl, the female half of the Ometeotl complex and therefore the consort of Tonacatecuhtli (Sullivan et al. 1997:140–141, n.16). She is identified with the day 7 Flower in the Florentine Codex (Sahagún 1950–1982, Book 4:7; Quiñones Keber 1995:187), the calendar date associated with embroiderers for whom she was patroness. She is prominent during the Atamalcualiztli ceremony held at Cholula, where she is depicted weaving with her back strap loom connected to a flowering tree, perhaps in reference to Tamoanchan (Sahagún 1993:Folio 254r). In a related text, Xochiquetzal was specifically identified as patron deity of Cholula (Sahagún 1950–819, Book 2:177–178). The identification of the Great Pyramid with the glyph 7 Flower may therefore represent both Tonacatecuhtli and Xochiquetzal as the supreme Ometeotl duality.

In 1535, Motolinía (1951:138–139) was called upon to exorcise the Great Pyramid because repeated attempts to raise a cross on the summit had failed because of storms and lightning. He excavated and found many buried idols, including giant conch shell trumpets (see also Rojas 1927). After removing these and warning the local people, Motolinía was able to erect a large bell, and the lightning stopped.

Diego Durán described the Great Pyramid in a section of his *Book of the Gods and Rites* that dealt with mountain worship during the month of Tepeilhuitl: "This hill was much hallowed; there were the usual and unceasing adoration, the prayers, the great sacrifices, offerings, and slaying of men" (1971:257). During this festival, mountain images were made out of amaranth seed, decorated to resemble earth and water deities, and consumed. Durán went on to add that the purpose of mountain worship was to ascend to a level from which to pray to the "Lord of Created Things, the Lord by Whom They Lived," a reference to Tonacatecuhtli. This tradition compares well with the widespread association of the Great Pyramid with the Tower of Babel. It also provides a conceptual link with the Nahua *axis mundi* of Coatépec, the serpent hill that acted as a portal connecting the mortal world with supernatural realms (Gillespie 1989:87).

A final ritual important for pre-Columbian Cholula that included the Great Pyramid was during the Atamalcualiztli ceremony that took place every eight years. Atamalcualiztli, or "the feast of the water tamales," was dedicated to Centeotl, the young maize god, and was observed as a time of fasting in which corn was allowed to rest (Sahagún 1950–1982, Book 2:177–178). Cholula is mentioned prominently in the colonial accounts of the ritual (McCafferty and McCafferty 1995). A detailed illustration of the festival in the *Primeros Memoriales* includes a drawing of the Pyramid of Quetzalcoatl alongside the Great Pyramid (Figure 11.21) (Sahagún 1993:Folio 254r). The pyramid features twin *tlaloque* rain spirits on its summit, along with a knotted *maxtlatl* loin cloth with rounded ends in the style identifiable of Quetzalcoatl. A possible cave inside the mound features a face over a glyph consisting of a paw with claws and four dots, perhaps a calendrical date for 4 Jaguar.[14]

Following the Spanish Conquest, the Great Pyramid continued as a religious center when the shrine to the Virgin of the Remedies was built (Olivera de V. 1970). This was one of the principal icons carried by the *conquistadores*, but in its new home it soon took on indigenous meanings. Within the context of local usage, the Virgin presides over curing and especially rain and fertility. The annual pilgrimage to the shrine is one of the largest in contemporary Mexico, with as many as 350,000 visitors attending the September fair in order to climb to the shrine on the pyramid (Olivera de V. 1970). The Virgin of the Remedies periodically descends from the pyramid to visit different parish churches in the Cholula urban zone in rituals that unify the diverse *barrios* of the city (Bonfil Batalla 1973). Colonial period representations of the Virgin show her emerging from a maguey plant (Durán 1971:230), in a motif very similar to that of the pre-Columbian goddess Mayahuel.

Apart from the religious significance of the shrine of the Virgin, the Great Pyramid itself remains an important symbol of the Cholula community. Early accounts and drawings of the pyramid mound attest to its

Figure 11.21   Detail of the Great Pyramid in Atamalcualiztli ceremony
(Sahugún 1993:Folio 254r)

prominence. An image was even reproduced onto mid–nineteenth-century transfer print pottery as part of the movement to create a Mexican national identity. In recent years heated and even violent conflict has continued between the neighboring communities of San Andrés and San Pedro Cholula over the historical origins of the Great Pyramid. Ethnohistorical and ethnographic evidence indicates that this rivalry may date back to the ethnic invasion at the end of the Early Postclassic period, with the two communities maintaining to some extent their separate Olmeca-Xicallanca and Tolteca-Chichimeca identities (Olivera de V. and Reyes 1969; McCafferty 1999a). At stake are the economic resources of tourism associated with the archaeological zone and the annual fair. On a more profound level, the question relates to the origins of the community and ancestral claims to the symbolic resources of the pyramid. The struggle over the Great Pyramid is currently an important political issue because the urban development of Cholula directly threatens the archaeological site, and competing factions of merchants, politicians, citizens, and archaeologists all search for a common ground to settle these issues.

Conclusions and Speculation

The Great Pyramid of Cholula has undergone numerous structural changes in its long history, both in terms of its architectural and its symbolic composition. A diachronic perspective on the evolving cosmological meanings of the pyramid offers valuable insight into the history of Mesoamerican religion, as well as provides important clues into the role of religious ideology in the organization of the Cholula polity. Unfortunately, the available data on the Great Pyramid is so fragmentary that solid conclusions are few and rather tentative, and so we are left with a range of speculation.

During the period of active pyramid construction, a variety of iconographic motifs were employed: Larval insects metamorphosed into skeletal images; intoxicated priests became transformed into animal spirits; the juxtaposition of terrestrial and celestial motifs established the pyramid as a corridor linking the natural and supernatural worlds (this was reinforced by the geomantic placement of the pyramid over a spring); architectural elements proclaimed power over time and the calendar; repeating mat motifs made an international statement of political authority; and the south stairway on a greca frieze became a 200-foot-tall place glyph for the city. The Great Pyramid was a complex symbolic statement of cosmological, political, and religious messages directed to a multinational audience. An overarching theme was of passage between states of being, precisely the ideas embodied in the *coatepetl* concept as a portal linking the different planes of existence.

Numerous themes occur at the pyramid: transformation, rain/fertility, feathered serpents, calendrical cycles, and political authority. Even though these themes are found at other ceremonial centers of Mesoamerica, they do not easily fit into a single ideational model, nor should they be expected to. With the long duration of occupation/utilization of the Great Pyramid, including several changes in ethnic composition for the surrounding city, the rituals and symbolic meanings associated with the pyramid undoubtedly underwent profound changes as well. With all this potential for variation, it becomes significant when themes remain constant over long periods of time. Such an example of continuity might relate the *pulque* ritual depicted in the *Bebedores* mural when linked to the representation of the Virgin of the Remedies as the pre-Columbian *pulque* goddess Mayahuel.

Another long-lasting significance of the pyramid relates to water resources. The geomantic reason for building the pyramid, and perhaps even for the rise of Cholula as a ceremonial center, was the spring beneath the mound. The spring was still prominently illustrated in the early Colonial *Historia Tolteca-Chichimeca* and is now an important shrine on the side of the mound. For the Aztecs, the goddess Chalchiutlicue was associated with water from the earth, with springs emerging from her womb:

> These [rivers] . . . issue from the goddess named Chalchiuhtlicue . . .
> [M]ountains were only magic places, with earth, with rock on the
> surface; they were only like ollas . . . they were filled with the water
> which was there. If sometime it were necessary, the mountains
> would dissolve; the whole world would flood. And hence the people
> called their settlements *altepetl* (Sahugún 1950-1982, Book 11:246).

According to the Tlaxcalteca account of the Cholula massacre (Muñoz Camargo 1948), the Cholultecas believed that if anyone attacked the holy city, the pyramid would burst open, and flood waters would wash away the attackers.

The Great Pyramid was also associated with water from the sky, as represented through the deity 9 Rain and the general mountain-worship theme discussed by Durán (1971). Mountains were the domain of the god Tlaloc and his *tlaloques*, or dwarf water spirits, who are depicted on the Great Pyramid in the *Primeros Memoriales* (Sahagún 1993:Folio 254r). One of the important reasons that pilgrims still attend the Cholula fair is to petition the Virgin for rain. Skyrockets fired from the summit of the pyramid are now used to summon the rain.

If earthly waters emerge from beneath the pyramid, and celestial waters are controlled from the summit, then the Great Pyramid itself would be a material and symbolic pathway connecting the Underworld with the Upperworld. The mediation between heaven/earth, sun/moon, and male/female is at the core of the Ometeotl principle of divine duality, embodied by the deities Tonacatecuhtli and Tonacacihuatl/Xochiquetzal. Both of these deities were identified at the Great Pyramid by their calendrical name 7 Flower, which can therefore be identified as Tonacatepetl, "mountain of sustenance" (see also Manzanilla et al. 1996:255).

The concept of the Great Pyramid as a passageway linking the Underworld with the Upperworld is repeated in the historic tradition of the pyramid as a New World Tower of Babel. It also leads back to the Aztec model of a serpent mountain, or *coatepetl*, as a mediator between the vertical layers of the cosmos (Gillespie 1989). As Davíd Carrasco observed:

"The [Great P]yramid was believed to be the opening to celestial forces as well as the covering over the primordial waters of the underworld" (1982:135). Ultimately, attempts to interpret the contextual meanings of the Great Pyramid result in more questions than solutions. Too little research has been done at the site, too little of what has been done has been adequately analyzed, and too little of that has been published. Was the Great Pyramid of Cholula an *axis mundi* for the pre-Columbian cultures of central Mexico? Based on such empirical criteria as overall size, longevity, and historical tradition, the answer is an unqualified yes. But to understand how and why the symbolism was acted out in practice, I can simply emphasize the need and urgency for further study.

Acknowledgments

Research contributing to this paper was funded in part by a Mellon Post-Doctoral Fellowship and by the Brown University's Undergraduate Teaching and Research Assistantship program. Preliminary drafts were presented at meetings of the College Art Association (New York) and the Society for American Archaeology (Anaheim). Interpretations presented here benefited from discussions with Linda Schele and her many talented disciples. I was grateful for the opportunity to show Linda around Cholula shortly before her untimely death. And of course I profusely acknowledge the fundamental contributions that my wife Sharisse has made in all phases of research, interpretation, artwork, and mental well-being.

References

Acosta, Jorge R.
>   1970a Sección 3. *Proyecto Cholula*. Edited by I. Marquina. Serie Investigaciones 19. México, D.F.: Instituto Nacional de Antropología e Historia. 47–56.
>   1970b El Altar 1. *Proyecto Cholula*. Edited by I. Marquina. Serie Investigaciones 19. México, D.F.: Instituto Nacional de Antropología e Historia. 93–102.
>   1970c El Altar 2. *Proyecto Cholula*. Edited by I. Marquina. Serie Investigaciones 19. México, D.F.: Instituto Nacional de Antropología e Historia. 103–110.
>   1970d Patio Sureste. *Proyecto Cholula*. Edited by I. Marquina. Serie Investigaciones 19. México, D.F.: Instituto Nacional de Antropología e Historia. 57–66.
>   1970e Sección 1. *Proyecto Cholula*. Edited by I. Marquina. Serie Investigaciones 19. México, D.F.: Instituto Nacional de Antropología e Historia. 119–128.
Anders, Ferdinand, Maarten Jansen, and Gabina Aurora Pérez Jiménez.

1992 *Codex Vindobonensis Mexicanus* 1 (facsimile). Graz, Austria: Akademishche Druck und Verlagsanstalt.
Berlo, Janet Catherine.
1983 The Warrior and the Butterfly: Central Mexican Ideologies of Sacred Warfare and Teotihuacan Iconography. *Text and Image in Pre-Columbian Art.* Edited by J. C. Berlo. Oxford: BAR International Series 180. 79–118.
Bonfil Batalla, Guillermo.
1973 *Cholula: La Ciudad Sagrada en la era industrial.* Instituto de Investigaciones Historicas. México, D.F.: Universidad Nacional Autonoma de México.
Byland, Bruce E., and John M. D. Pohl.
1994 *In the Realm of Eight Deer: The Archaeology of the Mixtec Codices.* Norman, Okla.: University of Oklahoma Press.
Carlson, John B.
1981 A Geomantic Model for the Interpretation of Mesoamerican Sites: An Essay in Cross-Cultural Comparison. *Mesoamerican Sites and World-Views.* Edited by E. P. Benson. Washington, D.C.: Dumbarton Oaks. 143–216.
Carrasco, Davíd.
1982 *Quetzalcoatl and the Irony of Empire: Myths and Prophecies of the Aztec Tradition.* Chicago: University of Chicago Press.
Carrasco, Pedro.
1971 Los barrios antiguos de Cholula. *Estudios y documentos de la región de Puebla-Tlaxcala* III:9–87.
Caso, Alfonso.
1966 *Codíce Colombino.* Interpreted by Alfonso Caso, glosses by Mary Elizabeth Smith. México, D.F.: Sociedad Mexicana de Antropología.
1979 *Reyes y Reinos de la Mixteca, Volume II: Diccionario biográfico de los señores Mixtecos.* México, D.F.: Fondo de Cultura Economica.
Contreras, Eduardo.
1970 El Altar 3. *Proyecto Cholula.* Edited by I. Marquina. Serie Investigaciones 19. México, D.F.: Instituto Nacional de Antropología e Historia. 111–118.
Diáz del Castillo, Bernal.
1963 *The Conquest of New Spain.* Translated by J. M. Cohen. New York: Penguin Books.
Durán, Diego.
1971 *The Book of the Gods and Rites and the Ancient Calendar.* Translated by F. Horcasitas and D. Heyden. Norman, Okla.: University of Oklahoma Press.
Fash, William L.
1991 *Scribes, Warriors, and Kings: The City of Copán and the Ancient Maya.* New York: Thames and Hudson.
Furst, Jill Leslie.
1978 *Codex Vindobonensis Mexicanus I: A Commentary.* Institute for Mesoamerican Studies Publication 4. Albany, N.Y.: State University of New York.

Furst, Peter T.
  1981   Jaguar Baby or Toad Mother: A New Look at an Old Problem in Olmec
         Iconograpy. *The Olmec and Their Neighbors: Essays in Memory of Matthew
         W. Stirling*. Edited by E. P. Benson. Washington, D.C.: Dumbarton
         Oaks. 149–162.
García Cook, Angel.
  1981   The Historical Importance of Tlaxcala in the Cultural Development of
         the Central Highlands. *Handbook of Middle American Indians, Supplement
         1: Archaeology*. Edited by V. R. Bricker and J. A. Sabloff. Austin, Tex.:
         University of Texas Press. 244–276.
García Cook, Angel, and Beatriz Leonor Merino Carrión.
  1987   Condiciones existentes en la región Poblano-Tlaxcalteca al surgimiento
         de Cholula. *Notas Mesoamericanas* 10:153–178.
  1990   El "Epiclasico" en la region Poblano-Tlaxcalteca. *Mesoamerica y Norte de
         México: Siglo IX-XII*. Edited by F. Sodi Miranda. México, D.F.: Museo
         Nacional de Antropología, Instituto Nacional de Antropología e Histo-
         ria. 257–280.
Gillespie, Susan D.
  1989   *The Aztec Kings: The Construction of Rulership in Mexica History*. Tucson,
         Ariz.: University of Arizona Press.
Heyden, Doris.
  1981   Caves, Gods, and Myths: World-View and Planning in Teotihuacan.
         Mesoamerican Sites and World Views. Edited by E. P. Benson. Washing-
         ton, D.C.: Dumbarton Oaks. 1–40.
Ixtlilxochitl, Fernando de Alva.
  1975–1977   *Obras Historicas*. Edited by E. O'Gorman. México, D.F.: Instituto
         de Investigaciones Historicas, Universidad Nacional Autonoma de
         México.
Jansen, Maarten.
  1996   Lord 8 Deer and Nacxitl Topiltzin. *Mexicon* XVIII(2):25–29.
Kirchoff, Paul, L. Ogden G., and L. Reyes G., editors and translators.
  1976   *Historia Tolteca-Chichimeca*. México, D.F.: Instituto Nacional de
         Antropología e Historia.
Klein, Cecilia F.
  1975   Post-Classic Mexican Death Imagery as a Sign of Cyclic Completion.
         Death and the Afterlife in Pre-Columbian America. Edited by E. P. Benson.
         Washington, D.C.: Dumbarton Oaks. 69–86.
Kubler, George.
  1990   *The Art and Architecture of Ancient America*. 3rd edition. New Haven:
         Yale University Press.
Lagunas R., Zaíd, Carlos Serrano S., and Sergio López A.
  1976   *Enterramientos humanos de la zona arqueológica de Cholula, Puebla*. México,
         D.F.: Instituto Nacional de Antropología e Historia.
Lind, Michael.
  1990   The Great City Square: Government in Ancient Cholula. Paper pre-
         sented at the Mesoamerican Network Meeting, Riverside, Calif.

Lockhart, James.
1992 *The Nahuas After the Conquest: A Social and Cultural History of the Indians of Central Mexico, Sixteenth Through Eighteenth Centuries.* Stanford: Stanford University Press.
López Austin, Alfredo, Leonardo López Luján, and Saburo Sugiyama.
1991 The Temple of Quetzalcoatl at Teotihuacan: Its Possible Ideological Significance. *Ancient Mesoamerica* 2(1):93–106.
López de Gómara, Francisco.
1964 *Cortés: The Life of the Conqueror by His Secretary.* Translated and edited by L. B. Simpson. Berkeley: University of California Press.
Manzanilla, Linda, Claudia López, and AnnCorinne Freter.
1996 Dating Results from Excavations in Quarry Tunnels Behind the Pyramid of the Sun at Teotihuacan. *Ancient Mesoamerica* 7(2):245–266.
Margain, Carlos R.
1971 Pre-Columbian Architecture of Central Mexico. *Handbook of Middle American Indians, Volume 10: Archaeology of Northern Mesoamerica, Part 1.* Edited by R. Wauchope, G. F Ekholm, and I. Bernal. Austin, Tex.: University of Texas Press. 45–91.
Marquina, Ignacio.
1939 Exploraciones en la Pirámide de Cholula, Pue. *27th Congreso Internacional de Americanistas Volume II.I.* México, D.F.: INAH-SEP. 52–63.
1951 *Arquitectura Prehispanica.* Memorias del Instituto Nacional de Antropología e Historia 1. México, D.F.: SEP-INAH.
1970a Pirámide de Cholula. *Proyecto Cholula.* Edited by I. Marquina. Serie Investigaciones 19. México, D.F.: Instituto Nacional de Antropología e Historia. 31–46.
1971 *Los Murales de los Bebedores en Cholula, Puebla.* México, D.F.: Artes de Mexico.
1975 Cholula, Puebla. *Los Pueblos y Senorios Teocráticos: El período de las ciudades urbanas, primera parte.* By E. Matos M. et al. México, D.F.: Departamento de Investigaciones Historicas, SEP-INAH. 109–122.
Marquina, Ignacio, editor.
1970b *Proyecto Cholula.* Serie Investigaciones 19. México, D.F.: Instituto Nacional de Antropologia e Historia.
McCafferty, Geoffrey G.
1984 A Middle Formative Feature in San Andrés Cholula, Puebla. Report submitted to the Centro Regional de Puebla (INAH).
1992 *The Material Culture of Postclassic Cholula, Mexico: Contextual Analysis of the UA-1 Domestic Compounds.* Ph.D. dissertation, Dept. of Anthropology, State University of New York at Binghamton.
1996a Reinterpreting the Great Pyramid of Cholula, Mexico. *Ancient Mesoamerica* 7(1):1–17.
1996b The Ceramics and Chronology of Cholula, Mexico. *Ancient Mesoamerica* 7(2):299–323.
1999a The Mixteca-Puebla Stylistic Tradition at Early Postclassic Cholula. *The Mixteca-Puebla Concept in Mesoamerican Archaeology: A Further Examina-*

tion. Edited by H. B. Nicholson and E. Quiñones Keber. Culver City, Calif.: Labyrinthos Press. 53–78.

1999b The Rome of Anahuac: Change and Continuity at Classic and Postclassic Cholula. *The Classic Heritage: From Teotihuacan to Tenochtitlán.* Edited by D. Carrasco. Boulder: University Press of Colorado. 341–370.

McCafferty, Sharisse D., and Geoffrey G. McCafferty.

1991 Spinning and Weaving as Female Gender Identity in Post-Classic Central Mexico. *Textile Traditions of Mesoamerica and the Andes: An Anthology.* Edited by M. Schevill, J. C. Berlo and E. Dwyer. New York: Garland Publishing. 19–44.

1994 The Conquered Women of Cacaxtla: Gender Identity or Gender Ideology? *Ancient Mesoamerica* 5(2):159–172.

1995 The Feast of the Water Tamales as Ritual Performance at Postclassic Cholula. Paper presented at the Annual Meeting of the American Anthropological Association, Washington, D.C.

1999 The Metamorphosis of Xochiquetzal: A Window on Womanhood in Pre- and Postconquest Mexico. *Manifesting Power: Gender and the Interpretation of Power in Archaeology.* Edited by T. Sweely and U. Lauper. London: Routledge Press. 103–125.

McVicker, Donald.

1985 The "Mayanized" Mexicans. *American Antiquity* 50(1):82–101.

Messmacher, Miguel.

1967a Los Patrones de asentamiento y la arquitectura en Cholula. *Cholula, reporte preliminar.* Edited by M. Messmacher. México, D.F.: Editorial Nueva Antropología. 6–17.

Milbrath, Susan.

1988 Birth Images in Mixteca-Puebla Art. *The Role of Gender in Precolumbian Art and Architecture.* Edited by V. E. Miller. Lanham, Md.: University Press of America. 153–178.

Motolinía, Fray Toribio de Benavente.

1951 *History of the Indians of New Spain.* Translated by F. B. Steck. Washington, D.C.: Academy of American Franciscan History.

Mountjoy, Joseph, and David A. Peterson.

1973 *Man and Land in Prehispanic Cholula.* Vanderbilt University Publications in Anthropology 4. Nashville, Tenn.: Vanderbilt University.

Müller, Florencia.

1972 Estudio iconográfico del mural de los Bebedores, Cholula, Puebla. *Religión en Mesoámerica.* Edited by J. Litvak King and N. Castillo Tejero. México, D.F.: Sociedad Mexicana de Antropología. 141–146.

1973 La extensión arqueológica de Cholula a través del tiempo. *Comunicaciones* 8:19–22.

1978 *La Alfarería de Cholula.* México, D.F.: Serie Arqueología, Instituto Nacional de Antropología e Historia.

Muñoz Camargo, Diego.

1948 *Historia de Tlaxcala.* México, D.F.: Ateneo Nacional de Ciencias y Artes de México.

Nagao, Debra.
1989   Public Proclamation in the Art of Cacaxtla and Xochicalco. *Mesoamerica After the Decline of Teotihuacan, A.D. 700–900*. Edited by R. A. Diehl and J. C. Berlo. Washington, D.C.: Dumbarton Oaks. 83–104.

Nicholson, Henry B.
1971   Religion in Pre-Hispanic Central Mexico. *Handbook of Middle American Indians, Volume 10: Archaeology of Northern Mesoamerica, Part 1*. Edited by R. Wauchope, G. F. Ekholm, and I. Bernal. Austin, Tex.: University of Texas Press. 395–446.

1982   The Mixteca-Puebla Concept Re-Visited. *The Art and Iconography of Late Post-Classic Central Mexico*. Edited by E. H. Boone. Washington, D.C.: Dumbarton Oaks. 227–254.

Noguera, Eduardo.
1937   *El Altar de los Craneos Esculpidos de Cholula*. México, D.F.: Talleres Gráficos de la Nación.

1954   *La cerámica arqueológica de Cholula*. México, D.F.: Editorial Guaranía.

1956   Un Edificio Preclásico en Cholula. *Estudios antropológicos publicados en homenaje al Dr. Manuel Gamio*. México, D.F.: Dirección General de Publicaciones. 213–224.

Olivera de V., Mercedes.
1970   La importancia religiosa de Cholula. *Proyecto Cholula*. Edited by I. Marquina. Serie Investigaciones 19. México, D.F.: Instituto Nacional de Antropología e Historia. 211–242.

Olivera de V., Mercedes, and Cayetano Reyes.
1969   Los Choloques y los Cholultecas: Apuntes sobre las Relaciones Étnicas en Cholula hasta el Siglo XVI. *Anales del INAH*, Epoch 7, 1(1967–68):247–274.

Paddock, John.
1987   Cholula en Mesoamérica. *Notas Mesoamericanas* 10:21–70.

Pohl, John M. D.
1994   Mexican Codices, Maps, and Lienzos as Social Contracts. *Writing Without Words*. Edited by E. H. Boone and W. D. Mignolo. Durham, N.C.: Duke University Press. 137–160.

Quiñones Keber, Eloise.
1995   *Codex Telleriano-Remensis: Ritual, Divination, and History in a Pictorial Aztec Manuscript*. Austin, Tex.: University of Texas Press.

Rojas, Gabriel de.
1927   Descripción de Cholula. *Revista Mexicana de Estudios Historicos* 1(6):158–170.

Sahagún, Bernardino de.
1950–1982   *Florentine Codex: General History of the Things of New Spain*. Translated by C. E. Dibble and A. J. D. Anderson. Salt Lake City: University of Utah Press and School of American Research.

1993   *Primeros Memoriales* (facsimile photographed by F. Anders). Norman, Okla.: University of Oklahoma Press.

Sharp, Rosemary.
    1978   Architecture as Interelite Communication in Preconquest Oaxaca, Ver-
            acruz, and Yucatán. *Middle Classic Mesoamerica: A.D. 400–700.* Edited by
            E. Pasztory. New York: Columbia University Press. 158–171.
Simons, Bente Bittman.
    1968   *Los mapas de Cuauhtinchan y la Historia Tolteca-Chichimeca.* Serie Investi-
            gaciones 15. México, D.F.: Instituto Nacional de Antropología e Histo-
            ria.
Smith, Mary Elizabeth.
    1973   *Picture Writing from Ancient Southern Mexico.* Norman, Okla.: Univer-
            sity of Oklahoma Press.
Suárez C., Sergio.
    1985   *Un entierro del clásico superior en Cholula, Puebla.* México, D.F.: Cuaderno
            de Trabajo 6, Centro Regional de Puebla, INAH.
Suárez C., Sergio, and Silvia Martínez A.
    1993   *Monografía de Cholula, Puebla.* Puebla, Mexico: H. Ayuntamiento Munic-
            ipal Constitucional de San Pedro Cholula.
Sullivan, Thelma.
    1982   Tlazolteotl-Ixcuina: The Great Spinner and Weaver. *The Art and Iconog-
            raphy of Late Post-Classic Central Mexico.* Edited by E. H. Boone. Wash-
            ington, D.C.: Dumbarton Oaks. 7–36.
Sullivan, Thelma D., with H. B. Nicholson, Arthur J. O. Anderson, Charles E. Dib-
            ble, Eloise Quiñones Keber, and Wayne Ruwet.
    1997   Paleography of Nahuatl Text and English Translation. *Primeros Memori-
            ales.* By Fray Bernardino de Sahagún. Norman, Okla.: University of Ok-
            lahoma Press.
Super, John C.
    1988   *Food, Conquest, and Colonization in Sixteenth-Century Spanish America.*
            Albuquerque, N.Mex.: University of New Mexico Press.
Tichy, Franz.
    1981   Order and Relationship of Space and Time in Mesoamerica: Myth or
            Reality? *Mesoamerican Sites and World-Views.* Edited by E. P. Benson.
            Washington, D.C.: Dumbarton Oaks. 217–245.
Torquemada, Fray Juan de.
    1975–1983   *Monarquía Indiana.* México, D.F.: Instituto de Investigaciones
            Historicas, Universidad Nacional Autonoma de México.
Villagra Caleti, Agustín.
    1971   Mural Painting in Central Mexico. *Handbook of Middle American Indians,
            Volume 10: Archaeology of Northern Mesoamerica, Part 1.* Edited by R.
            Wauchope, G. F. Ekholm, and I. Bernal. Austin, Tex.: University of
            Texas Press. 135–156.
Wheatley, Paul.
    1971   *The Pivot of the Four Quarters: A Preliminary Enquiry into the Origins and
            Character of the Ancient Chinese City.* Chicago: Aldine.

Notes

1. Similar hummanmade, or at least modified, caves with flower-shaped chambers have been discovered in the Tepeaca region of Puebla, near the source of the *Historia Tolteca-Chichimeca* account (Patricio Davalos, personal communication 1999).

2. A continuation of the same motif may be present on the tablero of Stage 3b on the west side of the Great Pyramid (Sergio Suárez Cruz, personal communication), although this is probably from a later stage of construction.

3. Amalucan, another Formative period site on the eastern frontier of the Cholula kingdom, apparently attempted a similar claim to symbolic significance as its inhabitants channeled an irrigation canal beneath the principal pyramid in an effort to establish it as an *altepetl*.

4. Rex Koontz (personal communication 1999) points out that this is an architectural trait also present at El Tajín.

5. Stage 3b is known as the Edificio Tolteca, not for its cultural affiliation but because of the liberal use of Tolteca-brand cement in its reconstruction. In fact, the front portion of this building, including its staircase, was removed in antiquity when Stage 3c was built, and therefore the reliability of the reconstructed front facade is unclear. In an earlier publication (1996a), I suggested that Stage 3b postdated Stage 3a, but on closer inspection of the joints between the two structures it is apparent that Stage 3a was built onto the existing Stage 3b.

6. Altar 3 was erected at the base of the pyramid staircase during excavation in the 1960s, even though the lower half was found near Altar 2 (Contreras 1970:111). It is equally plausible, therefore, that the stela was originally attached to Altar 2 as a complementary stela/altar group (McCafferty 1996a:10), although Acosta (1970c) considered and rejected this possibility because of the size difference between the two monumental slabs.

7. The top of Altar 3 angles to a triangular point so that its shadow could have served as a sensitive measuring device of the solstice, conceptually similar to a sundial.

8. It is also very similar to painted volutes recently found at the La Ventilla compound of Classic period Teotihuacan (Rubén Cabrera, personal communication).

9. No evidence of this mural can be found at the archaeological zone, although remnants of murals are stored in tunnels of the Great Pyramid.

10. Based on representations of the ceramic vessels in the murals and actual archaeological vessels, Müller (1972) suggested that the murals dated to ca. 200 AD. Alternatively, reinterpretation of the pyramid construction sequence, especially the Patio of the Altars, indicates that the murals date to the Epiclassic period, between 600–900 AD (McCafferty 1996a).

11. The head is also similar to a carved stone *ñuhu*, a Mixtec water spirit, that was found at San Juan Diuxi in the Mixteca Alta (Byland and Pohl 1994:11–12, Figure 3).

12. Until recently, dried toad effigies were a popular tourist item sold in Cholula. They were usually posed and mounted in a scene, such as in a cantina or as mariachis.

13. The Great Pyramid is also identified as 7 Flower in Folios 9v–10r and 14r of the *Historia Tolteca-Chichimeca* (1976), although there are only 6 flowers in Folio 7v, perhaps because the paw of the frog is obscuring the other flower. Map 2 of the *Mapas de Cuauhtinchan* also identifies the Great Pyramid as 7 Flower (Simons 1968:65–66).

14. Jansen (1996) has discussed the association of the Chichimec Lord 4 Jaguar, who appears prominently in the Mixtec codices as an ally of Lord 8 Deer "Jaguar Claw" and who may also appear in Nahua texts from Puebla/Tlaxcala as Nacxitl, an avatar of Quetzalcoatl. It was 4 Jaguar who perforated 8 Deer's septum at Cattail Frieze, which Jansen identifies as Cholula. The jaguar paw and numeral 4 may represent the Great Pyramid from the Atamalcualiztli ceremony as the site of 4 Jaguar.

A Sense of Place at Chichén Itzá

CYNTHIA KRISTAN-GRAHAM

For more than a century, archaeologists, art historians, ethnohistorians, and epigraphers have been studying Chichén Itzá, and a new picture of that site is emerging. Ongoing excavations indicate that Chichén Itzá is larger in area than was ever imagined, with a much more complex layout and more diverse inventory of buildings and imagery. Moreover, it appears that this late Maya capital that was home to a diverse group of Maya peoples forged a new social order with innovations in governance and public art and architecture. Although earlier Maya history has been reconstructed as a series of regional kingdoms based on royal genealogy, episodic warfare, and conquest, Chichén Itzá seems to have pioneered a new form of rulership shared among elite lineages that transcended dynastic and ethnic boundaries and that valued the rules of cooperation as much as the rules of engagement.

However, our picture of Chichén Itzá is not quite complete. A few crucial ingredients not usually considered as part of the study of Chichén Itzá proper—notably the conception of the site as a spatial nexus and the place of the original populace—can deepen an understanding of this ancient center. This emphasis on space follows recent advances in philosophy, architectural history, geography, and archaeology, wherein space is understood as a crucial link between people and social formation and as a catalyst for memory. Together, citizenry and space can be examined by asking several questions: 1) how does the plan of Chichén Itzá—essentially a constellation of terraced architectural platforms connected by a network of roads—intersect with habitation and ritual? 2) how are principles of self, family, and community embedded in the architectural landscape? and 3) how are social relations fostered and reproduced in the settlement?

In this chapter, an overview of the nature of space precedes a discussion of Chichén Itzá within the context of Maya society. Then follows an examination of the settlement of Chichén Itzá and the manifestation of governance, identity, and family in planning, architecture, imagery, and writing. Finally, there is a consideration of how these components were integral to a sense of place and a sense of belonging at Chichén Itzá.

The Politics and Poetics of Space

Space is both a natural phenomenon and an invisible cultural product, the latter by virtue of spatial conceptions and uses. Although we may never know how the ancient Maya precisely conceptualized their spatial environs, at Chichén Itzá platforms, buildings, and roads are vestiges of how space and landscape were planned and partitioned for a range of visions and uses. Following is a presentation of some ideas that can help lead to a refined understanding of the symbolic and social dimensions of space at Chichén Itzá.

Any settlement can be understood through the unique manner in which the population interacts with the spatial world. Such an inquiry may lead to an understanding of what architectural historian Christian Norberg-Schulz (1980:10) calls *genius loci*, or "the spirit of place" after the ancient Roman concept. The idea of *genius loci* conjures a complete sense of space wherein natural and cultural properties merge to form a sort of spatial personality. *Genius loci* is very similar to the concept of the aesthetic values of a landscape explained by Kathryn Reese-Taylor and Rex Koontz (chapter 1 in this volume). Components of a spatial personality may include natural terrain, landscaping, planning, traffic patterns, architecture, and related imagery. Even though some psychological and visceral aspects of *genius loci* may remain lost in prehistory, we shall see that Chichén Itzá's spirit of place encompassed a general plan and visual program that not only united the sacred and the mundane but was also conducive to everyday movement and special rituals in which notions of self, family, and state were acted out in both private and public venues.

A case in point involves the use of a *tz'onot*, the natural limestone sinkholes that perforate Chichén Itzá and other Yucatec sites. A *tz'onot* had a pragmatic use—to supply water—and a sacred referent as a portal to the Otherworld; their commingling may have suggested proximity between the earthly and spiritual realms. This sinkhole may also be understood as an aesthetic trope that enmeshed physical and spiritual geography. At Chichén Itzá, small ritual buildings were often built beside sinkholes, and both were integrated into the system of roadways that ran throughout the site. This repeated construct might be read as a visual and spatial metaphor regarding the access to, and necessity of, natural and supernatural resources.

Understanding space and architecture as aesthetic tropes may be complemented by treating space as a dimension of social relations. In this century, space has been analyzed from a variety of stances. For example, Walter Benjamin's Passagen-Werk, or Arcades Project, sought to examine how nineteenth-century Parisian industrial culture dialectically permeated, and was permeated by, public space. Specifically, Benjamin investigated how commercial areas with covered walkways, store displays, and advertisements—the ancestors of our cavernous shopping malls—may enter the unconscious and give shape to attitudes about the world. In an early note for his unfinished project, Benjamin notes:

> Streets are the dwelling places of the collective. The collective is an eternally restless, eternally moving essence that, among the facades of buildings endures . . . experiences . . . learns, and senses as much as individuals in the projection of their four walls (in Buck-Morss 1989:304).

Crucial to Benjamin's ideas is his belief that repeated movements and vistas, and concomitant ideas, can be quietly internalized and normalized as part of daily life. Like the Parisian arcades, Chichén Itzá was a capital space that encompassed roads, planned spaces, and three-dimensional pictorial programs. An analysis of its plan and traffic pattern may show what the populace spatially and visually experienced in their environs, notably the ways in which natural and humanmade features, along with movement and visual frames, imbued collective notions about social life.

In addition, space is a force in the exercise of power. As Michel Foucault (1986:23) has explained, buildings are more than just edifices; structures and spatial relationships are part of a field of social relations, and these relations help to delineate sites and inform a technology of power. Foucault has shown, for example, that the institution of the prison can embody and enforce social rules through tangible forms, such as cell blocks, and through intangible means, such as regulations, to form an intricate web of power. In discussing the Panopticon, an innovative nineteenth-century prison design in which the inmates could be observed at any time by the guards, who themselves were not visible to the prisoners,

Foucault observes that it is in the domain of rules, sight lines, and architecture that power relations are acted out:

> Power has its principles not so much in a person as in a certain concerted distribution of bodies, surfaces, lights, gazes; in an arrangement whose internal mechanisms produce the relation in which individuals are caught up (1977:202).

Following Foucault's paradigm that space and architecture can be read as part of an equation of power, it is possible to begin to look at the physical remains of Chichén Itzá as a clue to the construction and practice of social relations. In particular, a consideration of building location, ownership, and use may help lead to an understanding of Chichén Itzá as a physical, social, and psychic dwelling place.

Space is also a vital force in the formation of individuality and community. Architectural historian Dolores Heyden (1995:9) has explained how public spaces in the United States are closely linked with notions of self and group. Because natural topography and human artifacts spatially frame us and our vistas, Heyden reasons that settlements can be catalysts for and fonts of collective memory. In this sense, spaces have the capacity to foster a public memory of place and time in the form of communal territory and visions. Moreover, Heyden cites recent cognitive studies regarding the important role of space and place in engaging the senses and the intertwining of social relations into spatial perceptions:

> If place does provide an overload of possible meanings for the researcher, it is place's very same assault on all ways of knowing (sight, sound, smell, touch, and taste) that makes it powerful as a source of memory, as a weave where one strand ties in another (Heyden 1995:18).

In a related vein, the philosopher Edward Casey (1987, 1993) has interrogated the metaphysical dimensions of space and devised the idea of "place memory," wherein memory is place-determined, with place helping to determine who and what we are. Place in this sense is not necessarily cartographic but an experiential dimension in which one's surroundings, primarily landscape and architecture, are active agents in the formation of identity (Casey 1993:13–16; see also Bachelard 1964:8). If space is a catalyst for collective memory, identity, and experience, might it be possible to determine some of the images and visions Chichén Itzá offered its occupants and visitors?

Some recent studies of the politics of space, such as those by geographers Jacques Leclerc (1993) and Rudiger Korff (1993), have measured the effects of governmental policies upon the construction of modern urban centers in Jakarta, Indonesia, and Bangkok, Thailand, respectively. Using a wealth of documents, they have tried to understand the use of space as an extension of governmental programs because modern cities are consciously designed as loci of political symbolism and allegiance. However, to approach space only as a direct reflection of political forces may exclude more nuanced aspects of space, for example the experiential capacity of natural and cultural features in the landscape to impart a range of thoughts and activities beyond politics.

A sense of place, at Chichén Itzá or anywhere, therefore is connected to vision, memory, identity, and social relations. Throughout this chapter, space and place will be explored as the physical and symbolic terrain on which Chichén Itzá was built.

Chichén Itzá and the Late Maya World

Political History

Chichén Itzá emerged as a preeminent power during the Terminal Classic-Early Postclassic periods (ca. 800–1200 AD) when Lowland Maya society underwent a radical transformation. The site reached its political and economic apogee long after the burgeoning of Maya civilization in the highlands of Guatemala and in the southern lowlands of Mexico, Guatemala, Belize, and Honduras when population and monumental art production were centered at spectacular sites such as Palenque, Tikal, and Copán and at more humble sites such as Ceren, El Salvador. Beginning in the ninth century, the overall Maya population precipitously declined, for reasons still unclear; common explanations are drought, famine, disease, economic distress, invasion, internal rebellion, and ineffectual governance (Culbert 1973; Schele and Freidel 1990; Demarest 1992).

The subsequent Terminal Classic period was a vortex of peoples, places, and power. As the southern sites gradually declined and then were abandoned, the focus of power shifted to the northern lowlands of Yucatán and remained there until the conquest in the sixteenth century. Koba, Uxmal, Yaxuná, and Chichén Itzá became new hubs of Maya life in the north. Although the Yucatec Maya are not directly implicated in the Classic collapse, they took advantage of the vacuum left by their Classic predecessors by forming new political alliances and participating in new exchange networks with Central Mexico and Central America to establish themselves as formidable powers (Freidel 1986).

For several centuries, Chichén Itzá was a regional Maya capital, a sprawling hub of population and exchange. Although the site is yet to be fully mapped, it covers at least 25 square kilometers (Andrews, personal communication 1998). Its growth was paralleled by declining population in some of the other northern centers, and by about 950–1000 AD Chichén Itzá seems to have absorbed peoples into its sphere of influence from elsewhere in the Maya area.[1] The Chichén Itzá domain very probably stretched from Campeche across the Yucatán peninsula to northern Quintana Roo (Andrews 1990:26). Located near the center of northern Yucatán, Chichén Itzá was strategically located to regulate trade across the peninsula and around the coast as economic activity shifted northward; the varied and sumptuous trade goods and exotica found at Chichén Itzá and at its port of Isla Cerritos on the north coast of Yucatán confirm its role as a center of exchange and its status as one of the wealthiest of Mesoamerican centers (Ball and Taschek 1989:188; Robles C. and Andrews 1986:88).[2]

Ethnohistory

The central place of Chichén Itzá in the late Maya world is confirmed by many ethnohistorical sources. Although Diego de Landa's *Relación de las Cosas de Yucatán* was written in the sixteenth century, when Chichén Itzá had long ceased to be a dominant Maya center, his informants conveyed a strong memory of Chichén Itzá as a premier Yucatec city, recounting its former ruling lineages and political and economic clout, as well as its continuing importance as a ritual center in the period just before the Spanish Conquest (Tozzer 1941b). The *Books of Chilam Balam*, a collection of colonial-period Yucatec manuscripts written in the Latin alphabet with memories of the pre-Hispanic and colonial past and prognostications for the future, record that Chichén Itzá had been the focus of political allegiance and tribute in pre-Hispanic times (Roys 1967:74–75; Edmonson 1982:6, 166; 1986:117). The *Relaciónes de Yucatán* list the many towns and provinces in northern Yucatán that were tributaries of Chichén Itzá, as well as some towns in Mexico and Guatemala that likewise paid tribute to Chichén Itzá (de la Garza 1980, Volume I:164, 182, 200, 305).

It appears that Chichén Itzá was in part populated by outsiders who made a series of incursions into the site, set themselves up as new rulers, and subsequently abandoned their new capital in the Early Postclassic period (Tozzer 1941b:22; Roys 1967: 161; de la Garza 1980, Volume I:182). These peoples have come to be called the Itzá on the basis of ethnohistorical documents and hieroglyphic inscriptions. By the time of the Spanish Conquest, the name "Itzá" had been incorporated into the place name Chichén Itzá, "the well of the Itzá," referring to the Sacred Cenote in the site center that was the focus of pilgrimages. At least some the ancient inhabitants there called themselves by the name Itzá; the name Itzá Ahaw, or Lord Itzá, appears in inscriptions from Chichén Itzá (Schele and Mathews 1998:203, 354 n.6). Apparently the Itzá had a longer time-depth in the Maya world; the word "Itzá" is included on texts from pots from the Lake Peten Itzá region of the Southern Lowlands and appears in hieroglyphs in the Southern Lowlands by the Early Classic period (Schele et al. 2000:23).

The Itzá probably were either Mayas from the southern lowlands (Schele and Mathews 1998:201–203) or Chontal Maya or Gulf Coast peoples from Tabasco and Campeche (Thompson 1970; Andrews and Robles C. 1985:64–67; Kowalski 1989). The Itzá were accomplished traders whose exposure to a range of regions and peoples helped to forge a culture at Chichén Itzá that was influenced by both Mayan and Mexican elements. In addition, the cultural climate of the Terminal Classic—including new economic networks and loci of power that formed after the Classic period—made up a unique infrastructure at Chichén Itzá that was sensitive to the question of origins and to the fragility of alliance.

Ethnohistory and Visual Culture

Another group of foreigners, Toltecs or Central Mexicans, also have been embroiled in the history of Chichén Itzá. Some of the ethnohistorical sources relate that a Mexican captain named K'ak'upacal or a Mexican priest-deity named Kukulcan came to rule at Chichén Itzá, although they disagree substantially on many details (Tozzer 1941b:20–23;Roys 1967:161; Kelley 1968; de la Garza 1980, Volume I:182, 200, 216). This alleged Mexican presence at Chichén Itzá was supported by U.S. diplomat and explorer John L. Stephens (1843, Volume II:312), who noted two distinct styles at Chichén Itzá, attributing the buildings there and even much of Maya architecture in general to the migration of Toltecs from Mexico. Later in the century, French explorer Désiré Charnay (1885) noted striking visual similarities between Chichén Itzá and the Central Mexican site of Tula, Hidalgo, and suggested that the Toltecs had introduced Mexican traits into Yucatán. These observations led to the famous

Tula-Chichén Itzá debate. Framed as a unilineal equation, it was thought that one of the two sites had to have influenced the other, but the exact nature of the relationship remains a mystery (Kubler 1961; Ruz 1962).[3]

Ironically, Ralph Roys (1966) and Marvin Cohodas (1978:88) have shown that there is no actual mention of a Toltec invasion of Yucatán in the sources and that the notion of a Toltec presence in Yucatán has resulted from a misreading of primary sources. The idea of a Toltec invasion had nevertheless been accepted as an attractive way to account for a seemingly Maya-Mexican visual language at Chichén Itzá. Many scholars have been predisposed to accept a Maya-to-Toltec occupation at Chichén Itzá and have used planning, architecture, and imagery to support this scenario. For example, in scenes of battles such as those on the famous embossed gold disks found in the Sacred Cenote, interpreters invariably labeled the victors as Toltecs and the vanquished as Maya (Lothrop 1952).

The core of the alleged original Maya occupation at Chichén Itzá is in the south, in "Old" or "Maya" Chichén Itzá (Figure 12.1). There, so-called Chichén-Maya buildings parallel the Puuc style of the Northwestern Lowlands found at Uxmal and other sites; they feature relatively small, low, multichambered structures with interior spaces spanned by corbel vaults and exterior embellishment that includes hieroglyphic inscriptions and stone mosaic facades with geometric patterns or three-dimensional masks (Cohodas 1978; Lincoln 1986; Wren and Schmidt 1991). The famous Temple of the Three Lintels embodies many of these features and may be considered an exemplary Chichén-Maya building (Figure 12.2).

Other, supposedly later buildings are constructed in the Chichén-Toltec style, so named for the apparent Mexican flavor. The hallmark features include colonnades, a single- or double-chambered structure atop a stepped pyramid base, pyramid summits with decorated pillars supporting wooden roofs, and such alleged Mexican motifs as atlantid and *chak mol* sculptures and bas-reliefs with glyphs near the heads of figures (Lincoln 1986; Wren and Schmidt 1991). In contrast to the Chichén-Maya style, the Chichén-Toltec style is essentially a figural art tradition emphasizing crowded carved or painted panoramic compositions or single figures on stone pillars. The well-known Temple of the Warriors Complex has most of these traits and has been considered to be an exemplary Chichén-Toltec structure (Figure 12.3). (See Tozzer 1957 for his detailed chronology of Chichén Itzá.)

This traditional paradigm of Chichén Itzá as a sequential Maya-to-Toltec center is far too reductive to explain such a large and complex site;

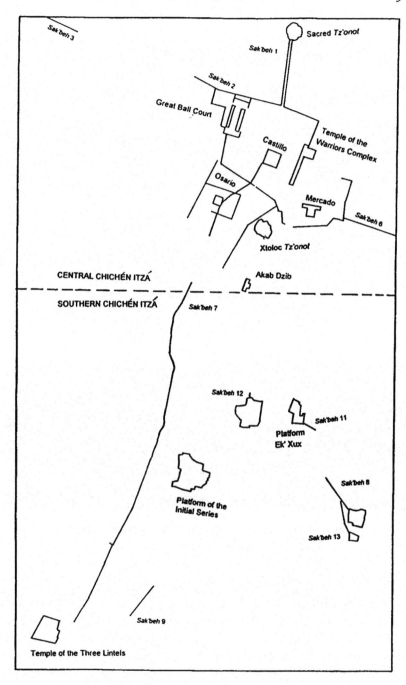

Sak'beh 3

Sacred *Tz'onot*

Sak'beh 1

Sak'beh 2

Great Ball Court

Castillo

Temple of the
Warriors Complex

Osario

Mercado

Sak'beh 6

Xtoloc *Tz'onot*

CENTRAL CHICHÉN ITZÁ

Akab Dzib

SOUTHERN CHICHÉN ITZÁ

Sak'beh 7

Sak'beh 12

Sak'beh 11

Platform
Ek' Xux

Sak'beh 8

Platform of the
Initial Series

Sak'beh 13

Sak'beh 9

Temple of the Three Lintels

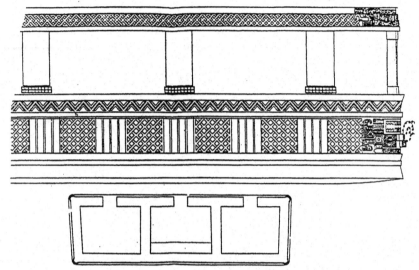

Figure 12.2   Plan and facade, Temple of the Three Lintels
(after Ruppert 1952:147)

Figure 12.3   Facade, Temple of the Warriors Complex
(photograph by Kristan-Graham)

surely military intrusion is not the only plausible explanation for the syn-cretic style there. Daniel Brinton (1887), Tatiana Proskouriakoff (1951), Ed-ward Kurjack (1988), Charles Lincoln (1990), and others are skeptical about a Toltec invasion or occupation and suggest instead that Chichén Itzá was home to an aggregation of Maya-speaking groups. One persist-ent problem has been that Chichén Itzá presents examples of art that do not comfortably fit our current notions of Maya and Toltec or Mexican art;

surely it is these categories, and not Chichén Itzá itself, that have been the real obstacle in attaining a finer understanding of visual culture there.

A New Picture of Chichén Itzá

The widespread "Toltecization" of Chichén Itzá has tended to obscure its full art tradition; clearly the architecture and art there have references that are not expressed by the Toltec-Maya opposition. Moreover, the Toltec and Maya categories are not mutually exclusive. For example, the famous Temple of the Warriors, an alleged Chichén-Toltec structure, combines both Maya and Toltec traits as they are traditionally understood (Figure 12.3). A corbel vault spans part of a colonnade, and the stone mosaic temple walls depicting Maya deities enclose carved stone pillars that display Mexican-style figures and glyphs. This consistent blending of so-called Maya and Toltec traits is so prevalent that it is integral to the art tradition there, and their contemporaneity in the same building undermines the very notion of a Maya-Toltec sequence. (Later, the Temple of the Warriors Complex will be discussed in more detail in order to show how one particular building and decorative program embodied and promoted the values of the Chichén Itzá polity.)

Archaeology, too, bears out the ambiguous nature of any Maya-to-Toltec sequence at Chichén Itzá. Ceramic chronologies show that the Maya and Toltec portions of the site overlap at least partially (Ball 1979). Settlement patterns indicate that the site was planned as a large, integrated entity and was built and occupied in one long phase spanning the Terminal Classic–Early Postclassic period (Garza and Kurjack 1980:25; Lincoln 1990; Schele and Mathews 1998:199; see also Cohodas 1978). David Freidel (1986:421) has noticed similarities between the plans of Chichén Itzá and such Puuc sites as Uxmal, Sayil, and Kabah, and he considers Chichén Itzá to be a basically northern Mayan center (cf. Taube 1994 on the Toltec nature of Chichén Itzá). If we accept this new paradigm of Chichén Itzá as a northern Maya cosmopolitan center, it is no longer necessary to sort out the Maya features from the Toltec ones. The aggregation of architectural forms and art styles are not necessarily evidence of a foreign intrusion; instead, they can signal different uses, occupants, or even aesthetic preferences. Richard Diehl (1993) suggests that given the contours of the Early Postclassic period, Mesoamerican centers were predisposed toward establishing a more synthetic culture and sharing key traits with other formidable powers, and this is a profitable way to understand Chichén Itzá, both as a capital and as an art tradition.

This cosmopolitan nature at Chichén Itzá was tied to a new strategy of rulership whose features are recorded in ethnohistorical documents and in monuments and imagery from Chichén Itzá. In a departure from the lengthy Classic-style inscriptions that charted royal history through portraits, titles, names, dates, genealogies, and events in narrative texts and images, the hieroglyphic inscriptions at Chichén Itzá are shorter, record a more circumscribed series of peoples and events, and are nearly devoid of imagery.

Several buildings in Southern Chichén Itzá have lintels or facades whose inscriptions feature dates that cluster between 867 and 881 AD, with the earliest recorded date at 832 AD (Krochock 1995:2). As Ruth Krochock (1988, 1991) has shown for the Temples of the One, Three, and Four Lintels, the texts typically record one or two dates in the Yucatec style of dating; building ownership; the names of a few male protagonists; their filial relationship; and a ritual event such as a building dedication, bloodletting, or sacrifice. For example, a transliteration of a portion of Lintel 2 from the Temple of the 4 Lintels reads: "On 12 K'an, the day of 7 Sak, sunrise, it was finished/incised the lintel in the doorway of his holy house, K'inil Kopol" (Krochock, personal communication 1997). Krochock further explains the significance of these inscriptions:

> [Each lintel] seems to highlight a different individual and that, in this way, the lintels seem to be "owned" by those individuals. One might view this as a way to permanently glorify and single-out the most important of the current ruling class without referring to the hierarchical status differences that may exist among them ... [the texts] may record the actions of several high-ranking personages of possible equal status. This evidence suggests that the Maya political social structure of Terminal Classic Chichén Itzá, before any presumed foreign invasion, must have diverged fundamentally from that of the southern Classic Maya Lowland sites (1988:13).

In a departure from Classic-period texts, only descent in the female line seems to be recorded in the inscriptions, and David Stuart (1993) and Erik Boot (1995) have observed that the protagonists are brothers or male companions.

The new social order at Chichén Itzá seems to have been based on multepal, or joint, rule, a new strategy of rulership that was in part a response to the political failures of the Classic period. In the Southern Lowlands, political power was directly linked to the royal dynasty that controlled each polity; the inability to form lasting alliances or to share power did not equip them to successfully confront growing social problems or the endemic fighting between competing realms (Schele and Freidel 1990; Demarest 1992). Chichén Itzá subsequently pursued a strategy of assimilation over that of conflict; instead of social hierarchy being overtly featured in decorative programs, imagery stressed the families and groups that formed the polity (Schele and Freidel 1990:348; Wren and Schmidt 1991:201).[4]

The Settlement of Chichén Itzá

In this discussion, the traditional ethnic labels "Maya" and "Toltec" and the chronological labels "Old" and "New" are replaced with more neutral terms to describe the three main zones of the settlement: Southern, Central, and Northern Chichén Itzá. When freed of the restraints of the Maya-versus-Toltec question, other concerns emerge, notably the codes of cosmology and community embedded into the architectural landscape.

Cosmological and Symbolic Referents

Chichén Itzá seems to have been planned in part with the template that ordered Tikal, Copán, and other Classic Maya centers. According to Wendy Ashmore (1992), common features of this plan include: (1) a strong north-south axis; (2) a formal and functional dualism in which large buildings and plazas for public rituals are concentrated in the north, whereas enclosed groups reserved for more private royal activities are concentrated in the south; and (3) a cosmological scheme in which the north symbolizes the celestial sphere and the south the mundane or underworld sphere.

Chichén Itzá is a variation of these basic principles. Architectural platforms are distributed in an uneven pattern, and they are connected by *sak beob*, or masonry roads, laid out in an arterial arrangement (Figure 12.1). Some of the longest roads run roughly north-south, creating a pronounced north-south axis. In contrast to the periphery of the site, the site core is monumental in scale, with plazas, broad avenues, temples, range structures, ballcourts, and some anomalous buildings; the large scale and central locale seem designed as an arena for huge public spectacles. Smaller platforms, roads, and buildings radiate from this "downtown" area; scale, siting, and building inventory are smaller, yet the basic

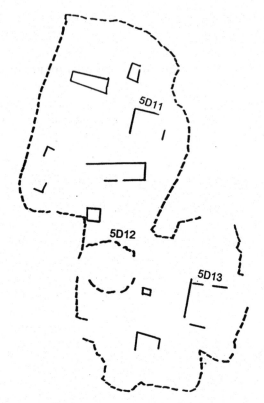

Figure 12.4   Plan of major buildings on Platform Ek'Xux:
Structure 5D11—colonnade; Structure 5D12—temple mound;
Structure 5D13—gallery-patio
(after Lincoln 1990:Map 1)

arrangement of buildings echoes the downtown area (Figure 12.4). These
platforms are probably residential compounds and may have been the locus of lineage festivals, administration, manufacturing, cooking, and the
collecting of tribute (Schele and Mathews 1998:29).

Maya sites have also been interpreted as cosmic maps in which topography, planning, and architecture are correlated with Maya myths and
cosmology. According to Freidel et al. (1993), the North Platform was the
major stage for ritual activity at Chichén Itzá and was characterized as
the Primordial Sea of Creation from Maya cosmogonies (Figure 12.5). The
Castillo, a monumental radial pyramid, is the Mountain of Creation that
embodies the four-fold partitioning of the world at the beginning of time.
North of this, the Sacred Cenote pierces the surface of the earth to reveal

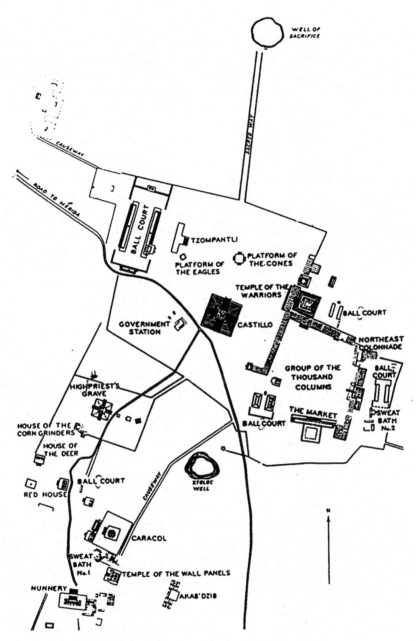

Figure 12.5   Plan, Central Chichén Itzá
(after Ruppert 1952:Figure 1)

the watery depths of the Otherworld. The connecting *sak beh* ("white road") symbolizes the Milky Way, the path traveled at the beginning and end of time. Two nearby structures frame this architectural cosmogram. The Great Ball Court recalls the setting for the *Popol Vuh*, a Maya creation myth; carved panels lining the playing alley plausibly represent rituals of the type held there, which recall the act of creation and mediate between the earthly and celestial realms. The temples that frame the ballcourt have carved and painted embellishment that commemorates Itzá battles associated with the founding of Chichén Itzá, the charter by which the Itzá rules, and the accession of lords (Schele and Mathews 1998:197–255). Across the plaza, the Temple of the Warriors Complex follows the plan of a Maya council house, or *popol nah*, where state business was conducted; decorative programs there likewise embody political interests.

These cosmological/mythic readings both link Chichén Itzá with earlier Maya sites and attempt to merge seamlessly its mythic past with its political present. But little attention has been paid to how Chichén Itzá was planned for social and political activity or to its everyday and symbolic use by a real population. A careful look at buildings, decorative programs, and traffic actuates a Chichén Itzá we can no longer see: People and architecture intersect to create a virtual ritual nexus that embodies new concepts of self, family, and community. The settlement can thus be viewed as an extension of the Maya cosmological and political universe, and compelling parallels with Yucatec literary traditions about Chichén Itzá add other nuances.

Central Chichén Itzá

The site center is the origin and center of the network of roadways (Garza and Kurjack 1980:25) (Figure 12.5). The large scale, central siting, decorative programs, and type of writing on buildings all suggest that Central Chichén Itzá was intended for public spectacles. The buildings here have referents aside from the cosmological ones just cited. Other scholars have suggested that the Castillo was a royal or calendrical monument; the North Temple in the Great Ball Court was a monument of royal inauguration; the Caracol was an astronomical marker; the Mercado and Akab Tzib were palaces; and the Monjas was a palace or council house (Coe 1993:146–151; Sharer 1994:392–396; Wren 1994; Henderson 1997:214–223). Some building types occur more than once in the site center. The Temple of the Tables is a smaller version of the adjacent Temple of the Warriors. The High Priest's Grave or Osario replicates the Castillo in miniature;

this radial pyramid is on axis with the Xtoloc Cenote and is connected to it by a *sak beh*. The Osario and part of the *sak beh* were once enclosed by a wall, so that at some point this complex was separated from the rest of Central Chichén Itzá (Schele and Mathews 1998:204). This isolation may indicate that the Castillo and the Osario were used by different groups, or that the former was for public use whereas the latter was perhaps reserved for more private use.

To account for this juxtaposition in scale and location between the Castillo and the Osario, Linda Schele (personal communication 1995) has invoked the concept of the galactic polity. Essentially, the galactic polity (also called a segmentary state, *negara*, theater state, or exemplary center) is an explanatory model for understanding politics and settlement patterns in traditional Southeast Asian societies. The galactic polity is a central governing body whose policies, rituals, and visual culture are reproduced in miniature by satellite centers, or by sectors within sites, to demonstrate incorporation into the larger political system. The primary center often is constructed as a cosmological model, and it seeks to encompass an ever-changing network of human and economic relations that flow from the capital to the hinterland and back again. The center and its satellites often share physical similarities and a symbolic rhetoric that accentuate their conditional relationship (Tambiah 1977; Geertz 1980).

The idea of the galactic polity has already proven useful in understanding the ancient Maya, especially to explain the web of relations between a primary center and its secondary and tertiary satellites as they spread across the landscape (Fox 1987; Demarest 1992). At Chichén Itzá, the Osario may have been used as a secondary ceremonial center or a "primary partner among equals" in the multepal system of governance. Rafael Cobos's (personal communication 1997) recent work mapping and excavating of portions of the site north of the Sacred Cenote provides new evidence of Chichén Itzá as a galactic polity. Around Chichén Itzá, secondary and tertiary sites radiate out from the site center equidistantly, just as causeways radiate out from the site center. At Chichén Itzá proper, architectural groups joined by causeways often contain similar structures—usually a temple, an altar, and a gallery-patio or a patio—that simulate part of the site core in miniature. Moreover, it seems that the manner in which goods were distributed fits a galactic polity pattern. Cobos (personal communication 1997) suggests that the flow of goods, such as obsidian, from Isla Cerritos to the central government at Chichén Itzá and on to family heads residing at different architectural compounds was

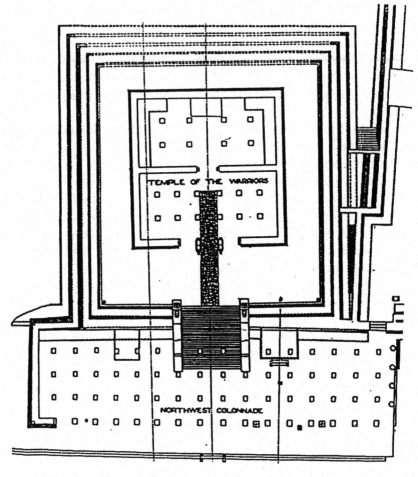

Figure 12.6   Plan, Temple of the Warriors Complex
(after E. Morris 1931:Plate 3)

relatively equal, thus indicating that the members of the polity were generally treated in kind.

Besides being the nucleus of a galactic polity, Central Chichén Itzá
(variously called the North Platform or the Gran Nivelación) seems also
to have been the spatial and economic center of the site, reserved for the
practical and ritual business of state. This is exemplified by the Temple of
the Warriors Complex, which commemorates polity membership. The
Temple of the Warriors and the adjoining Northwest Colonnade unite to

form the Temple of the Warriors Complex, which in appearance and theme transcends traditional ethnic styles (Figure 12.6).

The Temple of the Warriors itself encases an earlier building, the Temple of the Chak Mol. The Temple of the Warriors measures 38 meters on each side of the base and rises 11.41 meters from a terraced platform. The stepped pyramid is composed of four terraces and an 8.17 meters-wide central stairway on the main, or west, facade. A Puuc-style double-chambered temple sits on the pyramid summit. The outer temple walls are 21 meters in length and are embellished on the exterior with stone mosaic masks and reliefs of feathered serpents and other mythic animals, whereas the interior walls are decorated with murals. The temple interior has two spaces, an anteroom with twelve stone pillars and a rear chamber with eight pillars, all of which probably once supported a wooden roof. Two columns in the form of descending feathered serpents frame the entrance to the temple, perhaps an allusion to K'uk'ulcan or to rulership in general (Gillespie 1987). Stone standard bearers once probably stood on the corners of the temple. A *chak mol* sculpture now at the top of the stairs probably served variously as a sacrificial platform, a receptacle for sacrificial blood and hearts, and a podium for priests and rulers. The rear temple chamber contains a stone table or altar supported by small atlantid figures (Charlot 1931:265–266; E. Morris 1931:13, 37, 43–45).

The Northwest Colonnade serves as the foyer to the temple. The colonnade, 48 meters long and 14.8 meters wide, rests on a low-stepped platform above the plaza floor and joins the temple on its main west facade. The colonnade once measured 6.89 meters from floor to roof, and its 61 stone pillars once supported a wooden roof. Abutting the pyramid base are battered and decorated stone benches. A long corbel vault, now destroyed, probably formed a covered walkway at the base of the pyramid. The colonnade platform is connected to the adjacent Temple of the Tables to the north. The Northwest Colonnade is also connected to two others, the West and the North Colonnades, both with little preserved decoration (Charlot 1931:267; E. Morris 1931:45–68).

Some features of the Temple of the Warriors Complex indicate that it may have served as a *popol nah* (literally "mat house," community house, or council house). Like known Maya council houses, it faces a major plaza with an open facade punctuated by architectural supports and contains interior benches that provide a rectangular seating arrangement for meetings and feasting (see Fash 1991:131, and Stomper, chapter 8 in this volume, for a discussion of the *popol nah*). Unlike the benches found in

Classic Maya buildings, the ones at Chichén Itzá are larger and provide ample space for sitting. Maya council houses often have exterior mat motifs that announce the function of the building, where lords sat on woven mats as a sign of office. There are no extant mat designs in the Temple of the Warriors Complex, but the stone benches could have been overlaid with real woven mats to serve as thrones or seats of honor.

The pillars that form the open facade make up the most extensive portion of the decorative program. Their uniformity in size—approximately 3.74 meters high and 69 centimeters wide—consistent figural imagery, and regular placement in rows create a unified and vivid appearance. As elements in a visual composition, the carved and painted pillars mesh to form a huge panorama, perhaps the largest and certainly one of the most complex in the Maya world.

The siting of the pyramid on a vast open plaza, as well as the open plan and original bright polychrome decoration, made ritual visually exciting and inviting. Ritual, in fact, is the very subject of the temple's embellishment. The regimented stone pillars together represent key roles in the Chichén Itzá body politic: noble, warrior, and priest. These so-called pillar figures participate in a crowded procession that seems to move through the colonnade, generally from right to left and south to north. Some pillars at the bottom of the stairs represent prisoners bound by rope; perhaps they await the sacrifice that in typical Maya fashion would have occurred at the top of the stairs. According to Schele and Freidel (1990), this panorama depicts the ritual resolution of battle, when Maya foes were given the choice of joining the polity in return for allegiance and noble status, or of facing grimmer consequences. Additionally, bloodletting may be referenced here (D. Stuart 1988). Murals inside the temple that represent lords both seated and in procession, battles, human sacrifice, and tribute items are appropriate backdrops for a performative space where rites of the polity would have been acted out. The entire complex integrates notions vital to the polity's sustained power: conquest, alliance, and tribute.

Central Chichén Itzá is marked at the north by the Sacred Cenote, the axial and ritual focus of this zone given its position on axis with the Castillo and its connection with the largest *sak beh*. As the locus of pilgrimages and offerings, the Cenote was a repository for ritual goods, such as copal incense. But some of its contents—especially worked gold and carved jade—also were valued items of tribute and long-distance exchange. It may be that some tribute for Chichén Itzá, from subjugates and newly initiated polity members, was offered at the Cenote, which was both a symbolic entry to the Otherworld and a material entry to the polity. This is reinforced by the architectural vistas that frame the ceremonial way, especially the Great Ball Court and the Temple of the Warriors Complex, and that resonate with the themes of foundation, rulership, and tribute.

Southern Chichén Itzá

In comparison with the site center, the periphery of Chichén Itzá remains rather obscure. In the 1980s the Peabody Museum-Harvard University Archaeological Project directed by Charles Lincoln (1990) in collaboration with the Centro Regional del Sureste of the Instituto Nacional de Antropología e Historia (INAH), mapped portions of Southern Chichén Itzá; this augmented previous work by the Carnegie Institution of Washington and INAH. Lincoln and his associates excavated several platforms and noted that in configuration and building inventory, Southern Chichén Itzá parallels the basic plan of the site core, and it may be understood as a secondary ceremonial center. Changes in construction quality and scale between platforms may be an index of status.

The variety of buildings indicates a range of uses. The ballcourts and temples probably were used in ways analogous to those in the site center, but the range structures and gallery-patio buildings are more problematic. Range structures are enigmatic Maya buildings. They do not follow a strict plan, but like the Mercado tend to be long and rectangular and to contain rooms arranged in rows (Figure 12.7). Range structures have often been identified as palaces or elite residences, but not all of them may have served the same purposes. Lincoln (1990:605–609) notes that the Akab Tzib, with its relatively spacious rooms and isolation from other buildings, may have been a palace. In contrast, the Monjas, with its grand facade, more public location, and series of remodelings, seems to have had a primary function as a temple or council house, with elite residence as a plausible secondary function. If these larger, better-understood range structures probably served both residential and religious purposes, perhaps the smaller versions did too.

Gallery-patio buildings are another enigmatic type of building with a probable residential function. This T-shaped building type, such as the Akab Tzib, consists of a square patio, usually with a central sunken courtyard surrounded by a row of columns; attached is a longer walled gallery or colonnade (Ruppert 1943, 1950) (Figure 12.8). The largest gallery-patio structure at Chichén Itzá is the Mercado, ornately embel-

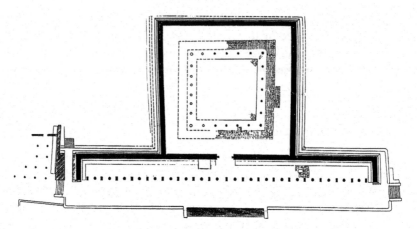

Figure 12.7   Plan of Mercado
(after Ruppert 1943:Figure 1)

Figure 12.8   Plan of Akab Tzib
(after Ruppert 1952:Figure 60)

lished inside and out with figural imagery. The Mercado has been variously interpreted as a judicial court building (Ruppert 1943:230), an elite
residence (Freidel 1981), a public ceremonial space by virtue of affinities
with contemporaneous buildings at Tula (Healan 1974), and a ritual
space for auto-sacrifice based on comparisons with later Aztec architecture (Klein 1987). Lincoln (1990:633, 1994:168) proposes that the gallery-
patio may be a type of palace distinct from range structures.[5]

Who used these buildings in Southern Chichén Itzá? Their relatively
small scale and their location away from the downtown area suggest a
private, perhaps familial use. Lincoln (1990:633) proposes that architectural groups with a similar assemblage of buildings—usually a small

temple, a gallery-patio, and a range structure—were discrete residential/religious spaces. Given the Maya emphasis on filial institutions and organization, it may be that families or lineages occupied these smaller platforms. In galactic polity fashion, the regularity of plan and structures may signal participation in multepal rule, with size and location an index of status.

Northern Chichén Itzá

This sector of the site is the least understood. Neither the Carnegie Institution nor INAH mapped it in the 1920s and 1930s. In the 1990s, the Proyecto Arquelogico Chichén Itzá-INAH has been mapping and conducting settlement pattern surveys in the area north of the Sacred Cenote; thus far 125 structures and 45 causeways have been uncovered and mapped. Like the southern portion of the site, architectural terraces here support a medley of buildings that are connected to each other, and ultimately to the site center, by a system of roadways (Cobos, personal communication 1997). Such general parallels with the rest of the site may indicate that the galactic polity model extends to the northern portion of the site.

Writing and Identity at Chichén Itzá

Two types of writing are found at Chichén Itzá: hieroglyphs and logographs. In the past, these two types of writing were ascribed to different cultural occupations, the hieroglyphs to the earlier Maya occupation and the logographs to the subsequent Toltec period. However, given our current understanding of Chichén Itzá as an integrated settlement with one long occupation period, it seems more likely that the two types of writings were contemporaneous, perhaps directed to different audiences and purposes. In general, hieroglyphic inscriptions appear on lintels, panels, and pillars of buildings in the site core (e.g., the Osario, Akab Tzib), and in a few buildings in the south (e.g., the Temples of the One, Three, and Four Lintels) (Figure 12.1). It seems reasonable to suppose that these texts found in probable palaces that recount genealogy and communal rituals are elite in nature. In contrast, single name glyphs are found on more public, monumental buildings in the site center with a presumed wider audience. This pattern suggests that at least two types of literacy existed at Chichén Itzá, hieroglyphs for elites and single glyphs for the entire population.

Southern Chichén Itzá

Classic-style hieroglyphic texts were found on the Temples of the One,
Two, and Three Lintels; the Initial Series; the Owls; the Wall Panels; the
Hieroglyphic Jambs; the Osario; Structure 6E; and at the nearby sites of
Yula and Halakal that were in Chichén Itzá's sphere of influence (Proskouriakoff 1970; G. Stuart 1989) (Figure 12.9). Ruth Krochock's (1988,
1991) decipherment of some of the hieroglyphs from Chichén Itzá indicates that they record ninth-century elite persons and their ritual activity. Yucatec lineage names recently identified in these texts include
Cauil, Cupul, Hau, and Kokom; because they are sometimes found in
conjunction with the word *holpop* ("at the head of the mat"), a title for in-
termediaries between townspeople and the ruling lord, it may mean that
individuals from these families held administrative positions (Ringle
1990:236, 239).

Other types of writing have different referents. Some buildings that
lack elaborate Puuc facades typically feature detailed exterior moldings
and cornices decorated with a row of carved stones that repeat the same
emblem (Figure 12.9). Some facades are variously embellished with rows
of carved turtles, heads, vases, and birds and have thus been called the
House of the Turtles, the House of the Little Heads, and so on. These emblems also correlate with Yucatec Maya lineage names, and hence they
iconically recall Maya family names and encode lineage in architecture
(this will be discussed in greater detail in the following section).[6]

At least five buildings in the southern portion of Chichén Itzá feature
facade details that may be read as family names (Table 12.1). *In situ* stone
masks are on the facade of the north temple in the Chultun Group (Ruppert 1952:152). On Structure 5C14, the House of the Phalli, a range structure, George Vaillant (in Ruppert 1952:160) observed one vestibule embellished with carved stone feather fans and a southern room extension

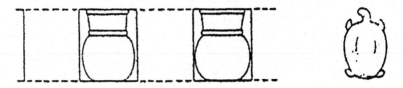

Figure 12.9   Carved cornice moldings of vessels and turtles,
Structure 5B2
(after Ruppert 1952:199, Figure 141b)

**Figure 12.10   Rollout drawing of Pillar 19,
Northwest Colonnade**
(after Charlot 1931:Plate 87)

embellished with a frieze of stone shells. The House of the Little Heads, Structure 5C3, has an exterior frieze of stone birds or bats and human heads or masks (Vaillant in Ruppert 1952:158). Structure 5B2, the Temple of the Turtles, has a band of stone vases and turtles (Ruppert 1952:99, Figure 141b). For these last two buildings, it may be possible that the juxtaposition of two or more emblems could signal descent from more than one lineage or a marital alliance.

At Chichén Itzá, then, each writing system tends to occur in different building types and to record different types of information. The Temples of the One, Three, and Four Lintels are range or double-chambered structures, whereas the buildings with decorated cornices and friezes are small temples or multichambered buildings (Ruppert 1952). If they are contemporaneous, then they may denote ethnic, functional, or social differences. It may be that the hieroglyphic inscriptions recorded the activities and marked out the houses occupied by families from the Southern Lowlands who retained a strong memory of Classic Maya civilization or who may have been original or early participants in conjoined rule at Chichén Itzá. The facade emblems, in contrast, may have marked the houses occupied by Maya families from other parts of the Maya area

Table 12.1   Chart correlating cornice emblems with Yucatec lineage names in Southern Chichén Itzá (information compiled from Ruppert 1952 and Roys 1940)

Building	Facade Emblems	Patronymic
North Temple, Chultun Group	Heads or masks	*Koh* (mask), *Pol* (head) or *Ich* (face)
Structure 5C14, the House of the Phalli; vestibule frieze	Feather fanes	*P'ot* (plume), *Iuit* (feather) or *Ybit* (feather, derived from Chontal Maya)
Structure 5C14, The Houe of th ePhalli; southern room extension frieze	Shells	*K'an* (shell)
Structure 5C3, the House of the Little Heads	Bats and Birds	*Zotz* (bat); the birds are rendered to generally to identify by species, but many patronymics were names of birds
Structure 5B2, the Temple of the Turtles	Vases and turtles	*Cumii* or *Chuil* (bottle); *Ac* (turtle)

where phonetic writing was not as prevalent, or by those who held different positions in the multepal system. In addition, the facade emblems occur on building exteriors whereas the hieroglyphic writing appears on lintels and pillars, both more private locations.

This pattern of writing suggests that dwellings at Chichén Itzá may have been something more than houses. With lineage emblems or names, dates, and events inscribed on facades, there is little doubt that a home was associated with a particular lineage, especially because the multepal system accepted and acknowledged membership through families rather than individuals. In this system, Maya families would have received titles, privileges, or prerogatives; would have joined in alliance with the burgeoning polity; would have retained or have been promoted to elite status; and would have been memorialized in public monuments. A named residence therefore served multiple functions; aside from providing shelter and space for domestic and ritual business, it iconically identified the occupants by lineage, and by extension membership in the Chichén Itzá system of shared rulership.

How can we understand the phenomenon of a "named house," especially in relation to filial, political, and social structures? The Chichén Itzá system of noble families associated with houses via descent is somewhat reminiscent of what Claude Lévi-Strauss (1983) has called "sociétés de maison" or house societies, a specific form of social organization that is not yet part of traditional nomenclature in the study of kinship. Lévi-Strauss first noticed structural similarities between medieval European noble houses and indigenous Kwakiutl and Yurok houses in western Native North America. In all three cases, he observed that the houses have a specific name, a patronymic in Europe and a functional name in the Americas. The house group endures through time as a social grouping and is the mechanism by which names, titles, wealth, and rights are transmitted. "House" in this context does not so much refer to a physical edifice but to the principles that define and organize house occupants. In fact, Lévi-Strauss neither analyzes nor compares the physical houses of the societies he studies, a situation that is being rectified in more recent anthropological studies of the house (Carsten and Hugh-Jones 1995).

Building upon his earlier pioneering work on kinship, Lévi-Strauss describes the house as a unit of social organization that does not fit easily into normative anthropological categories of kinship or social organization. He views this particular type of institution as a transition between kin- and class-based societies, noting:

> The whole function of noble houses, be they European or exotic, implies a fusion of categories which are elsewhere held to be in correlation with and opposition to each other, but are henceforth treated as inter-changeable: descent can substitute for affinity, and affinity for descent (Lévi-Strauss 1983:187).

Specifically, he suggests that the house merges through the uniting of two or more lineages with classification principles that are seemingly antithetical, including filiation/residence, patrilineal descent/matrilineal descent, and endogamy. The house society presents a new type of unity by physically incorporating opposing abstract principles into a system of equivalence that stresses alliance.

Another important characteristic of the house society is its innovative role regarding lineage. Although a family may reside in a house, its occupants do not form a true lineage, according to Lévi-Strauss. Instead, the house society is a hybrid descent group that is bilateral. The house society moves away from defining itself strictly on the basis of genealogy and incorporates an array of societal concerns, including status, wealth, and power. Even though blood ties are never totally disregarded, filiation becomes more equivalent to social standing.

What relevance does the concept of the house society have for Chichén Itzá? Although Lévi-Strauss has studiously avoided studying the supratribal cultures of ancient America and has never confronted the archaeology and time-depth of mythology and ethnography, some of the core characteristics Lévi-Strauss uncovers for the house society may apply to the multepal system. Given some striking similarities between house societies and Chichén Itzá, Lévi-Strauss' model is a useful explanatory tool for discovering some of the ways that genealogy and social organization intersect and for understanding some of the symbolism and nuances that dwellings had beyond practical housing.

First, at Chichén Itzá some named houses subsumed the individual to focus on the group. This fact is evident in the facade emblems that identify lineage rather than individuals. This also follows a general trend after the Classic period to focus less on individuals and their accomplishments and more on groups as a strategy of rulership that may have been more effective in fostering alliances and cooperation. Second, the house may signal the union of nominally opposing principles, such as matrilineal and patrilineal descent, or matrilocality and patrilocality. At the time of European contact, the Yucatec Maya reckoned descent in both the male and female lines (Roys 1940). Houses with more than one facade emblem thus may reference descent from both the male and female line in one lineage. Third, the houses symbolize social relations and alliance. Multepal rule at Chichén Itzá involved more than just blood descent. Conjoined rule was plausibly offered initially, and perhaps almost exclusively, for Maya families of high status, wealth, and power. To live in a named house proclaimed as much about the social standing of the current occupants as it did about their ancestors, who are not memorialized there directly.

The house, perhaps more than any other edifice or planned space, has the potential to inform deeply perceptions of the world. As a three-dimensional model, the house can embody taxonomic principles of the family and the world at large, which then may be internalized via spatial relationships, imagery, and movement (Bachelard 1964:4–5; Bourdieu 1977:89–90; Waterson 1995:57). In Southern Chichén Itzá, the consistent locating of residences on architectural platforms with other structures that are linked by a network of causeways stresses unity and spatial and

Figure 12.11   Rollout drawing of Pillar 37, Northwest Colonnade
(after Charlot 1931:Plate 103)

visual sameness; this pattern was diagrammatic of lineage as a vital component of the polity and of the entire settlement.

Central Chichén Itzá

Following the same pattern observed at Southern Chichén Itzá, two types of writing, hieroglyphic inscriptions and single glyphs, are found in the site center. The hieroglyphic inscriptions appear at the Great Ball Court, the Osario, the Casa Colorada, the Caracol, the Akab Tzib, and the Monjas, and they tend to record the same type of information as they

Figure 12.12   Name glyphs from Northwest Colonnade.
Left to right: Pillar 6 North, *Tzab* ("snake rattles"); Pillar 9 North, *Na(l)*
("corn"); Pillar 17 North, *Ta* ("knife"); Pillar 37 North, *Tzel*
("to grind maize") (after Charlot 1931)

do in Southern Chichén Itzá (G. Stuart 1989). But by far the most prevalent type of writing is a single glyph next to the heads of carved and
painted figures on single pillars or in crowded figural compositions.
These glyphs are concentrated in the Temple of the Warriors Complex
on benches and pillars (Figure 12.11, 12.12). They have been variously
interpreted as name glyphs (Tozzer 1930:151; Charlot 1931:311; Coggins
1984:162–163; Lincoln 1986:154); as personifications of personal attributes (Charlot 1931:313); or as signs for a variety of concepts such as
name, title, tribe, military order, lineage, or clan (Proskouriakoff
1974:209–210).

These hypotheses about the precise nature of the glyphs have never
been tested systematically. This lack is curious, given the long tradition in
Mesoamerican writing, especially in Oaxaca and Central Mexico, of using a single glyph near the head of a figure to identify it by name.[7] One
pattern is apparent for the Chichén Itzá glyphs: Most represent flora and
fauna, and a small number depict artifacts and human actions (Figure
12.13). In both content and frequency, this pattern corresponds to Yucatec
lineage names, either the *ch'ibal* (patronymic) or the *naal* (matronymic)
names (Roys 1957:3–5). An inquiry into Yucatec naming patterns will
clarify how the glyphs record lineage.

One enduring feature of ancient Maya society was the concern with
reckoning and recording individual identity. Lineage was not only the
fundamental component of the kinship system, it was the single most important mark of personal identity. Indeed, the Yucatec past recorded in
ethnohistorical sources takes the form of an interlocking network of family deeds and interests prominently featuring some elite individuals and

Figure 12.13   Detail of mural showing a battle, Temple of the Warriors
(after A. Morris 1931:Plate 139)

lineages. After the Spanish Conquest, Yucatec kinship was organized around the male line for corporate land ownership and residence patterns (Fariss 1984:132–135). Hence, the *ch'ibal* was the only indigenous name consistently preserved, and it was used as a surname preceded by a Spanish baptismal name (Roys 1940:35–36).

Although the colonial practice of retaining only the male name may reflect the patriarchal practices of the conquerors, it does not necessarily indicate that it was the most important name in the precontact period. The *naal* or matronymic name may well have been of equal status before it faded in the colonial period. There is epigraphic and ethnohistorical evidence that the Lowland Maya traced and recorded descent in both the male and female lines. Ethnohistorical sources indicate that the Itzá migrants to Yucatán arrived without wives and married local women. This fact may account for an emphasis on the matrilineal line in hieroglyphic parentage statements at Chichén Itzá that may have added an aura of Yucatecan legitimacy to the Itzá newcomers (Schele and Mathews 1998:203). Even though the hieroglyphic inscriptions at Chichén Itzá highlight female descent, it is unclear whether this reflects a widespread Yucatec pattern or a short-lived innovation. Landa (in Tozzer 1941b:71 n.156) reported that the Itzá were patrilineal and that they questioned the legitimacy of neighboring peoples who were matrilineal; it is unclear whether such a barb was based on fact or was an insult.

We may never know with confidence whether *ch'ibal* or *naal* names are inscribed in the temple, but their identification as lineage names leads to a clearer picture of the Temple of the Warriors Complex. There is considerable overlap between *ch'ibal* and *naal* names (Roys 1940:37), but because only male lineage names were consistently used in the colonial period, this is the only sizable corpus of names to use for comparison at the present time.

A sample of Yucatec *ch'ibal* names is provided in Roys's (1940, 1957) lists of more than 250 Yucatec patronymics compiled from colonial tax lists, many of which were written by Yucatec clerks. Roys translated about half of the names he collected, identifying many as specific plants and animals, but he was unable to pinpoint the exact species for others. His translation of surnames with actions or objects as referents is more straightforward. Although the tax rolls date to a century and a half after the Conquest, the patronymics they record appear to be valid for the precontact period lineage name as well because they correspond to precontact names recorded in Landa and the *Books of Chilam Balam* (there is even a close correspondence with names in the Quiche Maya *Popol Vuh*). Lineage names found in both the Temple of the Warriors Complex and the *Books of Chilam Balam* include Balam, Can/Chan, Chel, Ek, Na, Tok, Tun, and Xiw (Roys 1967; Edmonson 1982). Most are popular names from colonial and modern times and seemingly from prerecorded history as well.

There is a remarkably close correspondence between Roys's list of personal names and the glyphs at the Temple of the Warriors Complex. It

Name Glyph	Pillar	Patronymic
	2 North	*Cuy* (Owl)
	9 South	*Eb* (stairway)
	10 North	*Iuit* (feather; this is one of the few Nabuat lineage names used in Yucatán)
	13 North	*Balam* (jaguar)
	33 South	*Can* or *Chan* (serpent; this is a popular lineage name in both Yucatec and Chontal Maya)
	37 South	*Chimal* (shield; this is one of the few Nahuat lineage names used in Yucatán)

Table 12.2   Chart correlating selected name glyphs
with Yucatec lineage names from the Northwest Colonnade
(illustrations after Charlot 1931 and lineage names after Roys 1940)

has been possible to correlate many glyphs with *ch'ibal* names (Kristan-Graham 1989:197–200, 2000). Eighty-six of the two hundred seventy-eight extant pillar figures have glyphs, eleven from the Temple of the Warriors and seventy-five from the Northwest Colonnade; sixteen glyphs are flora, twenty-four are fauna, sixteen are objects, four depict human heads, and the remaining twenty-six glyphs are badly damaged or otherwise defy identification at this time (Table 12.2). Because the glyphs consist of one meaningful, recognizable unit, such as an animal, they are logographs as opposed to phonetic glyphs (Sampson 1985:32–33). Logographs appear in Classic Maya hieroglyphic texts along with phonetic glyphs, but at Chichén Itzá the logograph can stand on its own as a form of writing.

The linguistic variety of lineage names recorded by the glyphs and in ethnohistorical documents reflects the variety of ethnicities in residence at Chichén Itzá and mirrors the cultural mosaic of Yucatán after the Classic period. Most of the lineage names are Yucatec, but a few are Nahuatl and Chontal. Beyond lineage, there is no written indication of a specific individual's name, such as that of K'ak'upacal or Kukulcan.

Names may be inscribed in the temple complex in other ways as well. A distinctive yellow and green *kokom* vine sprouting from the headdresses of a group of pillar figures located together in the Northwest Colonnade may identify the figures as affiliates of the famous Kokom family, who once were rulers of Chichén Itzá (Kristan-Graham 1988). This family name is also found in hieroglyphic inscriptions at the Akab Tzib and the Casa Colorada (Grube and Stuart 1987:8), in colonial documents, and in the *Books of Chilam Balam*. Joseph Ball (1986:384) has suggested that in light of the rich metaphorical texture of the Yucatec language, Kokom might be synonymous with Itzá. If this is so, might the figures in question portray actual founders or leaders of the polity? Identity and writing are integral parts of the Temple of the Warriors Complex; the name glyphs are a plausible method of record keeping, forming a roster of polity membership and possibly even tribute obligations. Because the name Kokom occurs here and in Southern Chichén Itzá, it may be that some families associated with private buildings in the south are commemorated downtown in a monumental, public program.

Hence, whereas architectural compounds in Southern Chichén Itzá are generally marked out for individual families, the Temple of the Warriors Complex in Central Chichén Itzá focuses on lineage. In both cases, the writing very probably identifies specific individuals and lineages participating in the multepal system. The name glyphs deviate from the hieroglyphic inscriptions found elsewhere at the site. Writing is kept to a minimum, and imagery is entrusted to narrate most of the story of alliance. The logographic writing system is akin to an international sign system that cuts across linguistic boundaries to be intelligible to different groups at this new political capital. This turn away from the Classic concern with lengthy texts telling of supernatural history and genealogy fits a new social order wherein efficient alliances, trade, and tribute systems served more effectively than old patterns.

Design and Ritual

It was through design that the essential principles of the multepal system were embodied and realized at Chichén Itzá. The natural topography was leveled and overlaid with platforms connected by roads that marked out private and public terrain, regulated traffic, and led the ways to public celebrations.

Sak Beob

The network of roads served a multitude of functions. Aside from being ritual roads, they served political and economic functions by connecting political centers with outlying communities and by providing conduits between rural production areas and central markets (Robles C. and Andrews 1986:70). Further, the roads and their connections enable site plans to be read as organizational charts of social structure, as Kurjack (1994:308) has suggested.

Sak beob also may be physical records of kin and corporate alliances because in Northern Yucatán they often joined sites united by marriage and joined sectors within sites likewise related (Kurjack 1977). If sak beob had a similar function at Chichén Itzá, then some architectural platforms linked by causeways may be emblematic of marriage alliance; it also is possible that other interests, such as geographic origin or occupation, may be marked by causeways. Important links made by roads are illustrated by the Temples of the One, Three, and Four Lintels, the Temple of the Initial Series, and the Monjas, all united by Sak beh 7 and all sharing thematic similarities in their hieroglyphic inscriptions (Krochock 1988:129).

Causeways may also mark out political relations. According to a Maya myth, in ancient times roads united Chichén Itzá, Uxmal, and Koba and carried bloodlines to feed the rulers (Tozzer 1941a). The reference to blood vividly recalls how political relations provide economic sustenance and is a useful picture for understanding both the arterial network of the causeways and the wealth they provided. Whether this story is myth or metaphor, it underscores the link between roads, alliance, and tribute.[8]

If roads are symbols of political and marital alliances, then dismantling or "erasing" roads may mark a disruption of such alliances. Krochock (1995) has observed one instance of a road abruptly ending before it reaches the platform where the Temple of the Hieroglyphic Jambs and Structure 6E1 are located. She suggests that the road may have been dismantled or ritually terminated to kill symbolically the group and shut it off from the site; in addition, some masonry at the doorway to the Temple of the Hieroglyphic Jambs may indicate construction that was meant to seal off the inscriptions about the founding of Chichén Itzá. Lincoln (1990) adds that at some point someone excavated away the masonry to see the inscriptions again, but the date for this is unknown. Cobos (personal communication 1997) has observed that one *sak beh* near the Mercado was dismantled. Might the phenomenon of erasing roads have been the result of some rupture among a martial or political alliance?

When the element of human movement is added to the system of roads at Chichén Itzá, other mythic and ritual associations emerge. In a sense, ritual, especially processions, is an assumed element of the site plan, and although a sense of movement must be inferred from the physical remains, it is no less important in attempting to understand how ancient Chichén Itzá worked. Certainly the site as it exists today seems ready-made for spectacles and processions, and it is not difficult to imagine, on ritual occasions, a crowd gathering along the *sak beob* as it moved, congregating at residential compounds and the Sacred Cenote, and then dispersing back home

The movement of peoples along the *sak beob* parallels the social formation and rules of governance of Chichén Itzá. A traditional Yucatec riddle equates time with walking along a road, and traversing a *sak beh* adds temporal and symbolic elements to rituals. Walking along the network of roads, past named buildings, and resplendent visual panoramas could recall the passage of time in several ways: the path of the Milky Way; pilgrimages; waves of migrations; and the founding of Chichén Itzá as a center of conjoined rule. Processions that moved from outlying compounds toward the site center could repeatedly simulate the familial and centrifugal construction of the institution of the multepal system. The monumental scale of the North Platform could have accommodated thousands of people, and crowds formed a significant component of rituals. Crowds allow the populace to act as a body politic and create the effect of equality (Canetti 1978:16, 29), much as the polity aimed at binding different social and ethnic groups together.

The political dimensions of travel along the roadways would have been complemented by cosmological referents. Anthropologist David Kertzer has observed that rituals couple natural with social phenomenon:

. . . ritual structures our experience; it guides our perceptions and channels our interpretation of those perceptions. Through ritual, as through culture more generally, we not only make sense of the world around us, but we also are led to believe that the order we see is not of our own (cultural) making, but rather an order that belongs to the external world itself (1988:84–85) [parentheses original].

At Chichén Itzá, the site layout replicates the union of the social and cosmological universes. The populace moving along the roadway paralleled the way the universe worked, equating the immutable order of the cosmos with the natural social order. The network of roads converging on the Sacred Cenote emphasized the site core as the nucleus of the polity, and it linked the portal to the Otherworld with tribute, which contributed to the continued spiritual and economic health of the polity.

Moreover, it is tantalizing to think that ritual movement at Chichén Itzá could have acted out a fundamental Yucatec literary trope: migration. Many myths from around the globe link migrations to political beginnings, and this is part of standard Yucatec ethnographic fare. The *Books of Chilam Balam* mention migrations around the Yucatán peninsula and toward Chichén Itzá, replete with Maya families whose names are inscribed at the site. One passage states:

. . . they departed and arrived at Ppoole, where the remainder of the Itzá were increased in number; they took the women of Ppole [sic] as their mothers. Then they arrived at Ake; there they were born at Ake. Ake it was called here, as they said. Then they arrived at Alaa; Alaa was its name here, they said. Then they came to Tixchel . . . these are the names of whatever towns there were and the names of the wells, in order that it may be known where they passed in their march to see whether this district was good, whether it was suitable for settlement here (Roys 1967:70, 72).

Such migrations also are recounted in other Maya sources, notably the *Relaciónes and the Highland Popol Vuh* (Tedlock 1996) and *Anales de los Cachiqueles* (Recinos and Goetz 1953). Although it is unclear how accurately these sources record actual demographics, there can be no doubt that migration was a vital component of the Maya collective memory and the ways in which ancestry and political foundations were reckoned. Given the power of place and sight that, according to Heyden (1995) kindles senses, memory, and identity, walking along the *sak beob* during informal and formal occasions could help to stir emotions and recall the Yucatec past amidst an architectural landscape that was at once a symbolic map of the world and of Yucatec political geography.

Hence, the *genius loci* of Chichén Itzá might include the unique ways in which private lineage compounds, public venues, and roadways provided an arena for individuals to reckon their filial and communal identities. The outlying platforms and monumental downtown vistas visually recalled family and polity respectively. Connecting roadways marked out alliances and provided access to the spaces in which elite lineages were transformed into the larger body politic and a Foucauldian diagram of social relations. In a manner that may not have been unlike the nineteenth-century Parisian public amidst the Arcades, the Chichén Itzá populace in its vast architectural landscape could have internalized attitudes about selfhood and social relations. It was in these spaces, and during these rituals, that "presencing" could have occurred, where individuals could see and act out their roles as family and polity members against an architectural backdrop that recalled the mythic, ancestral past and the political present (see Buck-Morss 1989 and Norberg-Schultz 1980 for a discussion of presencing).

The Temple of the Warriors Complex

As one of the focal points of Central Chichén Itzá, the Temple of the Warriors Complex resonates with concerns of multepal and tribute. Murals and decorated benches and pillars enact a narrative about the ritual aftermath of battle and two material benefits of subjugation: prisoners and tribute. Building plan and figural imagery cue the reading order and action. The pillars, each placed 2.5 meters apart on the temple summit and colonnade floor, provide ample room for real actors to mingle with and infinitely transform the painted spectacle. The profile poses of the pillar figures imply movement through the aisles of the temple and colonnade that are formed by the pillars themselves. Most pillars are composed of two pairs of figures on opposite sides who face the same direction (Figure 12.11a, 12.11b). About half of the figures face the center aisles of the temple summit and colonnade that are on axis with the stairway, whereas the rest face west, or out toward the plaza (Anderson 1994).

In the colonnade, the figures stand in discrete groups, with warriors filling most of the north and south areas, and priests and nobles filling in the northwest corner and far south side (Charlot 1931). Prisoners bound at the wrists are carved on eight pillars that cluster in front of the stairway, where they are met by the gaze of the figures who face the center aisles. The central placement of the prisoners just below the temple stairway suggests that they are poised to climb the stairs, ushered by a crowd of warriors, and then greeted by a *chak mol* on the temple summit. Their ultimate fate may be forecast by two small murals inside the temple that depict human sacrifice; in one mural, sacrifice is performed atop a Maya temple not unlike the Temple of the Warriors (A. Morris 1931:Plate 145).

It would seem that although the decorative program shows a display of captives and captors, it is the threat of sacrifice and not sacrifice itself that is highlighted. Notwithstanding religious imperatives to perform sacrifice, in an emergent tributary system like Chichén Itzá, dead prisoners may not have been as valuable as living ones. The prisoner-sacrifice tableaux may have been calculated to win submissive individuals into becoming tributaries, not sacrificial victims, and in the temple complex the hundreds of warriors in Maya costumes and regalia may be new polity members who opted for this choice. It has been suggested that such figures may be *cahalob* or lower order nobles who became titular rulers in return for allegiance to the growing polity (David Freidel, personal communication 1988). In this sense, some figures may have entered into a forced détente relationship with Chichén Itzá.

Here the prisoners retain some dignity in contrast to Classic Maya representations of nude captives in humble postures. Their bound wrists are the only clue to their subjugated status because their ornate costumes and regalia are arguably the fanciest in the composition. The prisoners are allowed to stand with their captors and other ritual actors in the sacred temple space, and their prominent placement at the hub of activity signals their celebrity status, as they are named and paraded to the polity at large. There is a growing consensus that the temple complex commemorates a Yucatec Maya conflict (Charlot 1931:310–311; Ball and Taschek 1989:188; Kristan-Graham 1989; Anderson 1994:4;) in opposition to the traditional reading of a Toltec conquest of Yucatán (Tozzer 1957:177; Coe 1993:128).

In this scenario, it is no coincidence that the name glyphs incised on pillars cluster along the east/west axis of the temple complex, the spatial and narrative center of the composition. Without this writing, the composition may appear to depict just another story, but instead the entire temple complex attains an aura of specificity regarding polity membership and possi-

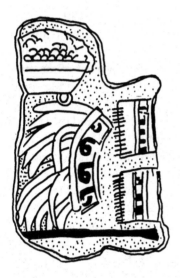

Figure 12.14   Fragment of mural showing tribute items, Temple of the Warriors (after A. Morris 1931:Plate 154)

ble tribute obligations. Likewise, murals inside the temple are diagrammatic of economic interests of the polity. One famous mural of a battle shows Maya merchants traversing a road along a coastline; they have striped bodies like those of the captives, but with headdresses and loincloths intact. In another mural, merchants with their characteristic walking stick, tumpline, and back burdens appear in a more bucolic maritime setting (A. Morris 1931:Plate 159; Blom 1933:435; Thompson 1971:76; Kristan-Graham 1995) Krochock (personal communication 1998) has observed that this scene may well represent salt manufacture, which of course was one of the most important commodities that the Yucatec Maya traded throughout Mesoamerica.

The theme of exchange is continued by another mural in the temple that shows colorful cotton mantas, feathered headdresses, and bowls of copal or jade beads, all highly prized items of tribute throughout Mesoamerica (Landa in Tozzer 1941b:94–95; de la Garza 1980, Volume I:269). The flattened bird's eye view perspective is strikingly similar to pages from the *Codex Mendoza*, a contact-period Aztec painted manuscript that records scenes of conquest along with tribute items such as mantas, costumes, feathered headdresses, and food (A. Morris 1931:409) (Figure 12.14). This mural is in marked contrast to others in the temple and elsewhere at the site, which are represented *en face*. Might not this singular mural denote a shared Mesoamerican visual convention, or even a precedent, for representing tribute items?

Merchants throughout Mesoamerica collected tribute, distributed goods, and secured new markets and trading partners, and it is intriguing that one mural may visually locate a scene of tribute at Chichén Itzá itself. Near the scenes of merchants and tribute is a schematic mural of a *tz'onot*, which may be the Sacred Cenote, the ultimate destination for many local and foreign luxury goods brought to the site as tribute (A. Morris 1931:409). Benches in the colonnade on the north and northwest sides feature carved and painted processions of figures bloodletting or making offerings, both sacred rites of state craft (Charlot 1931:Plate 124). Such scenes are frequent in the site core, and they parallel the content of some hieroglyphic inscriptions regarding group rituals (Krochock and Freidel 1994:360).

In general, the figural imagery in Central Chichén Itzá is more prominent and colorful than imagery from elsewhere at the site. If a building can function as a mnemonic device, with memory and meaning grounded in its narrative character as Heyden (1995:38–47) suggests, then the Temple of the Warriors Complex may encode a charter for Chichén Itzá. More than outright conquest, the theme of alliance pervades formal and iconographic properties of the temple complex. The overall scenes are Lowland Maya in flavor, but Classic types of sculpture seem to be transformed and updated. The ubiquitous carved pillar can be understood as a variation on the Classic Maya stela, the dynastic monument par excellence. The stela, typically carved on one face with a portrait of a ruler and related hieroglyphic genealogy, was literally stretched into a pillar, a towering geometric volume that provided architectural support and expanded the sculpted surface into four equal surfaces for individual portraits. The pillar is an appropriate type of sculpture to emphasize hallmarks of the new social order at Chichén Itzá; it showed that the group rituals replaced the Classic cult of the royal ruler and that the body politic was formed by elite lineages. Furthermore, the aggregation of pillars quite literally formed a standing army and portrait gallery of the polity. Given the capacity of the pillars to provide architectural support, accommodate large groups, and display visual programs, the colonnade is one of the most widespread structures at the site; Kurjack (1994:315) even suggests that the colonnade seems to supplant the Classic Maya palace as the space for conducting state business.

The Temple of the Warriors, given its function as a performative space and its embellishment of individual portraits and vignettes in the life of the polity, could have helped viewers and ritual actors alike share a common past, present, and trajectory for the future. Casey's (1993:13–16) notion of emplacement may also be applicable here; emplacement is a perpetual process of anchoring people to their environs and to each other and of construing a particular vision of the past within the contours of the here and now. In the Temple of the Warriors, real people would have shared the stage with painted backdrops and portraits of polity members. This place may be considered a core of "Itzá-ness," of becoming a member of the Itzá polity, with the asset of elite status and the requisite tribute obligation.

The Temple of the Warriors panorama, like other instances of Maya art, does not present a wholly happy image of a peaceable polity. It is one of the largest visual spectacles in the Maya world, and even though it may be a grandiose council house with an innovative visual program about governance, the particular reading of the narrative episodes is dependent upon social status, and no doubt is not equally palatable to all. Some apparent political tensions—notably the prominent display of prisoners, tribute, and sacrifice—do not evince a seamless alliance. Some characteristics that Benjamin noted for the modern urban panorama as form of montage are instructive here, such as his remark that the panorama "creates an illusion by so successfully blending units into a whole that evidence of contradiction is eliminated" (in Buck-Morss 1989:67). To the Yucatec Maya, hegemonic growth, subjugation, or paying tribute may not have been desirable fates, but in the Temple of the Warriors Complex, they are presented as tolerable or even desirable alternatives to servitude or death. It would seem that the panorama presents a picture of formal visual unity and social difference at the same time. It is perhaps while wandering the physical site, and in pondering the recesses between visual culture and realpolitik, that citizens and visitors alike were able to comprehend and envision their sense of place in the burgeoning polity.[9]

In this reading of Chichén Itzá, much of the ethnohistorical overlay through which we have come to understand Chichén Itzá does not seem entirely relevant. We might ask how the ethnohistorical and archaeological records intersect at Chichén Itzá and how closely we should follow the written sources as a guide to understanding an ancient settlement. Just as Roys and Cohodas found no primary source that told of a Toltec conquest of Yucatán, there are no extant epigraphic data or figural imagery to support this traditional Mexican conquest paradigm. The traditional myths and legends do not recount much about trade, tribute, or political organization, which certainly seem to be a major concern of visual programs at Chichén Itzá. In order to better understand Chichén Itzá amidst a sea of primary and secondary texts, normative definitions of Toltec ought to be redefined. References to a Toltec or Mexican incursion into Yucatán are not borne out by material culture. Clearly, planning, architecture, artifacts, imagery, and *in situ* writing at Chichén Itzá implicate a Terminal Classic Maya world in which Yucatec Maya, not Central Mexican, prerogatives were enacted. Today, Toltec may more profitably be understood as (1) an innovative tradition of visual culture that was engendered within the unique parameters of Terminal Classic Mesoamerica; and (2) as an honorific or metaphorical allusion to ancestors or foreigners, the latter a plausible reference to the Itzá, Chontal Maya, or another "Mexicanized Maya" group.

Given our growing body of knowledge about Chichén Itzá, primarily through archaeology, art, and epigraphy, it is apparent that visual culture there was vital in integrating notions of mythic, filial, political, and economic foundations and informing a sense of identity to the populace.[10] The reconstruction of rituals and even casual movement there demonstrate that the makeup of the polity—especially the peopling of Chichén Itzá, the move toward the multepal system, and attendant benefits and obligations—very probably were enacted and reproduced at every turn with recollections of family and community. The settlement of Chichén Itzá asserted its Maya identity while it forged an innovative union of politics and art to unite disparate interests and peoples in the late Maya world. All of this created a sense of being and of belonging, in short a sense of place, at Chichén Itzá.

Acknowledgments

Thanks to Anthony Andrews, Annabeth Headrick, Ruth Krochock, Mark Miller Graham, and Kathryn Reese-Taylor for reading an early version of this paper and providing valuable comments; to Linda Schele for providing insightful feedback on some of the ideas presented here; to Rafael Cobos for generously sharing information about recent archaeological work at Chichén Itzá; to David Merten for helping with some of the illustrations; and to the Atlanta College of Art for providing faculty development funds to attend the College Art Association meeting in San Antonio in 1995, where an earlier manifestation of this paper was presented.

References

Acosta, J.
 1956 Interpretación de algunos datos obtenidos en Tula relativa a la epoca 57 Tolteca. *Revista Mexicana de Estudios Antropologicos* 14(2):75–110.
Anderson, P.
 1994 Interpretations of Conflict at Chichén Itzá. *Seventh Palenque Round Table.* Edited by M. Robertson and V. Fields. San Francisco: Pre-Columbian Art Research Institute. 33–37.
Andrews, A.
 1990 The Fall of Chichén Itzá: A Preliminary Hypothesis. *Latin American Antiquity* 1(3):258–267.

Andrews, A., F. Asaro, H. Michel, F. Stross, and P. Cervera R.
1989	The Obsidian Trade at Isla Cerritos, Yucatán, Mexico. *Journal of Field Archaeology* 16:355–363.
Andrews, A., and F. Robles C.
1985	Chichén Itzá and Coba: An Itzá-Maya Standoff in Early Postclassic Yucatán. *The Lowland Maya Postclassic.* Edited by A. Chase and P. Rice. Austin, Tex.: University of Texas Press. 62–72.
Andrews, A., T. Gallereta N., F. Robles C., R. Cobos P., and P. Cervera R.
1988	Isla Cerritos: An Itzá Trading Port on the North Coast of Yucatán, Mexico. *National Geographic Research* 4(2):196–207.
Ashmore, W.
1992	Deciphering Maya Architectural Plans. *New Theories on the Ancient Maya.* Edited by E. Danien and R. Sharer. University Monograph 77. Philadelphia: University of Pennsylvania. 173–184.
Bachelard, G.
1964	*The Poetics of Space.* Translated by M. Jolas. Boston: Beacon Press.
Ball, J.
1979	Ceramics, Culture History, and the Puuc Tradition: Some Alternative Possibilities. *The Puuc: New Perspectives.* Edited by L. Mills. Scholarly Studies in the Liberal Arts 1. Pella, Iowa: Central College. 18–38.
1986	Campeche, the Itzá, and the Postclassic: A Study in Ethnohistorical Archaeology. *Late Lowland Maya Civilization.* Edited by J. Sabloff and E. W. Andrews V. Albuquerque, N.Mex.: University of New Mexico Press. 379–408.
Ball, J., and J. Taschek.
1989	Teotihuacan's Fall and the Rise of the Itzá: Realignments and Role Changes in the Terminal Classic Maya Lowlands. *Mesoamerica After the Decline of Teotihuacan A.D. 700–900.* Edited by R. Diehl and J. Berlo. Washington, D.C.: Dumbarton Oaks. 187–200.
Blom, F.
1933	Commerce, Trade and Monetary Units of the Maya. *Smithsonian Institution 34 Annual Report.* Washington, D.C.: Smithsonian Institution. 423–440.
Boot, E.
1995	Recent Epigraphic Research on the Inscriptions at Chichén Itzá, Yucatán, Mexico. Paper presented at the Advanced Workshop, Maya Meetings, Austin, Texas.
Bourdieu, P.
1977	*Outline of a Theory of Practice.* Translated by R. Nice. Cambridge: Cambridge University Press.
Brinton, D.
1887	Were the Toltecs an Historic Nationality? *Proceedings of the American Philosophical Society* 24:229–241.
Buck-Morss, S.
1989	*The Dialectics of Seeing: Walter Benjamin and the Arcades Project.* Cambridge, Mass.: MIT Press.
Canetti, E.
1978	*Crowds and Power.* Translated by C. Stewart. New York: Seabury Press.

Carrasco, D.
   1982   *Quetzalcoatl and the Irony of Empire: Myths and Prophecies in the Aztec Tra-dition.* Chicago: University of Chicago Press.
Carsten, J., and S. Hugh-Jones, editors.
   1995   *About the House: Lévi-Strauss and Beyond.* Cambridge: Cambridge University Press.
Casey, E.
   1987   *Remembering: A Phenomenological Study.* Bloomington, Ind.: Indiana University Press.
   1993   *Getting Back into Place.* Bloomington, Ind.: Indiana University Press.
Caso, A.
   1947   Calendario y escritura de las antiguas culturas de Monte Alban. *Obras Completas.* Edited by M. O. de Mendizabal. México, D.F.: no publisher. 1:113–143.
Castañeda, Q.
   1997   *In the Museum of Maya Culture: Touring Chichén Itzá.* Minneapolis: University of Minnesota Press.
Charlot, J.
   1931   Bas-Reliefs from the Temple of the Warriors Cluster. *The Temple of the Warriors at Chichén Itzá, Yucatán, Mexico.* Carnegie Institution of Washington Publication 406. Washington, D.C.: Carnegie Institution. 230–346.
Charnay, D.
   1885   *Les anciennes villes du Noveau Monde.* Paris: Hachette and Cie.
Cobos, Rafael.
   1994   Katun and Ahau: Dating and the End of Chichén Itzá. Paper presented at the 93rd Meeting of the American Anthropological Association, Atlanta, Georgia.
Coe, M.
   1993   *The Maya.* 5th ed. New York: Thames and Hudson.
Coggins, C.
   1984   *The Cenote of Sacrifice: Catalogue. Cenote of Sacrifice: Maya Treasures from the Sacred Well at Chichén Itzá.* Edited by C. Coggins and O. Shane III. Austin, Tex.: University of Texas Press. 23–155.
Cohodas, M.
   1978   *The Great Ball Court at Chichén Itzá, Yucatán, Mexico.* New York: Garland.
Culbert, T., editor.
   1973   *The Classic Maya Collapse.* Albuquerque, N.Mex.: University of New Mexico Press.
Davies, N.
   1977   *The Toltecs Until the Fall of Tula.* Norman, Okla.: University of Oklahoma Press.
Demarest, A.
   1992   Ideology in Ancient Maya Cultural Evolution: The Dynamics of Galactic Polities. *Ideology and Cultural Evolution in the New World.* Edited by A. Demarest and G. Conrad. Albuquerque, N.Mex.: University of New Mexico Press. 135–157.

Diehl, R.
  1993   The Toltec Horizon in Mesoamerica: New Perspectives on an Old Issue. *Latin American Horizons*. Edited by D. Rice. Washington, D.C.: Dumbarton Oaks. 263–293.
Edmonson, M., editor and translator.
  1982   *The Ancient Future of the Itzá: The Book of Chilam Balam of Tizimin*. Austin, Tex.: University of Texas Press.
  1986   *Heaven Born Mérida and Its Destiny: The Book of Chilam Balam of Chumayel*. Austin, Tex.: University of Texas Press.
Fariss, N.
  1984   *Maya Society Under Colonial Rule*. Princeton: Princeton University Press.
Fash, W.
  1991   Scribes, Warriors and Kings: The City of Copán and the Ancient Maya. New York: Thames and Hudson.
Foucault, M.
  1977   *Discipline and Punish: The Birth of the Prison*. Translated by A. Sheridan. New York: Vintage Books.
  1986   Of Other Spaces. Translated by J. Miskowiec. *Diacritics* Spring 1986:22–27.
Fox, J.
  1987   *Maya Postclassic State Formation: Segmentary Lineage Migration in Advancing Frontiers*. Cambridge: Cambridge University Press.
Freidel, D.
  1981   The Political Economics of Residential Dispersion Among the Lowland Maya. *Lowland Maya Settlement Patterns*. Edited by W. Ashmore. Albuquerque, N.Mex.: University of New Mexico Press. 371–382.
  1986   Terminal Classic Lowland Maya: Successes, Failures, and Aftermaths. *Late Lowland Maya Civilization*. Edited by J. Sabloff and E. W. Andrews V. Albuquerque, N.Mex.: University of New Mexico Press.
Freidel, D., L. Schele, and J. Parker.
  1993   *Maya Cosmos: Three Thousand Years on the Shaman's Path*. New York: William Morrow.
Garza, M., de la, editor.
  1980   *Relaciones historicos-geograficas de la governacion de Yucatán (Mérida, Valladolid y Tabasco)*. México, D.F.: Universidad Nacional Autonoma de Mexico.
Garza, S., and E. Kurjack.
  1980 *Atlas arqueologico del Estado de Yucatán*. Mérida, Mexico: SEP, INAH.
Geertz, Clifford.
  1980   *Negara: The Theatre State in Nineteenth-Century Bali*. Princeton: Princeton University Press.
Gillespie, S.
  1987   Feathered Serpents and the Origin of Kingship. Paper presented at the 86th Annual Meeting of the American Anthropological Association.
  1989   *The Aztec Kings*. Tucson, Ariz.: University of Arizona Press.
Grube, N., and D. Stuart.
  1987   Observations on T110 as the Syllable ko. *Research Reports on Ancient Maya Writing* 8.

Healan, D.
1974　Residential Architecture at Tula. *Studies of Ancient Tollan: A Report of the University of Missouri Tula Archaeological Project.* Edited by R. Diehl. Columbia, Mo.: Department of Anthropology, University of Missouri. 16–24.

Henderson, J.
1997　*The World of the Ancient Maya.* Ithaca: Cornell University Press.

Hers, M.
1989　*Los Toltecas en Tierras Chichimecas.* Cuadernos de Historia del Arte 53. México, D.F.: Instituto de Investigactiones Estéticas, Universidad Nacional Autónoma de México.

Heyden, D.
1995　*The Power of Place: Urban Landscapes as Public History.* Cambridge, Mass.: MIT Press.

Jones, L.
1993　The Hermeneutics of Sacred Architecture: A Reassessment of the Similitude Between Tula, Hidalgo and Chichén Itzá, Yucatán, Part II. *History of Religions* 32:315–342.

Kertzer, D.
1988　*Ritual, Politics and Power.* New Haven: Yale University Press.

Klein, C.
1987　The Ideology of Autosacrifice at the Temple Mayor. *The Aztec Templo Mayor.* Edited by E. Boone. Washington, D.C.: Dumbarton Oaks. 293–370.

Korff, R.
1993　Bangkok as a Symbol? Ideological and Everyday Constructions of Bangkok. *Urban Symbolism.* Edited by P. Nas. Studies in Human Society 8. Leiden, Netherlands: E. J. Brill. 229–250.

Kowalski, J.
1989　Who Am I Among the Itzá? Links Between Northern Yucatán and the Western Maya Highlands and Lowlands. *Mesoamerica After the Decline of Teotihuacan A.D. 700–900.* Edited by Richard Diehl and Janet Berlo. Washington, D.C.: Dumbarton Oaks. 173–185.

Kristan-Graham, C.
1988　Identification of Lineage in the Art of Chichén Itzá. Paper delivered at the 53rd Annual Meeting of the Society for American Archaeology, Phoenix, Arizona.

1989　*Art, Rulership and the Mesoamerican Body Politic at Tula and Chichén Itzá.* Ph.D. dissertation, Department of Art History, University of California, Los Angeles.

1995　Trade, Tribute and Art at Chichén Itzá. Paper delivered at the 60th Annual Meeting of the Society for American Archaeology, Minneapolis, Minnesota.

1999　Surveying Time at Chichén Itzá: A New Look at the Murals from the Temple of the Warriors. Paper delivered at the 64th Annual Meeting of the College Art Association, Los Angeles.

2000　Name Signs at the Temple of the Warriors, Chichén Itzá. Unpublished manuscript.

Krochock, R.
1988 *The Hieroglyphic Inscriptions and Iconography of Temple of the Four Lintels and Related Monuments, Chichén Itzá, Yucatán, Mexico.* M.A. thesis, University of Texas at Austin.
1991 Dedication Ceremonies at Chichén Itzá: The Glyphic Evidence. *Sixth Palenque Round Table.* Edited by V. Fields. Norman, Okla.: University of Oklahoma Press. 43–50.
1995 Cross-Correlation of Epigraphic and Archaeological Data at Chichén Itzá. Paper presented at the 60th Annual Meeting of the Society for American Archaeology, Minneapolis, Minnesota.

Krochock, R., and D. Freidel.
1994 Ballcourts and the Evolution of Political Rhetoric at Chichén Itzá. *Hidden Among the Hills: Maya Archaeology of the Northwest Yucatán Peninsula.* Edited by H. Prem. Mockmuhl, Germany: Verlag von Flemming. 359–375.

Kubler, G.
1961 Chichén-Itzá y Tula. *Estudios de Cultura Maya* 1:47–80.

Kurjack, E.
1977 Sacbeob: parentesco y el desarollo del Estado Maya. Los Procesos de Cambio. *XV Mesa Redonda de la Sociedad Mexicana de Antropologia* I (Guanajuato 1977):217–230.
1988 On the Toltec Invasion. *Merida-Mesoamerica,* Winter 1988:31–35.
1994 Political Geography of the Yucatecan Hill Country. *Hidden Among the Hills: Maya Archaeology of the Northwest Yucatán Peninsula.* Edited by H. Prem. Mockmuhl, Germany: Verlag von Flemming. 308–315.

Leclerc, J.
1993 Mirrors and the Lighthouse: A Search for Meaning in the Monuments and Great Works of Sukarno's Jakarta, 1960–1966. *Urban Symbolism.* Edited by P. Nas. Studies in Human Society 8. Leiden, Netherlands: E. J. Brill. 38–58.

Lévi-Strauss, C.
1983 *The Way of the Masks.* Translated by S. Modelski. London: Jonathan Cape.

Lincoln, C.
1986 The Chronology of Chichén Itzá. *Late Lowland Maya Civilization.* Edited by J. Sabloff and E. W. Andrews V. Albuquerque, N.Mex.: University of New Mexico Press. 141–196.
1990 *Ethnicity and Social Organization at Chichén Itzá, Yucatán, Mexico.* Ph.D. dissertation, Department of Anthropology, Harvard University.
1994 Structural and Philological Evidence for Divine Kingship at Chichén Itzá, Yucatán, Mexico. *Hidden Among the Hills: Maya Archaeology of the Northwest Yucatán Peninsula.* Edited by H. Prem. Mockmuhl, Germany: Verlag von Flemming. 164–196.

Lothrop, S.
1952 *Metals from the Cenote of Sacrifice, Chichén Itzá, Yucatán, Mexico.* Memoirs of the Peabody Museum of Archaeology and Ethnology10. Cambridge, Mass.: Harvard University.

Marcus, J.
1976   The Origins of Mesoamerican Writing. *Annual Review of Anthropology* 5:35–67.
1992   *Mesoamerican Writing Systems: Propaganda, Myths, and History in Four Ancient Civilizations.* Princeton: Princeton University Press.
Morris, A.
1931   Murals from the Temple of the Warriors and Adjacent Structures. *The Temple of the Warriors at Chichén Itzá, Yucatán.* Carnegie Institution of Washington Publication 406. Washington, D.C.: Carnegie Institution. 348–485.
Morris, E.
1931   Description of the Temple of the Warriors and Edifices Related Thereto. *The Temple of the Warriors at Chichén Itzá, Yucatán.* Carnegie Institution of Washington Publication 406. Washington, D.C.: Carnegie Institution. 11–227.
Nelson, B., J. Darling, and D. King.
1992   Mortuary Practices and the Social Order at La Quemada, Zacatecas, Mexico. *Latin American Antiquity* 3(4):298–315.
Nicholson, H. B.
1957   *Topiltzin Quetzalcoatl of Tollan: A Problem in Mesoamerican Ethnohistory.* Ph.D. dissertation, Department of Anthropology, Harvard University.
Norberg-Schulz, C.
1980   *Genuis Loci: Towards a Phenomenology of Architecture.* New York: Rizzoli.
Proskouriakoff, T.
1951   Some Non-Classic Traits in the Sculpture of Yucatán. *The Civilizations of Ancient America. Selected Papers of the 29th International Congress of Americanists.* Edited by S. Tax. Chicago: University of Chicago Press. 108–118.
1970   On Two Inscriptions from Chichén Itzá. *Monographs and Papers in Maya Archaeology.* Papers of the Peabody Museum of Archaeology and Ethnology 67. Edited by W. Bullard. Cambridge, Mass.: Harvard University Press. 459–467.
1974   *Jades from the Cenote of Sacrifice, Chichén Itzá, Yucatán.* Memoirs of the Peabody Museum of Archaeology and Ethnology 10. Cambridge, Mass.: Harvard University.
Recinos, A., and D. Goetz, translators and editors.
1953   *The Annals of the Cakchiquels.* Norman, Okla.: University of Oklahoma Press.
Ringle, W.
1990   Who Was Who in Ninth-Century Chichén Itzá. *Ancient Mesoamerica* 1(2):233–243.
Robles C., F., and A. Andrews.
1986   A Review and Synthesis of Recent Postclassic Archaeology in Northern Yucatán. *Late Lowland Maya Civilization.* Edited by J. Sabloff and E. W. Andrews V. Albuquerque, N.Mex.: University of New Mexico Press. 53–98.

Roys, R.
1940   *Personal Names of the Mayas of Yucatán.* Carnegie Institution of Washington Contributions to American Anthropology and History 31. Washington, D.C.: Carnegie Institution.
1957   *The Political Geography of the Mayas of Yucatán.* Carnegie Institution of Washington Publication 523. Washington, D.C.: Carnegie Institution.
1966   Native Empires in Yucatán. *Revista Mexicana de Estudios Antropologicos* 20:153–175.
Roys, R., editor and translator.
1967   *The Chilam Balam of Chumayel.* Norman, Okla.: University of Oklahoma Press.
Ruppert, K.
1943   *The Mercado, Chichén Itzá, Yucatán.* Carnegie Institution of Washington Publication 546. Washington, D.C.: Carnegie Institution.
1950   Gallery-Patio Type Structures at Chichén Itzá. *For the Dean: Essays in Honor of Byron Cummings.* Edited by E. Reed and D. Reed. Tucson, Ariz., and Santa Fe, N.Mex.: Hohokam Museums Association and Southwest Monuments Association. 249–258.
1952   *Chichén Itzá Architectural Notes and Plans.* Carnegie Institution of Washington Publication 595. Washington, D.C.: Carnegie Institution.
Ruz L., A.
1962   Chichén Itzá y Tula: comentarios a un ensayo. *Estudios de Cultura Maya* 2:205–223.
Sampson, G.
1985   *Writing Systems.* Stanford: Stanford University Press.
Schele, L., and D. Freidel.
1990   *A Forest of Kings: The Untold Story of the Ancient Maya.* New York: William Morrow.
Schele, L., N. Grube, and E. Boot.
2000   Some Suggestions on the K'atun Prophecies in the Books of Chilam Balam in Light of Classic-Period History. Unpublished manuscript.
Schele, L., and P. Mathews.
1998   *The Code of Kings: The Language of Seven Sacred Maya Temples and Tombs.* New York: Scribner's.
Sharer, R.
1994   *The Ancient Maya.* 5th edition. Stanford: Stanford University Press.
Stephens, J.
1843   *Incidents of Travel in Yucatán.* New York: Harper and Brothers.
Stuart, D.
1988   Blood Symbolism in Maya Iconography. *Maya Iconography.* Edited by E. Benson and G. Griffin. Princeton: Princeton University Press. 175–221.
1993   Historical Inscriptions and the Maya Collapse. *Lowland Maya Civilization in the Eighth Century A.D.* Edited by J. Sabloff and J. Henderson. Washington, D.C.: Dumbarton Oaks. 321–349.
Stuart, G.
1989   Introduction: The Hieroglyphic Record of Chichén Itzá and Its Neighbors. *Research Reports on Ancient Maya Writing* 23:1–6.

Tambiah, S.
1977   The Galactic Polity: The Structure of Traditional Kingdoms in South-east Asia. *Annals of the New York Academy of Science* 293:69–97.
Taube, K.
1994   The Iconography of Toltec Period Chichén Itzá. *Hidden Among the Hills: Maya Archaeology of the Northwest Yucatán Peninsula.* Edited by H. Prem. Mockmuhl: Verlag von Flemming. 212–246.
Tedlock, D., translator and editor.
1996   *Popol Vuh.* 2nd edition. New York: Touchstone.
Thompson, J.
1970   *Maya History and Religion.* Norman, Okla.: University of Oklahoma Press.
1971   *Maya Hieroglyphic Writing.* 3rd edition. Norman, Okla.: University of Oklahoma Press.
Tozzer, A.
1930   Maya and Toltec Figures at Chichén Itzá. *Proceedings of the 23rd International Congress of Americanists.* New York: Science Press Printing. 155–164.
1941a   *A Comparative Ethnology of the Mayas and the Lacandones.* New York: Archaeological Institute of America and Macmillan.
1941b   *Landa's Relación de las Cosas de Yucatán: A Translation.* Papers of the Peabody Museum of Archaeology and Ethnology 18. Cambridge, Mass.: Harvard University.
1957   *Chichén Itzá and Its Cenote of Sacrifice.* Memoirs of the Peabody Museum of Archaeology and Ethnology 11 and 12. Cambridge, Mass.: Harvard University.
Waterson, R.
1995   Houses and Hierarchies in Island Southeast Asia. *About the House: Lévi-Strauss and Beyond.* Edited by J. Carsten and S. Hugh-Jones. Cambridge: Cambridge University Press.
Whittaker, G.
1980   *The Hieroglyphics of Monte Albán.* Ph.D. dissertation, Yale University.
Wren, L.
1994   Ceremonialism in the Reliefs of the North Temple, Chichén Itzá. *Seventh Palenque Round Table.* Edited by V. Fields. San Francisco: Pre-Columbian Art Research Institute. 25–31.
Wren, L., and P. Schmidt.
1991   Elite Interaction During the Terminal Classic Period: New Evidence from Chichén Itzá. *Classic Maya Political History.* Edited by P. Culbert. Cambridge: Cambridge University Press. 199–225.

Notes

1. Cobos (1994) argues that Chichén Itzá had ceased to be a formidable power by the end of the tenth century.

2. Materials excavated from Isla Cerritos include ceramics from the Gulf Coast, Caribbean area, Southern Lowlands, and Guatemala; obsidian from Central Mex-

ico and Highland Guatemala; greenstone from Highland Guatemala; turquoise from North Mexico or the Southwestern United States; basalt from Veracruz or Belize; and gold from Costa Rica (Andrews et al. 1988:204).

3. The Tula-Chichén Itzá problem has been a persistent and intriguing issue in the study of Mesoamerican ethnohistory and prehistory, but it generally falls outside the parameters of this chapter. See Kristan-Graham (1989) and Jones (1993) for discussions of the Tula-Chichén Itzá issue. See Nicholson (1957), Davies (1977), Carrasco (1982), and Gillespie (1989) for discussions of the ethnohistorical literature, especially the relationship between Kukulcan and the Central Mexican deity-priest Quetzalcoatl.

An examination of obsidian distribution provides a compelling tie between Tula and Chichén Itzá. At Chichén Itzá's port, Isla Cerritos, 17 percent of the obsidian came from Highland Guatemala, and 82 percent of the obsidian is from Central Mexico (48 percent is from Pachuca, Hidalgo, which probably was controlled by Tula during the Terminal Classic and Early Postclassic periods, and 28 percent is from Ucareo, Michoacán). This particular distribution pattern has parallels at Tula and Chichén Itzá but has few parallels with the Maya area. At Chichén Itzá this is an abrupt shift away from the use of obsidian from the Guatemalan Highlands during Classic times and indicates that the Itzá had commercial ties with Central Mexico, probably via a series of outposts along the coast of Yucatán to the Gulf Coast of Mexico (Andrews et al. 1988:204; Andrews et al. 1989:359–361).

4. In alternate views, Cobos (personal communication 1997) and Boot (1995) argue for the possibility that one supreme lord ruled Chichén Itzá, and Lincoln (1990, 1994) suggests that the site had two corulers.

5. Gallery-patio structures were once thought to have been a purely Yucatec phenomenon, but such structures also are found in North and West Mexico. For example, the Hall of Columns from the Acropolis at La Quemada, Zacatecas, appears to be very similar to the gallery-patio structure (Hers 1989:162–166). La Quemada is mainly an Epiclassic site (600–900 AD); recent excavations have uncovered ritual architecture, elite residences, burials, a ballcourt, and a road system linking La Quemada to at least 200 other sites nearby (Nelson et al. 1992:298–301). La Quemada's dating, large size, complexity, and location along a trade route between the Southwestern United States and the basin of Mexico warrant further study between it and the rest of Mesoamerica.

6. A precedent for named buildings is found at Copán. Barbara and William Fash (in Fash 1991:129–134) suggest that buildings on the Acropolis decorated with specific sculptural motifs are the "House of Bats" and "Razor House," both mentioned in the *Popol Vuh*.

7. The earliest form of this type of glyph appears on the Danzantes reliefs on the exterior of Building L at Monte Albán, Oaxaca (500–400 BC). About 50 out of 300 carved stones portraying slain enemies are associated with glyphs in the form of human heads, animals, or objects next to the heads. There is general agreement that the glyphs identify the figures either by name or territory (Caso 1947; Marcus 1976; Whittaker 1980:20–21). At Tula, logographic writing is roughly contemporaneous with that of Chichén Itzá. Monumental stone pillars atop Tula's Pyramid B depict rulers or warriors who are identified by single

glyphs near the heads. These glyphs have been read as totems, names (Acosta 1956), tribes, or towns (Tozzer 1930). It is more probable that the glyphs record personal names: Deer or Rabbit, Eagle, Serpent, Coyote, Jaguar, and Merchant (Kristan-Graham 1989:205–217). Later Aztec art had a similar system of identifying individuals with small glyphs near the heads of human figures in sculpture and manuscripts. Most often the glyphs identify an Aztec ruler by his personal name. For example, a glyph of an eagle posed head down identifies the Emperor Cuauhtemoc, "Descending Eagle" (See Marcus 1992 for a discussion of name glyphs in Mesoamerica).

One specific example from the Temple of the Warriors Complex reinforces the nominal function of the glyphs. A carved figure is accompanied by a glyph of a profile rabbit head atop two vertical bars (Charlot 1931:Plate 59). In the Central Mexican bar-and-dot numeral system, in which a dot denotes a coefficient of 1 and a bar 5, this can be read as "10 Rabbit," a date citing month and day; in Mexico, it was common for individuals to have both a personal and a calendrical name, the latter equated with their birth date.

There are still some questions about how figures are to be more fully identified at the Temple of the Warriors Complex. Each pillar/figure is individualized by physiognomy and costume, but less than half have a name glyph. Are there distinctions between named and unnamed figures?

8. New maps of Chichén Itzá may allow political relations to be seen more precisely.

9. The Temple of the Warriors also may have been a locus for katun rituals, which commemorated the beginning and ending of twenty-year calendrical cycles; this intersects with the political and ritual affinities of the building, as Maya lords and priests played important roles in timekeeping (Kristan-Graham 1999).

10. The work of Castañeda (1996) has added to the ongoing dialogue about Chichén Itzá. His study of the modern town of Pist, which is adjacent to Chichén Itzá, and of scientific work at the archaeological zone proper, indicates that ethnography, ethnohistory, and archaeology have been conducted there in concert with concerns of Maya identity, modernity, and nationalism.

INDEX